DAVID
The Testimony of a Holocaust Survivor

EZRA BENGERSHÔM

DAVID

The Testimony of a Holocaust Survivor

Translated from the German by
J. A. Underwood

OSWALD WOLFF BOOKS
Berg Publishers Limited
Oxford/New York/Hamburg

Distributed exclusively in the US and Canada by
ST MARTIN'S PRESS, New York

First English edition published in 1988 by
Berg Publishers Limited
77 Morrell Avenue, Oxford OX4 1NQ, UK
175 Fifth Avenue/Room 400, New York, NY 10010, USA
Schenefelder Landstr. 14K, 2000 Hamburg 55, FRG

Reprinted 1989

Originally published as *Den Netzen entronnen. Die Aufzeichnungen
des Joel König,* Verlag Vandenhoeck & Ruprecht, Göttingen, 1967
German paperback edition published as *David. Aufzeichnungen eines
Überlebenden,* Fischer Taschenbuch Verlag, 1979
All German editions © Vandenhoeck & Ruprecht, Göttingen
This English edition, and editions in all other languages,
© The Inter Homines Foundation, Rotterdam

British Library Cataloguing in Publication Data

BenGershôm, Ezra
David: testimony of a Holocaust survivor.
1. Germany. Jews. Persecution, 1923–1942.
Personal observations
I. Title II. Den Netzen entronnen: die
Aufzeichnungen des Joel König. *English*
943.085'0924

ISBN 0–85496–222–0

Library of Congress Cataloging-in-Publication Data
Ben-Gershôm, Ezra.
[Netzen entronnen. English]
David: testimony of a Holocaust survivor/
Ezra BenGershôm: translated
from the German by J. A. Underwood.
p.   cm.
Translation of: Den Netzen entronnen.
ISBN 0–85496–222–0: $28.00 (est.)
1. Holocaust, Jewish (1939–1945)—Germany
—Personal narratives. 2. Jews—Germany
—History—1933–1945. 3. BenGershôm, Ezra.
I. Title.
DS135, G33B38413—1988   88—10441
940.53'15'039240—dc19   CIP

Printed in Great Britain by A. Wheaton & Co. Ltd., Exeter

Contents

A Note to the Reader

In the first edition of this book I referred to myself as 'David' and signed as 'Joel König'. For simplicity's sake I have now dropped these pseudonyms.

This book came about in two stages. The record of my experiences during the war years is based on relatively fresh memories; I began to make notes for it as soon as I was free of the Nazi sphere of influence. The memoirs of the years 1922–39 were not added until long after the war.

The chronological table at the back of the book is intended to help the reader fit my personal testimony into the wider context of historical events. At the same time it illustrates the extent of my unawareness of that context both before and during the period when I was literally fighting for my life.

Conversations, thoughts and letters are reproduced here as faithfully as I can recall them — often, for the sake of vividness, in direct speech. In no case do I lay claim to verbatim accuracy.

Names of persons, descriptions of small towns and villages and private addresses have for the most part been altered in order to preserve confidentiality. However, I have been careful to avoid making any changes that might detract from the documentary value of my account.

Some additional footnotes have been added for the English edition. The author gratefully acknowledges the assistance of his translator in compiling these notes.

E.B.
Spring 1988

Foreword

The memoirs of Ezra BenGershôm are most certainly not in the tradition of those war books capable of interesting only a specialised public for a limited period.* Their validity derives from an unusual source, namely the author's utter sincerity and moral candour and the way in which both are reflected in his style. It would be hard to imagine a less 'professional' piece of writing than this — and what a relief that is after all the self-conscious literature with which we are bombarded from every quarter.

In these pages the author presents himself exactly as he was without the least attempt at embellishment: a middle-class boy who is both very German and very Jewish, that is to say enamoured of the earthly order of things and at the same time rigidly faithful to an age-old rule of moral and ritual conduct. This initial contradiction (and others emerge as the story goes on, for what makes Ezra and his family so human is that they are so full of contradictions) gives rise to an involuntary and entirely unexpected comicality that colours the author's narrative in a quite startling way as it unfolds against the grim background of the progressive strangulation of European Jewry. This is the very nub of the book, the quality that makes it unique and new.

Ezra hides nothing; nothing is covered up. The pages devoted to the way in which Nazism spread to the remotest corners of Germany make us stop and think, as do his observations on the fascination (from which no one was immune, not even he) of marching in step, the spell of drum-rolls and torchlight processions. Yet his hero, as he emerges in what follows — complete with the nickname 'Rooster' — is cast in the Chaplinesque mould: simultaneously innocent and wily, ever ready to resort to imaginative improvisation, never abandoning hope, fundamentally incapable of hatred, violence, or deceit, in love with life, with taking chances, and with having fun. He slips through every net as if by a miracle, as if God's covenant with the people of Israel had found practical application in his person and for his benefit, as if God Himself, in whom he believes, were guiding him with a

---

* This Foreword was first printed in the Italian edition, Milan: U. Mursia & C., 1967 and is reproduced here by kind permission of the publishers.

hand upon his head, as He is said to do with children and with Jews.

I met the author years ago and found him delightful company — like all men of gentle views who nevertheless show great strength and determination in putting those views into practice and in enduring adversity. He told me the sequel to his extraordinary adventure,[†] culminating in his arrival in the land of his fathers where — supreme paradox — the British Secret Service refused to believe his story (it is indeed incredible), interning as a suspected German spy the young Jew who had made his way across most of wartime Nazi Europe without the Gestapo touching so much as a hair of his head.

It is my earnest hope that the author will one day find the time and the inclination to complete the story of his absurd and happy fate.

PRIMO LEVI

[†] As summarised in the Epilogue to the present volume.

Preface

This book is a testimony, not an autobiography. I must begin therefore by examining myself, as a witness who cannot possibly be impartial, and by reflecting on my ambiguous identity and my relation to my former homeland.

Who am I, in fact? The answer would be difficult to accommodate within the blank spaces of an official form. In this I am not unlike some of the ex-generals of Hitler's army who have presented themselves to the post-war public in autobiographies. From behind the smouldering heaps of debris in the death-haunts of Europe, heads have been popping up one after another — cautiously at first but latterly with less and less diffidence, less and less dissimulation.

I have read the memoirs of some of these people. I have read their apologias, ideological justifications, and advice about how best to defend civilisation in the future. It strikes me that they, the men of power in army and government, and I, the powerless individual, have something in common, namely a past crammed full of cock-eyed situations. The top army officers who under Hitler's supreme command destroyed Germany (and have since excused themselves on the grounds that it is a soldier's duty to obey orders) make me wonder how they got into their cock-eyed situations.

We have something else in common, they and I: the need to unearth a deeper significance in our experiences. The efforts and the blood-sacrifice of the German army must possess some deeper historical meaning, insist its surviving commanders. What, I ask myself, was the meaning of the deportation and extermination of my friends, those eighty young people in whose company I worked, suffered, and hoped amid the Brandenburg countryside up until May 1942? What was the meaning of all the SS atrocities that came to light after the war — for example, the murder of 14,000 Khar'kov Jews in No. 9 tractor factory? Were the members of the German task forces was it necessary for their officers in the SS and the police to spur them on with offers of extra leave and special rations of *schnapps*? You may still be alive, you men who arrested my mother, my father, my brothers and my sister and herded them into those death camps. You may be going about your honest business unmolested, somewhere in present-day Germany or Austria. Compare yourselves for a moment with those (to me) unforgettable

Germans who placed their lives in jeopardy in order to save mine. Explain precisely why you hated my parents and my siblings — or, if you didn't hate them, why you murdered them.

I vividly remember the way in which many well-meaning Germans were held in thrall by the terrorism practised by the Hitler regime, but I still cannot comprehend how millions of Germans were able to remain silent and let the rest do what they did.

It must have been some time between November 1938 and May 1945 that I shook off the habit of saying 'we Germans' and began to speak merely of 'Germans'. But that does not define my relationship to my former country with sufficient precision. The question 'How was it possible?' will haunt me till my dying day. It affects me more deeply than it affects survivors from other countries whose experience of Germany was exclusively evil.

What did the Germans do and what did they neglect to do, that Weimar Germany was able to degenerate into the Nazi Reich? What was it that led from the 'Christian-Germanic' monarchy of Friedrich Wilhelm IV to Hitler's 'Aryan', 'racially pure' state? Did the playground pogroms that I suffered at my secondary school in Silesia contain the seeds of Auschwitz and Bergen-Belsen?

Yet the history of the German people up to 1933 is not simply a prelude to the Third Reich. Many good things, many sublime human achievements have come out of Germany — not merely in the age of Goethe but right down into our own day. I had to find my way back to that realisation. I had to acquire it afresh. And it shook me more deeply than my bitter experiences had done on their own.

CHAPTER 1

Boyhood in Heilbronn

After the Second World War many commemorative books were published about Germany's Jewish communities. My own home town of Heilbronn on the Neckar devoted a volume to the fate of its Jews.* It relates the history of the German Jews from the eleventh century, when the power of the church grew so enormously under Pope Urban II, to the time when the largest share of power in Europe lay in the hands of Adolf Hitler. It begins with the anti-Jewish pogroms of the early crusaders and ends with the gas-chambers of Auschwitz.

How utterly innocent was my boyhood in Heilbronn of any presentiment of the persecutions to come, let alone any awareness of their connection with the medieval tradition of anti-Judaism! The early years of my life fell in what, in millennial terms, was a brief period of light for German Jewry. Friendly co-existence between Christians and Jews was something I took for granted, never having known anything else. I still believe today that my early memories reflect authentic reality, not merely the naïvety of childhood. No childish trust, no real love of one's birthplace can flourish in a country that is wholly evil.

The Jewish religious tradition had had roots in Swabia for a long time. In my parents' house it governed the daily round from the time we rose to the time we went to bed. When I reflect on the pious way of life of the Jews of southern Germany, I find much to criticise in retrospect. What I cannot find is any intelligible reason why it had to lead to the mass murder of those who lived it.

Yet the persecutions suffered by the Jews are said to be religious in origin. Christian and Jewish historians have shown that anti-Judaism constituted a reaction on the part of non-Jews to the Jews'

* H. Franke, *Geschichte und Schicksal der Juden in Heilbronn 1050–1945*, Heilbronn (Archiv der Stadt), 1963.

conviction that they are the Chosen People. This protest against the Jewish belief in divine election gave rise, among other things, to the charge that the Jews were responsible for crucifying Jesus. Racially motivated hatred — the anti-Semitism of the nineteenth and twentieth centuries — together with resentment against Jewish usurers, did not enter the picture until long after the Church had already deeply disrupted relations between Jews and Christians.

Knowing this, and knowing that my parents — murdered by Hitler's henchmen — were indeed devoted believers in the divine election of the Jewish people, prompts me to take another look at my childhood years. What was it about our way of life that can possibly have seemed so offensive to non-Jews? The question continues to haunt me even today.

My earliest memories are of no help to me here. They are as idyllic as the childhood memories of anyone who grew up in a secure home.

My father had left his own home in Bavaria during the inflationary period that followed the First World War to take up the office of rabbi in Heilbronn, a small town some twenty-five miles north of Stuttgart. Consequently we children grew up on the banks of the River Neckar. For my sister Toni and myself, the two youngest members of the family, the distinctive Heilbronn dialect became our mother tongue. But our elder sister Ruth and our elder brothers Jakob and Leon, despite the fact that they had reached school age before leaving Bavaria, also came to speak the purest Swabian. For this we largely had our Heilbronn-born maid Frieda to thank, as well as our Christian playmates from the houses round about.

Our house stood in a street named after the nineteenth-century German statesman Bismarck. The garden and the poultry yard attached to the house occupy an important place in my idyllic childhood memories. They were where we played and made friends with the neighbourhood children and spent countless hours observing the idiosyncrasies of the poultry flock. We made the discovery, quite without parental assistance, that hens drinking water repeatedly look skywards to thank God for each gulp. One bird that commanded special attention was a cockerel with the most magnificent colouring. His beak, spurs and talons were capable of making even adults keep a respectful distance. More than once we refused to set out for kindergarten until the cockerel had been thrown a distracting handful of barley.

A fresh phase in my exploration of the world began when I was tall enough to open the garden gate unaided. My usual destination was Kaiserstrasse, 'Emperor Street', the main thoroughfare of the town. That was the place — the precise place — where the world

2

promised to present itself at its most absorbing. Kaiserstrasse was a seething mass of clanking 'electrics' (our word for trams). In addition a dense procession of carriages, bicycles, motor cars and delivery carts squeezed through its narrow defile. Flanking the street, towering upwards to their pointed overhanging gables, were the façades of ancient half-timbered houses. Double flights of stone steps with wrought-iron balustrades stood there for the sole purpose of being clambered up and clambered down again. The street led to the town centre, where the huge tower of St Kilian's church went soaring into the sky.

No one could have failed to linger in the market-place to stare in wonder at the stall-keepers. They had a knack of handling fish, chickens, potatoes, bunches of grapes, or whatever it was as if they had had not one but three pairs of hands — and of accompanying their gestures with richly expressive remarks, couched in fruity Swabian, that had their customers laughing out loud. Only when twelve o'clock struck did traders and housewives pause and turn towards the town hall. The sight of the astronomical double clock as its figures jerked into motion was one nobody wanted to miss. Once the angels had finished blowing their trumpets and flourishing their sceptres and the bronze rams had struck the hour with their horns, all eyes returned, reassured, to the rows of bloaters and cabbages.

I cannot provide a more comprehensive account of the treasures of medieval Heilbronn, for I saw them only through the eyes of a child. Yet I was left with the purest of affections for the town of my earliest youth. Heilbronn gave me everything a home town can give anyone.

The holy and the shadow of the holy

Our life was woven through and through with Jewish customs. When we got home from school at lunchtime on a Friday, the meal mother set before us was almost frugal. She deliberately kept it simple in order to make Friday evening's feast seem all the more delicious. In any case, everyone in the house was far too busy to waste much time over lunch.

Most of the work fell to my mother, with the maid and my elder sister and brothers lending a hand. Naturally there was nothing for us little ones to do. Not that Toni and I were left in peace. Wherever we looked someone was either scrubbing or sweeping, and wherever we went we were in some busy grown-up's way. 'Will you get out of here with those filthy shoes!' was our greeting at the doorway of each room in the house.

The sense of anticipation became hourly more acute. Father played a major part in whipping up the tension. He 'dashed out' for fruit; he 'quickly' cut flowers; the barber was going to have to 'get a move on'. How thankful we were when mother finally lit the *shabbat* candles!* All the worry and the flurry were over then. For the next twenty-five hours not only was every kind of work forbidden but also every kind of workaday haste. Washed and dressed in our best clothes, off we went with father to synagogue.

Prayers at an end, we set out for home again through the twilit streets of Heilbronn. Occasionally we would hear the muffled bell of a distant tram. The garden was already dark; a straining eye might perhaps still detect a shovel or a rake propped against the fence. The hens already had their heads tucked under their wings. Mother opened the front door and led us into what only a short while before had been the living-room. In our absence it had been metamorphosed into a miniature banqueting hall.

With the advent of Friday evening the world underwent a radical transformation, and it remained in this transfigured state until Saturday evening, when it resumed its everyday guise. On that holy day we might stroll into town and thread our way through the noisy market-place. Drivers of carts and motor cars, customers, market-women, postmen and delivery boys were all going about their work as usual, but their doings were somehow removed from reality. To us children, all that bustling activity was now no more than a puppet show.

What was behind this miraculous change? Father's explanation was that the change had taken place not in the streets of Heilbronn, and certainly not in the outside world, but within ourselves. All people had received one soul from God. On the Sabbath, however, everyone who kept the day holy was lent a second soul, so that until nightfall on Saturday evening he or she rejoiced in a double soul. It was that second soul that accounted for the astonishing change.

The explanation made immediate sense — nor did I have any objection whatever to dressing up on a Saturday morning and, equipped with my double soul, trotting off to synagogue while my Christian school-mates had to shoulder their satchels and mooch along to school with their single souls.

However, the privilege of the double soul was associated with a great many restrictions and stipulations. We were not allowed to draw or to cut out paper figures. Catching butterflies and May bugs

---

* The Hebrew *shabbat* comes from *shavat*, 'to rest'. The English form 'Sabbath' and its pronunciation are the result of learned association with the Hebrew form.

was likewise forbidden, since the Sabbath was a day of freedom for animals, too. No further work could be done on the wooden hut that we children were erecting in the garden. We were not even permitted to touch any of the planks and battens that lay around, let alone the hammer and pincers, lest we be tempted to put them to use.

This 'do not touch' ban extended to all objects that one was not allowed to use on the Sabbath. Such objects were said to be *mukze*. All tools were *mukze*, and that included matches, scissors, slates and slate pencils. They must simply be left where they lay as if they had belonged to Sleeping Beauty's enchanted castle. The boxes and sacks and all the rest of the lumber in the cellar were *mukze* because they were too ugly and dirty for the holy day. Unfortunately, some of our playthings were *mukze*, too — Leon's airgun, for instance.

There was something rather extraordinary about this quality of being *mukze*. Presumably it adhered to the objects concerned all the time, yet it became apparent only on the Sabbath and other holy days. Take a rusty coal scoop, for example: you could see all week long that it was rusty, but that it was also *mukze* was something you became aware of only on the Sabbath, because you were then in possession of a double soul. You had been raised up to the realm of the holy; the coal scoop remained behind, *mukze*.

I assume there is no need to explain why money was *mukze*. It would be difficult to think of anything more *mukze* than money. When the postman brought a cash transfer on a Saturday morning, father had him count it out on the table-top and took no further notice of it till the evening.

It would no more have occurred to us to take a tram on the Sabbath than it would to go into a shop and buy a bag of sweets. We should not even have consented to travel gratis, because not only were the fare money and the ticket *mukze*; so was the tram itself. Trams, on the Sabbath, could do nothing for us beyond providing something interesting to look at.

My Christian classmates envied me for being allowed to miss school on Saturdays. What they failed to realise was that I had to catch up on my lessons at home on the Sunday. Nor did they have the slightest idea what awaited me at synagogue on a Saturday morning. Being squeezed into a pew with a whole lot of other children under all those watchful adult eyes and having to remain still and silent for two interminable hours was not exactly a pleasant experience. We were too young to be able to follow the reading from the Torah, the Jewish Law incorporated in the five 'Books of Moses'. Instead we used to amuse one another — and of course get caught — making faces beneath the pew.

My father climbed the steps to the pulpit. During the sermon we little ones were allowed to stand on the pew. Moreover, no one tried to stop us as we stolidly and quite shamelessly stared that august congregation in the face. The moment when the men sat down provided us with a welcome change. From our elevated vantage-point we proceeded to inspect the serried ranks of top hats (head-wear is obligatory in synagogue), spectacles, beards and moustaches as though all those severe-looking gentlemen had sat down with the express purpose of giving us nippers a better view. The transition was astonishing. There they sat, abruptly silent, hands clasped on paunches as, breathing visibly, they turned eyes and ears to the pulpit and allowed themselves to be treated to an address sprinkled liberally with quotations from the Bible and the Talmud.

After the sermon we stood again for more singing and prayers. At last everyone was streaming towards the exit, a cheerful, chattering throng exchanging handshakes and Sabbath greetings.

Back home again, we found the table laid for a feast. It was a while before we could eat, however, because father first wanted to know what the postman had brought. Business letters were placed on one side; they must wait until evening. Letters whose appearance made it impossible to tell whether they were of a business or personal nature were also left unopened to avoid any risk of profaning the Sabbath.

It was not always easy to maintain a holy nonchalance under this kind of pressure from the workaday world. Precisely those letters whose contents remained in question had a way of arousing the most stressful expectations. I wonder how many times I saw my father hold an envelope up to the light in an attempt to gain some approximate foreknowledge of its contents and, the attempt having failed, spend a moment in thought before perhaps trying the light test once again.

Having sorted out the personal letters, my father handed them to Frieda, our maid, who promptly drew a hairpin from her *coiffure* and used it to slit open the envelopes.

Frieda, the good-natured daughter of a Swabian farmer, did other jobs for my parents that she, as a Christian, was allowed to do on a Saturday, but we were not. She made up the fire, put the food on the stove, switched the electric light on and off — that sort of thing. She loyally and willingly performed every task my parents asked her to perform. What she thought about it all — whether she felt slighted or privileged at not being subject to the Sabbath restrictions — I simply do not know. What I do know is that we lived amicably under the same roof and that Frieda was devoted to our family.

6

When Frieda had cleared the breakfast table our official visiting time began. My father took great pleasure in receiving people, not only at visiting time but also at other times, whether on the Sabbath or on a weekday. A figure would appear at the door; it might be a friend or a stranger, a boy delivering groceries or the plumber come to thaw out the frozen water pipes. Invariably he would be greeted with an 'Ah!' of delighted surprise: 'Ah, good morning!' or 'Ah, good evening!' So effusive was my father's welcoming 'Ah!' that the figure at the door would break into a smile or respond with a look of astonished gratitude.

There was plenty of opportunity for such welcomings on Saturday mornings. But however much my father felt in his element receiving people, we children took little pleasure in the stream of visitors. In fact, we used to make vain efforts to escape the torrent of avuncular pleasantries.

It was at times like these, when (so far as we were concerned) unwelcome guests arrived, that the cockerel, without actually coming to our aid, did give us a certain amount of satisfaction. That bird was quite capable of holding at bay an entire party of elegantly dressed ladies and gentleman. We would have hugged him in gratitude had we not been so scared of him ourselves. Inevitably mother would reach smartly for a handful of barley, thus enabling our visitors to make it to the front door and be greeted by my father's 'Ah! Good Sabbath!'.

First news of the New Testament

I learnt my ABC in the Karlstrasse school. When the teacher left the classroom, I picked up some other things as well. I would suddenly find myself embroiled in a tangle of scuffling boys screaming at one another in high-pitched voices. In other words, our school was very much like schools the world over. The only difference was that the battle of words that formed the prelude to the actual brawling was conducted in the inimitably earthy* terms and tones of the local Heilbronn dialect.

For my part, when it came to a scrap I swallowed no swearwords and pulled no punches. After several tussles I began to realise that I was not among the strongest in the class — but nor was I among the weakest. In addition to what I might call these run-of-the-mill hostilities, I was to experience a special kind that I must go into in rather greater detail.

* And untranslatable! [Tr.]

7

One day as I was sauntering home from school with my satchel on my back, three boys from my class joined me at a street corner where I did not normally meet them. For a while we walked along side by side, saying nothing. Then suddenly they threw down their satchels and set upon me. With the odds so heavily against me, there was little I could do. Grazed, dirty and tearful, I made my way home.

Similar incidents occurred in the days that followed. Why were they out to get me in particular? Were they jealous because I was ahead of them in reading and writing? Or was it that one of them — Wolfgang, his name was — could not stomach my having thrashed him once in the playground? The reasons behind the assaults did not become clear to me until much later, although the torrent of insults with which the boys always accompanied their blows featured one phrase that should have opened my eyes: 'Dirty Jew!'

'Make sure you keep out of their way,' was my mother's advice. 'If anyone shouts "Dirty Jew" after you, tell him: "I'm the Jew, and you're the dirty one!" And if they go for you, you fight back just as hard as you can!' Mother also resolved to see to it that my brothers came to meet me occasionally on the way home. Jakob was then twelve and Leon ten.

These measures, while they improved matters to some extent, did not entirely prevent the three boys from spoiling my homeward journey from time to time. Accepting this philosophically as 'just one of those things', I consoled myself with the thought that my tormentors enjoyed no great standing at school. During breaks, whether in the classroom or out in the playground, they left me in peace. The presence of the other children, who had strict rules about what constituted fair and unfair fighting, was sufficient to intimidate them.

I got on with most of my school-fellows extremely well; with some of them I had even struck up friendships. On only one occasion, in the winter of 1928–9, did I become aware of anything approaching a general mood of hostility towards me. 'Dirty Jew!' several voices called out as I entered the classroom late that day. 'You Jews crucified our saviour!'

The accusation was new to me — and completely incomprehensible. However, some instinct warned me that caution was in order. Lessons over, I did not take my usual route home; I turned off down a side street. But the boys had spotted my manoeuvre. This time I had a whole crowd of them on my heels. What was I to do — make a run for it? No, they mustn't see I was scared. And anyway, maybe Jakob and Leon would come and meet me in time. Help, they weren't coming! I groaned inwardly. If only I was already at our garden gate, the wicked boys couldn't do anything to me! The cockerel would soon show them! I stole a glance over my shoulder. No, my friends were not in the crowd. But neither were they anywhere around to stick up for me. There was no escape. A couple of the boys grabbed me and pinned me against a fence by my outstretched arms. The rest quickly made snowballs and proceeded to pelt me with such a hail of snow and ice that I had difficulty in protecting my eyes.

This revenge for the crucified saviour ended only when some passing grown-ups intervened. I was aware of their scolding voices as I shook the snow from myself. They made the boys brush me down, then sent them packing.

Next day, some of my attackers attempted to make reparation by being especially friendly towards me.

Puzzling though this sudden outbreak of hostility was, I took it for little more than an isolated manifestation of ill-will. The grown-ups had stepped in; my school-mates showed remorse; justice was reinstated. Before long we were larking and scrapping together as we had always done.

First acquaintance with the Torah

When I first went to school in April 1928 I could already read and write a little — and do so in two languages. I had mastered the German alphabet through joining my sister Toni at her homework, purely out of curiosity. Even before that, however, father had taught me the Hebrew alphabet. We used Hebrew not for conversation but solely as the language of prayer and of the Torah. Gratefully as I recall all that early instruction today, at the time I did not think much of the privilege. It irked me to have my leisure time curtailed. While my Christian school-mates romped outside to their hearts' content, I had to wrestle with interminable prayers and familiarise myself with the story of Adam and Eve and their offspring. The times I had my ears boxed before the world was safely created! The strokes of the cane that fell before Noah finally got his ark built!

I remember one of those agonising hours of domestic Bible study with particular vividness. It was a sunny spring day. I can see myself now, wedged between table and chair, a reluctant right forefinger following the text of the Torah, my father's eyes holding me in a steely grip from the other side of the table. Word by word, I was having to work through the story of the wicked people of Sodom and Gomorrah, whereas my thoughts were all with the cable railway that Leon had just finished constructing. The little car was travel-

9

ling back and forth between the window of the next room and one of the stronger branches of the pear tree outside. The whirring, squeaking noise it made was like a magical force drawing me into the garden. I pleaded, protested, implored. Father remained adamant, employing every stratagem from threats to promises to keep me at my Bible. My despairing glance wandered over the walls and clung to the pictures hanging there.

Above the sofa was one of a girl decked out in tiara and earrings and dressed in an ample and luxurious gown. Holding aloft a bowl of fruit, she was looking over her right shoulder into the room, unmoved by my tears. (When I was older I discovered that the picture was a print of one of Titian's portraits of his daughter Lavinia, *Girl with a Fruit Dish*.) Below and slightly to one side of the girl, a picture of reapers returning home from the fields attracted my attention. With their scythes slung over their shoulders, they were trudging tired-eyed through the gathering dusk back to the village.

The day's Bible story concerned a city in which strangers sought shelter in vain, since hospitality was considered a crime there.* Nevertheless, one citizen dared to provide two weary travellers with some food and a roof over their heads. Instantly, he found his house surrounded by angry townsfolk. 'Bring them out!' they shouted. 'Bring those two strangers out this minute, or we shall deal worse with you than with them!'

My wandering gaze once again encountered the returning reapers, and suddenly I believed that these were the wicked men of Sodom I saw before me. I misread the end-of-the-day weariness in their weather-beaten faces as hardness of heart. Shouldering their scythes, they were marching over the fields with grim intent, heading for Sodom, which must be somewhere in the vicinity of Heilbronn. Anger boiled up inside me against the people of Sodom, not so much because they would not tolerate Lot's offer of hospitality as because those spoilsports with their long scythes stood between me and Leon's cable railway. By the time our well-thumbed Bible was back in the bookcase, page 28 — together with Lot, the two angels and the men of Sodom — was well and truly saturated with tears.

* Genesis 19:1–11.

10

CHAPTER 2

The Brown-uniformed World

A small town in Silesia

One Saturday in the spring of 1929 the postman brought us a momentous letter. It contained news of my father's appointment to the position of a district rabbi in Upper Silesia. A few months later we made the 450-mile train journey across Germany. Thanks to this premature leave-taking from Heilbronn, nearly all my memories of our time there are happy ones.

My father's new base was a little town with the rather grand name of Gross-Strehlitz. It and the other eleven villages that made up the rabbinical district lay in the Upper Silesian plain, midway between — as they were then called — Breslau and Krakau.*

Gross-Strehlitz and its surrounding villages led an inglorious existence well away from the mainstream of world affairs. After all these years, I have seen them mentioned only once in the international press. Towards the end of the Second World War, when I was already in Palestine, I found them listed in the official Soviet communiqué, together with a great many other places, as having been liberated the previous day. That must have been in January or February 1945, because the survivors of Auschwitz were freed by Soviet troops on 26 January, and my father's former district was situated about fifty miles north-east of Auschwitz.

In 1929, of course, which is when my family arrived in Upper Silesia, no one would have dreamed of using Auschwitz as a geographical reference point. Who had even heard of the place?

---

* The town is now called Strzelce Opolskie and lies in Poland (midway between Wrocław and Kraków). Most of Silesia was transferred to Polish administration under the Potsdam Agreement of 1945, which redrew the eastern frontier of Germany, from the Baltic to Czechoslovakia, along the line formed by the rivers Oder and Neisse. Technically, the so-called Oder–Neisse Line is still provisional.

It was in Gross-Strehlitz that my family was to live through the end of the Weimar Republic and the beginning of the Third Reich. How little we suspected what the future held in store as we moved into our new home!

The town, with its 12,000 or so inhabitants, had probably begun as a typical ribbon village, growing up along a traffic artery. The main road running through it still constituted its lifeline. In the centre of the town the road widened to form a sort of square bounded by four rows of houses, the so-called Ring. In the Ring stood the town hall and the war memorial for the citizens of Gross-Strehlitz who had fallen in the 1914–18 war. On market days farm-carts from the surrounding villages clattered over its cobble-stones and cries of 'Whoa there!' rang out from all sides, interspersed with the grunts, clucks and quacks of the livestock being offered for sale.

On Sundays the little town used to swarm with church-goers. Occasionally the veterans' association would hold a parade, marching up to the war memorial and performing solemn rituals around it. The rest of the time the town lay under a blanket of tedious tranquillity. Shopkeepers stood in their doorways, dreamy-eyed, gazing idly after the passers-by.

'Not a lot happens in Gross-Strehlitz', was a familiar complaint from the townspeople themselves. Yet it was the centre of an administrative district, with all that that implied. It had a mayor and a district council. Doctors, lawyers, teachers, a priest, a minister and a rabbi discharged the duties of their respective offices. The town contained a primary school, a girls' secondary school or *Lyzeum*, a classical secondary school or *Gymnasium*, a synagogue that could seat about 500, a Protestant church of around the same size and a very much larger Roman Catholic church.

Measured against a former *Reichsstadt* such as Heilbronn, a 'free imperial city' with a thousand years of history behind it, Gross-Strehlitz not unnaturally cut a poor figure. Similarly the country round about, with its pine plantations and ponds, presented a monotonous appearance in comparison with the Neckar Valley.

On all the roads leading out of the town lay villages with Polish-sounding names. In Gross-Strehlitz itself German civilisation reigned supreme. The farmers spoke only a very imperfect German, their proper language being a Polish dialect known as 'Water Polish'. The townspeople spoke a relatively correct German containing only a few Polish expressions. But to our ears it had a hard, spiky sound. We missed the idiosyncratic warmth of our native Swabian.

That was not the only thing we had lost by moving. We no longer had our own house. The apartment my father rented in Gross-Strehlitz, though it occupied a whole floor, was a poor substitute for the little world of our own that we had left behind in Heilbronn. Still, it was in a fairly smart building, virtually on the Ring; we could see part of the town hall from our living-room window. Our neighbours in the house were people of 'standing': above us lived *Studienrat* Dr Paulus, a member of staff at the classical *Gymnasium* (he later taught me Latin),* and the flat below was occupied by a veterinary surgeon.

Our south-German dialect and the strange customs we had brought with us from Heilbronn made the people of Gross-Strehlitz smile, and occasionally they would even make fun of us. Not that this in any way chastened my childish arrogance. I made it quite clear to my new school-mates that I expected to be treated with the respect due to a native of the immeasurably nobler former dukedom of Swabia. Whenever 'our common Germanness' was under discussion, I hastened to point out that I was no ordinary German; I was a Swabian.

My elder brothers and my sister Ruth also tended to look down on the Upper Silesians. My father, however, appeared to take a different view. Our repeated reproaches — why, of all places in Germany, we wanted to know, had he picked this out-of-the-way little market town with its stuck-up breed of men? — prompted him to give us a more detailed explanation.

We ought not, he told us, to despise the Upper Silesians or dismiss them intolerantly on the grounds that they were less friendly than the people of Württemberg. Life had always been difficult for them. For many generations they had had repeatedly to switch their colours and to profess successively Polish, Austrian and Prussian patriotic sentiments. No one could expect the children of so hapless a region to be as trusting and straightforward as children in southern Germany. We must simply be patient; they would come to seem less odd in time.

The call to Gross-Strehlitz was one my father had obeyed willingly. He felt it was his vocation to win over the Jews of those little Upper Silesian towns for the holy Jewish Teaching. For our benefit he put it like this: he wished to make them godly again.

Three-day Jews

What my father meant by 'making them godly again' was something

* As a *Studienrat* Dr Paulus was on the third rung of the secondary-school teaching ladder and enjoyed considerable status.

I felt closer to understanding as I began to attend services in synagogue daily and to frequent Jewish homes in Gross-Strehlitz.

As a building, the Gross-Strehlitz synagogue was very much larger and more splendid than the synagogue in Heilbronn. On most days in the year, however, it presented a somewhat desolate picture. The few individuals who appeared for worship on the Sabbath were dotted here and there among the pews — isolated figures shivering in the gloom. If you wanted to see the members of the Jewish congregation on the Sabbath, you were best advised to seek them in their shops, for most of them were shopkeepers and on the holy day it was 'business as usual'. At the Jewish New Year, on the other hand, there was scarcely a vacant seat in the place. The Bible and Jewish tradition regard the Sabbath as a more holy day than the festival of the New Year. But the Jews of Gross-Strehlitz made the Sabbath a working day and saved all the honours for three days in the year: the two days of the New Year festival and the Day of Atonement, Yom Kippur. Hence the scornful nickname — 'three-day Jews' — applied to them by Jews faithful to the Torah, as the traditionalist German Jews were.

The Gross-Strehlitz congregation included a handful of god-fearing Jews. The vast majority, however, were of the three-day variety. There were also a number of Jews who by marrying Christian women had broken completely with the Jewish religious community.

The behaviour of the three-day Jews raised various nagging riddles in my young mind. The life of the solidly traditionalist Jewish congregation in Heilbronn had given me a clear idea of what distinguished Jews from Christians. Now, for the first time, I saw that there were also people who paid only lip-service to Judaism. Their worship was not exactly play-acting, but neither was it in earnest; it was something I lacked the words to describe. They were quite capable of breaking off in mid-prayer for a cosy chat from pew to pew. Yet when the cantor intoned the prayer for the souls of the departed they would be moved to tears. This confused and offended my childish simplicity, especially since the Gross-Strehlitz Jews themselves shrugged their shoulders over their religious exercises and at the same time expected to be looked up to for performing them.

They were glad to have a cantor who conducted for them the ceremonies they felt incompetent to conduct themselves — and who also knew his way around such rites as were necessary to ensure the salvation of the soul. The cantor, a salaried synagogue official, possessed skills of a kind that in Gross-Strehlitz were expected only of a professional expert: he had Hebrew, was familiar with the set prayers, and knew how to recite them melodiously and with feeling or alternatively rattle them off with amazing lingual agility, as required. He further provided the younger members of the congregation with elementary religious instruction and slaughtered hens and geese in accordance with the prescribed ritual. He was happiest, though, when officiating at his prayer-desk. In fact, he could occasionally be prevailed upon to demonstrate his singing and praying skills even in the privacy of his own home.

Yet the way in which the three-day Jews behaved towards the cantor was curiously ambivalent. They had engaged him on condition that he fulfilled all the above functions, and they rewarded him for doing so with a respect that was more than a little ironic.

As a proud little Swabian and rabbi's son, I was quick to condemn the Jews of Gross-Strehlitz. My earliest notions of what constituted a proper Jewishness had been formed in the context of the Heilbronn congregation at a time when I was far too young to be aware of failings of any sort in its traditionalist members. After that the behaviour of the three-day Jews struck me as so absurd that I was in two minds whether to be outraged or amused by it.

However, I do not think my boyish judgment was entirely in error. Every child develops a sixth sense for whether the gravity of grown-ups reflects a true seriousness or merely a conflict-ridden feebleness of mind.

Was it an accident, I wonder, that among those who attended the Gross-Strehlitz synagogue it should have been a harmless imbecile that most fascinated me? His way of staring open-mouthed at the lame rituals enacted there made a profound impression on me.

Hans Hirschfeld (that was his name) was in fact twenty-three years old, but everyone called him by the pet name 'Guli'. He had not learnt to speak until he was fifteen, and even at this time, eight years later, his speech was still very slow and long-drawn-out. He began most of his sentences with the words 'Well, for instance . . .'. Lost for an expression, he was capable of stating with infinite regret, 'Well, for instance, I don't know how to put the words together.'

Guli's helpless awkwardness disappeared without trace the moment my brother Leon turned his attention to him. Then he would grunt with pleasure and might even laugh so loudly that his voice cracked. The nonsense those two used to get up to together! It was hilarious.

Guli was always Leon's most devoted 'court jester'. When father eventually gave up his position in Upper Silesia and moved to another job, we lost contact with him. Shortly before the war, however, as life became more and more intolerable for Jews in small towns, my parents sought refuge in Berlin. So too, a little while later, did the Hirschfeld family, and Guli once again became a regular visitor to our home.

Poor Guli! With the same look of bewilderment which the synagogue formalities of the three-day Jews had brought to his face, he wondered at the misfortunes visited ever more cruelly upon himself and upon all the Jews of his acquaintance — until one day, with his yellow star on his chest, he was sucked into one of the German extermination camps. And it is with a similar bewilderment that I now reflect upon the suffering that God inflicted on that innocent creature. For me, he stands for a great many others who were swept up, all unsuspecting, in the maelstrom of the Nazi persecution of the Jews.

Rescue attempts

My father, then, had set himself the task of converting the small-town Jews of Upper Silesia to Judaism. He was a great believer in the persuasive power of the spoken word. Travelling by train to each of the twelve congregations of his district in turn, he tirelessly harangued them from the pulpit. He also visited individual members in their homes and shops. When he was invited to give religious instruction to the Jewish pupils at the secondary schools of Gross-Strehlitz, he welcomed the opportunity. In fact, he delivered his lessons with such passion that his Bavarian dialect was more than usually in evidence. The pupils listened impassively, startled that anyone could speak so enthusiastically about such ancient customs as wearing phylacteries or eating kosher food. Some of the girls, tickled by his quainter Bavarianisms, used to nudge one another and giggle behind their hands.

What my father sought to do from pulpit and podium, I set out to imitate on a more modest scale. Filled with a child's religious zeal, I proceeded to lecture my Jewish school-mates and play-fellows in similar terms.

Klaus Friedburg went to the same school as I did, and since his homeward journey took him past our flat, we often covered that part of the route together. Sometimes we would get into an argument so heated that we dumped our school bags against a convenient advertising pillar in order to leave our hands free to hammer the point out there and then. My school-friend had no idea of the potentially far-reaching consequences of our discussions. It was vital that all Jews — even those living in such remote dumps as Gross-Strehlitz

— should return to the traditional Jewish way of life.

My father had explained it to us something like this: The Jews are condemned to live in exile, exactly as threatened in the Torah, because they have not obeyed God's teaching. One day, however, that exile will end. The end will come about through God's Anointed, the *mashiach*,* who will lead the Jewish people home and rule over them as their king. This will represent redemption not only for the Jews but for all mankind — including the Christians, who erroneously believe that the *mashiach* (or, as they call him, Christ) came 1,900 years ago. The true *mashiach* will put an end to all wars and lead the Jewish people and the whole of mankind in establishing the Kingdom of God. He will be no superhuman figure, no saint, but a man, a descendant of the Davidian dynasty. No one knows where David's descendants live now, for the genealogical tables have been lost, and the majority of the Jews living today stem, like King David himself, from the tribe of Judah. In fact the only Jews who can be excluded from King David's issue are the Levites and those descended from purely proselyte stock. Where and when the *mashiach* will appear, no one can say. His birth might be in twenty years' time. But possibly he has been born already and is wandering the earth as a stranger until his hour shall come. God will send the *mashiach* as soon as the Jewish people abides by the Torah.

Father's words put me in pensive mood. Our family did not belong to the Levites. Nor, so far as anyone knew, did we stem from purely proselyte stock. So it was by no means out of the question that Davidian blood might flow in our veins. I must strive to keep myself pure of all sin and free from all vulgarity. For who knew? Perhaps I was the appointed *mashiach*?

Making the mulish inhabitants of Gross-Strehlitz godly again turned out to be a harder task than I had imagined. The astonishing thing was that my father's efforts were not entirely without fruit. He did manage to persuade a growing number of Jewish families to make their eating habits conform to the ritual laws. He did not, however, manage to persuade the shopkeepers to close on the Sabbath. Here his homilies had only a limited effect: the three-day Jews, instead of showing themselves openly in their doorways on

* The Hebrew *mashiach* means literally 'anointed' and was originally applied in a general sense to those who were appointed — by anointment — high priests or kings (e.g. Cyrus, King of Persia). Later, under the influence of the visions of Isaiah and other prophets and seers, the term was used in an increasingly specific way to denote the *future* anointed king who would redeem the Jews and usher in the era of world peace. Later still, the *messias* or 'messiah' (Greek: *christos*) of the Church was believed to be a divine person, the 'Son of God'.

17

Saturdays as they sought to keep an eye on the market-place, shrank back in embarrassment into the interiors of their shops when father walked by.

The Treaty of Versailles

No one could live in Upper Silesia at that time without continually being made aware of Germany's loss of the valuable industrial areas in the eastern part of the province. After the First World War the victorious allies decided that the Upper Silesian population should make up its own mind in a plebiscite as to whether it wished to belong to Germany or to Poland. The majority declared for Germany. However, when the Poles opposed the decision with armed force, the League of Nations gave in and Upper Silesia was partitioned. While that partition took account of the ethnic affiliations of the population, it totally destroyed the economic coherence of the region.

Barely a decade had passed since those events. The German inhabitants of Upper Silesia were still smarting from them. The violence that had followed the plebiscite, the weakness of the League of Nations and the sudden partition and impoverishment of their province were as fresh in their minds as a robbery suffered only the day before.

Then, on top of everything else, came the great economic crisis. Banner headlines in the newspapers announced how many thousand million gold marks Germany still owed the Allies. The jobless figures began to increase at an alarming rate. The agitation this provoked in our parents and teachers led us children to suspect that terrible things must lie concealed behind the word 'unemployment'.

If you had asked me then to list the most calamitous events in the history of the world, I should have put the Fall of Man first, Titus's destruction of the Temple in Jerusalem second, and in third place the Treaty of Versailles.* Indeed, how could we ever have become reconciled to that fundamental evil when scarcely a day went by without some mention of it? At school we heard about the Treaty of Versailles in German, in our local history and geography lessons, and even in singing. At such moments of shared, impassioned resentment we became oblivious to all that separated us as Jews,

* Under the Treaty of Versailles, imposed by the victorious Allies after the First World War, Germany lost a great deal of territory as well as being required to admit to 'war guilt' and pay unspecified reparations. Many Germans felt humiliated by the treaty and never forgave the Weimar government for signing it on 28 June 1919.

Roman Catholics and Protestants.

I remember asking my father once, 'Why is it that we are always, without fail, on the weaker side? We're in a minority as Jews, and we have to suffer as Germans, too!' His pious reply — 'It is better to suffer wrong than to do wrong' — failed to satisfy me. So we decided, my brothers and I, that we would do something about the reality that was a daily offence to our feelings as child patriots. The Treaty of Versailles had been made possible by Germany's military defeat. Ergo, the military outcome of the war must be reversed.

I do not know how many times we set up our tin and papier-mâché soldiers in order to re-enact the First World War. But one thing I remember: *our* war always ended the way we thought it ought to have done. After the enemy's ground forces had been trounced all over the carpet, there would be mighty sea battles in the bath — leading inexorably to the same result.

My parents appeared to attach no more significance to these manifestations of German patriotism than to any of our other games. Mother left us alone as long as we did not allow our supper to get cold. Father was delighted to see us doing so much carpentry. He even paraded our home-made fleet before his visitors, who responded in thoroughly approving if not always very expert terms.

I had only one major disappointment. We had built a particularly powerful-looking battle cruiser, largely inspired by imagination. After all our trouble I felt a need to have the thing admired. I determined to show it off to the next visitor who came along. As chance would have it, this turned out to be none other than Herr Fried, a Polish Jew from Beuthen* who 'travelled' the towns of Upper Silesia once a month with two large leather suitcases full of kosher sausages.

Fried had scarcely set eyes on the ship before his face froze. 'What for you put those crosses on it?' he demanded.

'What crosses? You mean these here? They aren't crosses! They're the fighting masts!' The man was a picture of silent fury. 'But, Mr Fried — that's the masthead and the fire-control post!'

Fried only repeated even more angrily, 'What for you put those crosses on it, huh?' He had no eyes whatever for the intricate superstructure and the electrical installations of which I was so proud. I buried my head in my hands. How could I have been so stupid as to show my ship to such a dimwit! The man had no idea about battle cruisers!

* Now Bytom in Poland, a town about thirty miles south-east of Strzelce Opolskie.

Dear old Herr Fried! Unswervingly loyal to the Jewish religious tradition, he was equally close to all Jews, regardless of political frontiers. He felt himself to be neither Pole nor German. His home-land was the Yiddish small town. How could he possibly have appreciated our German patriotic feelings?

The Hitlers start to multiply

The frequent changes of government in Berlin and the tumultuous party struggles that preceded the advent of the Third Reich had their repercussions in Gross-Strehlitz. What my young understand-ing made of them I can relate only in the broadest outline. The speed and complexity of events were so bewildering that even adults had difficulty in keeping abreast of what was going on. Possibly my memory has in many cases compressed and amalgamated what were actually quite separate experiences.

School, with its firm framework of organisation and discipline, sustained us in the belief that we lived in a solid world resting on sure foundations, despite the fact that rowdy gatherings and violent, bloody clashes were the order of the day on the streets of Gross-Strehlitz.

Shop windows, walls and hoardings disappeared behind an ever-changing display of propaganda posters. What the political parties responsible for these crude mutual recriminations were really after was of course beyond the understanding of a ten-year-old. But whatever it was, we knew they must be in deadly earnest. We saw with our own eyes how savagely they beat one another up over it.

When yet another election day loomed and the little town suc-cumbed to a state of mounting turmoil, it was a bore having to go to school. We would far rather have watched the punch-ups. However, not all the clashes occurred in the mornings; there were plenty of them in the afternoons and evenings, too. Having located the focus of activity, we would climb a tree or scramble up a wall and sit there with our feet dangling down, studying at close quarters the energetic fashion in which the Communists and the 'Hitlers' pelted one another with insults, brickbats, rotten eggs and lumps of dirt or worse.

The terms 'National Socialist' or 'Nazi' were not yet current among school-children. When we saw an SA or an SS man we called him a 'Hitler'.* I might say at supper, 'Know what I saw this afternoon? A boy was chanting "Red Front, Red Front" — in

---

* The Sturmabteilung (SA) and the Schutzstaffel (SS) began life as illegal paramilit-ary organisations of Hitler's Nationalsozialistiche Deutsche Arbeiterpartei

Krakau Street, it was — and three Hitlers came along and beat him up.' On another occasion I went to a mass meeting, partly out of curiosity and partly because I got swept along by the crowd. At home I reported: 'Did anyone see the parade of Hitlers today? Chief Group Leader Heines was in town and gave a speech.* The market-place was packed. People were saying there were 10,000 Hitlers there from all over Upper Silesia!'

Our school — since Easter 1932 I had been a proud first-year at the Gross-Strehlitz *Gymnasium* — did not wholly escape the hulla-balloo of the party-political struggle. Senior boys used to get in-volved in fierce arguments in the playground, though these would stop short of actual violence. The staff behaved correctly on the whole, as long as they were on school premises. Nevertheless, we first-years had a pretty good idea of individual teachers' political allegiances.

There was little scope for political discussion at home. Before an election, father would gain some idea of the various parties' pro-grammes from the newspapers or by asking close friends. He relied on his friends to know far more that he did about such thoroughly secular matters.

During the critical period when the government was constantly changing, father voted for the Roman Catholic Centre Party 'be-cause it steers clear of all extremism and because it counts many God-fearing men among its members'. Even after Hitler's appoint-ment as chancellor, in the short time before Jews were deprived of the vote, he remained loyal to the Centre, as it was called. And what did the Centre do on 23 March 1933 but vote for Hitler's Enabling Act, thus helping to bring about its own demise as well as that of the Weimar Constitution!

My father's political table-talk was not particularly instructive. For the most part he simply repeated what he had read in the *Berliner Tageblatt* or what people were saying. He went rather more thoroughly into the attitudes of the various parties — particularly the NSDAP — towards the Jews. As anti-Semitic outrages became more commonplace, father saw them as part of a divine dispensation

---

(NSDAP), the National Socialist German Workers' Party. The SA was Hitler's political fighting force in the early years, its task to terrorise political opponents. It reached the peak of its power in 1933–4, declining in importance after that time. The SS, after breaking away from the SA in 1925, rose in power and authority under Himmler to become an independent army and a mainstay of Hitler's regime. The concentration camps became its special responsibility.

* The rank of *Obergruppenführer* was equivalent to that of general in the army.

intended to prompt Jews who had lost touch with their Jewishness to take stock and mend their ways. Moreover, the Hitler movement brought with it a further advantage. Its hostility towards the Jews would inevitably set anti-Semitism back a long way, not only in Germany but throughout the world, for — my father reasoned — who would want to admit to anti-Semitism in the company of that murderous riffraff? He regarded it as quite out of the question that President Hindenburg would entrust the government of the country to such a party or that the sensible majority of the people would tolerate such a government taking office.

Mother was less inclined always to look on the positive side. To mention a trivial example, one day the sound of a distant parade of Hitler Youth reached the windows of our flat. The lads were singing as they marched. 'Do you hear what they're bawling?' said mother. '"Jews out!"'

'No, you're wrong,' father countered. 'It's "*Youth* out!" They want young people to come out and join them.'

But, however carefully we listened to the oft-repeated refrain, there remained some doubt as to whether the words were in fact 'Juden heraus' or 'Jugend heraus'. Mother, refusing to discuss the matter further, retired to her room.

One day it was announced in school that there was to be a celebration that evening. Anyone who wanted to was invited to take part. When I arrived at school at the appointed time the pupils were already formed up in columns, class by class, and were preparing to march through the town behind their teachers. I quickly got into line and, like all the others, had a torch thrust into my hand.

I was not sure what we were celebrating. Still fresh in my mind was the memory of another procession that the pupils of the school had staged about a year previously. Then they had been led through the streets by the school band, and I had hugely admired the way in which members of the band managed to play the violin while marching along. Obviously such evening festivities were a school custom. I was 11 years old and it gave me enormous pleasure not to be an onlooker for once but actually to be taking part in the procession. This time they were even letting us march in step behind a military band, holding blazing torches in our hands.

As we reached the more brightly lit streets of the town centre, I noticed that the procession included other schools beside our own — and not just schools but also Hitler Youth and SA detachments. The 'military band' turned out to be a regular SA formation. What was going on? Was this whole thing organised by the Hitlers? What was I doing there, then? No, this could not possibly be a Hitler gathering. The invitation would not have come from school if it had been!

It was not until long after that memorable evening that I realised the truth: our torchlight procession had been to celebrate Hitler's appointment as chancellor. But why, in that case, had Dr Paulus taken part, along with other teachers whom everyone knew to be decent men? Had they been as naïve as we first-years?

Within weeks one became aware of people exchanging news in whispers, having first looked round to make sure all doors and windows were shut. Such reports often began with the words 'They've taken . . .' (whomever it might be) or 'They came for him in the middle of the night. . .'. What it all meant, we children were never told. But this much we could work out for ourselves: terrible things were happening, and they had something to do with the brown-uniformed Hitlers who wore white armbands bearing the words 'Auxiliary Police' and went around patrolling the streets, armed with rubber truncheons. Why the regular police were now regarded as inadequate and how and to what end the Brownshirts were meant to assist them remained mysteries to us.

What the whispers reported was that a number of the town's Communists and Social Democrats had suddenly disappeared. Some of them reappeared two or three days later with bandaged limbs; others remained in 'protective custody'. The terms 'auxiliary police' and 'protective custody' were completely new to us.

Outwardly Gross-Strehlitz seemed more peaceful than before. There were no more riots and no more fighting. Instead the streets frequently resounded to the roll of drums and the blare of trumpets. Swastika flags both large and small fluttered from windows and rooftops. The marching songs of parading columns drew crowds of curious onlookers into the streets. Przywacs the baker would abandon a shopful of customers without so much as a 'by your leave' and step out onto the pavement in his white apron, his pencil tucked behind his ear.

Our apartment commanded an excellent view of the processions. Even father would go running to the window. Our neighbour in the house opposite, a lawyer by the name of Dr Kurz, would also stick his head out. No swastika flag hung from his window. Kurz had not had any dealings with my father hitherto. But since Hitler's coming to power he had begun to greet him across the street, and whenever he met father out walking, he left him in no doubt as to his views on the new regime. As the brown-uniformed columns marched past below us with drums and trumpets, Kurz, at his window, would also swing his arm as if beating a bass drum and then break off the movement with a scornfully dismissive wave of his hand.

23

Father watched him with a gratified amusement that we children shared. 'No, we're not alone,' he would say then. 'There are still plenty of Germans who want nothing to do with the Nazis.' The sound of the Brownshirts' marching song receded into the distance as father withdrew from the window, smiling.

The Brown revolt in the school playground

Who can recall without horror the weeks that followed 30 January 1933?* Once again there was a chance of preventing a Hitler dictatorship — and by the most peaceful of means. The majority in parliament needed only to say 'no'; they said 'yes'.

We eleven-year-olds, looking out at the world from our first-year classroom, were not even aware that Hitler's Enabling Act was being debated in parliament. Life at school went on very much as usual. The teaching staff refrained from any mention of politics. The headmaster was a man called Bergmann, of whom I can speak only with the greatest respect. My judgement at the time may have been heavily reliant on vague feelings and other people's views, but to me Dr Bergmann was German probity and civilisation in person.

In the summer of the previous year work had begun on a new house next door to the school, presumably destined to be the headmaster's residence. By the early spring of 1933 the building was well advanced. It was possible to follow developments closely from the playground because the garden that had been newly laid out around the house was surrounded only by diminutive and currently leafless trees and shrubs. Occasionally the headmaster could be seen discussing something with the builders or with the gardener.

I gave these matters a great deal of my attention, and my break-times tended to be spent in the part of the playground nearest to the garden. Dr Bergmann was surely the kind of man to whom one could open one's heart; he would listen sympathetically. But since I could think of nothing I wished to say to him, I contented myself with hanging about in the vicinity of his garden, hoping that he would perhaps notice me there and speak to me himself.

Dr Bergmann had more urgent concerns than getting into conversation with first-years over his garden fence. Since Hitler's appointment as chancellor, certain of the older pupils as well as a number of teachers had ventured to make remarks that, as he saw it, went too

---

* The day when President Hindenburg was finally persuaded to receive Hitler in audience and appoint him chancellor. The event is often referred to in German simply as the *Machtergreifung* ('seizure of power').

far. Several of the most senior boys were said to have campaigned actively on Hitler's behalf, and they were now asking to have their forthcoming school-leaving examination 'marked up' because they had had to neglect their school work in favour of what they referred to as their 'service'. That was doubtless the occasion of the talk the headmaster gave us at assembly one day. 'This school,' he announced grimly, 'is a public institution open to all without regard to religious or political affiliation. No one is to be either preferred or discriminated against on grounds of his membership of a particular party. Within the walls of this school, peace and impartiality constitute the first commandment!'

It looked as though the headmaster's directive would be respected. Paschke, our music teacher, whose Hitlerite leanings were common knowledge, never said a word about politics. He taught us old folk songs and recommended that we sing a lot. Singing was healthy, he told us; it promoted proper breathing. Our classics master, Dr Paulus, went around with a very worried face in the days following the Reichstag fire.* He said nothing, however, and as he handed out our reports on the last day of term he gave us this piece of advice for the holidays: 'Use some of your free time to commit your Latin irregular verbs to memory. You will find they come in extremely useful.'

I met none of my classmates during the 1933 Easter holiday with the exception of Anton Krutzschek — and I could have done without him. Krutzschek was universally regarded as an idle, two-faced liar. I should scarcely have given him another glance had I not come across him several times in the street in an unusual get-up. Believe it or not, there was this craven coward marching at the head of a junior Hitler Youth column, bashing a drum. Apparently he enjoyed a more brilliant role in the Hitler Youth than he did in the classroom.

In defiance of every rule and convention the 1933 Easter holiday was extended several times. When lessons resumed in May, I crept especially unwillingly to school, my thoughts revolving round *Studienrat* Kasimir, about whom my elder brothers Jakob and Leon had told me a great many unpleasant stories. I was busy picturing to myself just how bad things might be if we got him for maths. Nursing a heartfelt wish — 'Please, anything but that!' — I reached the school and turned into the playground. The headmaster's house

* On 27 February 1933, a month after the *Machtergreifung*, the building that housed the German parliament (Reichstag) burnt down. Whether or not the deed was engineered by the Nazis, Hitler used it to gain a propaganda advantage and persuade the aged president to grant him his first dictatorial powers.

was finished; it looked as though he had already moved in. I entered the school building and hurried down the long corridor to my new classroom. The door was open. And there at the teacher's desk sat Kasimir.

I groaned inwardly: for a whole year, at the very least, we should be at the mercy of Kasimir's dirty tricks! Did my classmates, I wondered, realise what lay in store for us? I turned round with the intention of exchanging knowing looks with them. To my surprise, something like half the class had come to school in Hitler Youth uniform, or rather in the uniform of the *Jungvolk*, the organisation's junior section.

What had happened? Was it now permitted to 'bring politics into school'? That same day, for the first time, I saw two teachers in SA uniform, marching along the school corridor. One of them was Paschke, our music teacher; the other I did not know.

Kasimir lost no time in making it quite clear that he had no love for brown uniforms. For the rest, he swiftly confirmed his reputation as a classroom tyrant *vis-à-vis* all schoolboys indiscriminately. However, nothing appeared to incense him more than the kind of playing at soldiers indulged in by the Hitler Youth when it was coupled with incompetence at mathematics. In gruff tones he ordered Krutzschek to come to the blackboard. Naturally, the whole class knew why he had picked on Krutzschek. In his usual way, Kasimir first gave the pupil ample opportunity to demonstrate his uselessness at the blackboard. Meanwhile he directed a look of speechless indignation more at the class than at the squirming victim out in front. 'Just look at that!' was the message clearly legible on his angrily compressed lips. He took out his pocket watch. 'Enough!' he barked. 'Put the chalk down! Come here!' He glared down at the hapless Hitler Youth drummer, examining him from head to foot without saying a word. Krutzschek, intimidated by Kasimir's silence and even more by his contemptuous stare, shuffled his feet in embarrassment. 'Attention!' Kasimir roared, shattering the silence. 'Forward . . . march!' With the whole class looking on, Krutzschek was made to parade up and down the room. 'About . . . turn!' His classmates could scarcely contain their glee as Krutzschek was marched between the rows of desks and back up to the blackboard, not once but several times. 'Dis – miss!' Kasimir thundered. A crestfallen Krutzschek returned to his seat. Through it all I was careful to keep a straight face. Experience had already taught me that, as a Jew, one had to be more on one's guard against the wounded vanity of a Krutzschek than against the capable self-assurance of one's other fellow pupils.

Much as I disliked Krutzschek, fortunately he was the only one of his kind. On the whole, my relationships with the other members of my class were not bad. Nor, at first, did this change when something like two-thirds of them joined the Hitler Youth. What did change dramatically was the way in which I was treated by Hitler Youth members in other classes.

One break-time a first-year started baiting me in the playground. 'Saucy little squit', I told him (he was half a head shorter than me). 'I'll show you! Give a second-year cheek, would you? Are you daft or something?' And he duly got his ears boxed.

The first-year became steadily more insolent. I had no alternative but to hit him again. Before long we were surrounded by onlookers. They came running from all over the playground — first-years, second-years, even some fifth-years — and formed a dense ring around us. Voices were raised. 'Come over here! The Jew's bashing up someone smaller than him!' 'Hit him! Don't let the Jew walk all over you!' A lanky fellow detached himself from the crowd and tried to trip me up. When I did not fall, someone else grabbed my ankles and threw me to the ground beside the first-year. He now began to get the upper hand. The crowd howled. The unequal struggle ended only when the bell rang for the end of break. Dirty, grazed and out of breath, I dragged myself up the steps of the building through a hail of jeers and insults and found my way back to the classroom. Dr Paulus began his lesson by expounding a point of Latin grammar. I found it hard to listen. I was shaking with emotion.

Next day the same first-year went for me again. By now I had discovered his name: von Hörig. Soon we were rolling on the ground again, surrounded by curious onlookers. The fifth-years had almost helped the first-year to 'victory' when the crowd parted and the master on duty appeared. In no time the fifth-years got off me and melted into the crowd. The teacher stood watching for a while, evidently gained the impression that the fight was a fair one, and wandered off to another part of the playground. The fifth-years promptly returned to the fray, and things began to go badly for me again.

The pattern was repeated in the following days. At last I began to see through it. The fights were actually being instigated not by the first-year but by the fifth-years, who 'discovered' von Hörig's 'plight' as if by chance and came to his aid. I recognised the same faces over and over again. Now I understood the part being played by von Hörig; it was a case of stooge by name and stooge by nature.

What I could not understand was my own role. What did those great tall fellows want with me? They did not even know me, nor I them.

My father was all for going to see the headmaster. I resisted this. Fights are the accepted thing among schoolboys; no one goes and complains to the headmaster about a fight. And with the best will in the world Dr Bergmann could not have prevented the fifth-years from coming after me on my way home and wreaking 'vengeance'. Besides, a further consideration held me back. Things had been happening in Germany recently that counselled caution. A vague premonition told me: 'Don't go to the headmaster. He's having to be careful himself. If he helps you, the Hitlers in the school will start saying, "Bergmann is a Jew-lover."'

If things had got as bad as that while a man of the calibre of Bergmann was still headmaster of the school, what could we expect, we wondered, when in the late summer of 1933 Bergmann was ousted and an SA man placed in charge?

I could not even look to my brothers for help. Jakob, the eldest, was in the fifth year himself and, of course, knew the three 'Hitlers' in his class. But he dismissed my suggestion. 'If Leon and I and a couple more of the bigger Jewish boys stood up for you, don't you see where it would lead? The three louts from my class would also fetch reinforcements. And what would your scrap have turned into then? A battle between Christians and Jews! Three hundred against nine!'

I perceived with alarm how my role had changed. The days when I had enjoyed challenging other boys to stand-up fights were now gone. This new defencelessness against treacherous assaults and against the jeers of the crowd unsettled me. I avoided walking home alone, preferring to leave the school premises together with my two Jewish classmates, who sought my company for the same reason.

A new law came in, restricting the permitted percentages of Jewish pupils at secondary schools. But it was not for that reason that the number of Jewish pupils at my school soon shrank to three; as sons of war veterans, most of them were exempt from the *numerus clausus* provisions. What made them — and my elder brothers with them — leave the Gross-Strehlitz *Gymnasium* early was the constant harassment and mob-rule in the playground. In the lower classes I was the only Jewish pupil left.

The humane attitude of the headmaster and one or two of the staff and the more or less peaceable behaviour of my classmates had provided me with a certain amount of support in my increasing isolation. However, even my relations with my fellow pupils were affected by the change. Before, I had enjoyed a certain comradely approval. Now they put up with me — I cannot think of a better way of putting it than that. My fellow pupils — with the exception of

Krutzschek and a couple of other loudmouths — tolerated my presence in their midst. They exempted me, so to speak, from the officially propagated ostracism of all Jews. I gave them credit for doing so, and I drew a certain amount of comfort from it. I wonder how many times I was told, 'Do you know, looking at your face and your fair hair, no one would ever take you for a Jew!' I found such remarks flattering and began rather to fancy my appearance, not realising that I was thus, in effect, giving credence to the delusions of racism.

CHAPTER 3

'Dad, Everyone's Emigrating!'

Adler and Kohn discover the Jewish question

Had my eyes been opened since my eleventh birthday, I wondered, or did it have something to do with Hitler's coming to power that the differences of opinion within Judaism were now more in evidence than ever before? My childish intellect had simply drawn a crude distinction between godly Jews and three-day Jews. I had scarcely even heard of a 'Zionist Organisation' or a 'Central Union'. Suddenly Gross-Strehlitz was the scene of fierce arguments between these two bodies.*

A major change was observable in the Gross-Strehlitz synagogue during the spring of 1933. For many years the House of God had stood there like a cemetery — silent, sad, venerably moss-covered, tended by a handful of officers and seldom visited. Now it became

---

* Hitler and his followers spoke indiscriminately of 'the Jews'. In reality, Jewry had for generations been split into many different religious and political factions. Most German Jews subscribed to the Central Union of German Citizens of the Jewish Faith, founded in the 1890s to counter anti-Semitic slanders. After the First World War a second, related organisation grew up alongside the Central Union, the '(*Reichs*)League of Jewish Veterans'. It worked for the resettlement of Jewish ex-servicemen on the land as farmers and it founded sports and youth clubs.

The first principle of anti-Semitism is: 'Jews are and always will be foreigners.' A smaller group of assimilated Jews had assented to this proposition, out of necessity at first but subsequently with pride. Alienated from the essentially religious content of Jewish culture, they could think of nothing better to stick on their flag than a secular Jewish nationalism modelled on the nationalist movements of Central and Eastern Europe. In this way German Jews contributed in the 1890s towards the emergence of political Zionism, of which Theodor Herzl became the chief exponent. The overwhelming majority of German Jews, however, continued to give their national loyalty to Germany.

For an account of the various shades of opinion represented among German Jews, see *The Jewish Response to German Culture from the Enlightenment to the Second World War*, ed. Jehuda Reinharz and Walter Schatzberg, University Press of New England, 1985.

30

what it should always have been: a focus of life. You no longer had to wait for the New Year to see the congregation assembled. Few weeks went by without the upstairs prayer-hall filling with people.

I can see them now, entering the room one by one and striding between the rows of pews: wholesalers and retailers, solicitors and transport workers, disabled ex-servicemen with wooden legs and leather hands, school-children of all ages and sizes, solid matrons and nubile daughters. One even saw people who otherwise did not appear even for three days in the year — the truly peripheral figures of the congregation.

However, the men and women whose small talk used to echo on the stairs and in the cloakrooms did not afterwards push their way into the prayer-hall in order to hear a sermon or attend some tearful ceremony for the souls of the departed. They came to attend debates about the situation of Jewry.

'Are the Jews a people or a religious community?' 'Our way ahead as Germans and Jews.' 'A Jewish problem or an anti-Semitic problem?' Most of them were ill-equipped to ponder such questions, lacking both knowledge and the habit of thought. Their knowledge of Judaism was limited to the externals of synagogue ritual and something of the customs surrounding domestic life. As to whether it was an ethnic faith or a world religion, they had always left such matters to scholars. But now the unheard-of was happening: Hitler's appointment as chancellor had made such seemingly abstruse questions so burningly topical that even Adler and Kohn found their way back to the Jewish congregation in order to confer and take counsel.

Eberhard Adler and Siegfried Kohn had both contracted mixed marriages with Christian women. On the football field and at the rifle club they were familiar figures, but they had not been seen in synagogue since their parents died. Now they both suddenly became spokesmen for Jewish organisations, Adler for the local Zionist group, Kohn for the League of Jewish Veterans. Moreover, they discharged the duties of their respective offices with a solemn dignity quite surprising in a pair of businessmen.

A group better equipped for debating was the handful of practising Jews who remained faithful to the Torah. They knew a great deal more about Jewish history, and they were familiar with the sources of the sacred tradition. Their Jewishness had never ceased to affect their everyday lives. But the self-styled 'Torah-true' Jews kept strangely quiet, looking on passively and leaving it to the three-day Jews to wrestle with definitions and political programmes. My father did not occupy the rabbi's seat, as he did during services, but sat in one of the pews in the middle of the hall, contributing to the discussion only rarely. As a gesture of modesty, his action had my approval, but I felt some disappointment at the fact that my father, particularly in this situation, was leaving his congregation to its own devices, as it were, rather than advising it as to which way to go or at least chairing its discussions. As for our cantor, the small, chubby singer and master of ceremonies, he sat, unrobed and unobtrusive, in one of the very back pews and never said a word.

After a few discussion evenings there was talk of the congregation splitting into two camps. On the one hand the local Zionist group was attracting adherents. On the other hand people were flocking to the banners of the 'Central Union of German Citizens of the Jewish Faith' and the 'League of Jewish Veterans'. Under the influence of the latter a local branch of the 'League of German-Jewish Youth' was set up. The Zionists, too, founded a youth group.

I was too young to study the ideological literature. But I zealously attended the lecture and discussion evenings at which the different cases were passionately stated or at which their advocates met head-on in heated argument. I recall two occasions that clearly reflected the clash of views. One of them featured Adler and the other Kohn.

As chairman of the League of Jewish Veterans, Kohn was to speak at a ceremony of remembrance for the World War dead. The members of the League had gathered in synagogue, top-hatted and dressed in solemn black. In his whining voice the cantor recited a prayer for the souls of the fallen. Then Kohn climbed the rostrum, wearing his Iron Cross, First Class.* He cleared his throat and began to speak — stumblingly, haltingly and with a very red face.

This age, he said, had many trials in store for us Jews. 'We fought and bled for Germany, yet our Germanness is now being challenged and we are not allowed to defend it in public. It is my belief that we cannot more fittingly refute these calumnies nor more worthily honour the memory of our fallen comrades than by showing proof, throughout this difficult period, of unswerving loyalty to Germany. Our watchword is "fatherland, faith and combat discipline!"'

The occasion that featured Eberhard Adler also took place in synagogue. Shortly after the notorious boycott of 1 April 1933[†] the Zionists organised a discussion evening. Adler asked for the floor and made a speech in which he renounced his Germanness and at the same time announced his return to the bosom of the Jewish

---

* Prussia's and subsequently Germany's highest military honour was awarded in two classes.
† On that day the NSDAP organised a nation-wide boycott of Jewish businesses.

community. 'If Germany, for which we were ready to lay down our lives,' he roared, the balding pate on which his skull cap perched gradually turning a deeper and deeper red, 'If Germany does not even treat us as guests, then let us get out of here! Out of this ungrateful and barbaric land! Nor do we want its orders and decorations any more, if it is only to have our honour sullied by lies and slanders!' Saying which, he pulled something from his coat pocket, flung it to the floor, and proceeded to stamp on it. It was his Iron Cross. His colour turned even deeper as he did so, and the veins at his temples became visibly swollen and blue.

Adler's sensational conversion to Zionism was no isolated phenomenon. Many people joined him in pinning the blue-and-white badge of the Zionists to their lapels. People who had trouble reading the Kaddish prayer for their departed loved ones now set about learning colloquial Hebrew. The cantor found himself much in demand. Already functioning as master of ceremonies for the Veterans' League, he also contrived to make himself useful to the Zionists as a language teacher.

Moritz Adler, Eberhard's 28-year-old nephew, was the object of much astonishment and not a little mockery. 'Didn't that young dandy mean to have himself baptised a Roman Catholic?' the German patriots asked derisively. 'And now he fancies himself as a Zionist youth leader!'

Dr Seligmann, the dentist, was almost obsessed with Zionism. One might be talking to him about the Sino-Japanese war, the film *Mädchen in Uniform*,* even false teeth. Somehow or other the dentist always managed to steer the conversation round to anti-Semitism and Theodor Herzl.[†] He used to preach Zionism to his Jewish clients when, with their faces pulled into grimaces under the drill, they were in no position to argue.

I needed some dental treatment myself in the summer of 1933. Along with a couple of fillings I received a lecture on the part played by the French clergy in the Dreyfus Case.[‡]

---

* A German film ('Girls in Uniform') produced in 1931. Directed by Leontine Sagan, it dealt boldly with the oppressive discipline of a boarding-school for the daughters of Prussian army officers and the lesbian relationship between a girl and a teacher that arose out of it.

† Theodor Herzl (1860–1904) was the father of modern Zionism as a political movement laying claim to a Jewish homeland in Palestine.

‡ In 1894 a Jewish officer in the French army, Captain Alfred Dreyfus, was convicted on a spying charge and sentenced to solitary confinement for life on Devil's Island, the notorious penal colony off the coast of French Guiana. Two years later evidence of the captain's innocence began to emerge. That evidence grew to overwhelming proportions and eventually, in 1899, Dreyfus was pardoned — but not before

Poor Dr Seligmann! There may be Gross-Strehlitz Jews living in Israel today who quite literally owe their lives to his tireless zeal for Zionism. During the Second World War my brother Leon had to work in a Berlin munitions factory. There, at the beginning of 1943, he met Dr Seligmann, heavily disguised as a factory worker. The dentist had failed to obtain the coveted immigration certificate for Palestine. Leon saw him in the factory daily from then until that fateful 27 February 1943 when the last remaining Jewish munitions workers were fetched from the factory — to be deported to Poland.

Campfires and solemn promises

There had been an unpretentious Jewish youth club in Gross-Strehlitz for years. Now, with matters Jewish suddenly coming in for such fierce debate, we youngsters were no longer content to hike through the woods of Upper Silesia to the accompaniment of singing and lute-playing or to organise parlour games in a side-room of the synagogue. We wished to harness our activities to higher objectives. A key member of the club, fifteen-year-old Friedel ('Freddy') Nötling, began to speak of 'experiences', of 'shaping one's existence' and of 'fresh ways of life'. We young ones listened with rapt attention, though we had only the haziest notion of what such solemn words implied. 'Higher objectives' related to the realm of the inconceivable. They aroused a vague longing but offered no satisfaction. So the effect was like that of a dazzling revelation when the longed-for ideal sent us some visible harbingers. They arrived in grey-green uniforms, marching in step beneath fluttering pennants to the sound of drums and trumpets: a troop of Jewish Boy Scouts from Breslau.

The thing that bound us all together, our uniformed visitors explained, was our loyalty to our German homeland and to our Jewish faith. Their purpose in coming to Gross-Strehlitz was to invite our organisation to affiliate to the 'League of German-Jewish Youth'.

Most of the boys and girls in our club voted for affiliation and swore an oath of allegiance in a solemn ceremony that involved touching the flag. We thus fell victim, by insensible degrees, to the poison of romantic longing, wallowing in very German emotions and conceiving an enormous enthusiasm for campfires and what we saw

'l'Affaire Dreyfus' had become a national scandal, effectively splitting French society into two factions: the 'Dreyfusards' and the anti-Semitic, anti-Dreyfusard camp. During the First World War Lieutenant Colonel Dreyfus was decorated with the *Légion d'honneur*. But the anti-Dreyfusards, exposed as anti-Semitic liars and forgers, were unable to forgive and forget.

as a primitive, tribal way of life. In the process we ducked completely the questions with which the Hitler regime was increasingly confronting Jewry.

How childish we were — and, as I say, how German! — even more childish and even more German than the model on which we unwittingly patterned ourselves: the Wandervogel (Bird of Passage) youth movement of pre-Nazi days.* The boredom and striving ambition of the middle-class life-style was the bugbear of the 'Bird of Passage'. Our bugbear was the life-style of the German-Jewish bourgeoisie with its predominance of businessmen and small shopkeepers. The only part of it we wished to adopt was the patriotism of the Jewish Veterans. Otherwise we needed only to think of the uncle-and-auntyish figures of the synagogue congregation to know how we did *not* want to live.

We preferred to look back in time to the world of our forefathers and the rude splendour of the Middle Ages. When we did, however, it was not so much the stifling confinement of the ghettos and the Jewish expulsions that we saw — more the knights and pirates, the minnesingers and the lansquenets!

And yet we liked to think we were bravely looking the reality of the year 1933 in the face. For did we not regularly attend the discussion evenings in the synagogue, and had we not opted for the standpoint of the League of Jewish Veterans? Only a few of our former youth-club members joined the Zionist youth group. The new age now dawning appeared to smile on our anti-bourgeois endeavours. Millions of young people throughout Germany were devotees of living rough, of campfires and route marches and troopers' songs. In all but their anti-Semitic watchwords, were we not in harmony with them?

I had quickly made up my mind in favour of the League of German-Jewish Youth. However, I ought to explain why my father placed no obstacle in the way of my joining, despite the fact that he had reservations about both parties that had formed within the Jewish congregation.

By what right, he would ask, did one party call themselves 'German citizens of the Jewish faith'? The Jewish faith was just an empty word to them. They had become so thoroughly assimilated to their non-Jewish environment that German Jewry might well have

* The Wandervogel, a romantic, anti-modernist movement, was founded around the turn of the century and went from strength to strength until the movement was disbanded in 1933. It cultivated a youthful life-style with the emphasis on folk music and dancing and amateur theatricals. The movement enjoyed a limited revival after the Second World War.

disappeared completely, had they had their way. The others — the Zionists — were even more dangerous assimilators. They wanted to establish a state as profane as any other. Such a course would most certainly lead to the end of Judaism. Both parties — the Zionist and the German-Jewish — sought to solve the Jewish question purely at the political level, without God. To that extent both courses were unrealistic, the Jewish question having come about through God's will because the Jews had rebelled against the Torah. The Jews had a mission: to bring all mankind to honour God. If they lived up to that ideal, father said, God would solve the Jewish question himself.

My father's visionary way of thinking nevertheless allowed him to exercise a benevolent tolerance, and he found some good in both parties. Most of his sympathies were with the patriotic loyalty of the German-Jewish camp. But he hoped that Zionism would have the effect, through its misguided nationalism, of bringing Jews back to the faith. There was in fact a movement already in existence that professed a religiously motivated Zionism: it was called 'Misrachi', though it had no supporters in Gross-Strehlitz.

Anyone who, as my father did, walks the earth with his eyes fixed on the Messianic future will find patience comes more easily. The contradictions between rival parties lose some of their importance. The battle-lines become blurred. The struggles of the nations are but steps on the way, their highest national objectives mere intermediate stages on the many routes leading to God.

My father raised few objections when I joined the League of German-Jewish Youth. He raised even fewer when, in 1939, I switched my allegiance to Misrachi.

In April 1933, then, I marched proudly through the streets of Gross-Strehlitz in my new get-up, the silver ring of the League of German-Jewish Youth and the Young Sportsman's badge of the League of Jewish Veterans both flashing on my shirt-front. To give myself a more military look, I wore a bread pouch and a canteen at my belt, even for indoor evenings in that side-room of the synagogue. However, neither the badges nor the field equipment gave my boy-scout outfit quite enough military panache to measure up to the ideal I had in mind.

By bombarding my mother with repeated requests, I managed to persuade her to purchase a length of field-grey material and make me a 'proper officer's jacket', complete with gleaming buttons, exactly the way I had conceived it and even got it down on paper. The only thing that bothered me about the jacket — though at the same time it delighted me — was the fact that I was the only person in Gross-Strehlitz, if not in the whole of Germany, to be wearing such a uniform.

But there was still something missing. I addressed myself to our platoon leader. 'Listen, Freddy, the Gleiwitz branch have two trumpeters and two drummers. I reckon we ought to have at least one trumpet. I think I could play the trumpet pretty well, actually.'

'You're absolutely right', Freddy replied, 'but we simply haven't got the money.'

That same day I became a fanatical saver. In three months I saved enough to buy not a trumpet but at least a bugle. I arrived at our next meeting in a state of happy excitement, carrying the gleaming brass instrument. Outside the door I had a brief conference with our platoon leader, during the course of which he asked whether he might 'have a blow'. Then we stepped inside and Freddy made an announcement: 'Ezra is hereby appointed bugler of the Gross-Strehlitz branch.'

With my 'officer's jacket' and my bugle, my dreams were still a great way short of total fulfilment. But at least, so it seemed to me, like this one could let oneself be seen. Or would it have been better to keep a low profile? One day as I was strutting through the streets of Gross-Strehlitz I was stopped by an SA man: 'Well, little fellow, and what sort of uniform is that?'

'This is the uniform of the League of Jewish Veterans.'

'Hah! Don't make me laugh!'

'I mean the Young Sportsmans' Association of the League of Jewish Veterans,' I corrected myself. He went off shaking his head.

In the summer of 1933 the League of German-Jewish Youth in Upper Silesia organised a provincial gathering in the vicinity of the little town of Tost.* Arriving in the forest, I made extensive use of my bugle. But hark! What was that? Away off in the distance a second horn replied. I sounded my instrument again, and again the reply came back. What could this mean? Was it another Jewish youth group marching into camp? At length they came into view. Ah — now I was less keen to meet them. They were a detachment of Hitler Youth.

In the crossfire between Hitler, Herzl and Rathenau

The battle between the Zionist and German-Jewish camps was fought in many private homes. Brothers and sisters fell out, friends turned against each other, sons with Zionist leanings rose in revolt

* The Polish Toszek, some ten miles to the south-east of Strzelce Opolskie on the railway line to Gliwice (Gleiwitz).

against their fathers. Conversions of German patriots to Zionism were not unknown, despite the torrent of mockery and gossip with which those provincial townspeople punished every apostasy.

The countless private and public arguments that I heard in the early years of the Third Reich addressed my emotions more than my intellect. I felt them more than I understood them. Whenever I try to reproduce them from memory, my recollections are inevitably contaminated by subsequent insights and retrospective analyses. But those stormy discussion evenings in the Gross-Strehlitz synagogue remain vivid memories and I can see the speakers as if they stood before me now. I also believe that I followed the arguments with greater understanding than might generally be expected of an eleven-year-old.

Why was that? I received little encouragement from my brothers. Rather than try to form a mature opinion and reach a personal standpoint on the problem of being Jewish, Jakob and Leon applied themselves to reducing all ideologies and partisans to their comic aspects. Nor was there any shortage of things to laugh at, for the Jewish petty bourgeoisie of Gross-Strehlitz were possessed by their ideologies as if by demons. Yet neither the grotesquely wagging forefinger of a licensed victualler nor the absurdly emotional rhetoric of textile salesmen and cereal merchants could wholly obscure the seriousness of the problem.

What caused me to reflect were the conflicts of opinion between Jews and Christians and among Jews themselves, the glaring disparity between what the National Socialists said about the Jews and what I knew from my own experience. Wherever I went, whether at home, at synagogue or at school, I was assailed by the most contradictory theories. To take just one example, at school I heard three different accounts of the history of the Crusades in the space of a few years.

First we had the crusaders portrayed as the noble and magnificent army of Christendom, setting out to liberate the Holy Land from the Muslim infidel. The history and reading textbooks of the Prussian Education Department, which at that time was responsible for the schools of Upper Silesia, were full of the tradition of romantic Christianity.

In Jewish religious instruction we learnt that the First Crusade sparked off appalling persecutions of Jews. The crusading armies, scratch mixtures of knights, adventurers, desperadoes and alley thieves, left a trail of blood, smoke and destruction behind them wherever they went, be it France, Germany, Hungary or the Holy Land itself. As our teacher pointed out, the pope at that time, Urban

II, had never mentioned — let alone condemned — these atrocities. The First Crusade had thus set the pattern for the others as well as for all subsequent pogroms. The deep alienation between Jews and Christians, from which neither side had ever entirely recovered, dated from that time.

The third version was offered to us after the curriculum had been rewritten by the National Socialists. The crusades had been preached, so our brown-uniformed history teacher assured us, purely in order to harness the knightly classes of the West for the 'alien purposes' of various popes. In fact, the popes were not interested in liberating the Holy Sepulchre but only in extending their political power and plundering the fabled wealth of the East.

Further food for thought was provided by my father's table talk, in which he would expose the inconsistencies and downright contradictions of both the Zionist and the German-Jewish ideologies. Above all, however, it was the debates in the upstairs prayer-hall of the Gross-Strehlitz synagogue that made me prick up my young ears.

Everyone attended — young and old, adherents of the different ideologies and those who had yet to make up their minds. The Zionists usually occupied the left-hand third of the hall, with the boys and girls of the Zionist Youth Association, conspicuous in their blue-and-white uniforms, filling the front few pews. Those of the German-Jewish persuasion took up the right-hand third of the hall, and we youth members likewise sat at the very front in our grey-green boy-scout outfits. Crowded in behind us were the men of the League of Jewish Veterans, together with their wives.

In Eberhard Adler and Dr Seligmann, the Zionists had two gifted defenders of their cause. No one on the German-Jewish side was any match for them. But then we received reinforcements — or rather, a reinforcement. Rudi Halpern, the group leader of the League of German-Jewish Youth in Beuthen and a very gifted young man in his last year at school, began to visit Gross-Strehlitz regularly to step into the breach. It used to fill me with pride that our cleverest spokesman at parrying the Zionists' attacks was a member of the Youth League. The Zionist youth organisation never sent a champion into the arena.

I remember one particular evening when the topic under discussion was 'Causes and Control of Anti-Semitism'. People glared at one another across the room like the parties of left and right in parliament. The air was hot and the atmosphere highly charged. Rudi Halpern's remarks were punctuated by jubilant applause. The correctness of the German-Jewish view seemed to me to have been proved beyond question. Suddenly there was a commotion on the Zionist benches. Eberhard Adler and Dr Seligmann were demanding the floor with upraised arms and clicking fingers.

Adler mounted the rostrum. He turned to Rudi Halpern, his face bright red, and said flatly that the anti-anti-Semitic defence policy pursued by the Central Union for many years had proved a failure and that German-Jewish patriotism was now reduced to ignominious absurdity. A year ago, he told us, he had himself believed that the anti-Semites were common riffraff and that the real Germany consisted of decent people. The police saw to it that anti-Semitic thugs were placed under lock and key. 'Today, ladies and gentlemen, we know better. The anti-Semites, far from being under lock and key, occupy key positions in government ministries!' As he said this, Adler pointed vigorously to his right, as though the ministries concerned had been situated in the immediate vicinity of the Gross-Strehlitz synagogue.

Thinking back, I am amazed at how openly people still dared to speak out against the Hitler regime. Of course, in our small-town congregation everyone knew everyone else; people who ought not to have been listening would have been immediately obvious. Moreover, the Brown spy network or system of informers that later became so pervasive an ingredient in the Nazi dictatorship was only beginning to be developed at that time.

During the discussion that I am attempting to reconstruct, I sat among my friends, resplendent in my fantasy uniform, and listened with bated breath. When Rudi Halpern had the floor I studied the face of Eberhard Adler, on which an expression of deep thoughtfulness alternated with one of derision. I kept a similarly close watch on Rudi Halpern while Adler was speaking. The idea that the Zionist might turn out to be right in the end filled me with apprehension.

Rudi Halpern mounted the rostrum with springy self-assurance, like a boxer entering the ring. He had to admit, he said with a courteous nod in Adler's direction, that, despite the blood sacrifice that Jewish soldiers had made for Germany, anti-Semitism had increased rather than decreased since the war. Did that prove that the work done by the Central Union to combat anti-Semitism was futile? Did Walther Rathenau's life of dedicated service to Germany mean nothing because he had been assassinated by anti-Semitic thugs?* That kind of arithmetical approach would never provide

---

* Walther Rathenau, son of the Jewish founder of the electrical industry giant AEG (Allgemeine Elektrizitäts-Gesellschaft), made a major contribution towards planning Germany's war economy in 1914–18. After the war he served for a time as

the right answer in our world. We were living in a period of moral reverses. Civilisation was under threat from brute elements the world over. Anti-Semitism was only one sign of those anti-intellectual tendencies, and it was currently astir in many countries, Palestine included. The forces of civilisation must never be permitted to capitulate anywhere to mindless violence. 'We Jews', he went on, 'are not alone in being persecuted. We are fellow sufferers with and allies of all Germans who stand up for the ideals of humanity and democracy. Would it not be desertion if, rather than fight side by side with our Christian comrades of like mind for the restoration of democracy, we were to look for a better life abroad — just when Germany needs us most? That kind of isolationism would play right into the hands of the anti-Semites, who seek to cut us off by violent means from the rest of the German people. Are we going to allow the anti-Semites a greater right to speak in Germany's name than the finest and worthiest representatives of that people?'

I was too young to distinguish between the validity of the arguments deployed and the rhetoric in which they were couched. Nor did it occur to me to examine whether the questions raised were appropriate to the situation in which the Jews found themselves. Since both men were good speakers, I found myself forced to agree with the one who currently held the floor. So I was particularly glad that Rudi Halpern had the last word. He concluded by quoting the Zionist's own words back at him to the effect that one could no more argue the anti-Semite out of his hatred than one could argue a man out of his love. Why then, he asked, were the Zionists attempting to argue us out of our love for Germany?

A smiling Rudi Halpern returned to his seat to be greeted with a hearty handshake by the branch president of the League of Jewish Veterans. Simultaneously Adler was received as if in triumph by his nephew Moritz and by Dr Seligmann. 'Didn't he speak splendidly!' was the general opinion expressed by the departing audience.

In minutes the prayer-hall was empty except for a handful of people who lingered among the pews, still locked in fervent discussion. The pleas and urgings of the caretaker finally persuaded them to depart.

I set out for home with my parents. As we came out of the synagogue, the whole of Gross-Strehlitz appeared to be asleep. The

Minister of Reconstruction. As foreign minister he was the architect of the Treaty of Rapallo (1922), which restored diplomatic and economic relations between Germany and the Soviet Union. In the atmosphere of mounting political violence that poisoned the early Weimar years, he was murdered by anti-Semitic agents in June 1922.

audience had dispersed and been swallowed up in the darkness of the surrounding streets. On one corner, however, two men still stood debating in the light of a street-lamp, their voices steadily rising in pitch. As I watched, they broke off and looked anxiously about them before continuing the debate in whispers.

So our German-Jewish view had carried the day! The thought filled me with happiness on my way home that evening. On other evenings it was with considerably less self-assurance that I returned from those public discussions. 'Who is right?' I would ask myself constantly. The question left me no peace. In fact, it caused me greater and greater torment the more implacably the Jews were excluded and defamed, in total disregard of their patriotic loyalty and service to their country. The warnings of the Zionists proved only too justified.

'Who is right?' How silly the question sounds today! What, I wonder, happened to Rudi Halpern? Did he get out in time, or did he remain true to his beloved Germany until he was reduced to ashes in Auschwitz? I can still hear his voice, ringing out from the rostrum: 'Would it not be desertion to look for a better life abroad — just when Germany needs us most?'

A Machtergreifung *in Gross-Strehlitz*

Let none of what I have to say in the next few pages about my teachers, about the headmaster, Dr Bergmann, and about his brown-uniformed successor mislead anyone into thinking that I saw through the staff of my school. At 11 or 12 years of age I was incapable of fully understanding the bewildering events of which I and my fellow pupils were witnesses. At first I was inclined to believe that our teachers held the key to what was happening. Yet the more I scrutinised their faces with my questioning stare, the more incomprehensible they became and the more baffling everything else appeared. Not that my incomprehension prevented me from rating them very differently and roughly categorising them as decent, malevolent or simply weak and fickle. The headmaster, Dr Bergmann, and our quiet, withdrawn art teacher, Lübke, enjoyed places of honour at the very top of my scale. They stood for something that I was not yet capable of putting into precise words. In later years, when I was trying to think of representatives of the humanist tradition in Germany, it was them I recalled.

Fate took its calamitous course, and Dr Bergmann was abruptly pensioned off, despite the fact that he was many years short of retiring age (we put his age at about 40). How did it happen? I was absent from school on that ominous day and had to rely on the reports of my school-mates.

For some reason all the staff and pupils were assembled in the hall. Dr Bergmann mounted the rostrum and began to address the school. Suddenly the sound of heckling arose from among the massed ranks of pupils. Shocked, people turned to see who had dared to interrupt the headmaster. The face they saw was a new one to the school. It belonged to the young officer in charge of the local Hitler Youth, who had taken a seat in the front row. He now rose to his feet and in front of the whole school ordered the headmaster to leave the rostrum immediately. The unheard-of then occurred: Dr Bergmann clearly felt obliged to comply with the order of the young man in uniform, whereupon the Hitler Youth leader took his place and announced that the headmaster had been dismissed for unreliability.

I should not have taken the reports seriously had they not been confirmed from all sides. And indeed, from that day on Dr Bergmann was never seen again. It was said that he had left Gross-Strehlitz and was looking for another post 'somewhere in Germany'.

For several weeks our school was without a headmaster. Rumours were rife on the subject of who might be appointed to succeed Dr Bergmann. In the end all our speculations turned out to be false. None of the existing members of staff was found to be suitable. The job went to a man who in all probability was as new and unfamiliar to our teachers as he was to us.

One day, there he was, a man of about forty introducing himself in the school hall as our 'provisional headmaster'. He was short, had a slight stoop, and wore a dark-brown, Hitler-style moustache. His protruding teeth and full lips gave the lower part of his face an almost Negroid appearance. From behind his glasses a pair of impenetrable steel-grey eyes radiated a quality of grim earnestness. His brisk walk was somehow out of character with his puny build. His name was Pierke, and he came from Gleiwitz, where he had taught maths and biology at a boys' secondary school. Word went round that Pierke had distinguished himself in 'the party' as an 'old campaigner'.

We were to hear Pierke give many speeches in the school hall as time went on. He spoke in short staccato sentences and showed a predilection for the inelegant words and phrases that Nazi usage was to make so hideously familiar.*

* As examples of expressions favoured by Pierke, the author cites *wesensgemäss*, *unverrückbar*, *unumstösslich*, *unerbittlich*, and *grundsätzlich* — literally, respectively, 'in

They rather suited his angular gait and his ascetic face. It was only when he mentioned 'race life' and talked about 'the Nordic blood in us Germans' that I stole a glance at the other teachers to see whether I could not catch a surreptitious smile or two. Most of them would be staring straight ahead in embarrassment as their provisional headmaster's fleshy lips spouted on and on. And Pierke did go on. He spoke with a solemn ardour. Not that there was anything new about that: even in Bergmann's day we had associated the school hall as much with such expressions as 'service to the state', 'fatherland', 'duty' and 'they died for Germany' as with the life-size paintings of Frederick the Great, Bismarck and Emperor William I that adorned its walls. But Pierke was capable of grandly flinging at his audience a sentence as portentous as 'Foreign protein is poison!'

Occasionally I would see Pierke looking out of a window of the house that had been built for Dr Bergmann or strolling in the new garden. At such times I was forcibly reminded of all the care and effort that the old headmaster had expended on his house and grounds.

In the early days Pierke used to go from class to class to familiarise himself with his new sphere of activity. I remember his first visit to us in the second year. Kasimir was in the middle of teaching us a theorem. Suddenly the door was pushed open, we rose to our feet, and there he stood before us, our new, hunchbacked headmaster. As he nodded to Kasimir, one side of his mouth went up. A smile was more than he could manage.

Pierke allowed his gaze to roam round the class. The expression on his face suggested that he was wondering how to put his second-years to the best use. His impersonal scrutiny, coupled with his silence, made us all extremely uncomfortable. At a sign from the headmaster, Kasimir resumed the lesson. Pierke stood by the door, listening. The eyes of the class remained glued to the blackboard, with only the occasional glance straying towards the door. It found Pierke looking round the classroom with an inquiring air, examining everything — the teacher's desk, the radiators, the windows, the pupils, the walls, the pictures on the walls, the ceiling, the lights and once again the pupils. His attention appeared to return to the lesson. Finally he remarked before leaving: 'I notice you have no picture of the Leader in here as yet. I shall see that you get a suitable one.' A few days later our classroom had its picture of the Führer.

Many other changes were introduced. New subjects appeared on the timetable, and of the old subjects few escaped some modifica-

---

conformity with [its] nature', 'immutable', 'irrefutable', inexorable' and 'as a matter of principle'. Needless to say, they lose their flavour in translation [Tr.].

tion. Our art education was henceforth supplemented by a handi-craft lesson, which was chiefly devoted to model-aircraft construction. Gymnastics took on an unmistakably military flavour as *Wehrsport*, with boxing, field exercises and hand-grenade throwing featuring prominently on the programme.

One entirely new subject was 'National Political Instruction'. For this lesson we were not only allowed but actually told to bring the newspaper. The teacher would read an extract aloud and proceed to explain how political events must be viewed if one was to arrive at a right judgement concerning them. He taught us to see why all the opinions voiced in the newspaper corresponded to something called 'sound popular instinct' and were therefore correct.

Certain deviations from the traditional school day enjoyed consid-erable popularity. Imagine our delight when, in the middle of a Latin lesson, a siren would summon us to air-raid drill! Once all the classes had assembled, we would be instructed in the use of sand-buckets and fire-extinguishers. The importance of such drills was made plain by a poster displayed in the main corridor. It showed Germany being invaded by flights of enemy bombers converging from every direction. The air-raid drills were actually more fun than the poster might have led one to expect. Providing first-aid for fictitious victims and dealing with imaginary incendiary bombs made an amusing pantomime. And the sight of the sixth-formers kitted out in their gas-masks — creatures half human and half phantom — was irresistibly comic.

A major innovation were school roll calls. I remember the first one. The school year was at an end and reports had been distri-buted. Just as we thought we were free, it was announced that staff and pupils were to assemble in the playground. Once the pupils had formed up and the staff as 'non-commissioned officers' had finished dressing the lines, 'Supreme Commander' Pierke had each teacher list his class. The flag was then raised, and Pierke made a speech. In it he pointed out that every pupil who put all his strength and all his abilities into his school work was not only contributing towards his own advancement but also assisting the Führer in his task of building up the nation.

As was to be expected, the speech concluded with the ritual cry of 'Unser Führer, Sieg Heil!' and the singing of *Deutschland, Deutschland über alles* and the 'Horst Wessel Song', all about flags held high and ranks closed tight.* As these songs resounded from 300 assembled

---

* Horst Wessel, a student member of the SA, was an early 'martyr' of the Nazi movement. His militant song became the second national anthem of the Third Reich, after the *Deutschlandlied*.

throats, all I could think of to do was to have a private look around for fellow sufferers. I was sure I was not the only person present who was pained by this coupling of the German national anthem with the battle-hymn of the Brownshirts. Indeed, several teachers were clearly very embarrassed at having not only to take part in the singing but also to hold their right arms in the air while doing so. Kasimir was staring into space above the pupils' heads. Dr Paulus, a practising Roman Catholic, had his arm raised but in a way that suggested he was in the last stages of exhaustion. Lübke, our art master, stood with lowered gaze. Schmiedhammer, who had already suffered a number of transfers because of his Social Democratic convictions, appeared to have developed a sudden interest in the clouds. Only Pierke and his supporters had their hearts in the business, and their outstretched arms were stiff with commitment. All in all, the staff hardly presented a picture of joyful unanimity.

Compared to the teachers, I was in a fortunate position. No one expected me to raise my right arm, let alone sing the SA song. As a Jew, all I was required to do was to stand in rank and file and listen to this profession of faith in the Führer until, with Pierke's 'School, dismiss!', we had our orders to begin the holiday.

Since 1945 it has been customary to speak of two phases in the history of the Third Reich. In the first phase, from 1933 to 1937, developments in Germany are said to have been disquieting but still to some extent civilised. It was only in the second phase — and particularly once the war had begun — that National Socialism took the final step into barbarism. 'Things got out of hand', we are told. 'The evil developed a momentum of its own.' Once they had become caught up in that momentum, there was no escape for the German people.

In the years 1941 to 1944 I saw my own and others' parents, brothers and sisters, friends and acquaintances — countless innocent people — deported to the death camps. And yet, alongside those ghastly memories, the dismissal of Dr Bergmann as headmaster of my school refuses to fade from my mind. Bergmann had his faults, certainly. And Pierke was no devil but simply a pushy careerist who, as was subsequently to emerge, did not shrink from partisan manipulation and gross perversions of justice. What was so outrageous was that the worse had been favoured above the better. Germany had changed course — and the new compass bearing was evil.

If you were to ask me, 'What were the worst crimes that Germans ever committed against Germany?' I should name in first place the hundreds of thousands of 'seizures of power' up and down the country in which the Bergmanns were forced out by the Pierkes.

In step, but with a poor conscience

Reorganising the curriculum of the Gross-Strehlitz *Gymnasium* would have been an uphill task had the 'provisional headmaster' — whose position, incidentally, was soon made permanent — not been backed up by a number of like-minded teachers. The staff that Pierke had inherited already included several Brownshirts. These now received reinforcements.

Eight new teachers were appointed to the staff in the period 1934–5. They were nearly all very young. Four of them made their SA affiliation public immediately. Another three showed themselves to be not particularly enamoured of the regime. The eighth, an older man by the name of Schmiedhammer, I have already mentioned. Schmiedhammer made no secret of his anti-Nazi persuasion. When teaching our class he used to make repeated references to the patriotic merits of the Social Democrats. He was not with us for long. He was probably given yet another transfer for disciplinary reasons, if not some worse punishment.

Schmiedhammer's boldly outspoken approach made him a somewhat isolated figure. The other non-Nazis, both among the new members of staff and among the old, familiar faces, initially adopted an attitude of extreme caution and reserve. Occasionally they would betray with a blush or a brief hesitation how reluctantly they complied with the directives of the National Socialist education authority. Such involuntary self-betrayals became particularly apparent after the introduction of the Hitler salute.

I still remember how I felt myself turn pale as the new directive from the Minister for Science and National Education was read out:

Staff and pupils shall give one another the German salute [i.e. the Hitler salute] both on and off school premises. At the start of each lesson the teacher shall face the standing class and give it the salute by raising his right arm and saying 'Heil Hitler'; the class shall return the salute by raising their right arms and saying 'Heil Hitler'. The teacher shall end the lesson, once the pupils have stood up, by raising his right arm and saying 'Heil Hitler'; the pupils shall return the salute in the same fashion.

Otherwise pupils shall salute members of staff on school premises merely by raising their right arms in a fitting manner.

Whereas Roman Catholic religious instruction has hitherto begun and ended with the versicle and response 'May Jesus Christ be praised' — 'For ever and ever, Amen', in future the German salute shall be given at the beginning of the lesson before and at the end of the lesson after the versicle and response.

Non-Aryan pupils may choose whethe or not they wish to give the German salute.*

However cynically the last sentence of the directive was meant, for the time being it rescued me from an appalling dilemma. 'Aryans', be they staff or pupils, were obliged to pay homage to Hitler ten or a dozen times a day. Anyone who refused could not remain at the school. And let me say right away that the Gross-Strehlitz *Gymnasium* did not produce a single recusant.

Even a practising Roman Catholic, Dr Paulus, learnt to pronounce those two words. Did not Paulus's lip-service, however shallow, contribute towards making an idol of the Nazi chieftain he so hated, thus helping to seduce the young people with whose education he had been entrusted? I should have thought he would rather give up his position than utter Hitler's name and the word 'Heil' in the same breath. However, he was responsible for a family of eight children. I knew them all, from lanky Franz in the lower sixth to Peter, who was still crawling. As I have said, they lived in the flat above ours. It was a painful moment when Dr Paulus first managed to utter the Hitler salute, for one saw clearly what agony it caused him. His face contorted with strain, he wrenched the phrase from his throat with a sudden lurch. 'HEIL! Htlr,' he cried, with the emphasis very much on the first word, as if to say, 'I don't mean Hitler at all, and I use the other word in the Christian sense of grace, salvation.'

Schmiedhammer showed less hesitation than Paulus, pouncing on the Hitler greeting as boldly as if he had been taking a bite out of a juicy apple. Afterwards, though, he would pull a face as if his teeth had encountered a maggot. I remember watching his cheeky pantomime with uneasy amusement.

When the Roman Catholic school chaplain, Father Zylka, lisped his 'Heil Hitler', his bald head used to flush pink all over while his watery blue eyes went as small and round as a hen's.

It cannot have been easy for Pierke to work with such a mixed bag of teachers. In the early years of the Nazi dictatorship there were so many sackings and early retirements in schools throughout Germany that it was not immediately possible to fill all the vacant posts with faithful Hitlerites.

Among the teachers who formed the inner core of Pierke's following was one called Matzgruber. For a year Matzgruber taught us

* The German text of the order is given in Werner Klose, *Generation im Gleichschritt*, Oldenburg, Stalling Verlag, 1964.

history. As he portrayed it, the story of mankind presented the spectacle of a constant battle between noble, powerful peoples and inferior, parasitical peoples. The noble peoples belonged without exception to the Aryan race. The significant achievements of the ancient Egyptians, Phoenicians and Assyrians were attributable to the occasional influence of proto-Germanic tribes, whose courageous sea voyages had sometimes brought them to the most remote parts of the world.

He offered these explanations without either emphasis or emotion. What we had been taught before Hitler's coming to power had been wrong, he told us. Matzgruber proceeded to discharge his office by pointing out, in calm, objective tones, just how untenable the old views had been before going on to expound, in equally unemotional tones, the view that had recently been found to be correct.

What Matzgruber did for history, a teacher called Billig did for German. The difficulties he faced were similar in that our reading book contained chapters in which 'wrong' opinions were expressed, opinions that ran counter to the 'national instinct'. A reading book more in harmony with current opinion was still in preparation. So Billig either arranged for the dubious passages to be omitted or, if that could not easily be done, simply pointed out, 'Nowadays we take a very different view!' He also supplemented our 'obsolete' reading book with more up-to-date 'literary sources'. These included speeches by the Führer, articles from National Socialist newspapers, and pronouncements by district political officers. I remember one lesson in which we had read to us, one after the other, a poem by Goethe and a poem by 'National Youth Leader' Baldur von Schirach. Goethe's poem was *Der Zauberlehrling*, 'The Sorcerer's Apprentice'. I was unable to recall the National Youth Leader's poem verbatim, though I remembered its approximate content. Recently, however, I came across the complete text in a yellowed German reader and recognised it instantly:

> *HITLER*
>
> Ihr seid viel tausend hinter mir,
> Und ihr seid ich, und ich bin ihr.
> Ich habe keinen Gedanken gelebt,
> Der nicht in euren Herzen gebebt.
>
> Und forme ich Worte, so weiss ich keins,
> Das nicht mit eurem Wollen eins.
> Denn ich bin ihr, und ihr seid ich,
> Und wir alle glauben, Deutschland, an dich!

(Behind me you are many thousands,
And you are me, and I am you.
I have not lived a single thought
That has not trembled in your hearts.

And, forming words, I know of none
That is not one with your desire.
For I am you, and you are me,
And we all, O Germany, believe in thee!)

Billig spoke in a sprightly, unassuming, conversational voice. To
see him struggling for the attention of the class, his glasses always
rather too far down his nose, one might have taken him for a kindly
village schoolmaster.

Our music teacher, Paschke, a long-standing member of the
National Socialist Motor Corps, clearly found no difficulty in working closely with the new headmaster. Back in 1932 he had recommended that we sing a lot because singing was healthy. Now
Paschke spoke even more persuasively of the value of song as a
propaganda instrument. His smooth face would shine with contentment as he wrote the words and music of the latest battle hymn on
the blackboard. It was the contentment of a man who is conscious of
enjoying the approval of his superiors. His hand would go up to
bring us in, and the pupil host would roar:

Ein junges Volk steht auf zum Sturm bereit!
Reisst die Fahnen höher, Kameraden!
Wir fühlen nahen unsre Zeit.
Die Zeit der jungen Soldaten.
Vor uns marschieren mit sturmzerfetzten Fahnen.
Die toten Helden der jungen Nation . . .

(A youthful people rises, ready to attack!
Haul the flags higher, comrades!
We feel our day approaching,
The day of the young soldiers.
Before us, with storm-torn banners, march
The dead heroes of the young nation . . .)

Spotting the NSDAP supporters among the members of staff
would have been a simple matter even if they had never shown
themselves in uniform. Nevertheless, I was surprised that the young
teachers gave expression to their Hitlerite views in such measured
tones. Under the influence of Hitler's and Goebbels' speeches, the
acts of violence for which the Brownshirts were notorious, and the
style in which the SA chose to portray itself on its propaganda

posters, I had formed a clear mental image of a National Socialist. He was equipped with furiously clenched teeth, massive jaws and an icy stare. His limbs moved in angular jerks. He was incapable of ever appearing informal, cheerful or relaxed. His deadly earnestness prohibited him from laughing. When he spoke he attempted to intimidate you with his fist or drown you out with his hysterical screeching. He proclaimed his truths in the voice of a sergeant major, so that his listeners' protests died in their throats. However, very few of these characteristics were observable in the young Brownshirts on the staff of our school. They gave an impression of moderation, if not humanity. The only one who came anywhere near the type of convinced National Socialist that I had imagined for myself was the headmaster, Pierke.

In the first year after Hitler's seizure of power, about half the teaching staff at our school remained unwilling participants in the Nazi cult. There was something comforting about that. Their deep embarrassment and obvious conflict of conscience showed that decency and human dignity were offended but not extinct. In the course of a school year our teachers had to render public homage to Hitler an estimated two and a half thousand times. Is it any wonder that Father Zylka was eventually able to say 'Heil Hitler' without turning red? Even Dr Paulus no longer appeared to be having such a struggle with himself. Little by little, I too became desensitised to the monstrosity of the Führer cult.

The Nordification of the Gross-Strehlitz Gymnasium

How can they ever have thought that I would blindly accept the dogmas proclaimed by Pierke and Matzgruber? Growing up in a Jewish family, I had been aware from an early age that authorities and majorities were not necessarily closer to the truth. Even so, I am amazed at the extent of my own naïve stupidity.

Billig told us one day that there was no more instructive occupation than to familiarise oneself with those to whom one owed one's being, one's faith and one's entire potential. The individual could form a correct understanding of his importance to his people only when he saw himself in the context of his ancestral line. The exercise was not compulsory, but he, Billig, would be delighted if each pupil were to draw up his own family tree. On it we should enter dates of birth, professions, details of war service and other significant events in the lives of our forefathers. Particular attention should be paid to their personal qualities — whether they were of violent or easy-going temperament, whether they tended to be adventurous or set greater store by a settled life.

Uttered in Billig's sprightly conversational tone, these words inspired me. Suddenly I was seized with a boundless curiosity as to what my ancestors had looked like, where they had lived and what had happened to them.

Father could do little to slake my thirst for knowledge. His information went back only four generations. The picture that emerged was as follows.

With one exception, all my progenitors had been rabbis. Only my great-great-grandfather had been in business. For two generations my forefathers had lived in Bavaria. They had moved there from East Prussia. Beyond that there was some evidence that my great-great-great-grandfather had originally come from Lithuania. No portraits of my ancestors survived. The only thing father could find in a drawer was a photograph of my grandfather. This was extremely blurred. In fact, one could make out only that it represented a man with a beard.

All my ancestors, as far back as they could be traced, had been Jews. And not merely Jews but, according to my father, devout and godly Jews. I promptly made a note of this under 'personal qualities'. I then entered all my notes neatly in the appropriate places on the tree that I had drawn up on a large sheet of paper.

I remember handing Billig the finished document at the end of a lesson. He gave it a cursory glance and appeared to have some difficulty in suppressing a smile. With a word of praise for my diligence, he folded the paper and put it in his briefcase, together with the contributions of several of my classmates. That was the last I heard of my family tree. The matter was never mentioned again.

By contrast, another stupid thing I did led to grave consequences. In 1936, as we went up into fourth year, it so happened that the headmaster's son Siegfried became my classroom neighbour. We got on well together. In the fourth year we had the headmaster for maths and biology. Once I had grown accustomed to seeing Pierke at close quarters almost daily my terror of him abated. Siegfried's father must surely be a good-natured fellow, I reasoned; otherwise he would not have been able to bring his son up to be such a pleasant, peace-loving lad. Nor was there any indication that Pierke felt any displeasure at seeing his son and myself sharing a desk.

What Pierke called biology ought really to have been called heredity. All he ever talked about was genetics. The charts he hung up showed the processes of cell division and fusion magnified many thousands of times. Pierke used technical terms that were new to us: chromosomes, cross-breeding, genotype and the like.

Why was so much importance being attached to these things all of a sudden? For anyone who heard Pierke's addresses in the school hall or had any inkling of Nazi ideology, the answer was obvious. These lessons in genetics were to lay the foundations for ethnology, and the purpose of ethnology was to instil in all our hearts a belief in the destination of the German people as the 'master race' and in the consequent need for a race policy.

Race, however, did not yet concern us. Initially it was a question not of Teutons and Slavs but of sea-urchins and fruit-flies, white mice and guinea-pigs. Red and white tulips and brown-speckled and black-speckled cattle were crossed with each other. Using a handful of simple rules, one could work out what kinds of tulip or calf would result. The decisive importance of the gene in determining the value or otherwise of the individual was thereby revealed, along with the fateful power of the chromosome.

At the same time this whole science was shrouded in the secrets of procreation and sex, and we 14-year-olds were now considered mature enough to be initiated in these mysteries. With the aid of the microscope we were given a glimpse into the way in which nature compiles the mosaic of qualities in her creatures. I was fascinated. Rarely did a biology lesson go by without my putting my hand up and making a contribution. In a while we had progressed to a point where Pierke could have the charts illustrating Mendel's laws taken down. In their place he had charts showing human races hung on the board. Neanderthal and Cro-Magnon men, Mongoloids and Negroids, Indian Veddas with their unkempt beards, saddle-nosed Slavs, Amerindian head-hunters of the Amazon Basin, and other dolichocephalic or brachycephalic representatives of the human race were arranged as neatly and clearly as the edible and inedible fungi in our nature-study books at home.

As Pierke expounded the characteristics of the different races my gaze wandered round the classroom, studying my classmates' chins and cheekbones, estimating their facial angles and comparing their ears and noses. I noticed that my classmates were doing the same. We continued these ethnological exercises during break-times, occasionally even using rulers and protractors. None of my fellow pupils came anywhere near the pure Nordic type, to say nothing of the headmaster himself. Some of them thought that with my long, narrow head, my facial shape and my fair hair I showed several Nordic racial characteristics. That rather appealed to my vanity. At the same time I regretted not being taller and not having blue eyes. I should have been delighted to think that, as a Nordic-looking Jew, I was a source of irritation to members of the Nazi Party — particularly those with dubious racial antecedents.

Our headmaster held forth on the virtues of the Nordic race in especial detail. In his eyes the Nordic Aryans were equipped with every imaginable good quality. Pierke, whom I never once saw make a joke or even smile, assured us that only Nordic man possessed a genuine sense of humour. There is no doubt that our headmaster was embarrassed by his own racial characteristics. Possibly that was why he came to school in uniform more often than his fellow party members on the staff.

Mind you, none of this occurred to me until it was too late and the damage had been done. Given a little more insight into Pierke's nature I would certainly have been more careful. I would have sat quietly at my desk and never once put my hand up.

Pierke decided to introduce us to two new technical terms: *Aufartung* and *Aufnordung*, respectively 'racial improvement' and 'Nordification'. *Aufartung*, he explained, was the opposite of *Entartung* ('degeneration'). It was what the cattle-breeder practised when he continually selected the relatively pure-bred animals for further breeding until he had a racially pure or thoroughbred stock. Similarly, *Aufnordung* meant giving preference to and enriching the Nordic racial component in a people. The 'Nordification' of the German people was one of the racial-policy objectives of National Socialism.

As he explained these terms to us Pierke walked up and down between the lines of desks. He would ask a question, pause, give the explanation, and after a further rhetorical pause resume his pacing. 'Nordification', he said in a voice full of meaning. 'Have any of you heard that word before?'

No one answered, so I put my hand up and said: 'You mentioned the opposite before: de-Nordification.'

Pierke stood for a moment in silent thought. Then he exploded. 'What do you mean by suddenly butting in with "de-Nordification"?' he shouted at me. 'I didn't ask you to speak! What outrageous insolence!'

'I'm sorry, headmaster, I didn't mean it like that. I only said it because you were talking about opposites before. I thought. . . .'

'Don't lie!' he barked at me. 'You simply butted in with your "de-Nordification"! You heard him, all of you!'

My classmates froze and said nothing. No one could bring himself to corroborate the lie. But neither did anyone dare to contradict the irate SA headmaster.

I hoped the headmaster could be persuaded to take a different view if I spoke to him alone. At the end of the lesson I ran out of the room after him. In the corridor I again stressed the perfectly innocent intention with which I had uttered the word 'de-Nordification'.

Pierke cut me off. 'You can't fool me. You knew perfectly well what you were doing when you butted in with your "de-Nordification". I am going to have to punish you for your insolence.'

I stared in bewilderment at his stony face.

The 'de-Nordification affair' became the talk of the school. Within days it was the talk of the town. First- and second-years shouted after me in the street: 'Hey, look! There goes the de-Nordifier!' Jewish businessmen stopped me as I passed their shops. They wanted to hear the whole story. For the space of a week I was the most sought-after member of the Jewish congregation. Even the half-witted Guli went round telling people: 'Well, for instance, he called out "de-Nordification!"' And he would laugh till his voice cracked.

I did not feel like laughing. What worried me was not the whispering in school, nor the talk in town and at synagogue, but the headmaster's silence. A week went by without his mentioning the subject. After a further few days I was summoned by one of the new teachers, a young man named Tillich, who was particularly well disposed towards me. I remember that he came from Cologne.

'Now listen to me, my lad,' he began. 'Just what have you been up to, eh?' He studied me anxiously.

'You mean with the de-Nordification, sir?'

'Of course! What else would I be talking about?' He paused for a moment. 'The headmaster brought your case up at the staff meeting. He wants to expel you. He didn't get much support. Keep that to yourself, though. Some of us even put in a good word for you. But it was no use — in fact, it only made him angrier. Now he's referring your case to the provincial education committee. It's a foregone conclusion what they'll say. But you don't have to wait for their verdict. That's what I wanted to tell you. Leave voluntarily! Do you understand? Otherwise you'll never be accepted at another school.'

'But sir', I stammered, 'I haven't done anything wrong! The whole class knows that! How can they expel me?'

'Believe me, lad', Tillich said kindly. 'I know our headmaster. He'll get his way. That's all I can say to you. I'm sure you understand why. Have a word with your parents and get them to withdraw you from school. It'll be the best thing for you. You told me yourself that your father's leaving Gross-Strehlitz soon in any case. So you'll have nothing to lose by quitting school a bit earlier.'

My final report contained some surprises. In several subjects I received far better marks than I deserved. Was that a silent protest, a demonstration of sympathy? When I think of the warmth with which certain teachers shook my hand as I left, I am inclined to think so.

'Dad, everyone's emigrating!'

The end of our time in Gross-Strehlitz was approaching. The Prussian Union of Jewish Congregations, on whose behalf my father exercised his office, found itself obliged through lack of funds to reduce his salary and finally to give him early retirement. Father, who was then 60, could not bear the thought of emigrating, with all that it implied in terms of domestic upheaval and getting used to the language and way of life of a foreign country. He wanted to spend the rest of his life in Germany. He sought to bolster his meagre pension by taking another job. He found one with the tiny Jewish congregation in Schönlanke, a small town some 130 miles east of Berlin.* There he hoped to be able to recover his strength after the difficult years in Gross-Strehlitz.

He had every intention of helping us children to emigrate. My eldest sister, Ruth, was already outside Germany. She had married a Czech Jew and gone to live in the Carpatho-Ukraine.† The rest of us were to be given some vocational training first, to enable us to earn a living in our future home. My brother Jakob wanted to be a violinist, so father arranged for him to have private lessons. He was also to attend a Jewish secondary school in Berlin in order to prepare for his school-leaving examination. I was to continue my education at the same establishment. Until then I went on studying by myself. My brother Leon was dispatched to a technical college in Czechoslovakia to study mechanical engineering. My other sister, Toni, was meanwhile helping mother with the housework.

Worse things had to happen in Germany before my father, despite his age, attempted to emigrate with the whole family. The exclusion of Jews from all areas of public life, their defamation in the press and on the radio, and their social degradation as a result of the 1935 Nuremberg Race Laws‡ had long since prompted many Jews, even in Gross-Strehlitz, to leave Hitler's Germany. Some of my Jewish

* Pomerania east of the Oder–Neisse Line was also transferred to Polish administration in 1945, and Schönlanke now appears on the map as Trzclanka.
† A province occupying the southern slopes of the Carpathian Mountains. At that time it belonged to Czechoslovakia. In 1939 it reverted to Hungary, and in 1945 it became part of the Soviet Ukraine.
‡ Laws passed by the Nazi Party's national conference in Nuremberg in 1935. These laws deprived Jews of their civil rights and forbade them to contract marriages or even form liaisons with citizens of 'Aryan' blood.

56

school-friends were already in Palestine with their parents; others had emigrated to America or Australia. Those left behind included patriots associated with the League of Jewish Veterans, persons who lacked the professional qualifications demanded by the countries accepting immigrants, and the very poor, who could not afford to emigrate. They also included the deaf and dumb transport worker Markus and the unfortunate, imbecilic Guli.

With the Jewish community of Gross-Strehlitz shrinking visibly I too began to worry. One day — my father had just come home from synagogue and was pacing thoughtfully up and down our living-room, still full of the sermon he had just delivered — I ventured to bring up the subject: 'Dad, everyone's emigrating. Wouldn't it be better if we emigrated, too?' But the question made my father cross, and I did not ask it again.

My father found life in Germany difficult but not intolerable. He was able to practise his profession as a rabbi unhindered. In fact, even after the promulgation of the Nuremberg Race Laws he bought himself a car to enable him to serve his twelve congregations more efficiently. He preached from twelve pulpits, and he had a great deal else to do besides. School-children had to be given religious instruction. Young couples wished to be married. On one occasion a Christian man came to see my father and said he wished to be received into the Jewish religious community — not in spite of but because of the new oppression of the Jews. The singular fate of the Jews, he explained, had inspired in him a conviction that they really were God's Chosen People.

The promulgation of the Nuremberg Race Laws had sown dismay in the Jewish congregation. My father was not dismayed, though. He was only sorry that he was obliged to dismiss our 'Aryan' maid, who was thoroughly competent and had given our family years of affectionate and devoted service. Her place was taken by a Jewish girl. The disadvantage was that the new maid could not be asked to switch the electric light or the hotplate on or off during the Sabbath, for the Sabbath laws are binding on all Jews. Ah, but what was the point of living in the age of technology? Father adopted the course taken by many practising Jews: he purchased two clockwork time switches, one for the light and one for the hotplate. As long as these were correctly set and we had remembered to wind them up, the lights and the hotplate came on and went off precisely as required.

Father saw the guiding hand of God even in the Nuremberg Race Laws. As he saw it, the anti-Jewish legislation of the Third Reich corresponded exactly to the laws of the Torah that the German Jews had so often transgressed. Jews opened for business on the Sabbath;

hence the fact that the first general boycott of Jewish shops fell on a Sabbath. They married people of other faiths; hence the Nuremberg Race Laws. The introduction of the compulsory first names 'Sara' and 'Israel' in 1938 was a divine corrective measure aimed at Jews who were ashamed of their Jewish names.

Armed with such beliefs, my father took the increasing disfranchisement of the Jews relatively calmly. Our domestic life in the years 1934 and 1935 might have given the impression that contemporary events had left us completely unaffected. Jewish and Christian visitors from all over the world called at the house and were met by my father's unfailingly cordial 'Ah!' of welcome. I remember the evening gatherings over a small glass of liqueur and a large helping of convivial gossip. If our visitors were drawn from the Jewish congregation, the talk would usually turn on people's family news, and of course anti-Nazi jokes formed an essential part of the proceedings. Some evenings were devoted to domestic music-making, when father would sing and play the piano and Jakob would play his violin.

In the summer of 1936, some two months after I had left Pierke's school, we moved to Schönlanke. There my father rented a modest flat from a Jewish landlord. The move went off without a hitch. The men from the removal firm grunted and groaned while father directed operations. He took personal charge of hanging the pictures. Titian's *Girl with a Fruit Dish* and the *Returning Reapers* went up in the living-room, where they had hung in Gross-Strehlitz and before that in Heilbronn. I remember father cocking his head on one side to check whether they were straight. I supervised the installation of our two time switches for Sabbath-day electricity.

I do not feel qualified to paint a fair picture of the non-Jewish inhabitants of Schönlanke. My dealings with them were almost without exception painful. In Gross-Strehlitz I had got to know a number of well-meaning people over the years. In Schönlanke, where I lived for a few months only, I had no success in this direction.

I spent the first three days after our arrival exploring the streets of the little town. No one molested me. But then one day, as I was crossing the market-place with a local Jewish boy, stones were thrown at us. From that day on I was treated to all manner of abuse, even when I was out alone. So as far as possible I avoided going out until I moved to Berlin. My brothers fared no better. They were glad when, soon afterwards, they too had to leave Schönlanke to continue their education elsewhere.

My father clung to his belief that the move had been a sensible step. He had no idea of the bitter experiences Schönlanke had in store for him.

My parents' social life was almost exclusively limited to the members of the local Jewish congregation. For me, Schönlanke was simply a stop-over on the way to Berlin; my youthful arrogance would not allow me to indulge in conversation with small-town Jews. I preferred to endure a semi-voluntary seclusion. Most of my day was taken up with preparatory work for the school I was to attend in Berlin. What free time remained I spent in conducting scientific experiments. This was not a new interest on my part; my room in Gross-Strehlitz had come increasingly to resemble a laboratory. Now Berlin, the capital of Germany, loomed before me as a great metropolis of chemistry and medicine. I worked out how many hours of leisure my new school timetable would leave me in which I should be able to hang around the university quarter. What I failed to notice was how my new hobby diverted my attention from the calamitous events that were continuing to take place in Germany.

CHAPTER 4

Exciting Berlin

Friendly reception in the capital

In April 1937 my father accompanied Jakob and myself to Berlin, found us a room and full board with a Jewish family by the name of Teitelbaum, and introduced us to the headmaster of the Jewish *Gymnasium*.

This school, which belonged to Berlin's 'Adass-Isroël' congregation, was situated in Siegmundshof. Five minutes' walk from Tiergarten Station in the direction of the River Spree brought you to the playground entrance. Beyond the playground rose the school building. It was an extensive complex, housing not only the secondary school but also a primary school and a synagogue, both of which also belonged to Adass-Isroël. From the classroom windows heavily laden barges could be seen passing on the river.

I found myself surrounded by excited fifth-years as soon as I set foot in my new classroom. 'A new boy! A new boy!' They could not wait to interrogate me. However, my account of the de-Nordification affair left them cold. 'Stories like that are old hat to us,' one of them assured me with a wry smile.

Many of my new school-mates had, like myself, previously attended state schools until brown-uniformed teachers and fellow pupils had made their lives a misery. Several members of staff had had similar experiences, I learnt. They had had to give up their state teaching posts in 1933. The Jewish *Gymnasium* was a place of refuge for both types of outcast, which explained why the teaching body even included former university lecturers.

I did not find it easy to keep up with the lessons in all subjects. My Greek was superfluous. My advantage in Latin proved of little use. I was a long way behind in French, and English was a new subject to me. But how trivial these problems appeared in the light of the blissful change that the Jewish school brought into my life! The ugly spectre of anti-Semitism was banished. Gone, too, were the Hitler pictures, the 'German salutes', the unfair fights and the Nazi battle songs. I felt I could breathe again, so relieved was I to be back in a normal school — or rather, the kind of school that had been normal throughout Germany before 1933. That such a thing still existed in Germany in 1937 was little short of miraculous.

I want to say a little more about three of my teachers in particular: Messrs Buchswedel, Breitstirn and Blitz.

Studienrat Buchswedel professed opinions of the sort that were prevalent in the Central Union of German Citizens of the Jewish Faith. He was proud of the decorations he had won at the western front in the 1914–18 war. He was proud of his academic rank, of his German culture and, as he claimed, of his Jewishness. Since Buchswedel often talked in sharply critical terms about 'the Jews' while giving no indication of any positive appreciation of the Jewish tradition, I was never able to take the words 'proud of my Jewishness' to denote anything more than a protest against anti-Semitism. In any case, it was a pride that stood on frail foundations. Buchswedel's repeated tirades against the Jews' alleged 'lack of mutual respect', together with the pedantic severity with which he felt he must assert his authority *vis-à-vis* his 'disrespectful Jewish pupils', made it look as if he was the one who was lacking — in self-respect.

Professor Breitstirn, our Latin master, wasted no words on respect and discipline as he strode between the rows of desks, his face wreathed in a subtle smile. He enjoyed teaching. He liked his pupils, and he controlled them with consummate ease. His shrewd eyes sparkled with wit and intelligence. A few ironic words from his lips would serve to show that he was exempt from both admiration for German power politics and Jewish feelings of inferiority. He was one of the most likeable men at the school.

Professor Blitz taught Jewish history. He might equally well have taught us Latin, physics or musical theory, for he was something of a polymath. His evening lectures to the local congregation or for the benefit of various Jewish societies were attended by, among others, large numbers of listeners who were incapable of following his arguments in any but the most fragmentary fashion. Blitz had the knack of presenting even seemingly dry academic material to gripping effect.

An exciting lecturer, he was also a much feared debating partner. Having amassed a battery of arguments in his encyclopedic brain, he would proceed with a smile of triumph to drive his opponent into a corner.

I heard critical and even disparaging remarks made about Blitz in

61

various quarters without understanding what it was that people had against him. That did not become clear to me until shortly before the outbreak of war, when I was 17. At that time I was plagued by all kinds of doubts about Rabbinical Judaism, and I took them to Blitz. He contrived, with the aid of a few laconic remarks, to scatter my doubts like chaff and demonstrate to me the unassailable validity of the Talmudic Law. I acknowledged defeat. And yet, though I could find no counter-arguments, I felt somehow cheated.

So what had happened? I had expressed my doubts. Professor Blitz, completely ignoring the possible motives behind my crisis of faith, had seized on my clumsy words. Quick as a flash, a couple of logical inferences had reduced my position to absurdity. I had been at a loss for a reply. Yet again, he had made me feel his superiority. I was clearly meant to draw the conclusion that, when my words were swept aside by a man of such towering intellect, right was very likely to be on his side rather than on mine.

If only he had used his towering intellect to help a disciple towards a better understanding of himself! I should have gone home not routed but enriched.

My joining the school also gave me entrée to the Adass-Isroël congregation, which met in the synagogue next door. In the praying congregation I found not only Nachman Schlesinger, the headmaster, but a number of other members of staff. Our music master doubled as the choirmaster in synagogue. A school-friend proudly drew my attention to the learned men in the congregation, for they included some internationally famous names. Every young man needs heroes, and it did me good to see men of such standing and repute assembled in the light of the synagogue lamps.

The bulk of the congregation consisted of shopkeepers, brokers, reps, tailors, bakers and coal merchants. In time, I came to know a number of them personally, though none so well as my landlord, Herr Teitelbaum.

Teitelbaum, an accountant by profession, occupied the unassuming position of a 'Baal Bayit' in the congregation. The phrase may be translated as 'paterfamilias', or 'head of the family'. In synagogue, he sat modestly in a pew near the back, gazing with respectful curiosity at the more prominent members of the congregation.

The Teitelbaums' table-talk turned for the most part on news connected with the Adass-Isroël congregation, on the emigrations and business careers of friends and acquaintances, and on snippets from the newspaper. The kind of conversation based on a subject from the Torah that is customary at table among many practising Jews was never held in the Teitelbaum household. Teitelbaum knew just enough to be able to live in accordance with Jewish custom but too little to embark on a theoretical discussion. In fact, he freely admitted his ignorance of all matters not bearing on the art of book-keeping. All the greater was his admiration for men who were his superiors in terms of talent and knowledge. He spoke with effusive admiration of Jewish Nobel Prize winners, and when Teitelbaum said, 'Gentlemen, Professor Cohen is an authority in the field of internal medicine!' you could tell from the look on his face what it did for his self-esteem. His wife, too, was capable of pausing in the doorway at such moments to listen with rapt attention, her mind a million miles from the empty soup tureen in her hands.

The Adass-Isroël congregation belonged to the Neo-traditionalist tendency that had emerged from the clash with the Reform Movement around the middle of the nineteenth century.* It aspired to a synthesis of the sacred Jewish tradition with the culture of modern Germany. That may sound strange today, but at the time I found Neo-traditionalism neither strange nor indeed new, having been brought up on it. It was the feeble professions of the Gross-Strehlitz three-day Jews and their ilk that struck me as strange, not to say absurd.

Although the policies of the Nazi government were directed against all Jews equally, the effects of persecution on Jewish self-awareness varied enormously. Three-day Jews — those, that is to say, who did not turn to Zionism — more easily lost confidence in themselves, and their congregations declined rapidly. 'Torah-true' Jews, as the German traditionalists called themselves, proved to be made of sterner stuff. They even began to exert a certain power of

---

* After the French Revolution, one effect of which had been to prepare the ground for the emancipation of the Jews, many Jews continued to see a decisive obstacle to their integration into west-European society in the traditional Jewish way of life, and in particular the belief that they were God's Chosen People. A major incentive behind the foundation of the Reform Movement was to remove these obstacles by 'cleansing' Judaism of its particularism and retaining only its universalist ideals and by assimilating Reform Judaism to the model of Protestant Christian confessionalism. A further incentive was provided by the desire to break out of the Jews' half-involuntary, half-willed state of seclusion and join fully in the rich cultural life of modern Europe. The trouble was that the Reform Movement was unable to prevent many of its adherents from abandoning Judaism altogether and so far integrating themselves into the dominant society as to accept Christian baptism and take Christian marriage partners.

To counter the self-destructive aspect of Reform Judaism, there emerged in Germany a modern traditionalist movement. This sought to demonstrate that not only was it possible, it was the religious and civic duty of Jews to participate in German culture and assume German patriotic responsibilities *without abandoning Jewish particularism or a way of life that conformed to the Torah*. This became the fundamental conviction of the 'Adass–Isroël' congregations that constituted themselves in a number of German cities and that inspired similar congregations throughout Western Europe and the United States.

attraction. Many a three-day Jew who had been forced to think seriously about his Jewishness for the first time after the events of January 1933 found fresh security in one of the traditionalist congregations. The Adass-Isroël congregation remained a powerhouse of Berlin's Jewry right up until 1939, even with its ranks thinned by the emigration movement.

The synthesis of Jewish tradition with German culture that formed the goal of Neo-traditionalism was reflected in the school curriculum, where Jewish religious instruction occupied an important place. The school further taught all the subjects that had been compulsory at every modern-language secondary school in Germany under the Weimar Republic. It continued to be recognised by the state and to come under the Ministry of Education. But even the minister stopped short of expecting Jewish teachers to revise their lessons in accordance with the tenets of National Socialism. I dare say there were not many schools in Germany in the years 1937 to 1939 at which German history, literature and art received such honest, unadulterated treatment as they did at the Adass-Isroël Jewish *Gymnasium*.

In a few weeks my brother Jakob and I were beginning to feel at home in our new surroundings. Life in Berlin agreed with us. Jakob, who had left the Gross-Strehlitz school long before me, had gone on studying on his own and had even made some progress. He was now able, as an only slightly over-age schoolboy, to follow the lessons at the highest grade in the Jewish school without too much difficulty. We enjoyed each other's company, even though Jakob was six years my senior and our interests differed widely. I learnt to get on with my homework without allowing myself to be distracted either by Jakob's violin practice or by the high-speed suburban trains that thundered past the house. In fact, I even came to enjoy that peculiar blend of string music and traffic noise.

I felt good in Berlin. My only irritation was that in that enormous city I had not yet found room for my chemistry laboratory. The chemicals and apparatus that I had collected over the years were still sitting in packing cases back in Schönlanke, waiting to be fetched.

The chemistry teacher, Dr Willy Halberstadt, with whom I was soon on excellent terms, helped me to find an unexpectedly simple solution. The Jewish school had its own chemistry laboratory. Designed for student experiments, it had been out of commission for years because of lack of funds. Dr Halberstadt had a word with the headmaster. Three weeks later I received permission to set out my bottles of chemicals on the shelves of the school laboratory. From then on I seized every available opportunity to conduct experiments in chemistry and physiology.

As soon as lessons were over for the day I would bolt my lunch and set out for the scientific second-hand dealers and the factories and institutes that I had spent the morning dreaming about in school.

I was particularly attracted to the part of the university quarter in which chemistry and medicine were taught. I would pause reverentially in front of the monuments to Robert Koch and Emil Fischer. The window displays of the specialist medical-instrument shops and the academic booksellers held me spellbound. I used to linger near the entrance to the Charité Hospital time and time again, gazing longingly up at the façades of the scientific institutes. Indeed, those serene façades were about all I did see. As a 15-year-old schoolboy in short trousers, I could hardly hope to get inside. I almost forgot that, as a Jew, I should have been thrown out in any case. Even 'Aryans' were admitted only on condition that they made obeisance to the Führer in the approved fashion.

The doorman at the main entrance to the huge Schering & Kahlbaum chemical works laid a friendly hand on my shoulder. 'What is it, then? — You want to see round the works? — Nay, lad, come back when you're a chemist. Then we'll let you in!'

At other times I had better luck. I was invited in to look around a factory in Wedding that made laboratory equipment, and from then on I became a regular visitor to its glass-blowing and engineering workshops. I often stayed until knocking-off time, when I would take my bicycle and mingle with the endless streams of office and factory workers wending their way homeward through Alt-Moabit.

What a delight it was to have a bicycle on which I could glide so silently and effortlessly through the streets of Berlin! The thing that delighted me most, though, was the rapid sequence of scene changes, the dreamlike transition from the familiar classroom, through the roaring traffic of the nation's capital, to the showrooms and workshops of that laboratory-supplies company.

Busy as I was with my school-work and despite my fascination with laboratories and factories, I was not inattentive to political events. In fact, I was very much alive to the elaborate state ceremonies that unrolled in public in the centre of Berlin. The arrival of Mussolini in September 1937 and the visit of the Hungarian Regent, Miklós Horthy, in August 1938 were events I witnessed at first hand — and at close quarters. Both statesmen were accorded a triumphal reception and a drive-past along the great avenue in the city centre, Unter den Linden. I also made a point of watching the military parades that marked the birthday of the Führer. I was driven by curiosity, but that was not my sole motive. I knew that people did not recognise me as a Jew, and I saw it as my simple duty to mingle with the crowd and be an eye-witness.

So dense was the crowd of spectators that there was no risk in neglecting to raise one's arm in the Hitler salute. The armoured cars clattered by. The ground shook beneath the weight of the guns. Overhead, squadrons of bombers roared past beneath the clouds. I was not proof against the spell of those demonstrations. In a corner of my heart, German patriotic feelings were still capable of being stirred. Germany was once again a force to be reckoned with; she was no longer at the mercy of her foes. The Treaty of Versailles had been torn up. Did that not represent the end of an immense and humiliating injustice? (Similarly, my first reaction to the *Anschluss*, Hitler's half-opposed, half-acclaimed annexation of Austria in March 1938, was to see it as reparation for the Allies' refusal at Versailles to allow the German-speaking remnant of the Austro-Hungarian Empire to unite with Germany.)

My enthusiasm for those parades also stemmed in part from a boy's sheer pleasure in all things military. But how many grown-ups were there in Germany at that time who did not feel a little bit like small boys? How many of them could have said of themselves that they stood and watched those magnificent military spectacles with pure misgiving, unalloyed by a tinge of delight?

After one such parade, I spotted a student from the Berlin Rabbinical Seminary whom I knew well. He had been standing near me in the crowd outside the College of Advanced Technology. As the crowd dispersed, he waved to me. His face wore the embarrassed smile of a person who, shamed by his own insignificance in the presence of some overwhelming event, is at the same time glad to have been present. I joined him, and we walked part of the way home together. He heaved a series of deep sighs but said nothing. I, too, was silent. We strode west along the Charlottenburger Chaussee.* The traffic, held up for hours and now unleashed, filled the park air with a lively din. Still I waited for a word from my companion. He gnawed at a finger. Finally, clearing his throat, he said, 'What colossal power they have, these Esau people! There'll come a time, though, when they see how stupid and futile it all is!'

---

* The main east–west avenue through the Tiergarten (now renamed Strasse des 17. Juni to commemorate the uprising by the people of East Berlin and other cities of East Germany against the Communist government of the German Democratic Republic on 17 June 1953). At its eastern end the Brandenburg Gate marks the beginning of the old city centre (now in East Berlin).

Fine words from a budding rabbi; yet why had he uttered them with that gleam in his eye? Was he really thinking only of the Messianic future?

Removals, confusions and shades of things to come

My brother and I regularly spent the school holidays with our parents. Each time we arrived in Schönlanke, father had scarcely finished greeting us before he began to bombard us with distressing news.

The Gestapo officers in Schönlanke, clearly not satisfied with the restrictions imposed at national level on Jewish rights, imposed further restrictions on the Jews living in their district.* On their orders, the men of the local congregation had to report in person regularly every Saturday, the holiest day in the Jewish calendar. They were required — young and old, the healthy and the sick — to stand in line for hours on end, perhaps only, after the ordeal of waiting, to have a fresh batch of harassing regulations read out to them. Long before the outbreak of the war, the Jews of Schönlanke were forbidden to leave town without the express permission of the Gestapo.

Staying in Schönlanke was never so odious to me as on the days for which a Hitler speech was announced. My father used to sit with his ear almost glued to the radio, anxious not to miss anything that Hitler might say about the Jews. The inflammatory screaming of the Führer, only momentarily doused from time to time by roars of applause and muffled shouts of 'Sieg Heil', had an all-pervasive quality. It made you feel you were no longer at home within your own four walls. On one occasion I began to find my parents' flat so unbearable that I fled into the street in search of a corner — any corner — where I might be spared the sound of that voice. I could not have embarked on a more hopeless quest. There was no such quiet corner in all Schönlanke. From every window and shop doorway, from every bar and workshop in the town the loudspeakers kept up the relentless howling until the speech culminated in a seemingly endless, alternately swelling and ebbing roar of 'Sieg Heil!' and the invisible, roaring masses raised their iron-hard voices in the anthem of the SA, the 'Horst Wessel Song'.

How glad Jakob and I were when, at the end of each holiday, we found ourselves sitting in the train once more, on the way back to

* Under the National Socialists, the Gestapo — an acronym of *Geheime Staatspolizei*, Secret State Police — had virtually unlimited powers to detain people in prison or concentration camp without trial and without legal guarantees of any kind.

Berlin! Only one thing still preyed on our minds: the knowledge that father and mother must stay behind in the poisonous atmosphere of Schönlanke.

The autumn of 1937 brought some important changes in our lives. A further drop in salary obliged my father to make even more drastic economies. He could no longer afford to pay full board for Jakob and myself and go on financing Leon's training. Leon had to drop his technical-college course and come to Berlin. He too was to take the school-leaving examination at the Jewish *Gymnasium*. Father rented a cheap room for the three of us. We were to furnish it ourselves and cook our own meals. Mother supplied pans and crockery, a spirit stove and a quantity of excellent advice. Each of us had only forty-five marks with which to keep body and soul together for a month, yet father still saw fit to warn me with a wagging forefinger, 'And no using it to buy chemicals and test tubes, do you hear?'

We became subtenants of a waiter named Kohn, occupying one room of his flat on the third floor of an apartment building in Moabit. There is not a lot I can say about Kohn. He was a bachelor who earned his living in an all-night restaurant in Alexanderplatz. During the day we rarely saw him in the flat awake. A small man, he moved with the bustling agility typical of his profession. Had his name not been Kohn, it would never have occurred to me that that blue-eyed, snub-nosed man could be of Jewish descent. His flat was not exactly dirty, but neither did it give the impression of being particularly clean.

The window of our room overlooked the courtyard. From the ground floor to the attic all that could be seen was windows and yet more windows with, between them, areas of peeling, smoke-blackened plaster. Looking up at the narrow rectangle of sky, one saw chimney-pots turning in the wind, and one might glimpse a pigeon or two. Down below in the courtyard stood a line of dirty-grey metal bins, which noisily and dustily received the contents of everybody's refuse buckets. After being dragged out through the entrance by the dustmen, the bins in turn yielded up their contents with a noise like thunder. Occasionally, the sound of carpet-beating would come up from the courtyard, and very occasionally the melancholy strains of a street organ.

The longer we lived in Kohn's flat, the more I became aware of a feeling of having come down in the world. All of a sudden it seemed to me that my Jewish friends on the other side of the Spree had an easier, more comfortable life. Without allowing myself to envy them, I caught myself more than once wondering whether I was treated with the same sympathy and respect as my better-off classmates.

How trifling were these real or imagined degrees of status in the light of what was happening to the Jewish people! In March and April 1938, immediately following the *Anschluss*, streams of Jewish refugees from Vienna and Burgenland arrived in Berlin in search of help from the Jewish organisations. In April a new decree made it compulsory for Jews to declare their assets. In June a further decree was introduced whereby Jewish ownership of shops and businesses was to be indicated on doors and in shop windows. Far more alarming, however, was the news that began to reach us in that same month: large numbers of Jews were being arrested without charge and dragged off to concentration camps. In many cases the relatives later received an urn containing the detainee's ashes.

In the summer of 1938, back in Schönlanke for the holidays, I could not help blurting out, 'Look, we've got to emigrate! There's no future for us here in Germany!' Father, though clearly annoyed, said nothing. Mother turned on him reproachfully: 'You see? Haven't I told you a dozen times that we have to get away from here? So what are you waiting for? Till we're all of us slaughtered or what?'

I was shocked at the effect my words had produced. Actually I had only the haziest idea of the seriousness of the situation myself. All I had done was to pass on what I had picked up from people in Berlin, and surely something of that must already be familiar to my parents? What surprised me was that they should have needed such a warning, living as they did in that dreadful hole Schönlanke, where Jews had a far worse time of it than in the capital. And I was astonished that the role of warning voice should have fallen to me, of all people — the youngest and least experienced member of the family.

In fact, my father did then begin to make preparations for us to emigrate to the United States. As a rabbi, he had a chance of obtaining an immigration affidavit (the document by which a citizen of the host country guaranteed a new immigrant) with priority. He established contact with a Jewish congregation that was willing to sponsor him. The negotiations looked like dragging on, so he applied for an ordinary affidavit just in case. He was then issued with a registration number by the American consulate and advised that he would be summoned as soon as it was his turn. However, he was able to work out for himself that the summons would not arrive before 1941. American immigration law allotted a restricted annual quota to each country, and the quota for Germany was already taken up for several years to come. Father consoled himself with the hope that, in view of the many thousands of victims of Nazi persecution, the American Congress would temporarily lift the restrictions. He clung tenaciously to that hope until the day when Germany forbade its Jews to emigrate.

In reality, my father did not pursue the matter of our emigration with any great enthusiasm or persistence. With his registration number in his hand, he was able to prove to himself and others that he had done what he could; it was not his fault that there was such a long delay.

Head-waiter Kohn had a more realistic outlook than my father. Yet all we did was laugh at him.

One evening, Leon greeted Jakob and myself with the question, 'Has either of you two noticed that our landlord has taken a new surname?' We had not. 'Ah, well. I must tell you about it. This very morning Mr Kohn changed his name. He did it with a screwdriver. You don't believe me? Come into the corridor and see for yourselves.'

Sure enough, Kohn's nameplate on the door of the flat had undergone a subtle modification: the upper part of the letter 'h' had been scraped away.

'What has he done that for?' we wanted to know.

'His name is now Konn. He has asked us — indeed, begged us — never to call him Kohn again, not even in the flat.'

'But that's ridiculous!'

'Call it ridiculous if you like. Just don't call him Kohn any more. He gets furious!'

'Yes, but it's utterly pointless. He's registered with the police as Kohn; he can't simply change his name.'

'He realises that. He just doesn't want all the strangers who walk past his door to know that a Jew lives behind it. He says, "You never know what might happen."'

A visit to a chemical works

I spoke of my father's naïvety. How innocent I was myself of any real conception of the dangers threatening us Jews will be clear from the following episode.

During the summer of 1938, as the Sudeten crisis began to stir world opinion* and Czechoslovakia, France and England called up their reserves, I was spending my free time as usual, conducting

---

* Sudetenland, a strategically important area straddling Bohemia and Moravia and largely inhabited by German-speaking people, had been taken from Austria-Hungary after the First World War and assigned to Czechoslovakia. Increasing Nazi agitation in the area during the 1930s led eventually to the Munich Agreement of September 1938, by which Sudetenland was assigned to Germany. To the British

chemical experiments. My current number-one interest was electro-plating; I had a passion for covering everything with a deposit of either nickel or copper. I got hold of a glass aquarium, a rectifier transformer and a grinding and polishing bench, and I set about nickelplating and copperplating spoons, forks, compasses, drawing-pens — in short, any metal object I could lay hands on that seemed to me to lack shine. I enjoyed myself enormously. I was also beginning to acquire a certain skill. However, I thought I could achieve even better results if I modelled my technique on the methods used by the major industrial galvanisers.

The Berlin business telephone directory offered me a list of such establishments. I took out my bicycle, rode to the nearest one, and marched into the office. 'Excuse me,' I said to the first man I saw, 'I'm at school here in Berlin, and I'm extremely interested in chemistry. I'd like to obtain permission to look around the galvanis-ing plant. May I speak to the manager, please?'

'I'm sorry, no — I can't let you do that,' the man replied in a tone of voice that suggested I was already speaking to the manager.

Expecting a few refusals, I had taken the precaution of jotting down more than one address. 'Goodbye,' I said, and out I marched again.

I was about to remount my bicycle when the man came running after me. 'Hey, wait a minute! Who sent you here? — Nobody? — Well, I'll be frank with you: you strike me as suspicious. I'm going to have to notify the police.'

As there happened to be a member of the force standing at the crossroads a few yards up the street, I did not think it advisable to leap on my bike and make a dash for it. The works manager took me up to the policeman and whispered in his ear. The policeman then ordered me to accompany him, pushing my bicycle. As we walked along, he began to ask me questions in his easygoing Berlin accent. This was a relief: he would soon see he was not dealing with a spy.

However, as we drew steadily closer to the huge Chausseestrasse police station and he showed no sign of being about to release me, my mind began to frame silent reproaches against both him and myself. To all appearances he believed me, so why was he bringing me to the police station? I had told him I was a Jew. Did he not realise that the merest suspicion could cost me my head? And what

---

prime minister, Neville Chamberlain, and to many people throughout Europe, Munich seemed to be a victory for peace. Others saw only that Czechoslovakia had surrendered its main line of defence. Indeed, six months later Hitler simply annexed half the country, making the Second World War inevitable.

an idiot *I* had been! What had I been thinking of, going along to a firm I knew nothing about and asking if I could look round their plant! They were bound to be working on arms contracts.

A grey-haired sergeant took down my details. In calm, level tones he questioned me about what had happened, making notes of my replies. I thought I could read in his eyes the point at which he became convinced of my harmlessness. What a piece of luck: an officer of the old school! He would never commit an injustice. His manner became friendlier by the minute.

When he had finished taking my statement the sergeant disappeared into the next room and left me waiting. I heard him talking on the telephone. After about a quarter of an hour, the door opened again and out came the policeman who had brought me in. He had the statement in his hand.

'Come along, then. Just write your name on this label quickly and tie it to your bicycle, so it won't get lost by the time you come back. I have orders to take you to headquarters for interrogation. Nothing to worry about, though. If you can clear yourself, they'll let you go soon enough.'

We took the tram to Alexanderplatz and entered the dirty red-brick building that housed the city's police headquarters. My escort seemed unfamiliar with the geography of the place. Through a maze of corridors, we came at last to a place where our way was blocked by an iron-barred gate. The policeman turned to a passing officer and asked, 'Are we right for the Gestapo?'

'Yes, you have to go through here. Hang on, I'll open the gate for you.'

The policeman thanked his colleague warmly, and I walked on at his side. Outwardly I was still quite calm, but the word 'Gestapo' had hit me with sickening force. I had heard of the cellars where the Gestapo tortured their victims.

I shall never forget the moment when the policeman handed me over. We had entered a large room that presented a scene of bustling activity beneath a pall of cigarette smoke. Voices speaking on the telephone or dictating blended with the clatter of typewriters in a dense wall of office sound in which I could make out only isolated words. The men wore casual civilian clothes. A very feminine-looking woman of about thirty sat at a desk, bent over a stack of papers. Three other shorthand-typists — young, female, wearing smart street clothes — moved about the room.

Someone referred us to an elegantly dressed, square-jawed man who was addressed as 'Herr Kriminalkommissar'. Accepting the statement, the chief inspector told me to stand in front of his desk and wait. This gave me more time to inspect my new surroundings. Superficially there was little to distinguish the room and its contents from any other office — in a commercial firm, say, or a factory — except that on the wall between the windows a large plaque bore a message in huge letters: 'Please keep calm'. A second door stood open, and I could hear more dictating and typing going on in the next room.

I became aware that the policeman who had brought me there, having duly exercised his function, was preparing to leave. I felt a wave of despondency wash over me. It was like one of those really agonising farewells. That policeman, without for a moment losing either his jovial manner or his good-humoured expression, had conveyed me first from the freedom of the street to the local police station and then from the local police station to the Gestapo. And here I was, suddenly convinced not only that he was the finest fellow in the whole wide world but that I had known him for ages. I dispatched a silent plea in his direction: take me away from here! Or at least take me back through the iron-barred gate — I'll find my own way out of the building! But if you really can't get me out onto the street again, please at least stay with me; don't leave me alone with this man!

Five minutes later I was made to take a seat in the middle of the room. Four Gestapo officers sat in a circle around me and began to fire questions at me. A typist took everything down. The chief inspector remained standing in a corner, saying nothing. I could feel his piercing gaze fixed on me throughout the interrogation.

'Who gave you the address of the electroplating works?'

'Have you been round other factories before?'

'Where were you going to conduct your experiments?'

'Where did you mean to get hold of the necessary chemicals?'

'Are you a Communist . . . a Freemason . . . a Spartacist?'

'No, I'm none of those things,' I replied. 'I don't even know what a Spartacist is.'*

'With which foreign organisation are you in touch?'

For three-quarters of an hour I was bombarded with questions. I answered them all with the simple truth, keeping back only that I had set up my laboratory at the Jewish *Gymnasium* and that I had the run of a number of factories in Berlin. There was hardly time to consider my replies in any case. Only once was there a pause in the

* 'Spartacist' — originally a member of the Spartacus League, the radical left-wing organisation out of which the German Communist Party crystallised in 1917 — was widely used as a synonym for Communist. Freemasonry was likewise anathema to the Nazis, and all Masonic lodges in Germany were dissolved as early as 1933.

questioning. During it, I heard a voice in the next room dictate the words, 'In Marienbad on 28 July 1938 the Jew Weissberg. . .'.

Then my interrogation was resumed.

'What does your father do?'

'My father is a rabbi.'

'Aha! A rabbi, eh? So he sent you there to do a bit of spying, is that it?'

'What have you got in your briefcase?' another of them wanted to know.

'Bread, jam, sugar and writing materials.'

'And how did you get hold of all that?'

'I bought it.'

'How "bought"? Like this?' And his hand performed a pantomine of stealing.

The crudeness of some of the questions was startling. But what surprised me even more was the fact that the whole interrogation was conducted in a relatively humane manner. Was this just a 'softening-up' process for the torture to come?

The Gestapo officers got to their feet. The typist handed the record to the chief inspector. He glanced through it and ordered me to sign. I was given no chance to read it myself.

'We forbid you to go into any factory ever again!' he barked at me. 'Is that clear?'

One of the officers who had taken part in the interrogation told me to follow him. He led me along corridor after corridor in complete silence. By now I was seeing everything through a kind of mist. . . .

I became aware of hurrying footsteps. A car horn sounded. A fresh breeze caressed my face. Forcing my eyes open, I looked for my escort. Nowhere to be seen. Above me, the bright blue sky. And behind me — was that the entrance to police headquarters? Alexanderplatz throbbed with the din of traffic as trams snarled and squealed their way through a maelstrom of buses, taxis and goods vehicles. The glass-fronted office buildings, the tower of the city hall and the entrances to the Underground were dimly perceived shapes in my clouded field of vision. I turned round, shook myself. I climbed aboard the tram. My fellow passengers took no particular notice of me. The ticket in my hand became first neatly folded and then crumpled into a ball, just like a real tram ticket.

Back at the Chausseestrasse police station, I saw the policeman who had taken me to the Gestapo. He greeted me cheerily: 'What, you back already? Aren't you the lucky one! They don't come back from the Gestapo that quickly as a rule. Well, maybe you'll have learnt your lesson: not to go round sticking your nose into everything. Come on, I'll give you your bike.'

Exhausted and famished, I rode straight to the nearest restaurant, turning to look behind me several times on the way. No one seemed to be following me. As I was eating my soup, though, I clearly felt eyes on my back. To avoid looking suspicious, I did not look round again until I reached the exit . . . No, no one appeared to be on my tail. However, wanting to be absolutely sure, I spent most of the next three days on my bicycle, criss-crossing Berlin like a mad thing. It really did seem that I was not being followed.

My leather-crazy brother

After that experience, I saw Berlin through different eyes. Hidden dangers lurked everywhere. Every civilian was a potential Gestapo agent, every policeman a potential accomplice of the Gestapo. The sight of police barracks or prisons, whenever I chanced to ride past them, filled me with foreboding. I no longer dared to go visiting factories, not even those to which I had enjoyed free access for some time.

As the weeks went by, however, my agitation subsided. I had alerted my brothers and poor Kohn/Konn for nothing; the dreaded house-search failed to materialise. Nor did my visit to the electro-plating works produce any unpleasant consequences for my parents or for my headmaster.

Soon the temptation was too strong for me: I went back to my old habit of frequenting various danger-spots in Berlin.

My brother Leon used to tell me I was being reckless. Yet basically we were both up to the same thing. Like myself, Leon defied all the laws of National Socialist ethnology by possessing an 'Aryan' skull and a nose that was not at all 'Jewish'. Consequently, we were attracted by the idea of being eye-witnesses in places where 'Jewish'-looking Jews could not venture without risk. The only difference was that Leon took it further than I did. He made himself a bogus uniform in which he even dared to enter the sports stadium and mingle with the SA and SS men when Goebbels was giving a speech.

The black boots and breeches looked as if he had been poured into them. No one would ever have thought that Leon had tailored his own 'SS trousers' from a couple of father's old overcoats. Roaring through the Tiergarten on his motorbike, he certainly looked more like an SS man than a student from the Jewish *Gymnasium*. Ah, but what if someone were to look more closely? Leon's get-up lacked the cap and badges of a real uniform.

Leon ignored my warnings. He kept up this 'military' style of dress for years. During the war his bogus uniform was to play an important role, and not once was he stopped by police or SS patrols. However, we had no way of knowing that in 1938.

It was not simply the incompleteness of his disguise that aroused my misgivings. If he felt he needed that kind of camouflage for his safety, at least he ought also to have felt a certain revulsion against wearing it. Yet revulsion was the last thing he showed. On the contrary, he took the most elaborate care of his 'uniform'. A whole ritual surrounded the daily polishing of his boots to a mirror-like shine, and he never wearied of making little improvements to the outfit here and there. It seemed almost every day that I saw him standing in front of the mirror, examining the fit of his clothes with a critical eye. Tirelessly, he would unpick yet another seam, re-sew it, iron it flat, and try the garment on again.

His love of uniforms went hand in hand with a partiality for various kinds of leather. 'That is real leather!' Leon was capable of exclaiming with heartfelt joy. Before long he possessed, in addition to his two briefcases, a leather toilet case, a leather case for his drawing-instruments, another for a sewing-kit, another for tools, and several more besides. And because, as Leon put it, the stupid, stick-in-the-mud saddlers and leather-goods manufacturers offered so limited a choice, my brother was obliged to cut out and stitch every single item himself.

One day in the summer of 1939 Leon showed me a small leather suitcase. 'What do you think it's got inside?' he asked me with a bashful grin. When he opened the lid I had to laugh. The suitcase was full to the brim with leather cases of all shapes and sizes.

How did Leon come to need so many leather cases? Or should the question have been turned round the other way: how did most people manage to get through life with so few leather cases? It was dreadful, the way they left useful and valuable objects just lying around, utterly exposed. Such objects literally cried out for protection from an uncaring world. Leon heard their cry, and he duly sheathed them, one and all, in suits of real leather armour.

When a person enjoys tailoring and cultivates a predilection for uniforms and leather cases, no one need be too surprised if one day he cuts and stitches a leather case for his own body. A uniform made entirely of real leather! However, even if that was Leon's ideal, it would have been useless as a disguise. Neither the German army nor the SS nor any other military organisation dressed in leather.

I was just as guilty of ignoring Leon's warnings about my reconnaissance expeditions as he was of ignoring mine.

The city authorities were said to have had the words 'Not for Jews' painted on the benches in the *Lustgarten*, the 'pleasure garden' near the cathedral. As soon as I heard of it, I hurried over there to see with my own eyes. 'But that's downright robbery!' I fumed. Had the Jewish taxpayers of Berlin not paid just as much towards the cost of the benches as the 'Aryans'? And I promptly sat down on one of them to look out for passers-by who shared my indignation. I saw none.

Entry to the popular Wannsee bathing-place on one of the lakes formed by the River Havel in south-west Berlin was forbidden to Jews. After lying in the sand for more than an hour, surrounded by milling bathers, I rode home disappointed. Instead of the revealing conversations I had hoped to overhear as part of my campaign to probe the mood of the people, I caught only the odd sentence here and there about the correct method of swimming backstroke, the composition of various bathers' sandwich fillings, and how best to acquire a quick tan.

When Jews were forbidden to frequent the government sector of the city, curiosity made that my natural target. The new Chancellery building was nearing completion. I cycled up and down Voss-strasse several times to give myself a closer look at it. The SS 'guard of honour' in their black uniforms stood motionless on the steps. I had gazed my fill and was about to remount when I spotted a black-uniformed figure heading straight towards me from the corner of what is now Otto-Grotewohl-Strasse (formerly Wilhelmstrasse).

As he approached, my fear dissolved. It was my brother Leon.

'What are you doing here?' he exclaimed. 'Are you crazy? Don't you know Jews are not allowed to set foot in these streets?'

'Well, what are you doing here?'

'Do you realise? This is the first time we've bumped into each other by accident all the time we've been in Berlin!'

He smiled as he spoke, but he did not seem too happy that I had found him there. 'Don't you know Jews are not allowed to set foot in there streets?' The facetious reproach did not fool me. What he meant was: do you *have* to turn up just as I'm playing the SS man? Are you trying to make me fall out of character?

After 9 November

The night of 9 November 1938, when synagogues all over Germany went up in flames, was cynically dubbed *Reichskristallnacht* — 'Crystal Night'.* Until that pogrom, Hitler had been concerned, for

* Not only synagogues but hundreds of Jewish shops, schools and homes were looted

77

reasons of political convenience, to maintain at least a semblance of constitutionality. The opinion of the world outside Germany still mattered to him. He was also well aware that many Germans condemned his methods. Very nearly all the maltreatment of Jews and political opponents had gone on in the secrecy of police cellars and concentration camps, and dire threats enjoined silence on those who were subsequently released. What made Hitler and Goebbels suddenly feel they could reveal the undisguised brutality of their terrorist regime? How were they able to get away with it? Had the country of my birth changed so dreadfully?

After 'Crystal Night', such questions plagued me all the time. I called to mind the many honest, upright people I had met since my childhood: the Christian neighbours with whom we had been on such good terms in Heilbronn and Gross-Strehlitz; the maids who had served my parents with such devotion; Bergmann, my old headmaster; my teachers Schmiedhammer and Tillich, and the thoroughly decent factory workers I had got to know recently in Berlin. Where were they now — and the millions like them? They could not simply have disappeared from the face of Germany.

I did in fact hear afterwards that during the pogrom a very considerable number of 'Aryans' had given help and sanctuary to their Jewish friends. This time, however, it was the righteous Germans who, through fear of the Nazi terror, shrouded their doings in secrecy and confined their protests to whispers.

The reflected glare in the sky and the news spreading rapidly from mouth to mouth drew me out of the house early on that morning of 10 November. I rode from synagogue to synagogue, passing through a number of business districts in Charlottenburg and in the city centre. In places the road was so thickly strewn with broken glass that I was obliged to dismount and carry my bicycle.

I had wanted to witness these wild doings, but I invariably arrived too late; the arsonists and the looting mobs had done their work. Wherever the SA vandals had spent their fury, silent crowds had now gathered to inspect the resultant scenes of desolation. At one crossroads there was a strong smell of scent, suggesting that the glutted and plundered shops nearby had included a perfumery. I mingled with the curious bystanders in the hope of catching something of what they were saying. But the few words that were spoken here and there were drowned by the noise of glass being shovelled up

---

and burnt that night, while many Jews were beaten up and a number murdered. The name 'Crystal Night' alluded to the thousands of panes of glass smashed during the SA's first orgy of violence for five years.

into heaps on the pavement.

Returning from my fact-finding trip, I noticed that the door of Kohn/Konn's bedroom was open. In the evening, I learnt that our landlord had been arrested.

Leon made better use of that day than I did. Leaving at the crack of dawn, he rode to Schönlanke on his motorbike. He could not have picked a better moment to arrive. Father had already been arrested, the Schönlanke Gestapo having rounded up virtually every male member of the Jewish congregation. He found mother in a state of shock in the flat that a couple of Hitler Youth bully-boys had ravaged only hours before. Damaged furniture and broken crockery and glasses still littered the floor. Our sister Toni was out buying food that could be eaten without cooking or lengthy preparation.

Leon was able to spend two days patching up the furniture. Then he had to make a quick getaway. A particularly conscientious member of the Jewish congregation, having got wind of my brother's arrival, had reported it to the Gestapo. Two officers were promptly sent round to arrest Leon. However, what the officers failed to notice was that the flat had a second exit. Fortunately Leon's motorbike started first time, and the Gestapo men were treated to the sight of a black-uniformed figure riding off in a great hurry. It probably did not even occur to them that the swiftly disappearing figure was the rabbi's son they had orders to bring in.

Some time later we heard from mother that the men who had been arrested in Schönlanke had been sent to Sachsenhausen concentration camp, a little way north of Berlin. Only on presentation of emigration papers could their release be expedited. I heard similar rumours in Berlin, where they sparked off much feverish activity in Jewish circles. I asked a number of Jewish friends for advice, and everywhere I went the talk was of little else but passports, release papers, affidavits, certificates and transit visas.

One month after our landlord's arrest we suddenly found him back in his flat. Questioned about his experiences in the concentration camp, Kohn/Konn gave only evasive replies. We did not press him too hard, for he was clearly a very sick man. The doctor diagnosed pleurisy. Not many months later, the former head waiter was dead.

Some six weeks after 'Crystal Night' we were surprised to receive a telephone call from father. He was free. Had he been released because he owned no assets for which the camp authorities could ransom him? Or because of the letter he had received from the American consulate? The condition of his release was 'immediate emigration'. But the consul had merely acknowledged that father's name had been entered on the immigration waiting list.

Whatever the reason, father was on his way home to Schönlanke. He had decided to break his journey in Berlin for a few hours to see his sons again.

Father was laughing as he came up the stairs. We too had to laugh as we ran down to greet him, though we had not imagined the reunion would be quite so hilarious an occasion. Oh dad, what must you have been through! And what a sight you are! You look like a clown! What did they do to you? Why is your coat so crumpled and your hat so creased? But our questions died on our lips, and father was still laughing as we entered the flat. He might deliberately have ruined his own clothing, purely in order to amuse us.

'You're probably wondering why I look like this,' he chuckled. 'It's because of the disinfection.'

But father had more important things to relate. He immediately started talking nineteen to the dozen — about the arrival at the concentration camp, the endless roll-calls, the cruel tricks played by the SS camp guards, meeting Jews from all over the country. . . .

'Dad, won't you have something to eat before you tell us any more?'

But father barely heard the question, so caught up was he in his own account. 'And do you know, they gave us no time to pray. But I said my prayers during roll-calls as we stood in line for hours with our feet turning numb with cold. I believe I only missed my evening prayers two or three times in all. Oh, and I must tell you about the millionaire. . . .'

Father came out with all this almost cheerfully. His words as well as his voice betrayed only a naïve amazement at a series of incredible experiences. He paused and started to laugh again. And, since father spoke so light-heartedly of the ghastly world of the concentration camp, we adopted the same flippant tone. Was it not our duty to keep father's spirits up after all that he had suffered? Rarely had we joked together as much as we did that evening. Yet underlying all our merriment was a creeping unease.

I have often thought about that meeting since. It was indeed a curious blend of joyful reunion, thanksgiving for father's deliverance and sheer, convulsive hilarity. It was only in retrospect that I understood the source of our unease. Father had been humiliated and robbed of his dignity. We had expected him to be bursting with indignation. Yet he was nothing of the kind. After his totally unexpected release, his mind was much more on the grotesqueness of his experiences than on the degradation they had brought.

I had been to look at our school on 12 November. The building was undamaged. Lessons resumed, after a fashion. But there was a general feeling that the roof might fall in on us at any moment. Three of our teachers had disappeared.

The family reunited

The November pogrom and the fresh anti-Jewish decrees that the Hitler regime promulgated in its wake gave a dramatic boost to the emigration movement. Anyone who was able to flee the country did so, even when no more salubrious place of refuge offered itself than Shanghai or Honduras. My father, too, was now determined to do his utmost to put Germany behind him. However, there was not a great deal he could achieve from an out-of-the-way place like Schön-lanke. If he wished to get anywhere with the American consulate, he would have to call countless times in person. Anyway, in Schönlanke my father no longer had a job to do; the congregation was in the process of disintegration.

So he applied to the Gestapo for permission to move to Berlin. He was told that permission would be granted only if he could present documentary evidence to the effect that the Berlin authorities accepted him as a resident. For their part, the Berlin authorities made it clear that any such acceptance would depend (1) on my father's first finding accommodation in Berlin and (2) on the Schönlanke Gestapo's granting him permission to leave their jurisdiction.

For weeks father shuttled backwards and forwards between the two authorities, reaping nothing but frustration and discouragement. To assist him, I took a day off school and called at the legal-advice bureau run by the 'Great Jewish Congregation of Berlin'. The legal adviser regretted that he had no advice to give me.

'There's no doubt about it, young man,' he assured me. 'The authorities are leading your father up the garden path! We have absolutely no recourse in law. If the Gestapo does not wish your father to move to Berlin, your father can do nothing about it. And neither, unfortunately, can we.'

I forget how the vicious circle was eventually broken. In May 1939, father instructed my brothers to give notice on our room in Moabit. He had accepted a position as rabbi at a Berlin synagogue, and the whole family would shortly be moving together into a flat in the capital.

In June the family was indeed reunited under one roof. We sublet rooms from a Jewish widow, Frau Polonski, in Wilmersdorfer-strasse, near the German Opera House. Emigration from Schönlanke had been achieved; our next goal was emigration from Germany.

Fitting a large household into three and a half rooms of a rented flat imposed many restrictions on all of us. Nevertheless, father rejoiced over the move. Had God not helped him to escape the clutches of the Schönlanke Gestapo? And would God not help him further?

In Berlin around that time we met a number of Jewish friends who had likewise left provincial towns and come to the capital in order to accelerate the progress of their emigration. Father saw this as confirmation of the wisdom of his own planning.

Among the friends with whom we met up again in Berlin was the Hirschfeld family with their good-natured imbecile son, Guli. Guli was overjoyed at being reunited with Leon, and we began to see a lot of him again. He had hardly changed at all; his vocabulary had taken on a few new expressions, but the years had not made him very much wiser. His parents meant to emigrate to the United States 'bag and baggage', as they put it. One could imagine them getting their baggage accepted, but what about Guli? What consul was ever going to give Guli an immigration visa?

On the brink of catastrophe

Every day the German newspapers reported Polish frontier violations and outrages committed against the 'ethnic Germans' in Poland. The Führer was striving, Britain's Mr Chamberlain was striving, Italy's *Duce* was striving — everyone was striving for a peaceful solution. It took only a little more intelligence than Guli possessed to see that war was just around the corner.

My Jewish friends treated the majority of the claims that appeared in the German press as propaganda lies. How could they forget the way in which, first in Austria and then in Czechoslovakia, Hitler's supporters among the 'ethnic German' populations of Germany's neighbours had used terror to provoke counter–terror until the Führer had had to come running to their aid? It was all too fresh in everyone's memory. Yet, to my astonishment, I heard after the war that many 'Aryan' Germans — even among those who had no time for the Nazi regime — had allowed the press to lead them by the nose. Did they really believe that the Poles were the authors of all those 'outrages'? The Jews, after years of persecution and public calumny, appear to have taken a more sceptical view of the claims of the National Socialist news service.

The threat of war spurred my father on to even greater efforts to secure the family's emigration. Not that they did much good. The officials at the American consulate pointed to the large numbers of would-be immigrants who had been on the waiting list for much longer than my father. 'There's really no point,' they told him, 'in your queuing here for hours. We have received your visa application, and we will call you without fail as soon as your number is next on the list.'

And when my father came home, exhausted and overwrought after a day of such vain endeavours, the pressure did not let up. Our new landlady, Frau Polonski, was a veritable fury. Every day she found a fresh pretext for a quarrel. 'Will you kindly tell your visitors not to tread so heavily in the hall!' 'Will you kindly plug your clockwork time switches in somewhere else! I can't sleep for the ticking!' 'Since you moved in here, my electricity bills have trebled. You're simply going to have to pay me the extra!' I would rather not mention the shameless insults she used to hurl at us, and I dread to think what went on in her mind. She had nothing but contempt for the Jewish faith. She used the vocabulary of Julius Streicher and his anti-Semitic smearsheet *Der Stürmer** to deride religious Jews. At the same time she regarded herself as a better Jewess because she knew Yiddish and we did not.

My father had too soft a heart. He was defenceless against so much ill-will. What was the use of his refusing to speak to Frau Polonski? Our landlady would simply pretend that *she* was the offended party who was not speaking to *us*. The woman was clearly incapable of living without quarrelling. One day there was a note under the door. Father picked it up and immediately went purple with rage. It read, 'If you leave your laundry basket standing in the hall once again, it and its contents will disappear!' Father wrote a few answering words on the back of the note and pushed it under Frau Polonski's door. It was the preamble to an exchange of notes that continued for several weeks, inflicting greater damage on my father's nerves than the reported exchange of diplomatic notes between Germany, Poland and the Western powers that filled the newspapers every day.

What were my parents to do? Frau Polonski's insolence left them speechless. To challenge a Jewish woman in the courts would have been madness, for the judges were all Nazi appointees. And a summons to appear before a Jewish court of arbitration would have been greeted by Frau Polonski with disdain. At a loss, father could

* *Der Stürmer* (the title means 'The Striker', except that in addition to sporting and military connotations the German word carries literary ones, from the 'Storm and Stress' period of early Romanticism) was founded by Julius Streicher, a friend of Hitler, in 1923. Spewing pornographic calumnies, it was a major weapon in the Nazi campaign to stir up hatred against Jews. The weekly, which was sold throughout Germany, was exhibited in special display-boxes.

think of only one solution: to look around for another flat. In Berlin that was a virtually hopeless undertaking. Who, by that time, was willing to rent accommodation to Jews?

The Jewish population of Germany shortly before the war numbered something over 200,000 — 200,000! It was pathetic in comparison with the number of German Jews before Hitler's coming to power, and it was additionally pathetic because those 200,000 persons constituted not a flourishing community but a demoralised mass of people with no future who were trying to make their escape as quickly as possible. On the other hand, 200,000 was an appallingly large number, given that there was no escape for those people other than to flee abroad and that the countries offering refuge had closed their doors to all but a few.

The question 'How is your emigration coming along?' was now as common among Jews as 'Hello, how are you?' Worries about our emigration prospects occupied our every waking moment, while longing for a swift escape from the Third Reich filled our dreams at night. With our minds preoccupied by German provocations against Poland, we sat at our school-desks and marvelled that there were Jewish men still capable of talking for hours on end without so much as a passing reference to the threat of war.

An air of unreality hung about everything our teachers had to say on such subjects as the geological structure of Central Europe and the abiding importance of the Investiture Contest! The one burning question in all our minds was: will Britain and France keep their word this time or will they leave Poland in the lurch just as they did Czechoslovakia?

A four-storey house across the road from the Adass-Isroël *Gymnasium* was commandeered for the use of Luftwaffe staff, and permission was granted for the parking of air-force vehicles on the Jews' playground. The ranks of the pupils were already much thinned by emigration, and the staff was shrinking too. But Schlesinger, the headmaster, would let nothing induce him to loosen the reins of school discipline — no message from Roosevelt to Hitler, no military pact with Mussolini, nothing. Hitler might be setting Europe ablaze, but lessons continued as usual.

As expected, the school eventually had to give up its independent existence. It was merged with the school belonging to the 'Great Jewish Congregation of Berlin' and moved to Wilsnakerstrasse, about a mile and a half away in Moabit. As a result of the merger, we received new teachers, and the classrooms were once again full of pupils.

November 1939. Poland was in the clutches of Hitler and Stalin, who had partitioned it between them. Goebbels was shaking out his wrath and scorn against the Western powers because they were neither prepared to fight, nor would they accept the 'hand of peace offered by the leader'.

Today we know what happened to the Jews in German-occupied Poland. Poland had a lively tradition of pogroms against the Jews. It went back to the policies of the tsars and the virulent anti-Semitism of the clergy. And it paved the way for the German campaign of Jewish persecution.

In the wake of the German armoured columns moved the lorries and motor-cycles of the *Einsatzgruppen*, the 'action groups' of the Security Police and SD, Heydrich's men who had organized the pogroms of November 9th, 1938. Pogroms indeed broke out in almost every town with Jewish inhabitants, and they began on the first day of the campaign. It was not hard for these experienced *agents provocateurs* to persuade the Polish population to console themselves for the miseries of defeat. But the 'little terror' of September–November, 1939, was not comparable with the methodical massacres undertaken in 1941 during the invasion of Russia. The outrages of 1939 lacked the signs of a co-ordinating touch; nor were they confined to the SS and police troops, for Wehrmacht units of every description indulged in them. They seem to have become worse after the fighting ended, and it was not until the establishment of a civil government in the middle of November that they were suppressed.*

Following the invasion [of Poland], systematic action over the Jewish question — as opposed to mere sackings and pogroms — began only after the introduction of the Jewish star.[†]

However, we were living in Berlin at the time. What did we know about what was going on in Poland? My homework finished, I would sally forth on my bike to patrol the streets of the capital. On the streets life seemed to go on much as it had in peacetime. Trams and buses rolled past at their appointed times, adorned with posters. The message those posters carried in enormous letters was not 'Germany drags Europe into the abyss' but 'Ata for that all-round shine!' I saw a new title on display in a bookshop window: *Deutsche*

---

* Quoted from Gerald Reitlinger, *The Final Solution*, London, Valentine Mitchell, 1968 (second edition), pp. 34f.

[†] *Ibid.* On 23 November 1939 the newly-appointed Nazi governor-general of German-occupied Poland, Hans Frank, decreed that all Jews must identify themselves by wearing a yellow star on the front of their clothing.

Dichter in Polen — 'German Poets in Poland'. The newspapers were short of sensational news after the conclusion of the Polish campaign. The Polish Jews scarcely rated a mention; only *Der Stürmer* made a great fuss about them. It looked as though they had nothing worse to fear than mockery.

Jews in Germany suffered no further losses of rights in the early months of the war. The flight from Germany continued, quite calmly, in dribs and drabs, limited by the paucity of immigration opportunities. I saw it happening. One of my classmates managed to emigrate to the United States. Another found his way to Argentina and a third to Shanghai. Suddenly I felt that I could no longer go on sitting quietly at my desk, concentrating on my school-work.

It was rumoured that there might be a further opportunity for Jewish youngsters: going to Palestine. My father took me along to the Misrachi section at the Palestine Office — the Zionist agency for promoting emigration to Palestine — to find out more about it. The religiously oriented Misrachi organisation was a body to which father had always had certain objections on ideological grounds. In the present situation, however, such subtle misgivings carried little weight; it was a question of getting out of the Nazi Reich.

The Palestine Office, which was situated in Meinekestrasse, off the Kurfürstendamm, presented a scene of frenzied activity. We sat down to wait on a bench in the corridor. Typewriters clattered ceaselessly in every room. Occasionally a door would fly open and someone would emerge to scurry past us carrying a pile of papers and disappear through another door.

Our turn came at last. A serious, motherly-looking woman received us. She asked a series of questions and examined me with a critical eye. Then she turned to my father. She had no more immigration certificates for Palestine, she told him, but I was young and strong: I might qualify for 'Aliyah Bet', a Hebrew phrase meaning approximately 'secret immigration'. It was secret, she explained, only so far as the British were concerned; there were no problems from the German side. However, the Zionist Organisation had only a very small number of ships at its disposal, and the British were doing everything they could to prevent refugees from landing in their mandated territory.

'I have to point out to you, sir,' she went on, 'that we are using old river steamers to make the trip through the Mediterranean to the coast of Palestine. Some of the vessels sail from ports in Greece or Yugoslavia, but the main route is down the Danube and through the notoriously stormy Black Sea. We can offer no guarantees. Passengers travel entirely at their own risk.'

At these words, father looked at me as if to say, 'Well, what about it?' When she saw that we were undeterred, the woman continued. Despite all the dangers, she told us, it was considered a great privilege to be granted a place on a refugee ship. Naturally, priority would be given to young people who had belonged to the Misrachi movement for years. But she was unwilling to turn us away. I must first receive an agricultural training at a preparation camp. If I did well there, I stood a good chance of getting on a refugee ship.

Father agreed to the terms immediately and asked for me to be given a training-camp place. On the way home he said to me, 'That's put paid to your chemistry, though!'

'Yes, well, we'll see about that', I remember replying.

From the Central Union of German Citizens of the Jewish Faith to the Zionist Organisation is a big step. What German Jew of any character could have taken it with an easy conscience? My step — from the League of German–Jewish Youth to the League of Zionist Pioneers — was simpler; seventeen-year-olds, looking back, tend to make light of the convictions of their 'awkward' years. A bugle blackened by the vapours of the laboratory is unhesitatingly classed as junk. But what about a boy's profession of loyalty to Germany? Was that just another childish trifle, to be hung on a nail like a boy–scout uniform now several sizes too small? After all that had happened in Germany since 1933, I did not feel any challenge in the question 'Can you still look upon and love Germany as your fatherland?' If I felt challenged at all, it was by the need to save my skin.

The Arab–British–Jewish conflict

Why was it that the National Socialist regime tolerated — indeed, even encouraged — the 'illegal' emigration of Jews to Palestine? As a British mandated territory, Palestine was for all practical purposes at war with Germany. More than 130,000 men and women in Palestine answered the call of the Jewish National Council and enlisted.

But how were the Zionists able to propose the formation of a Jewish division within the British army at a time when Britain's policy on Palestine had taken on a distinctly anti-Zionist complexion? Why did the British army then make only reluctant and very limited use of the Jewish volunteers? At the time I knew so little about these matters that I would not even have been capable of framing such questions. It was not until long after the war that things became clearer to me.

What was happening in Palestine at that time is usually described as a phase in the Arab–Jewish conflict. Britain, however, far from being a neutral arbiter, was itself very actively involved in the dispute as a third party. For that reason it would be more appropriate to speak of an Arab–British–Jewish conflict. Because of its power-political interests in the Near East, Britain set great store by the pro-British attitude of the Jews and even more by that of the Arabs.

During the First World War the British government had made extensive political promises to both sides. In the so-called Balfour Declaration of November 1917, the British Foreign Minister, A. J. Balfour, promised help towards 'the establishment in Palestine of a national home for the Jewish people'. In accepting the League of Nations mandate for Palestine in 1922, Britain reiterated the promises of the Balfour Declaration. In notes to Ibn Ali Hussein, the Sherif of Mecca, Britain made similar concessions to Arab aspirations towards autonomous statehood. The two guarantees were irreconcilable. All that they guaranteed was a future breach of promise. There was nothing unusual about airy assurances and irredeemable commitments; they are the standard currency of great-power politics. In this case, however, the British realised, too late, that they had deeply offended two national groups: the Arabs, who after centuries of Turkish rule were looking forward to a sovereign Arab state, and the Jews, who after one and half millennia of Christian and Muslim oppression saw in Britain's assurances nothing less than the fulfilment of their Messianic hopes. British politicians first became aware of their dilemma when the Arabs began to stage violent uprisings. Britain's attempts to reach a compromise resulted only in both sides — Jews and Arabs — feeling betrayed.

What made this development even more regrettable was the fact that power-political motives were not the only ones involved. There were genuine feelings of sympathy among the British people — for both the Arabs and the Zionists.

In the spring of 1939 the British government found itself in an extremely difficult situation. When the Germans marched into Prague Chamberlain's eyes were finally opened. The policy of appeasement vis-à-vis the aggressive Axis powers had failed. The Second World War was now imminent, and Britain felt ill-prepared. The latest attempt to reach a settlement between Jews and Arabs around a London conference table had come to nothing. There was reason to fear that the Arabs would come down on the side of Hitler and Mussolini (as in fact to some extent they did). The position of the Jews within Hitler's sphere of influence was desperate. For many of them, flight to Palestine was the only hope.

What was the British government to do? Humanity towards the persecuted Jews dictated that they should be given asylum as quickly as possible and on as generous a scale as possible. Strategic and political considerations, in the light of the grave danger threatening the British Empire, made it seem more advisable to mollify the rebellious and politically far more influential Arabs.

The Chamberlain government did what it had done in Munich eight months previously: it sought to buy peace by appeasing the powerful aggressor at the expense of the weaker victim. The British White Paper of May 1939 represented a break with the Balfour Declaration. It was to be made more difficult for Jewish settlers to purchase land. Jewish immigration to Palestine was to be sharply restricted and to cease altogether after five years.

The White Paper was censured not only by the Jews but also by the Mandating Commission of the League of Nations as well as by nearly half the British Parliament as being incompatible with Britain's commitments. The outbreak of war made League of Nations intervention impossible.

The lesson that the more militant Jewish extremists drew from British policy was that there was more to be gained from the British by terror than by legitimate means. Fortunately they were a tiny minority; most Jews took a different view.

Britain declared war on Hitler. In doing so it was defending not merely itself but civilisation — including Jewry — against barbarism. Britain's fight was therefore the Zionists' fight too. Hence the 130,000 Jewish volunteers in Palestine.

The White Paper was another matter. The Zionists were determined to fight too, but not by the tiny Jewish community in Palestine taking up arms against a great power. They wanted to show the British that they faced a choice between imposing the White Paper policy by force or abandoning it. Britain was no Hitler or Stalin dictatorship; its government was answerable to the people. It was scarcely thinkable that the fundamentally decent British people would insist on the morally very questionable White Paper if the only way to implement its provisions was at bayonet point.

Passive resistance, unarmed struggle on the part of refugees — that was the solution adopted by the Jewish majority. Aliyah Bet, the 'illegal' immigration movement, went from strength to strength.

In the early days of the war the German authorities gave encouragement to Aliyah Bet in order to accelerate Jewish emigration and embarrass Britain. At the same time, Nazi agents stirred up the Arabs against both the British and the Jews.*

* For a very readable account of Aliyah Bet that has the additional merit of being written without hatred, see Jon and David Kimche, *The Secret Roads*, London, Secker & Warburg, 1954.

CHAPTER 5

.

Preparing for Palestine

The training farm

It was the middle of December 1939 when I set out for the Steckelsdorf training farm. The village of Steckelsdorf lies between Rathenow and Stendal, about forty-five miles west of Berlin. I walked
from Rathenow station carrying my luggage. It was a long, weary
way. But once I had the town behind me and was striding down a
virtually deserted road between wintry fields, I began to enjoy the
feeling of solitude. In fact, so agreeable was the silence all around me
that I could almost forget the eerie silence that had fallen over
Europe: there was no fighting anywhere, yet the continent was at
war.*

'Is this the training farm — have I got the right place?' I asked
somewhat uncertainly (I had taken a number of wrong turnings) at
the entrance to a large group of farm buildings.

The strapping young fellow at the gate grinned broadly. 'You
have indeed, son. And you needn't look so worried. You'll learn
everything here — muck-spreading and all!'

'Hey, a new arrival!' another voice exclaimed. Several more
youngsters of both sexes appeared and gathered round to help me
with my bags and inspect the 'new arrival'.

'Hear that? He's from Berlin. Who's a pretty boy, then? Talks like
a scholar, this one!'

'From Berlin? Really? Here, we'll shake to that!'

With this cheerful babble going on around me, I had little
opportunity to take stock of my new surroundings. I was introduced

---

* Between 3 September 1939, when Britain and France declared war on Germany
following the latter's invasion of Poland, and 9 April 1940, when Germany attacked
Denmark and Norway, the opposing armies on the western front remained almost
completely inactive behind the Maginot and Siegfried lines. The period came to be
known as the 'phoney war'.

to the manager, a tall, lanky farmer with an oriental nose whom my companions addressed respectfully as 'Herr Blumenfeld'. Mr Blumenfeld certainly did not put himself out to give the new arrival a friendly reception. In a voice like a sergeant-major's, he demanded my papers, the change-of-address permit issued by the police and my ration card. He also asked me some questions. During the interrogation he marched up and down the room with much creaking of his leather gaiters. His expression left no doubt as to his low opinion of grammar-school boys from Berlin.

Lunch gave me my first sight of the young inmates of the preparation camp all together. We ate in a spacious room that opened onto a veranda. For seventy people, though, it was a tight squeeze. The room was cold and draughty, despite the beech logs crackling away in the two tiled stoves. I entered to find everyone already eating. The tables, lined with crude wooden benches, were arranged in a horseshoe. Two girls moved up to make room for me.

'Tuck in!' one of them said, pushing towards me a steaming bowl of potatoes boiled in their skins. I did so somewhat hesitantly, unnerved by the new faces all around me and aware of a great many pairs of critical eyes beamed in my direction.

As I did not appear to be making much headway with my potatoes, the girl who had pushed the bowl towards me offered to help me peel them. I accepted gratefully. She was pretty and I found her briskly straightforward manner charming. Her pert, country face was deliciously set off by her vigorous Baden dialect.

I perceived all this only dimly, as if through a sort of haze. The steam from the potatoes was partly responsible, but there was a second factor clouding my vision. For some reason I felt compelled to divert my gaze from the girl who was peeling my potatoes, as if I found all my other table companions far more interesting. In fact, I had to divert my gaze from her many times during lunch. Really, I said to myself, slightly ashamed, seventeen years old and you're smitten by that rustic poppet! Haven't you ever met a girl before? But at the next meal I sat down in the same place.

In the break after lunch I was introduced to the youth leader, Sholem Klein. I was also shown where I should sleep, and someone helped me arrange my belongings. After supper I found myself at the centre of a circle of friendly inquisitors. We talked until late.

Before the lights went out in the dormitory the fellow who had first greeted me at the gate came over and said in his rough-and-ready way, 'You report to me at eight in the morning, you hear? There's work to be done!'

'Where shall I find you?'

'Just ask for Fred. Anyone'll tell you!'

Next morning, my life as a farmworker began in earnest. And my first job really was muck-spreading. I felt hopelessly clumsy as the fully laden wheelbarrow tipped over after only a few steps. In fact, this was exactly what Fred had intended should happen. It turned out that work had not actually begun yet, and in any case it was not for Fred to give the orders. Fred's idea of a joke was to make every greenhorn push a lop-sided barrowload of dung. He tried to pull my leg about the 'four-seater', too, but he was too late: I had already gathered that the farm's 'four-seater' was neither a car nor a horse-drawn carriage but the multiple latrine in the wooden shed down by the frog pond.

It took me a few days to find my way around the training farm. The principal buildings were the farmhouse and what we called the 'summer villa'. They formed the two foci of our life and work, providing as they did the living accommodation for the entire workforce.

The ground floor of the farmhouse was occupied by the office and by the flats of the manager, Blumenfeld, and the head gardener. The upstairs room was furnished with bunk beds and served as the girls' dormitory. We males slept in the summer villa. The farmhouse, together with the adjoining cowshed, stable and toolshed and the barn opposite, constituted the farm proper. At a little distance were the greenhouse and the manure hotbeds of the market garden, and beyond them stood the hen house. Around the farm and the market garden, orchards and fields of vegetables and rye stretched away to the boundaries of the property. The estate also included a small pine wood, through which one walked to get from the farmhouse to the summer villa.

The original owner had no doubt spent many a pleasant week in his summer villa; its present occupants found it offered few amenities. A severe winter having set in, it took real determination to climb out of a cosy bed into that freezing-cold room each morning and go and fetch water from the hand pump in the farmyard.

Shivering, we would pull on our work clothes and go down to synagogue. The entrance hall of the villa had been adapted for this purpose. A simple cupboard housed two Torah scrolls. Readings from the Torah were given from a large lectern set up in the middle of the hall.

Morning prayers over, everyone sat down to breakfast. Everyone, that is, except the two people who had just come off duty as nightwatchmen. They went to bed in the nightwatchmen's room.

At the sound of a gong, we all trooped off through the wood to the farmhouse and formed up in rank and file outside the front door. The manager and the head gardener emerged from the office to allot jobs.

The names of those who were off sick were reported. If the sickness was not serious, the invalid stayed in bed. More serious cases were transferred to the 'sickroom'. If someone was really ill, the manager had to ask an 'Aryan' doctor to come out from Rathenow, knowing that he would hardly be overjoyed at having to visit the 'Jew camp'.

We lived in great seclusion. A broad belt of fields and woods separated the estate from the surrounding villages. One rarely met a soul on the sandy path that led to the farm. Steckelsdorf itself and another village called Neue Schleuse were only a couple of miles away, and Neue Schleuse was barely a stone's throw from the town of Rathenow. But most of us never got that far. Only Moshe Heilborn, the acknowledged boss of the stables, hitched up his horses two or three times a week to go into the village or on into town to deliver our produce. At the same time he would purchase our meagre rations. Two of us used to deliver milk to the village early each morning.

Visitors to the farm included the postman, the man from the electricity works (occasionally) and the doctor from Rathenow already mentioned. Once a month a barber came over from Neue Schleuse, and a room in the summer villa became a hairdressing salon for a day or two. A farmer would call on the manager every now and then to borrow a plough or a harrow. Otherwise we saw hardly anyone from the villages round about.

Peace and tranquillity surrounded our little domain for as far as the eye could see. Only in one direction was there any evidence of war. Along the northern boundary of the estate, about fifty yards beyond our rye field, railway lines cut through the landscape. I believe they formed part of the connection between the capital and the great industrial region of the Ruhr. At any rate, traffic on them was heavy. Trains passed every few minutes it seemed — passenger trains or goods trains laden with coal, tree-trunks, or farm machinery. Many of the passenger trains were painted with huge red crosses along their whole length. Goods vans rumbled by, probably carrying livestock, followed by open wagons bearing camouflaged armoured cars, guns and other military equipment. Then there would be another endless line of goods vans with soldiers of the Wehrmacht, the German armed forces, sitting in fours in the open doorways with their legs dangling down.

Not even the troop transports were capable of stirring our surroundings out of their peaceful stillness. The passengers sat quietly, looking out of windows or doors; the armoured vehicles squatted motionless on their flat-cars; the guns were idle. Smoothly, serenely, they filed past beyond the rye field like a silent parade.

At the heart of a Germany stiff with uniforms and bristling with weapons of war, there was a haven of peace in which police and SA men never appeared and where air-raid wardens were never seen. And we were the ones privileged to live there.

Not even loudspeakers invaded our calm. Germany's Jews had had to surrender their radio sets right at the beginning of the war, with the result that we were spared having to listen to the Goebbels propaganda put out by the government broadcasting station all day long.

Of course it also meant that we lacked an important means of finding out what was going on in Germany and the rest of the world. There were heavy penalties for anyone, not only Jews, caught listening to foreign broadcasts. No one at Steckelsdorf dared to keep a set clandestinely, because discovery would have meant disastrous consequences for us all.

But even without a radio all sorts of news got through to us. Our parents' letters were usually confined to private matters, of course, for we always had to reckon with secret censorship. The farm possessed a telephone — by official permission — though our calls were monitored. So our principal source of news remained the men from the Palestine Office in Berlin who visited our training camp from time to time.

Rathenow had its own daily newspaper, and a copy of that was available in the office for anyone to look at after work. But something really exceptional had to have happened to make us all pounce on the paper and apply our wits to reading between the lines of the official communiqué in order to work out what had actually occurred.

We took little notice of what the newspaper had to report in that first winter of the war. By contrast, every item of news that reached us from the Palestine Office caused great excitement. We were not greatly troubled by our ignorance of events. From now on, our lives in Germany were on a purely provisional footing. Deep down, we felt we already belonged to the Holy Land — which, since it was unknown to us, we painted in all the gorgeous colours of adolescent yearning.

Form and figures of a community

An establishment such as the Steckelsdorf training farm was known in Zionist terminology as a *kibbutz hakhshara,* a 'training collective'. Its purpose was to turn city youths into farmers, sons and daughters of the bourgeoisie into future collective settlers, children of German citizens of the Jewish faith into proud, Hebrew-speaking nationals of the Holy Land. People believed that so radical and fundamental a change could be brought about with the aid of 'training courses'.

If I am not mistaken, there were twenty such training establishments in Germany at the beginning of the war. Three were run by 'Bachad', the religious Zionist pioneers, the rest by secular Zionist associations.

The heart and head of the whole organisation was the Palestine Office in Berlin (the Palästina–Amt, or Palamt, as we called it for short). The Palestine Office acted for the Zionist associations, which were officially banned, *vis-à-vis* the Reichsvereinigung der Juden in Deutschland, the National Association of Jews in Germany.* Its chief task was to promote emigration to Palestine, but it also operated as a kind of cultural headquarters, issuing educational directives and supplying books for Hebrew-language teaching, maps for Palestinian studies and the words and music of Zionist songs. It further issued guidelines for the 'organisation of feast-days' and ran training programmes for youth leaders and course leaders.

How odd that Jews who were obliged to live in the Third Reich had not yet developed an allergy to such terms as 'cultural headquarters', 'organisation' and 'youth leader', whether couched in German or Hebrew! The way in which those terms were employed by the Palestine Office was painfully similar to the linguistic usage of totalitarian indoctrination. Behind them lay an idea that was alarming in its simplicity. The *kibbutz hakhshara* contained the 'human material'; the 'office' in Berlin supplied the recipes for the doctrinaire kitchen; the youth leaders cooked the soup by the book and fed it to the trainees. Could the Zionists not have found a more dignified way of winning Jewish young people for what was a highly dignified ideal?

However, there were very considerable differences between Zionist education and training and the totalitarian methods of 'orientation'. Zionism had no *Führerprinzip* or 'leader principle', and no blindly credulous 'following'. Nor did it proceed dogmatically but instead left room for different interpretations. In my first few weeks at Steckelsdorf I was only vaguely aware of all this. At first I was merely surprised at how readily my contemporaries adapted them-

---

* This was the only body that the National Socialist authorities allowed to continue to represent Germany's Jewish population and to promote Jewish emigration.

selves to a life-style that must have been alien to them, a life-style that had not grown up naturally but had been artificially pieced together. I found it far from easy to adjust to all the new customs.

The very language of the training farm had a dubious ring. The youth leader might announce after a meal: 'Chaverim, I have been informed by the merkas that an advanced Ivrith course for madrichim is being organised in Berlin.' What he was telling us 'comrades' was that 'headquarters' had sent word that an advanced Hebrew course for 'youth leaders' was being organised in Berlin. The Hebrew technical terms for the Zionist Organisation did not translate easily. On the other hand, none of us yet knew enough Hebrew to be able to communicate solely in that language. So we got by with an unlovely hybrid: Zionist German.

Even stranger were the 'songs and dances from Eretz Israel' that appeared to form an essential part of Zionist ritual. Most of the tunes were so sad and monotonous as to be in stark contrast to the joyful optimism and national pride embodied in the words. I discovered later how the songs had originated. They had been brought to the Holy Land by the earliest Zionist settlers from eastern Europe. As a result of this historical accident, Zionists the world over were now required not only to sing along with these pastiches of Hebrew words and Slavonic melodies and to dance the Rumanian *hora* but also to believe that this was Hebrew folk art.

It all struck me as slightly forced. But after my first few days at Steckelsdorf, as I became better acquainted with some of the workers there, my misgivings began to evaporate. Once I had got to know fellows like Friedel ('Fred') Krämer and Moshe Heilborn, I felt much more at home.

My new companions were far from being zealous adherents of the Misrachi movement. Fred, the joker of the pack, whose charming south-German dialect had greeted me on my arrival, was someone who defied classification. One sideways look from behind Fred's glasses said it all: this was no lad to embroil in an ideological discussion. I can see him standing there now in his coarse brown working trousers, positively bursting with life! His casual manner, his slight stoop, the way his baggy shirt used to hang down over his belt — it all combined to produce a comfortable, confidence-inspiring impression. Whether he was wearing his thick woollen sweater or, if it was Saturday, a white shirt and dark-blue suit, inside the clothes there was always the same thoroughly genuine fellow, whose every second sentence was spoken in jest.

He was the son of a cattle dealer. His father farmed his own land and walked behind his own plough. This was not unusual among the

Jewish cattle dealers of southern Germany. Accustomed to handling ploughs and scythes since childhood, Fred was in his element on the training farm.

At the evening classes in Hebrew his light shone less brightly. What a bore it was, this business of learning a foreign language! Even High German was an alien tongue to him. His native south German dialect was so much a part of him that one almost felt inhibited about speaking to him in what he called 'the writing'. In Palestine, restricted to Hebrew, would he be able to speak his mind so pithily?

The average age of our community was about 18. The youngest members were 15, and there was a small group of older ones between 25 and 30. Moshe Heilborn was one of these. On his birth certificate it said Moses, and undoubtedly Moses was what his parents had named him. Now that he was training to become a Hebrew-speaking settler, however, he had discarded the Latinised version of the name and restored the original Hebrew form, pronounced 'Moshé'. Isaac, Samuel and Rebecca were likewise no longer content with their names; as proud Hebrew speakers, they now called themselves Yitzhak, Shemuel, and Rifka. We soon learnt to find the Latinised names corrupt and ugly.

Moshe, having grown up as a farmer's son, had remained true to his father's calling. He did his work in the stables and out in the fields without wasting words. He groomed the horses, ploughed, mowed and loaded the hay-wagon. There was nothing odd about his being able to turn so brisk a hand to everything; the odd thing was what a man like Moshe was doing in an agricultural training camp in the first place. He knew all there was to know about farming, and he would surely have been hard at work in a settlement in Palestine already if the British mandatory authorities had allowed him into the country.

Meanwhile, until the time for his 'illegal' immigration came, Moshe went about the place doing his job. His skill and the sheer strength of his calloused hands earned him the respect of all the younger trainees.

On Saturdays Moshe put on his best suit like everyone else. He never looked more like a yokel than with that suit on his back. Fine clothes and leisure seemed to make him thoroughly uneasy. The horses were fed; what else was he to do with the holiday? He would thrust his right hand into his trousers pocket — and after a while pull it out again, as if he were unable to find a satisfactory place to put it.

Not many of us could compare with Moshe or Fred. Of the

seventy young people at Steckelsdorf only eight had grown up on farms, despite the fact that the selection process for admission had been weighted in favour of rural Jews. The vast majority were town-bred. But for the Hitler regime, their lives would doubtless have continued like their fathers'. We should have found them today practising as businessmen and tradespeople right across Germany from Saarbrücken in the west to Königsberg in East Prussia — in the textile and cosmetics industries, for example, or in furrier's workshops or possibly in silversmiths' studios. Under their name-plates we should read 'Closed on Saturdays'. Others would have become doctors, lawyers, journalists, teachers and the like.

Some of our trainees had just begun their professional training; others had still been at school when Jewish businesses were sub-jected to compulsory 'Aryanisation' and Jews were excluded from the state educational system. As a result, the Zionist watchword 'back to Zion — back to the soil!' had found a warmer welcome in their hearts. The Steckelsdorf training farm was now peopled with youngsters who had been knocked off course: secondary-school children without school-leaving certificates, shop girls with flowery dismissal notices, three-quarters-trained apprentices, and journey-men 'all but'. I came across two third-year grammar-school stu-dents, one fourth-year and two would-be secondary-school teachers who had been halfway through their training.

One might have expected that collection of washed-up city youths to be less than enthusiastic about agriculture. Yet most of them seemed by no means loath to take up the farming life. 'Retraining' might have been an alarming prospect to older people; adolescents with little or no experience of working life took to it much more readily.

But did all the *chaverim* who milked those cows so keenly and spread their muck so zealously mean to end their days as farmers? I for my part had come to Steckelsdorf with something else in mind. If in order to get to Palestine it was necessary to learn how to plough, then I would learn how to plough. Working outside for a year, I reasoned, would toughen my muscles; once in Palestine I would resume my studies. Other inmates, I discovered, harboured similar thoughts.

There was no coercion from the Palestine Office. It sought by every available publicistic means to win young people for the kibbutz movement in Palestine. But no one had to commit him or herself to staying in agriculture. Of course, someone who looked like becoming a particularly proficient kibbutz farmer had more chance of getting a place on a refugee ship.

Many of those at Steckelsdorf showed conspicuous enthusiasm for tilling the soil and for kibbutz-style communal living. There was never any knowing which factor weighed most heavily in individual cases: Rousseau-esque romanticism, the ethos of the Zionist labour movement or simple go-getting hypocrisy.

The older generation is usually expected to exercise a restraining influence on the younger generation's more radical plans. Our 'older generation', however, together with its whole bourgeois outlook on life, had come a cropper. The parents' bewilderment had the effect of boosting the ideological zeal of their offspring.

I shall never forget the day when the parents of some of the young trainees visited Steckelsdorf. It was a hot, sunny afternoon in June 1940, and we were all hard at work. Suddenly we became aware of them, tripping along between the fields towards us, looking lost, the men swinging walking-sticks, brows streaming with perspiration beneath the brims of their felt hats, the women breathing hard, fending off the rye stalks with their fashionable handbags. Every few seconds they stopped to peer about them, trying to identify their sons and daughters among all those youngsters in rustic garb. How perfectly they embodied the German–Jewish bourgeoisie — and how utterly out of place they seemed on that farm!

The scenes of greeting between parents and offspring, an uneasy blend of pleasure and embarrassment, were as irresistibly comic as the discomfiture of the third-former whose mother puts in an unexpected appearance in the school playground. Between the potato fields and the manure hotbeds, two epochs of Jewish history met, and it was the parents' misfortune to represent the one that had been stripped of all competence and authority.

Selection for deliverance?

Among the training goals of the Palestine preparation camp was the cultivation of team spirit. One strove with all one's might to emulate the Palestinian kibbutz. The kibbutz retained something of the ethos of early socialism. Indeed, it is possible that nowhere else have the ideals of comradely co-existence been realised in so pure a form.

The Hebrew word for the members of a co-operative fellowship is *chaverim* (sing.: *chaver*), which is what the young men and women at Steckelsdorf called one another. I prefer to leave *chaverim* untranslated, because despite the trace of phoney pathos that sometimes attaches to it, it seems to me to have become less devalued through misuse than, for example, the German *Genosse* or the English 'comrade'.

A feature of the kibbutz way of life is democratic self-government. Accordingly, this was something that we practised at Steckelsdorf. Once or twice every three months the membership was summoned to a meeting. The agenda might cover a wide range of subjects. How much money of his own ought each *chaver* to possess? When a *chaver* receives a food parcel from his parents, ought he to share it with his room-mates or ought he to hand it over to the kitchen?

The question 'Do we want to go on singing German songs or only Hebrew ones in future?' gave rise to vigorous debate. The majority wanted to go on singing German songs.

The meetings were chaired by the youth leader, Sholem Klein. Unlike most of the *chaverim*, Sholem was not a German Jew; he came from Miskolc in Hungary. As a Hungarian citizen, albeit a Jewish one, he enjoyed undiminished civic rights in Germany. He was a good-natured fellow with the engaging manner of the travelling salesman. His straightforward Jewish faith and his large, manly figure gave him an unchallenged position in the community. In word and deed — and above all in song — he professed the religious faith of Zionism, and since he had a powerful baritone voice his professions were clearly audible during community singing sessions. He performed his duties as youth leader willingly and to the best of his ability. Nevertheless, he was not the right man for the job. A course at the Talmudic college in Munkacs had made him familiar with the dialectics of the Talmud but not with the mentality and the problems of young Jewish people growing up in Germany. These remained essentially a closed book to him. Yet that was not the reason for the tensions that occasionally made themselves felt between the community and its youth leader; they were due more to his sophistical way of thinking.

Ours was a small community. Nevertheless, it offered an instructive model of democracy, with all the advantages and disadvantages of that system. Someone like Moshe Heilborn, for example, never opened his mouth. Fred, that merry fellow, was unrecognisable at meetings. His wit appeared to have deserted him; he would sit staring straight ahead of him with a bored expression, except when he was whispering some comment to his neighbour. Out of the seventy or so people present, it was always the same eight who took part in the discussions — rarely more than that.

A subject that cropped up repeatedly was 'How can we cultivate team spirit amongst ourselves?' On such occasions Lea Schwermann, a fiercely combative *chaverah* with an enormous bun, was sure to ask for the floor. That, too, was part of the democratic discipline we were to learn there: we must hear out Lea Schwermann's

100

relentlessly reproachful tirades without interruption.

One of the tasks of the general meeting was to elect a five-man committee that (again with the youth leader in the chair) took care of internal organisational matters. The committee allotted the set jobs, divided the community up into study groups and appointed the course leaders. Its principal task, however, was to select — or, as we used to say, 'confirm' — the candidates for immigration to Palestine.

Only those who were capable of doing all the jobs with the animals, in the fields and in the market garden competently and assiduously were eligible for selection. They must also have proved their worth in the context of the life-style of the collectivity. *Chaverim* who had been at the training farm for several years were also to have their 'long service' taken into account.

Everyone wanted to become a 'confirmee' because only confirmees were in line for a place on a ship. Considerable importance also attached to the sequence of confirmation. There might, for example, be room for four hundred passengers on the next refugee ship. There were twenty Palestine preparation camps in Germany. On average, therefore, twenty persons were taken from each camp. It mattered little whether a confirmee was number two or number three. But it mattered enormously whether he or she was number twenty or number twenty-one. The committee used to deliberate for nights on end.

I was to be involved in those deliberations myself. Five weeks after my arrival at Steckelsdorf, I was elected onto the committee! This trust, so quickly won, pleased me but at the same time rather alarmed me.

My misgivings increased when I attended my first meeting. A fine committee we were! Not one of us was above twenty years old. I had only just turned eighteen and did not even know the names of all the *chaverim* as yet. And we were expected to pass judgement on others and to have a hand in deciding the fates of seventy people!

The only person on whom I could confidently have passed judgement was myself. I certainly had no right to a place on the next boat — nor on the one after that, nor on the one after that.

There was a certain charm, I have to admit, in those lengthy evening sessions spent discussing, in snug comfort, the merits and demerits of people who, all unaware, lay tightly wrapped in blankets in cold, damp dormitories. But what was it that we actually discussed so animatedly each time? Was it not an imagined responsibility with which we felt ourselves burdened? Was it really up to us to decide who should emigrate to Palestine and who should not?

Moritz Schilling said it was, and his opinion counted for something because he was an important official in Berlin: a member of the Misrachi national board. Occasionally, to keep an eye on things, he would come out to Steckelsdorf on a visit. He always asked to see the people our committee had 'confirmed', because the last word — which set the seal on their selection, as it were — lay with him.

When Schilling visited us, he was fetched from the station in the wagon and received with full honours. He was not yet thirty-five years old, but his fiery expression and permanently strained features gave one an idea of how many and various were the activities under his control and how momentous the thoughts that preoccupied his mind. His appearance invariably gave rise to whispered conjectures and inspired a diffident awe.

Schilling once explained the organisation of Aliyah Bet to us in the following words: 'We in the Palestine Office collect the lists of confirmees that come to us from all the camps, and we submit them to the Gestapo for approval. So far the Gestapo have not struck a single name off any of our lists. Then comes the second stage. A Danube steamer has to be purchased — one that is reasonably seaworthy. With a war on, ships are becoming harder and harder to come by, and each time we have to pay a fortune. Once a ship is lying ready, the confirmees travel to Vienna by special train under a Gestapo/SS escort. The ships leave from Vienna, and it is in Vienna that all who are to embark have to meet. At this point, we have the business with the transit visas. The Yugoslavs, the Hungarians and the Rumanians create every conceivable difficulty when it comes to issuing a right of passage. It is as if they fear no enemy quite so much as a few hundred refugees whose only wish is to descend the Danube as rapidly as possible. The stretch from Vienna to the frontier goes quickly and smoothly. But weeks of agony may pass before the ship enters the Black Sea and subsequently the Mediterranean. Then, when all these obstacles have been overcome, we reach the final, most critical stage of the whole voyage. As the refugees approach the Palestinian coast, it will depend entirely on their skill, on a great deal of luck and on the help of the Jewish settlers whether they manage to reach the interior of the country without being spotted by the British.'

Moritz Schilling hinted that other things lay concealed behind his terse remarks — things he was not at liberty to divulge.

Twenty-four sacred hours

The excitement stimulated by Schilling's words lasted no more than a few days. The thoughts of the *chaverim* dwelt more on their

102

long-term objective than on the many dangers it involved. Besides, they did not live by their hopes and expectations alone. For believers, life has a sacred pivot, no matter where in the world they happen to find themselves.

The vitality of this feeling became particularly apparent in the training-farm community on *shabbath*. One could also feel how shared worship strengthened the bonds between the young people of Steckelsdorf.

Our rural seclusion lent a unique flavour to our Sabbath celebrations. Sunday was just as much a working day with us as Monday and Tuesday, as if the training farm had been situated in a part of the world where the Christian holiday was not observed. And when the Sabbath came, we felt it all around us. A solemn silence reigned over the whole estate, from the rye field to the woods and from the greenhouse to the plantations. Only the clatter of the trains would occasionally reach us, borne on the wind; or we might hear the drone of an aeroplane, high up above the clouds.

After Friday evening prayers, seventy young people shook one another by the hand and exhanged greetings — 'Shabbath shalom' — as their eyes radiated that special joy that comes from casting off the burdens of the working week.

We took our places at the simple yet festively decorated table (actually several tables arranged in a horseshoe). I always chose a place from which I could see everybody; I loved to look around me during the meal. Though I was already familiar with all the faces, I never ceased to delight in the way a lot of dirty, sweaty farm labourers had transformed themselves into a smart supper party. Ties and lipstick were taboo. The girls were quite capable of making themselves attractive without the aid of cosmetics, and as they lined the tables in their gaily coloured frocks they presented a thoroughly festive picture.

It never took us more than a few moments to dispose of the soup, fishballs and mashed potatoes. The helpings were woefully inadequate. Yet we hardly gave a thought to the fact in our impatience to strike up the traditional songs of praise and thanksgiving in honour of the sacred day.

Here Sholem Klein was really in his element. Sometimes he would get carried away and start to accompany the singing with rhythmic clapping, as he had been used to doing in the Chassidic congregations of his native Hungary.* It never seemed to occur to him that

---

* *Chassidim* ('the godly ones') is a name that goes back a long way in Jewish history. It was adopted by the followers of Rabbi Israel Baal Shemtob (Besht), who launched

anyone might find his enthusiasm off-putting. In fact, for all their unfamiliarity, his spontaneous outbursts of joy proved infectious. Some of the girls would begin to move their heads and necks in time to the tune, almost imperceptibly, while others rocked with such abandon that they ended up almost dancing in their seats.

The Friday evening meal was followed by an hour of Torah study. For this we were divided into six groups according to how much we already knew. The task of leading the study groups fell to those who knew most.

I had been agonising over the question of my further education ever since my arrival at Steckelsdorf. Which group should I join if I wanted to be sure of having a good teacher? When I went to the youth leader to ask his advice, he suggested that I should not look for a teacher so much as for pupils. With my knowledge I was just the person to lead a group myself. I was accordingly made a *tarbutnik*, a 'culture specialist', and my fond hope of assuaging my thirst for knowledge was ushered into an early grave.

In fact, I rather enjoyed being a group leader. My group was a somewhat heterogeneous affair. It included Herbert Frohwald, a skilled joiner from Bavaria who was the farm's carpenter. In the wake of the November 1938 pogrom he had spent several months in Dachau concentration camp. That was said to have been where he picked up his stutter.

We were reluctant to question Herbert about his memories of Dachau. He rarely broached the subject himself, and when he did so it was usually to speak of trivial matters only. Did he feel unable to share his dreadful experiences with us? Or had he already had to tell the story too many times? In spite of everything he had been through, Herbert was still up to all kinds of jokes and pranks, which made it easier for us to bridge any uncomfortable silences.

Sara Grossberg had the best educational background of the group. Her family were strict 'Torah-true' Jews. But while she was often able to make a pertinent contribution towards our discussion of the biblical text, her orthodoxy dripped boredom. Rosa Behrend, Sara's loyal friend, was another one who was just too meek and mild to be capable of injecting any life into the proceedings.

The group also included Moshe Heilborn, the farmer's son who read Hebrew only with difficulty, and a pretty girl named Liesel Gold, who spent the entire time wrapped in an impenetrable silence. Then there was Bruno Lipmann, an enormously tall young man

a 'charismatic' Jewish revival movement in the Ukraine in the eighteenth century. He preached the need for spirituality and a world-affirming mysticism.

from Berlin who never seemed to know what to do with his long arms and his big feet. Bruno distinguished himself neither at work nor in the study group, where he sat awkwardly in his place and looked pathetic. Was the course too difficult for him? Did his gawkiness get him down? Or was he simply suffering from hunger? Indeed, how could our meagre fare ever have satisfied a great body like his? Fred spotted him climbing into bed after lunch one day for a surreptitious snack — a mouthful of toothpaste!

It was not easy to get a brisk discussion going with people like that. How glad I was that Fred, the arch-joker, was put in my group as well as Hans Wiener, a cocky young fellow from Leipzig who knew very little and had even less patience to learn anything! At least between them they made sure there were a few laughs and that no one actually fell asleep.

On the morning of the Sabbath we got up an hour later than usual. As soon as the animals had been fed we went in to morning prayers, which included a reading from the Torah. The meal that followed, like that of Friday evening, consisted of a great deal of singing and not much food.

Lunch was followed by a period that we were free to spend as each of us thought fit. In bad weather we used to spread out over various rooms of the summer villa. Some made for the silent, unused kitchen, others for the reading-room; most people found no better place to spend the time than the sparsely and uncomfortably furnished dormitories. In the absence of any chairs or benches, people used their beds. Most of these were bunks, however, and since it was impossible to sit upright on the bottom one, many preferred to lie down and converse in that position or simply read a book. Others returned to the dining-room to play games of various kinds. You rarely saw anyone in the cold, damp synagogue.

When the weather was fine the dining-room had an empty, abandoned look. Groups of strollers dispersed in all directions, penetrating to every corner of the estate and out into the surrounding countryside. Some, moving at a leisurely, holiday pace, would amble through the plantations to the manure hotbeds and the greenhouse. Others might pay a visit to the poultry yard and the dovecot or wander, hands in pockets, into the stable and cowshed. There they would lean over the calf pen to let a calf suck on a forefinger or simply listen to the peaceful champing and snorting of the cows, pleased that the animals too were enjoying a day of rest. Afterwards they might stroll past the barn and the machine shed where the ploughs, harrows, rollers and seed drills all lay idle, looking like museum-pieces. Walking through the woods to the frog pond, one caught glimpses of those gaily coloured frocks between the trees. Shouts and snatches of talk were occasionally audible against a background of birdsong. In the more secluded spots one might surprise a couple, or possibly some youngster keeping his own company and shunning all conversation.

Since time immemorial Jews have been in the habit of spending the twilight hour that ushers in the end of the seventh day in song. The songs that belong to that time have a melancholy sound. It is hard to take leave of the sacred day. The Jewish mystics tell us why. After twenty-four hours in a pure, sublime world, man is thrust back into the grotesque confusion of everyday life. The other half of his double soul departs, leaving him doubly alone amid coal shovels, money-bags and jangling alarm clocks. Small wonder that the soul that remains behind resists the change with all its might. Hence the melancholy.

But at the same time there is promise of a reunion. Somehow or other one will get through the next six working days. Besides, the Sabbath from which one is taking leave has been an imperfect affair, a feeble foretaste merely of the unalloyed sacred day that shall come and shall never end. As well as melancholy, that last hour of the seventh day brings a twofold joy as the Jew looks forward to the following week's Sabbath and as he looks forward to the ideal Sabbath of the end of time.

The seventy young men and women assembled in the dining-room of the summer villa, sitting motionless on their benches in the timeless recurrence of Sabbath peace, strike up one song after another. And so hushed is their music that it is as though they are not singing at all themselves but listening to a song that comes floating down to them from the ceiling. The light fades. Shapes in front of the veranda windows become silhouettes, seen against the red glow of evening. The figures in the room give up their outlines to the gathering dusk. Only the faces of those sitting nearby remain recognisable. Some stare straight ahead of them, sunk in thought. Others, with eyes wide open, seem to be looking right through the walls of the room. It is as though they have succeeded in penetrating eternity itself.

The Patria

After the first winter of the war, the coming of spring was doubly welcome. It ended our imprisonment within the cramped and uncomfortable quarters of the summer villa and the farmhouse. And our training programme, which in winter was confined to the cowshed and the greenhouse and padded out with makeshift jobs and extra hours of theory, once again became rich and varied. The fields needed ploughing. The greenhouse contained thousands of seedlings that were waiting to be planted out in the open. Armed with spades and hoes, we spread out over the whole area of the farm and allowed work and the mild spring sunshine to warm our bodies. As if to spur us on to even greater efforts, there was good news from the Palestine Office in Berlin: it was thought that a Danube steamer would be leaving shortly.

All of a sudden, the shadow of momentous events fell upon our world and upon our hopes. The news struck us like bolts of lightning: German troops in Denmark and Norway! Germany attacks Holland, Belgium, France! Dunkirk in German hands! More than a million French and British prisoners!

Usually news reports reached us only in the lunch-break or after we had knocked off in the evening. On days such as these, however, *chaverim* who had seen the headlines in the newspaper in the office would come running out to us in the fields. Deeply shocked, we would pause in what we were doing to exchange looks of consternation and dismay. Then we would go back to planting out tomatoes and kohlrabi, though it struck us at the time as the most pointless activity imaginable. France, the whole of Western Europe, in Hitler's power? It seemed scarcely credible.

The flush of victory that affected the whole nation, the bell-ringing that reverberated through every German town for seven days following the capitulation of France, failed to penetrate our seclusion. Like the events that had inspired them, we only read about them in the newspaper. The environs of the training farm remained as tranquil as ever. The trees stood newly clad in green. There was a smell of fresh earth overlaid with the tang of resin. From the woods came the sound of birdsong, punctuated by the blows of an axe or perhaps accompanied by the singing of a saw.

A false feeling of confidence spread throughout Germany at that time to the effect that 'victory in the West' had brought peace a step nearer. Many of us believed it, too. But would peace also bring an end to our predicament as Jews?

The National Socialists' lust for power had, to all appearances, managed to achieve its objective. Might not their blind hatred of all things foreign, and in particular of us Jews, be assuaged? Thoughts such as these certainly found expression among us at Steckelsdorf, and even the people from the Palestine Office evidently harboured similar hopes. In fact, they thought it possible that, once the international situation had been stabilised, the way would be opened for us Jews to emigrate to Palestine.

While we still clung to such illusions, the first deportations had already taken place in the Reich. In October 1939 Jews from Vienna and Bohemia were dragged off to Poland. In March 1940 a similar fate befell some 1,200 Jews from Stettin.* In the night of 21–2 October 1940, thousands of Jews in Baden, Saarland and the Palatinate were taken from their homes by the local police, packed into goods trains and deported to the unoccupied part of France, where the Vichy government interned them in prison camps.[†] However, it was not until very much later that we learnt of all these terrible things.

Nor, consequently, did we have a proper appreciation of the quite extraordinary good fortune of other Jews who were allowed to embark on the journey to Palestine and were even helped on their way by the Gestapo. For in the autumn of 1940 we heard that in Vienna a ship was waiting to take 300 'confirmees' from training camps in Germany together with several hundred Jews from other groups in the country to the land of our dreams.

In several late-night sessions, our committee once again revised the list of confirmees for the Steckelsdorf training farm. The first fifteen on the list packed their bags and left immediately.

'How far have they got?' we wondered for a while. 'When will they be in Pressburg/Bratislava? When will they reach Budapest?' No letters came. We tacitly assumed that they had made a safe getaway, and before long we gave them scarcely another thought. Life at Steckelsdorf was arduous, and in the meantime we had heard about the deportations of Jews from Stettin and Baden. This terrified us. What lay behind the word 'deportation' was something we were not aware of at the time. But we had no doubt that the deportees would be experiencing quite as much cruelty as the Jews of Polish nationality who had been 'repatriated' in October 1938. They had simply been packed into lorries, dumped at the Polish frontier and chased away over the fields.

Six months after our *chaverim* had climbed aboard that Danube steamer we finally heard what had become of them. Moritz Schilling paid us a visit in the spring of 1941. He summoned a meeting immediately on his arrival, and after expressly enjoining us to the strictest secrecy he shared with us the news that had reached the

* Now Szczecin in Poland.
[†] Hitler's troops overran France in just five weeks in May–June 1940 (Paris fell on 14 June). On 22 June a new French government based in Vichy signed an armistice that left most of the country occupied by the German army with a small unoccupied (but inevitably still subservient) zone in the south.

Palestine Office in Berlin by way of Switzerland.

At the end of a two-month voyage, so Schilling informed us, the steamer had reached the coast of Palestine in November 1940. Before the refugees could go ashore the ship was stopped by British naval units, together with a second Jewish refugee ship that had arrived at the same time. The two ships were taken to the port of Haifa under close escort. Not a single refugee was allowed to disembark.

'Until now,' Schilling continued, 'the British have been admitting illegal immigrants, simply knocking a corresponding number of certificates off the next immigration quota. Now they have suddenly decided to transport all illegal immigrants to Mauritius.'

'Where's Mauritius?' It was Moshe Heilborn who asked.

'Mauritius is a British — formerly French — colony in the Indian Ocean, east of Madagascar. It is a small island with an atrocious tropical climate. There is still an old French prison on the island. They meant to intern the refugees there until the end of the war. After the war, they were to be taken somewhere else, but not under any circumstances to Palestine.'

'Please,' Schilling was forced to interrupt himself at this point, 'no further questions just now! When the refugee ships reached Haifa, an unmanned French ship, the *Patria*, still lay in the harbour. It was the intention of the British to use the *Patria* to transport 1,700 people to Mauritius. They forcibly transferred them to the French ship, which was to sail in a few days. Suddenly the port of Haifa was rocked by a massive explosion. Unfortunately the refugees had miscalculated their act of sabotage. They had not reckoned with the ship sinking in less than a quarter of an hour. As a result, 250 of them lost their lives.* The *Patria* affair, as you can imagine, unleashed tremendous bitterness against the British, both in Palestine and throughout the world. In the end, the British allowed the survivors to remain in Palestine. But they are still keeping them behind barbed wire. None of our fifteen *chaverim* from Steckelsdorf was killed in the incident. However, Liesel Gold's father was also aboard the *Patria*. Liesel has now lost her father.'

We all looked round for Liesel, but she was not in the room. Schilling had spoken to her before the meeting.

'I haven't finished yet,' Schilling went on. 'Shortly after this a third ship reached Palestine with 1,800 refugees. Those 1,800 people

* We now know that this account of the incident is incorrect. The sinking of the *Patria* was the work not of the refugees but of members of the Jewish paramilitary organisation, Haganah.

were then deported to Mauritius. *Chaverim*, as you can see, we now find ourselves in a very different situation!'

We had listened to Schilling's report with mounting dismay. We were accustomed to the persecutions of Jews in Germany by now, accepting them with a certain fatalism, almost as if they had been natural disasters. But we still judged the conduct of the British by the yardstick of humanity. We were deeply disappointed.

'You agree, then, that after the Nazis our worst enemies now are the British?' shouted one of the younger *chaverim*.

Schilling's reply was serious: 'Possibly. But at the same time they are still our allies. Imagine what Europe would look like now without the British. They are the only great power to have taken up arms against the Nazis.'

He ended on a challenging note: '*Chaverim*, in conclusion I just want to say one thing. We at Aliyah Bet headquarters intend to go on working. We shall show the British that no coastguard patrols and no forcible deportations are going to deter us!'

We dispersed in silence. Only four or five *chaverim* stayed to press Schilling with further questions.

A net is woven

In the late autumn of 1940, before we heard of the deportation of the Jews from Stettin and Baden, a rumour reached our ears that the Germans were planning to load all Jews onto ships, deport them to Madagascar, and turn them loose in the jungle. On the Jewish side, the Reichsvereinigung was said to have set up a special training camp already, where people could learn the necessary survival skills for the tropical wilderness: how to clear jungle, dig wells and so on.*

On the other hand, Jews in Germany were now more and more in demand for all kinds of work — in the munitions industry, for example, in road-building and in agriculture. The Reichsvereinigung reacted immediately, advising able-bodied Jews to set about making themselves indispensable in industry and commerce. Given the current shortage of labour, there was no surer means of self-protection.

Blumenfeld, the manager of the Steckelsdorf training farm, followed the same advice. He began to pace the floor of his office with an air of even greater importance than before. Blumenfeld clearly

* Hitler and some of his associates had indeed discussed such a plan before the war (see Reitlinger, pp. 79ff.). With the collapse of France, the political context required for its implementation seemed in part to be provided. In August 1940 Adolf Eichmann was given the task of drawing up a suitable 'resettlement programme'.

took pleasure in making the farmers and smallholders who came knocking at his door feel just how much depended upon his goodwill and upon his personal decision. His office in the farmhouse became a busy place. Market gardeners and landowners came and went. Even factory-owners from Rathenow asked to see Blumenfeld. His voice could be heard positively crowing down the telephone: '*So* sorry! I've no one left!' or 'I can't promise anything, but I'll see what I can do for you!'

Soon more of us were working off the premises than on. There were no longer the toings and froings between the summer villa and the farmhouse that there had been. Now the majority of the *chaverim* set out each morning with haversack and canteen, bound for new places of employment. Those who owned a bicycle rode to work. A sizeable group left for Rathenow each day, where they had jobs in the optical industry. Not until supper was the whole community reunited. The Steckelsdorf Palestine preparation camp had become a workers' hostel.

Actually, it was the best thing our manager could have done — to 'volunteer' our services before the labour department made it compulsory. That way he could pick and choose his employers. His authoritative manner lent him the necessary weight. Blumenfeld was even able to impose conditions, which the farmers and factory-owners accepted: 'No one is to work more than eight hours a day. And don't expect any help from us on Saturdays and other Jewish holidays — not even at harvest-time!'

The employers were so pleased to get hold of workers at all that they agreed to everything. Some farmers insisted that we should at least come to work on Sundays. Blumenfeld had no objection to that.

Willy-nilly, the rest of us had acquiesced in this changed situation. We did so with a troubled conscience, though, feeling that we were abandoning our true aim. After all, the sole justification for our existence at Steckelsdorf lay in the fact that it was temporary. Our real life would begin later, somewhere in the orange plantations between Tel Aviv and Haifa, or possibly manning a fishing boat on the waters of the Mediterranean. With our eyes fixed on such plans, we could put up with a lot: our seclusion, the spiteful village policeman, the anti-Jewish decrees, hunger. . . . Now, however, what had been temporary was beginning to drag on alarmingly.

Collective gripes

Suddenly our wretched bivouac in that transit station en route to the Holy Land began to look like a permanent state of emergency.

111

I shared a large room with seven other youths. We referred to it as 'the barracks'. The view out of the windows was blocked by a row of iron bunk-beds, giving the room the appearance of a cage. A peculiar, musty smell hung about 'the barracks' and all that it contained. There was no getting rid of it, no matter how much fresh air we allowed to blow through the room. Sweat-soaked socks and boots, damp towels and straw-filled mattresses kept it permanently 'topped up'. Rotting floorboards and mildewed walls added their own peculiar exhalations.

The other dormitories in the summer villa and in the farmhouse were smaller but equally barrack-like and uninviting. They accommodated four and six *chaverim* each. Yet it was not the cramped conditions or the discomfort that made life at Steckelsdorf so unedifying at times.

'It is not good that the man should be alone,' said the Lord God, contemplating Adam in the Garden of Eden. But is it good that he should never be alone? The question imposed itself more and more insistently. At the training farm we did everything collectively: we lived, slept, read, worked and relaxed collectively. In our eagerness to emulate a Palestinian kibbutz, we were suspicious of anything that smacked of individualism.

A person who yearned for solitude could, in fine weather, spend his free time walking in the woods. But he did so at the risk of inviting disapproval of himself as a 'loner'. It had clearly not occurred to the adherents of the kibbutz ideal that young people do occasionally like to be on their own.

Loving couples had a hard time of it. The community looked askance at confidential relations of any kind. Even friendships were frowned on. It was feared that the comradeship of all with all might suffer as a result. So loving couples and friends were forced to seek the most extreme seclusion. But how were they to do that when at almost all times and in almost all places they found themselves in the spotlight of collective curiosity?

Even so, during my first few months at Steckelsdorf I never heard a word of complaint about this lack of any private life. Among seventy youngsters there were naturally some representatives of the type that hates nothing so much as solitude and silence. The rest had been able to come to terms with the excessively communal nature of life on the training farm. However, as an end to this temporary state of affairs became an increasingly remote prospect, many grew weary of the everlasting camaraderie. Groups and cliques began to form. Struggles for power and importance led to all kinds of discord, even in the context of public debate. A free association of volunteers had become a coercive community. A number of young men — including myself — had had many reservations about the collective way of life long before our community was so fiercely put to the test. Our general meetings dealt with questions that impinged too deeply upon our private lives.

When I had been at Steckelsdorf for more than ten months I began to experience an oppressive feeling that we were going round in circles. Something was inhibiting the development of our mental and physical life-forces; I thought I could detect a kind of intellectual inbreeding. I believed the reason for it lay in our being so cut off from the world and in the relative ignorance of our 'culture specialists'. Yet that still did not explain why a feeling of staleness occasionally insinuated itself even between friends. Had we no more to say to one another? Was the illusion that we could see into the farthest corners of one another's hearts due solely to the pressure of a hostile outside world?

When I found myself in a Rumanian internment camp in 1944, many things about Steckelsdorf became clearer in retrospect. What happened to us on the training farm was what happens to people everywhere when they are forced to live together in the same room all the time, eat at the same table and forfeit all personal privacy: we suffered from camp psychosis.

CHAPTER 6

Schulze's Tree Nursery

Blumenfeld had assigned me and five other *chaverim* to a tree nursery. We wondered what sort of man our employer would turn out to be. He would be the first non-Jew with whom any of us had been in contact on a daily basis since the start of our lengthy seclusion. One of our number had heard that he was an SS man. Another claimed he was not SS but was a former party militant. Was there anything in what they said? Why was Blumenfeld sending us to him, of all people?

Cycling through Neue Schleuse on our way to the tree nursery, we had our first encounter with a group of French prisoners-of-war, marching under armed escort. We stopped and got off our bicycles. The Frenchmen were shuffling along out of step, staring resignedly at the rain. After following them for a while with our gaze, we remounted and rode on without a word. Later it transpired that the same thought had occurred to every one of us: those men are our brothers.

The tree nursery lay some way out of the village. The proprietor, Schulze, was a thin man of medium height. He wasted little time over greetings. After showing us where to put our bikes, he told us to pick up the six spades that stood ready, looked us up and down with a critical eye and proceeded to demonstrate how to dig up frozen young fruit trees with a couple of quick thrusts.

'Nothing to it,' he told us. 'First shove the spade in all round. Then, between two of you, heave ho and out she comes. Shake the earth off, and there you are. On to the next one.'

It was a hard day. The rain did not let up for an instant. The loamy soil caked our cuffs and trouser-legs. We dragged heavy clods of earth with us at every step.

Schulze was better equipped for the work than we were. High boots protected his legs, and he wore a green hunting hat and a loden coat. All right for him to say 'Nothing to it', we thought. He goes home to a warm room, and his wife serves him a proper meal. I wondered if Schulze really was a Hitler supporter. I studied him covertly all day, debating the question with myself.

His narrow face and thin lips, together with the taut muscles round his mouth, indicated tenacity and will-power. The pipe that he held clamped between his teeth the whole time would have lent him a jovial air had his grey-green eyes not scrutinised us quite so sceptically. However, he certainly did not look like an SS thug. (We found out later that he had never actually belonged to the SS, though he had been an SA man even before Hitler's rise to power.)

We were filthy, famished men when we got home that evening. At last we were able to wash our hands and pull out a handkerchief. I had never realised what a privilege it is to be able to blow one's nose as and when one likes. The day's incessant drizzle had been a source of pure delight to Schulze. 'Lovely planting weather — couldn't have asked for better!'

Next day we did indeed start planting. The rain was falling harder now, lashing us either in the face or on the back of the neck. The cold wind made our fingers stiff. The freshly dug field seemed very wide; lengthwise, it went on for ever. The saplings lay in heaps along the edge, waiting to be planted.

On the third day the rain and mist gave way to mild autumn sunshine. Our new workplace began to assume a friendlier air. It was only now that we were able to gain a view of the nursery as a whole. Close to the entrance stood a wooden house with a veranda and a terrace — the home of the Schulze family. At the back of the house was a small but well-equipped tool-shed. There, among a wide variety of hand tools, we came across a rubber truncheon. It consisted of a length of garden hose, a wooden handle, and some galvanised wire. Schulze had probably made it himself. The hose felt as if it was filled with small pebbles or lead shot. As to what Schulze used or had used his rubber truncheon for, we could only speculate.

Out in the middle of one of the fields, the wind whistled round a small latrine thatched with reeds and straw. Crudely, Schulze recommended it to our use.

I have a reason for describing Schulze and his domain at such length: we were to spend a good part of our lives in his tree nursery.

Chin up! No slacking!

The transformation of the Palestine training school into a labour camp imposed considerable extra burdens on us. There was no longer anything remotely educational about the work.

Only fifteen boys and girls remained on the farm. They had to till the fields, tend the animals and maintain the market garden and the orchards; they also had to staff the kitchen, the laundry and the sewing-room.

Those who now went out to work were given malt coffee and four thin slices of the inferior, spongy bread that the village baker supplied for Jewish consumption. Such were our rations for an eight-hour working day; they had to last us till suppertime. Two farmers for whom some of the *chaverim* worked used voluntarily to supply their famished helpers with milk and eggs. They were laudable exceptions. Most of our employers considered their duties discharged when they had paid for the work done at the official rate, using the worthless wartime currency.

Nor was hunger our only problem; our clothes and shoes now wore out more quickly. These were irreplaceable, for Jews received no ration coupons for clothes.

Also, we now had very much less free time. Many of us spent more than an hour travelling to and from work. In the evenings we found it difficult to follow our courses with proper attention. Things had virtually reached a point where our lives consisted of nothing but an endless round of work and sleep.

Alarm at this state of affairs spurred us into making a fresh effort. The general meeting voted by a large majority to reorganise our study and reading periods. The courses in Torah-study, Jewish history and Hebrew received new impetus. As the most powerful counterpoise to the slavery that threatened to engulf us, the Sabbath now assumed even greater importance.

Evening song recitals and dances also came into their own. There was a piano in the summer villa, and some of the *chaverim* owned fiddles, flutes and mandolines. A greater delight than the musical offerings of unpractised amateurs, however, were gramophone evenings, during which we gave ourselves up to the music of Haydn and Mozart. For many of those young people this was their first encounter with the masterpieces of Baroque and classical music. After such evenings, snatches of Beethoven's violin concerto were liable to come drifting out of the kitchen and the dormitories. Bits of themes from Wagner's *Tannhäuser* or a Mozart serenade might be struck up in the woods or on the way to work or in the tree nursery.

There were also repeated calls at the general meeting for more sport and games. We decided to get up twenty minutes earlier and start the day with open-air gymnastics. I was placed in charge.

Nearly eighteen months into the war the streets of Berlin resembled those of a peaceful provincial town. Traffic was very restricted and there were few pedestrians about. The inhabitants bore the nightly air-raid warnings with patient good humour. Bombed houses were still such a rarity that Berliners used to travel across town to see them.

I received only the most fleeting impression of Berlin at that time, for when I was granted two weeks' leave in January 1941 I spent almost the whole of it with my family.

Since the beginning of 1940 my parents had been the subtenants of a flat in Cuxhavenerstrasse, just down the road from Hansaplatz. I found that it was not far from my old lodgings with the Teitelbaums. The 'one and a half' rooms of the flat (in fact one ordinary-sized room and one tiny one) were stuffed so full that one had to pick one's way among the pieces of furniture. Titian's Lavinia peered out from the corner in which mother prepared lunch over a spirit cooker. The coal allowance was insufficient to heat the rooms properly. My father wore a blanket draped around his shoulders and spent most of the time in the immediate vicinity of the not very warm stove.

Despite the cramped conditions and the numbing cold, my parents were glad to have the flat — without a Frau Polonski to make their lives a misery with her insolence. Their 'landlord', a former Jewish businessman now working for the Jewish congregation's welfare service, was said to be courteous and helpful. I did not meet him myself as he was out of town at the time.

My brother Jakob was still employed in a paint works. Toni helped with the housework. Leon was diligently teaching himself modern languages. Ought they perhaps to consider themselves lucky that they had not been forced to work in the munitions industry? Such questions preoccupied many Jews in Berlin at that time. Optimists like my father were glad not to be involved in compulsory labour, for under the orders of Nazi superiors, Jews could expect nothing but constant humiliation. The pessimists saw their exclusion from war work as an additional cause for concern: did it not forebode an intention to organise fresh 'spontaneous outbreaks of popular anger' against 'useless mouths to feed'?

Who was right? Basically, none of us was very much wiser than Guli, who continued to seek my brother Leon's company and who would fatuously repeat the most contradictory rumours parrot-fashion.

Few people called on my parents except Jewish friends and

acquaintances. Their conversation touched on a thousand different subjects, but it always came back in the end to the most inexhaustible topic of all: the situation of the Jews. My father had marshalled a series of arguments to prove that things could not get much worse. His Jewish friends appeared less convinced, preferring to keep their spirits up by telling jokes against the Nazis.

I would listen to the jokes and laugh along with the rest, but I usually found — for some reason I could never quite identify — that they left a nasty after-taste.

The problem of the anti-Nazi joke continued to preoccupy me in the years after the war. Of course, the occasional surreptitiously whispered witticism did serve to take our minds off our misery. Intellectually, it offered the victims of persecution a chance to rise above their oppressors. For that reason it was as vital a necessity to us as bread and oxygen. But did not every one of those jokes have the side-effect of minimising and playing down the murderous reality of the Nazi terror? Did it not make it easier for the oppressed to accept their fate and permit them to squander their sense of outrage in a way that was politically sterile?

In the house where my parents lived, Jews were permitted to use the air-raid shelter in the cellar. Nevertheless, when the sirens went off my parents and my brothers and sister preferred to stay in the flat. The mere notion that someone might look askance at them as Jews deterred them from taking advantage of the facility. Moreover, in common with many Berliners they were confident that the bombs would fall at a safe distance from their flat.

As I was reading the Torah with father one evening, the sirens went off yet again. Anti-aircraft guns started up all around us. We let nothing distract us from our Bible study. Mother and Leon were just going to bed; Toni was in bed already.

Suddenly, in the space of a second, it happened. An eerie howl, a thunderclap — and all the lights went out.

'Hello, where are you?' we called blindly to one another. An ice-cold wind was blowing in at the window. We groped our way forward, stumbling over obstacles at every step. Eventually our eyes adjusted to the darkness. The obstacles turned out to be a jumble of smashed furniture, doors blown off their hinges, broken glass, bed-clothes, and fragments of paving-stones. Window-panes, drapes and blackout curtains were all gone. Snow blew into the room unhindered. In the reflected glow from the circling anti-aircraft searchlights, Leon finally found a torch.

Where was mother? No one had heard her voice. We searched and searched and finally dragged her unconscious from beneath what was left of a wardrobe. There was a gash on her forehead, and her right eye was covered with blood. Together we carried her down to the air-raid shelter and inspected her injuries by the light of a lantern. God, what a relief! The eye was undamaged, needing only to have the blood washed from it.

In a little while, mother came round. Then it was a question of freeing Toni, who was unharmed but had been pinned to her bed by heavy furniture falling on top of her.

Back in the cellar, we met the remaining occupants of the house. Not one of them made a face or passed any remark about the presence of Jews. Not that there was time for that, anyway. A number of wounded were brought down. We heard that there had been two deaths in the building. A doctor arrived and administered first aid; he also dressed mother's wound. After some hours, the occupants of the building were fetched in families by the welfare department for rehousing. Only we and a second Jewish family were left behind. Leon and I made several trips up to the shattered flat to salvage warm blankets and coats from among the debris. We spent the rest of the night in the air-raid shelter. But where were we to go once day dawned? Where should we live?

In the morning, father went to the office of the Jewish congregation for advice. Meanwhile Leon, Toni and I set about patching up the badly damaged flat. By the evening it was possible to walk through the rooms without stepping on broken glass. The window apertures were more or less sealed against the driving snow with the aid of an arrangement of cupboards, boards and blankets. But the cold wind still blew into the room, and there seemed little point in lighting the stove.

Fortunately, the cold and snow let up over the next few days, and the weekend even brought some dry, bright January weather. The sun tempted many strollers out, and a number of them bent their steps to Cuxhavenerstrasse to view the bomb damage.

Toni and I stuck our heads out above the boards and blankets and had a good laugh at the expense of the citizens of Berlin as they paused on the pavement opposite. One gentleman with a fat paunch pointed his walking-stick up at our faces and barked at the man standing beside him: 'Just look at that, will you? There are still people living there!'

My parents were obliged to go on living in that latest sight-seeing attraction for several more weeks until my father was at last allocated another home. It was to be his last.

My leave was nearing its end. I felt dreadful about leaving my loved ones in such wretched circumstances. It was some consolation, however, that though my parents might be ignored by the National Socialist welfare department, they were not ignored by everyone.

I had repeatedly heard my family speak in praise of a certain shoemaker. 'Who is this shoemaker you all keep talking about?' I asked. He lived in the next house, Toni told me. But for him, the family would be in a bad way. Nearly every week he got them something extra to eat. One time it would be bread coupons, another time butter or potatoes. And all they did in return was to go shopping for him. The shoemaker had no one else. His wife had been dead for many years and his sons were at the front. I could meet him if I wanted, Toni added. Mother's shoes would be ready the day after tomorrow; I could go and collect them.

The 'day after tomorrow' was the day of my departure. I did not even have a chance to look in the shoemaker's shop-window; like all the windows in the street, it had been boarded up after the bomb had fallen. Had I had any inkling of the fateful role that the shoemaker was to play in my life I should have gone out of my way to make his acquaintance before returning to Steckelsdorf.

The magic garden

Spring had come. The days passed with pleasing regularity. They started grey and overcast, but after a few hours our horizon widened; the cloud cover parted and everything around us began to gleam and sparkle.

The saplings we had planted in the autumn rain were now covered with buds. The fields glowed green. The chink of our spades and hoes was swept up in a tide of bird-song. The earth was one vast, luxuriant garden, with everything under the dome of heaven breathing peace. Not even the aeroplanes threading their way high overhead reminded us of the war.

What lay ahead? What did the future hold for us? We had ceased to ask.

The further spring advanced into summer, the more conversant we became with the cultivation of young fruit trees. I took a fancy to the work, despite all the hours of hard labour we put in on a virtually empty stomach. There were weeks, too, in which there was little else to do but pull up weeds and prune the young trunks of superfluous branches. We might spend hours on end working between rows that ran as straight as an arrow, never exchanging a word. We delighted in the way in which, under our care, insignificant-looking saplings were turning into slender yet sturdy young trees.

Schulze showed us the correct way to cut scions and buds. At

120

knocking-off time he gave each of us a couple of shoots and a budding knife in order — as he thought — that we might go on practising how to cut buds in our free time at home.

'When we were lads,' he added, 'we'd practise our grafting in church under the pew during the sermon. Bad enough having to listen to the preacher drivelling on. That way we were at least doing something useful. Preacher never noticed, anyway.'

We laughed.

'Here, what do you do on Sundays, then? Do you go to church and that?'

'On Sundays we work on the farm, in the market garden or out in the fields.'

'No, I mean on your Sunday — on Saturday!'

'We don't work then. We spend the day celebrating and saying our prayers.'

'Well, then, you can practise your grafting under the pew too, when your preacher's preaching in the Jew church!'

How quickly we got the knack of budding! We even grew accustomed to the backache that came from having to spend hours with our feet placed wide apart, bent double, dealing with one tree after another. Once I had grafted my first couple of hundred saplings, I began to see grafting as one of the most beautiful and commendable of all occupations. Back at Steckelsdorf in the evenings I would sometimes reach into my trousers pocket, pull out a budding knife, and with a craftsman's pride explain to *chaverim* who did not belong to our group exactly what constituted a good budding knife. I examined every tree I set eyes on around the training farm to see whether it had been grafted or budded. I even inspected large, mature trees to make sure they had been properly dealt with.

In my mind's eye I was already banging in the fenceposts around my own tree nursery in Palestine and starting to prepare the soil for planting. I meant to leave the study of chemistry to others, preferring to spend the day outside. The wide open spaces for me, I thought.

I stuck to that plan for years, through a great many vicissitudes of fate. It was not until I felt the Palestinian sun beating down on my head that I decided to opt for a job in the shade after all.

Escape into the net

Every month the Palestine Office dispatched new candidates to Steckelsdorf. There were still plenty of young people in Germany who wished to emigrate to Palestine. What about our prospects of actually getting there, though?

In the spring of 1941 Hitler and Mussolini extended the war to some of the countries through which our escape routes led. Rumania, Hungary and Bulgaria were already allies or satellites of Hitler. In April German troops invaded Yugoslavia and Greece. By the end of May the Balkans were in the grip of the Axis powers right up to the Turkish border.

We did not entirely give up hope. After all, the authorities approved of our emigrating to Palestine. Groups of Aliyah Bet refugees were even escorted to the frontiers of the Reich by SS and Gestapo units. Was it not conceivable that from now on they would escort them to the frontiers of the German–Italian sphere of influence?

However, a month before the German attack on Yugoslavia our organisation was threatened by a disaster of a different order. On 7 March a new law was passed obliging German Jews to perform forced labour. The law also affected the men from the Palestine Office, despite the fact that their activities were sanctioned by the Gestapo. In fact, they managed to evade the forced-labour law by leaving Berlin very promptly and distributing themselves among a number of Palestine preparation camps. Once in residence there, they came under the regional labour departments and were able to claim that they were already 'registered for agricultural labour duties'. This dispersal of the Palestine Office did not make official steps vis-à-vis the authorities of the Reich any easier, but it seemed to be the only way to continue the office's work.

One result of this development was that Moritz Schilling turned up on our doorstep one day, complete with wife, child and luggage. He announced that he was transferring the national headquarters of Misrachi to Steckelsdorf. We squeezed up and vacated a room in the summer villa for him.

I should say at this point that Schilling and his colleagues from the Palestine Office dispatched no further refugee ships to Palestine. In his time in the Berlin office, Schilling had made a major contribution towards helping Jewish young people. From now on he played an influential but rather less gratifying role at Steckelsdorf.

It was his misfortune to take himself far too seriously. His opinions became rulings, his announcements proclamations — even revelations. As long as he had been an infrequent visitor from Berlin, his relentlessly agitated face had inspired a certain awe. Once we had it before our eyes the whole time, day in and day out, the halo faded rapidly. Concern about his dwindling prestige drove him to seek out fresh leader roles. He became an active organiser wherever there was anything to be organised — and unhappily also where there was not. We had to exercise like a boy-scout troop in response to his Hebrew commands. In synagogue he performed as cantor and prayer leader. He also pushed himself forward as our music teacher and conductor, in which role his favourite activity was rehearsing Misrachi propaganda songs. We failed to see the point of this: the ideals of the Misrachi movement had long been taken for granted on the training farm.

Schilling's Zionist propaganda had the effect of shaking my own Zionist convictions slightly. However, my friends were able to prevent my confusing the nature and essence of Zionism with the nature and essence of Moritz Schilling.

Schilling was married to an attractive woman from Cologne, who showed great discretion in the way in which she adapted herself to the life of the community. She lent a hand in the sewing-room. Their eight-year-old son, as the only child on the farm, led a somewhat lonely existence, for all the affection that was showered on him.

Out of the blue, our training farm was asked to take ten *chaverim* from a Palestine preparation camp in Hesse, which had been disbanded. These were mature men, not lads. One brought his fiancée with him. The oldest member of the group was forty-two and had fought at the front in the final year of the 1914–18 war. Fitting them into our already overcrowded accommodation was not easy. However, with much patience and goodwill on both sides we managed it.

Imagine our horror when, shortly afterwards, a second group of seventeen *chaverim* turned up from a camp near Hamburg! Where were they all going to sleep, let alone stow their belongings? How were a hundred people going to squeeze into our dining-room?

But when we got a closer look at the newcomers, such worries struck us as mean and petty, for they were all very much younger than ourselves. In fact, we felt tempted to ask them, 'But, children, whatever are you doing in a labour camp? You ought to be at school!'

After a week the new boys and girls had overcome their shyness and were beginning to feel at home. It was only then that we realised what a significant addition had been made to our community — in numbers, in life, in cheerfulness and in conviviality. The dining-room was so packed that many of us could get only one hand to our plates; the other hand had to lie idle under the table. But what a delightful crush! My eyes never wearied of gazing at that jostling throng of faces, some laughing, some thoughtful, some childishly serious.

Blumenfeld had the wisdom to send the young ones to Habermann's to work. Habermann, who was regarded as the most humane of all our employers, ran a large market garden in Neue Schleuse, where he also employed French and Polish prisoners of war. He was rumoured to have received one official reprimand already for treating his prisoners too indulgently.

The Steckelsdorf training farm, from being a mere transit station on the way to Palestine, was increasingly acquiring an existence in its own right. The community now comprised young adults of both sexes, adolescents, an eight-year-old boy and several men in the prime of life. In the summer of 1941 we were joined by a seventy-year old doctor and a sixty-year old accountant. We were clearly on the way to becoming what amounted to a natural village community. The image of that community bore the stamp of youth, which gave us a feeling of growing.

What a world of difference there was between our way of life and that of the members of Jewish congregations in the towns and cities of Germany, who lived in a context of collapse and decay! By degrees, Steckelsdorf came to be regarded as a place of refuge from Jew-hating neighbours in the city and from the pitiless assembly lines of the munitions industry. The fathers and siblings of some of our *chaverim* came to see the farm manager to ask whether they too might be allowed to live and work on the training farm.

Richard Heymann

The groups from Hesse and Hamburg had arrived at the farm with their own youth leaders. Steckelsdorf now had a manager, a head gardener and three youth leaders, on top of the national administration of the Misrachi youth movement in the person of Moritz Schilling. This led to all sorts of disputes over jurisdiction and precedence. The one who wanted to be top dog was poor Schilling — to his own and our displeasure. However, it quickly emerged that the man who commanded the greatest respect was one of the newcomers: Richard Heymann, the 24-year-old youth leader of the Hamburg group.

A native of Berlin, where he had attended the Siegmundshof Jewish secondary school, he was now the only person on the training farm who had completed his *Abitur*, the school-leaving examination that was a requirement for university entrance. The guiding passions of his life were Hebrew and German literature and music. In the jealously guarded bookshelf that stood beside his bed, works by Nietzsche, Kierkegaard and Rilke occupied pride of place.

It was not until we had known each other for some months that

124

Richard confided in me that he wrote poetry. One day, with a smile, he showed me a volume of his poems. I could not read a word of them. They were written in a secret script of his own invention.

It goes without saying that even Steckelsdorf had its inmates to whom the well-articulated German of an *Abiturient* was inherently suspect. Richard's literary and artistic inclinations, his diffident glance and his high-pitched voice were insufficiently manly for the more robust among the Zionist pioneers.

I could see what it was that many of his admirers missed in him. Just occasionally he struck us all as being rather too unworldly. When he arched his eyebrows and subjected the most trivial, everyday questions to critical analysis, even I could not help teasing him. He might so easily have found himself dismissed as a wet aesthete! However, his manner was too modest for that. No job was beneath him. And when there were important decisions to be made, it was often Richard who took the lead.

When Richard heard himself described as an intellectual, he reacted with an ironic smile. Most people on the training farm pigeonholed him as the *tarbutnik* or 'culture specialist' of our kibbutz. This title, too, Richard would accept only with a smile.

His Torah lessons drew a large audience, and this was not only because Richard was a lively teacher. With his thorough knowledge of and philosophic approach to the subject, he was agreeably different from the usual kind of youth leader. His method of discussing biblical texts was characterised by a disciplined objectivity and a strict avoidance of rhetoric and pulpit pathos.

As to his own religious views, he was very reluctant to express himself. It gradually became clear to me that this reluctance stemmed from a sense of religious modesty. I cannot say how Richard behaved in synagogue during prayers, for I could never bring myself to look round at him; I sensed that, for him, prayer was a very private matter.

Richard exerted a wholesome influence on our community, neutralising much of the damage that might otherwise have been caused by Schilling's organising zeal. I owe a very special debt of gratitude to my association with Richard. Many of our conversations made an unforgettable impression on me. I was delighted when, in May 1941, Richard started coming to the tree nursery in place of one of my other workmates. Our seeing so much of each other led to a firm friendship. And when some time later Richard became engaged to Lotte Tauber, our friendship was even strengthened.

Where is Richard today? Where is Lotte? Where are all the other young men and women? In the two parts of Germany, in Austria, and in other supposedly constitutional countries thousands are still walking around unpunished who as SS camp guards and ghetto sentries once performed their indescribable 'duties'. *They* know what happened to my friends.

Tree-nursery talk

One evening in the late spring of 1941, the manager announced at supper, 'As from next week, work for everyone will commence at eight and continue until six!'

Three weeks later we had all grown accustomed to the new timetable and protests were no longer heard. Evening classes were cut short. Resignedly, groups of us would march or ride out of the gate at half past seven in the morning.

The new regime was hardest on those labouring on large farms. The group growing flowers and vegetables in Habermann's market garden had the least awful time of it. Our job in the tree nursery was hard, too, but there were always easier days in between, when the hours passed peacefully and smoothly amid the sun-warmed, sweet-smelling foliage.

We preferred to work in adjacent rows whenever we could. The conversations we used to have between one row and the next are among my happiest memories. With Richard Heymann, Fred the prankster, and a clumsy fellow by the name of Sabre in one work gang, there was no end to the merry nonsense that got bandied about!

Sabre was a skinny lad who had learnt his dairy farming in the Bavarian Alps. The most salient portion of his anatomy — a disproportionately long and ramrod-straight nose — provided Fred with an inexhaustible source of fun. The nose was the real Sabre, Fred would say; everything else was extra. And Sabre really ought to buy a scabbard for that snout to stop the air being constantly cut to ribbons!

The talk rambled from one subject to another — from food shortages to British mandatory policy in Palestine and from the moods and mannerisms of our employer, the tree nurseryman Schulze, to speculations as to when the war would end and what would become of us afterwards.

When Richard and I were alone, the conversation often turned to questions of literature and art. I particularly remember the musical discussions triggered by one or the other of us humming a tune as we hoed and weeded. Under the spell of a Bach cantata or a piece from Handel's *Messiah* that we had been listening to the previous evening, we never tired of analysing compositional structure and meditating on the twin miracles of musical creation and the listener's emotional involvement in music.

In the heat of debate our movements tended to become slower. The other *chaverim* began to get ahead of us with their hoeing, and when the gap grew too wide, reproachful looks would be cast in our direction. We needed no second warning, knowing full well that our talks must never lead to the others having to do more work than we did. They already looked at us slightly askance, calling us the 'highbrows'. So we would shut up and put our backs into the hoeing for a bit until we had drawn level with the others once again.

There were also conversations — some serious, some humorous — in which everyone took part. Once all the latest political jokes had been told, Fred would keep us constantly amused with his coarse pranks. And when Schulze joined us with spade or billhook, he contributed to the entertainment willy-nilly. During the winter months he had kept himself pretty much to himself. Now it happened more and more often that he began to chat about things that had little or nothing to do with the job in hand.

I recall with particular pleasure Schulze's sceptical remarks on the subject of archaeology. One afternoon when he was working with us, digging over a field — he positively radiated good humour that day — his spade hit a broken piece of flowerpot. Picking it up, he showed it to us with a sly smile: 'Look at that — 20,000 years old at least! The professor can have it for cash. He's had plenty of stuff for nothing.'

'Which professor is that?' I asked.

'Last year, it was — you hadn't come then — this fellow wanted to do some excavating. One of your real cleverdicks. Tried to tell me there used to be a village here 10,000 years ago. He'd got it all worked out.'

'Do you not hold with archaeology, then, Mr Schulze?'

'Oh, ay — they know it all, they do. They can work everything out. The moon's a million miles away, New Year fell on 1 January, and a pound of sugar'll cost you fourpence. Multiply by a hundred, and these bits of pottery come out at a thousand years old. What, you believe in all that figuring?'

'No', I replied, 'I don't believe it is possible to calculate precisely the age of excavated pottery. But the distance between the moon and the earth is an established fact. With a pencil and paper, I could show you the way they work it out. We learnt how to do it at school.'

'Blessed are they that believe, I say.'

'Do you think it's all rubbish, then, Mr Schulze? But how do you account for the fact that, in your calendar, the phases of the moon are calculated so exactly in advance?'

'I don't know about that, but no one's going to try and tell me how far away the moon is! Has one of these learned professors been up there, then?'

'There's no need to go to the moon for that. In science, many things are found out indirectly. This place where we are now, for example — a long time ago, this was all under water. Rathenow and Berlin once swarmed with whales and polyps and crustaceans. There was no one around to see it, but science was able to discover it was so.'

'Here, hold on!'

'Don't you accept that the sea once covered this place? What is all this chalk doing on dry land? How does shelly limestone get into the mountains?'

'How does cow-shit get on the roof? The damnedest things happen!'

An argument in which the clever party treats the less clever with amused indulgence is always entertaining. It is particularly so when both parties regard themselves as the cleverer.

Schulze had very decided views on everything: science, religion, different makes of spade and billhook, the village schoolmaster, the parish priest, the farmers of Neue Schleuse, the relative importance and status of different callings — that of tree nurseryman being immeasurably greater and higher than that of farmer, for instance — the risks of the war in the air and many other topics.

On one occasion the talk turned to the question of life after death. 'You believe in *that*?' Schulze asked in amazement. 'When it says in the paper, "He died for Führer and fatherland, his spirit lives on", you reckon it means his spirit goes on living up there, then' — he took his pipe out of his mouth and pointed skyward — 'somewhere behind the ninth cloud on the left? Never!' he chuckled. 'Doesn't mean a thing. All it means is, we'll remember him kindly.'

We laughed with him. But his example had made us think. He died for Führer and fatherland! What could be going through Schulze's mind at those words? Unfortunately, he did not pursue the matter. Sometimes his conversation seemed to be heading for the subject of Hitler, but he always took evasive action at the last minute. We should dearly have loved to know what the man for whom we laboured day in and day out thought of Hitler.

And what was Schulze's opinion of Jews? He was certainly no out-and-out Jew-hater; otherwise he would never have got into conversation with us and would not have allowed his five-year-old son to play with us. Still, the flood of anti-Jewish propaganda was unlikely to have swept over him without leaving some trace.

Yet surely we, his six assistants, were living contradictions of all the calumnies? He might deride us as 'educated city folk', but what, looking at us, could he discover of that 'inferior Jewish character'? And where were our 'Jewish racial characteristics' (as it happened, only one of us looked at all 'Jewish')? And what about the 'Jewish aversion to physical work'? He knew that we came from an agricultural training establishment, and he had found us to be good workers.

Well, one summer day it came to light, Schulze's opinion of Jews.

Early in the morning he summoned the butcher from the village to slaughter his one and only pig. Richard, Sabre and I were to help drive the sow out of the sty beside the tool-shed. Richard with a sow! The sight of that educated, highly-strung pig-tamer made me laugh. We teased one another mercilessly. In fact, none of us proved especially good at the job. The sow's piercing squeals and frantic looks rattled us so badly that at one point she came close to escaping from us altogether and running off through the plantations. An hour later, thank goodness, it was all over. The sow was no longer squealing or looking wildly about her. She was hanging up in the barn by her back legs, all fat and pink like some giant maggot. Her ears drooped harmlessly.

That afternoon, Schulze enthusiastically drew our attention to the many benefits of pig breeding. 'Nothing goes to waste, you see. Every little bit gets used.' He asked why we did not eat pork. We had to explain to him the meaning of 'kosher'. He made a scornful gesture. Years ago in Rathenow, he told us, he had known a Jew who had eaten ham and 'it hadn't done him any harm'. Furthermore, he had been 'a real Jew', with a hooked nose and horn-rimmed spectacles and always dressed just so.

'There was a wealthy bastard if ever I saw one — stank of money from every pore. Jews, you know, have a way of getting rich in no time at all. Arrive on the scrounge, and a couple of years later they've got fat bankrolls and posh villas and they're living like kings. Whilst our sort have to sweat and drudge all the way from cot to plot. And what's behind it all, eh? You can't fool me! Honest toil never made anyone rich. Jews'd rather not work at all. Far too strenuous for those fine gentlemen. They'd rather strut about smoking a fat cigar and have other people do their slaving. They know all about doing deals — crooked ones, for preference. Got contacts everywhere. Spend all day writing letters and talking to their cronies on the telephone. You show me a single Jewish craftsman — never mind about farming or horticulture! Oh, no — might get their nice white shirts dirty and damage their dainty fingers!'

During this speech, we looked at one another and laughed. We laughed because we were embarrassed and because what he said sounded so comical. He was not saying anything new about the Jews; we had just not expected to hear that sort of thing from his lips.

Why not, actually? Now that he was speaking the words, they seemed to suit him in precisely the same way as the green hunter's hat on his head and the everlasting pipe in his mouth. 'How perfect he is — in his way!' I thought in amusement. Whether he was talking about village schoolmasters or archaeologists, Jews or peach trees, he never denied his nature for a moment.

Not until several days later — I am afraid I have never been very quick off the mark — did it occur to me that we ought to have asked him: 'But, Mr Schulze, have you completely forgotten whom you are talking to? You're trying to tell *us* what Jews are like?'

Arguing religion among the espaliers

After the introduction of forced labour for Jews, there were no more rumours about imminent deportations. Many a Jew whom the labour department classified as unfit for work did everything in his power to get the verdict overturned and to make a useful contribution to the war effort.

Many believing Jews had — for the first time — to work on the Sabbath. There was no conflict of conscience involved, because a refusal would have been tantamount to suicide. According to the law of the Torah, it was even their duty to work.

Nevertheless, this enforced profanation of the Jews' holy day represented a gross invasion of the rest of their private lives. The cohesion of families suffered severely as a result. The synagogues were virtually empty, with only children, old men and invalids still attending. Hounded and harried by the treadmill of forced labour, Jews were left with little time — between sleep, air-raid warnings and the often long walk to work — for collecting their thoughts and saying their prayers.

Fortunately the new forced labour decree did not entail any fresh difficulties for us at Steckelsdorf. How glad we were that Blumenfeld had chosen our own employers while it was still possible! Those employers had grown used to and were still quite happy with conditions that had been agreed months previously. We were possibly the only group of Jews in the whole of Germany who did not

130

have to work on the Sabbath.

As the labour shortage became more acute, increasing numbers of agricultural businesses went over to Sunday working. Our employer, however, seemed to be determined to keep Sunday as a day of rest. We put it to him that he should let us work in his tree nursery on our own on Sundays; there was no need for him to have his day off disturbed. But our suggestion was rejected.

Schulze's inflexible attitude kept us guessing and caused us not a little concern, particularly since he had repeatedly said how far behind we were with the summer jobs. He had also hinted that a further increase in our hours would sooner or later be unavoidable. It was why we had suggested working on Sundays. So what was his objection?

A few days later, as we were pruning some young espalier apple trees, he finally came out with it.

'Listen, why do you have to celebrate your Sunday on a Saturday, of all days?' It clearly embarrassed him to put the question. His green eyes threw us only the briefest of glances before he bent back to the tree he was pruning. 'I mean, I don't want to take your religion away from you. But why on earth must you have a different Sunday from everyone else?'

'It's the other way around, Mr Schulze,' I replied. 'The Christian Sunday stems from the Jewish Sabbath. It was only afterwards that they moved it to Sunday.'

'You don't say!'

'It was. We learnt that at school. The early Christians knew no other holy day except Saturday. They celebrated the Sabbath the same as the Jews did.'

'Now wait a minute!'

'Have you never heard of the Council of Nicaea? One of the things decided at the First Council of Nicaea, some 300 years after Jesus, was to move the Sabbath to Sunday.'

'Never heard of that. Anyway, sounds as if it all comes out of a book, what you're telling me there. I haven't got that much education.'

In my scholarly enthusiasm, I began to explain it all in greater detail, but he cut me off after only a few sentences: 'If you don't mind my saying so, that's as may be — I'm not saying it isn't. But now everyone celebrates Sunday. You ought to go along with the majority.'

'The people who celebrate Sunday aren't anything like the majority! There are more non-Christians in Asia alone than there are Christians in the entire world. And even if they were the majority, that wouldn't be any reason for people of a different faith to go along with them. You wouldn't do something contrary to what you believed, would you, Mr Schulze, just because the majority believed something different from you?'

'Never mind what I believe! I'll tell you what I believe: seven pounds of beef make a damned good soup. . . .'

As Schulze went stalking off, we put our heads together to confer. What would happen now? Sabre reckoned that our employer was quite capable of going to the labour department and making us work on the Sabbath.

'He won't do that,' Richard said. 'He might lose all of us if he did. His tree nursery is hardly vital to the war effort, is it?'

That discussion with Schulze went round and round in my head for days afterwards. I asked Richard what he thought. His view was that while my argument to the effect that there were many more non-Christians in the world than Christians was perfectly correct, it had been out of place: as far as Europe was concerned, the Jews were in fact living among a Christian majority. I should have done better to concentrate on the inexchangeability of the day that was consecrated to the Lord and on the role played by the Sabbath in the religious controversy between Jews and Christians. For the Jews, it would have constituted an unprecedented denial of their faith suddenly to call Sunday the Lord's Day.

'Ah, but you'd have had to translate all that into tree-nursery language!' one of our number pointed out.

Hunger

We had to accept a further increase in the number of hours we worked per week. So did the *chaverim* who were working elsewhere. We were all now putting in up to eleven hours a day. That is nothing unusual for a farmworker. But who can work for eleven hours a day on a virtually empty stomach? Added to which, a new decree enacted by the authorities of the Third Reich said that Jews might no longer own bicycles. Now, at the beginning and end of a long working day we also had a long walk.

We had suffered from malnourishment in the days before there had been any talk of war work, whether 'voluntary' or compulsory. I remember my surprise, soon after arriving at Steckelsdorf in December 1939, to find that we endured worse food shortages living on a farm than my family did in the city. My new friends told me the reason for this. The training farm grew its own grain but had to have it milled under supervision. The hens were all accounted for and the egg supply calculated in advance. The milk had likewise to be delivered. The little we were able to retain for our own use without arousing suspicion might have sufficed for the manager and the head gardener; for seventy hungry stomachs it was not even enough to make a doughnut. Animals slaughtered in accordance with Jewish ritual were not to be had in Germany, so that such meat coupons as we were issued with remained unused. And the bread that the village baker supplied for us Jews was of very poor quality, even by wartime standards.

Our community now comprised 100 hungry stomachs, and with forced labour beginning to make extra demands on our strength, Blumenfeld toyed with the idea of simply keeping back more of the farm's own produce. But the risk attached seemed to him to be too great. He could not bring himself to take it.

The four girls who ran the training-farm kitchen put an enormous amount of effort and imagination into trying to keep a hundred hungry stomachs at least halfway satisfied. The only real improvement they came up with was a different distribution of the existing starvation rations. It was decided no longer to serve bread for breakfast but only a watery soup that, while it did nothing to still our hunger, at least put something warm in our stomachs. This made it possible to give those working away from Steckelsdorf three double slices of bread instead of two. Laid together, the three double slices measured about one and a half inches in thickness. It was up to each recipient to see how he or she got through a day's work on that. The supper that awaited us when we returned in the evening usually consisted of a hash of swedes, carrots and blighted potatoes.

An urgent consideration in these circumstances was how best to distribute the three sandwiches over the period from seven in the morning until six in the evening. Whichever way we distributed them, they did not take long to eat. This left us with something like ten minutes to spare in our breakfast and tea breaks and as much as twenty to twenty-five minutes in the lunch break. We got into the habit of spending the spare minutes reading.

We read partly to take our minds off our hunger but even more in order to satisfy a hunger of a different sort. We had literally no other time for reading. After an exhausting day's work, our evening classes claimed any energy we had left, and next morning we were obliged to rise at five, even though early-morning gymnastics had long since disappeared from the programme.

So we seized on those few minutes during breaks. We made a solemn pact not to disturb one another while reading. With the onset of winter, Schulze let us use a small, heated room beside the laundry in the cellar of his house as our 'coffee hut'. In fact, more books than coffee were consumed there.

Richard and I decided to read the same books and to discuss what we had read over our work. 'Life is short, and time is precious,' he said. 'So why not start at the top, so to speak?' His suggestion was Goethe's *Faust*.

We got hold of two copies of the play and of Friedrich's commentary, both in the inexpensive Reclam edition, and embarked on a systematic study of the work. Thanks to Richard's knowledge, our readings were followed by fruitful discussions. Our breaks became more precious to us than ever. One day, as we were absorbed in the scene where Faust and Mephistopheles are in Auerbach's cellar, Schulze poked his nose round the door of the 'coffee hut' and asked where we had put the whetstone for the billhooks. We found it hard to conceal our irritation at the interruption.

We needed to practise the greatest thrift with everything — time, food, muscle-power, whatever was vital to us. But no amount of thrift, no system of distribution, however sophisticated, could make up for being perpetually short of food. We often found ourselves in that state of unnatural tension in which the body labours on like a wound-up clockwork toy and one no longer feels hungry but only weak and light-headed.

Every available opportunity to lay aside one's spade for a couple of minutes and take a breather was welcome — even a visit to the latrine. When the loamy soil was just too heavy to work, we used to make for the little hut in the middle of the field without waiting for the call of nature. Gradually a tacit agreement emerged among us not to spend too long in there and never to go out of turn. None of us was to dodge work at the expense of the others. In time the straw-thatched thunderbox became a second reading hut.

Eventually Schulze noticed something. 'Huh! Must have dozed off in there!' he would mutter whenever one of our number was absent for too long.

Schulze, like the other employers, paid us for our work at the set rate. Out of our wages, the training farm covered all our shopping expenses, though since everything was severely rationed it was only possible to use part of the money. The greater part of our wages went to the state in the form of income tax and war taxes. What was left simply lay around as useless wartime currency. Swindled out of a proper return for our labour, we saw it as no robbery when we slipped in the odd illegal break. Indeed, we were deliberately stingy with our strength. Who knew what our undernourished bodies might yet have to face? The tempo of our digging used to speed up appreciably when Schulze approached. When he went away, back it dropped again. How degrading our existence had become! It was poor consolation to know that the prisoners of war and the countless other slaves of the war effort shared it with us.

One morning in June, as we were hoeing and weeding in the field beside Schulze's house, the sound of a radio reached us from the veranda. With a start, I recognised the Mozart *Divertimento* that father had so often played with my brother Jakob. Schulze turned the volume up and came out of the house, beaming all over his face. 'There, what more could you want? Music while you work! Put your backs into it, now! Ought to go a bit swifter to music.'

Our employer was occasionally gross but he was never rude. He clearly hated having to urge us on to greater exertions.

One day, when work was once again proceeding rather slowly, he asked for the first time: 'Tell me, how much do you get to eat a day?' When we told him, he pressed his lips together and was silent. Next morning he brought us a few bread coupons. His gift put us on the spot: should we keep the coupons and make use of them or not?

Sabre said fiercely, 'No, it wounds my pride to accept alms!'

Fred gave him a stinging rejoinder: 'It wounds his pride! The fine fellow won't accept alms! You're nothing but a workhorse, mate! They up your rations so they can get more work out of you! Ever seen a proud workhorse, eh?'

The dilemma resolved itself. We explained to Schulze that unfortunately we could not use the bread coupons ourselves. Jews were allowed to buy bread only with coupons stamped with a 'J'. Schulze merely shrugged. It never occurred to him to send his wife round to the baker for us. We had to be content with his gesture.

135

CHAPTER 7

Creeping Despair

The net starts to tighten

It happened one afternoon in June 1941.

The whole tree nursery was decked in bright green foliage. We were busy pruning young mirabelle trees. I remember the way the leaves clung to one's bare forearms, releasing their fragrance into the balmy summer air. Although we were working in adjacent rows, there was little conversation. All that could be heard was the click of our billhooks, the rustle of the foliage and the perpetual hum of insects.

Schulze came out, unsheathed his billhook and started on a row of trees. As he drew level with us he stopped working and stood up: 'Heard the news?' he said. 'One hundred and eighty German divisions have just invaded Russia!'

We stared at him in stunned disbelief. The news must have come as a shock to him, too. For the first time he spoke his mind to us on the subject of the war: 'Who wanted this war anyway? Tell me that!' he exclaimed in a voice that betrayed deep concern. 'Wasn't it peace we all wanted?'

Whether it was the carnage at the front that filled him with horror or the fear that he might be sent to the front himself, his whole demeanour expressed a genuine revulsion against the war. And as he gave vent to his feelings, how human he sounded! A deep sense of dread at the slaughter and destruction that now seemed to stretch into the unforeseeable future bound us together — him, the *Parteigenosse*, as Nazi 'party comrades' were called, and us, his Jewish forced labour.

'Wasn't it peace we all wanted?' It was a cry from the heart. We were sorely tempted to answer it and to have a proper conversation with Schulze, a real dialogue. But we merely heard his words and nodded in speechless agreement.

After that, there was an uncomfortable silence between the rows of mirabelles. Once again, only the click of the billhooks, the rustling leaves and the hum of insects could be heard. We kept stealing glances at Schulze through the foliage.

Did we guess his thoughts correctly? Did he guess ours? His complaint had been not about the Russians but about the war! Eight years of Nazi terror had given us a very keen ear. Was Schulze beginning to regret ever having voted for Hitler?

We felt ourselves wise by comparison. We had long known the truth about National Socialism. Now it was almost with sympathy that we looked across at the disillusioned *Parteigenosse* — a silent, anxious figure working his way along a row of plum trees.

When Schulze finally went away, we put our heads together: 'God! Where will it all end?' 'And what'll become of us?' 'They'll do to Russia what they did to Czechoslovakia and Poland!' 'Shall we *ever* get to Palestine?' 'More to the point, what's going to happen to the millions of Jews in Eastern Europe — and to Jews in Germany?' 'I don't think they'll have time to worry about Jews now. They'll have enough on their plate, dealing with the Red Army!'

How naïve were our fears, even at that late date! What Hitler's troops actually perpetrated in Poland and Russia far outstripped our worst forebodings. Today we know the whole story: Himmler and his henchmen did have time to worry about the Jews. Gestapo, Sipo and SD followed hot on the heels of the armoured divisions of the Wehrmacht. Outrages against Jews began to occur only days after the invasion of Russia. The German security police who staged those pogroms in the occupied towns behind the eastern front kept a low profile at first. In the bloodbath in Kaunas in Lithuania, they allowed released convicts to beat hundreds of Jews to death with iron bars.*

We knew nothing of all this at the time. But we were soon to find out that, Russian campaign or no Russian campaign, the rulers of the Reich were relentlessly pursuing their policy of persecution of the Jews. In September 1941, little more than two months after the invasion of Russia, the 'Police Ordinance Concerning the Marking of Jews' was promulgated. The news reached us as we returned from work one day. We saw a number of *chaverim* engaged in a heated discussion by the gate of the training farm. 'Have you heard?' they called to us. 'Jews now have to wear a yellow patch and aren't allowed to travel without police permission!'

We refused to believe them at first. Where had they heard that?

* See G. Schoenberner, *Der gelbe Stern*, Hamburg, 1960.

Clearly this was a masochistic figment of somebody's fear-ridden imagination!

But it was true. The newspaper was passed round; we all read it for ourselves. The paper also carried an illustration of the yellow patch. It consisted of a Star of David with the word 'Jew' written across it in a hideous parody of Hebrew script. Apart from the picture, the announcement looked like a page from the criminal code. It was neatly laid out in paragraphs and sub-paragraphs. A preamble in bold type was followed by the police authority's implementing regulations in typical officialese: 'In Paragraph . . . permanent domicile shall be deemed to mean. . . . A public place shall be construed as any place where. . . .' The document concluded with Paragraph 6: 'This police ordinance shall take effect on the fourteenth day after its promulgation'.

We read it, reread it, looked at one another and said nothing. For the first time even the optimists were speechless.

Two weeks later we marched off to work with the yellow Star of David on our chests. Each of us carried in his pocket a police permit conferring on him the special right to leave the training farm before six and eight o'clock in the morning to go to work and the further right to return to the farm before nightfall. The permits had been issued, stamped and signed by the village policeman in Neue Schleuse.

Our employers either 'did not notice' our badges or, like Schulze, made some witty remark about them — and that was that, as far as they were concerned. After a few days, everyone we had anything to do with took them for granted.

It was different in the towns. Schulze drove us into Rathenow in a lorry one day to collect horse manure from the police riding school, and for the first time we found ourselves subjected to ugly abuse as wearers of the star. But what we endured in that one hour was nothing in comparison to what Jews living in towns had to put up with all day and every day.

It did occasionally happen that 'Aryan' Berliners would whisper to their Jewish neighbours: 'Your badge is our shame.' The younger generation, though, educated in the new spirit, saw the yellow star as an invitation to throw stones. Some even made the cynical suggestion that Jews should be made to wear a second patch on their backs so that they could be recognised — and pelted — from behind.

Amongst themselves, Jews whispered, 'This is the beginning of the end!' Others cited those famous words of the Zionist leader Robert Weltsch, uttered in the context of the Nazi campaign to brand Jewish businesses in 1933: 'Tragt ihn mit Stolz, den gelben Fleck!' (Sport the yellow patch with pride!).*

Most Jews showed themselves in the street as little as possible. When they could not avoid going out, they used to slink along the walls of buildings. It was painful for them to feel the hate-filled glances of passing 'Aryans' directed at them. It was equally painful for them when decent 'Aryans' tactfully avoided looking at them, much as one avoids looking at cripples.

Many wore a permanent blush of shame. Their self-conscious smiles constantly begged forgiveness. They felt themselves to be guilty because it said in the papers that they were to blame for everything. They dared not lift their eyes because every loudspeaker within earshot was shouting that they were criminals. They felt ashamed of their dark hair and their 'Semitic' noses; they felt ashamed of their defencelessness against the street urchins; they felt ashamed because they were still walking around, in the flesh, with their stars on their chests; and they felt ashamed of their shame.

One day in October 1941 a message reached us from the Reichs-vereinigung that from now on Jews were forbidden to emigrate.

Sabre's reaction was immediate: 'Didn't I prophesy from the outset that Germany would soon be one big concentration camp for Jews? I'm telling you: we'll not survive this war!'

'Now we needn't fight for places on the Danube steamers any more,' Moshe Heilborn remarked sarcastically. 'And the British navy will no longer have to patrol the Palestine coast. The British government ought to send Hitler a thankyou telegram!'

So deeply embittered were we that we had almost ceased to differentiate between the men of the SS and the British soldiers and sailors who stood gun in hand, cutting us off from the Holy Land.

It was not the first time that we had talked about 'surviving the war' and 'getting away with our lives'. We had used such express-ions on the training farm back in December 1939. At that time, they had been virtually synonymous with 'reaching Palestine' and 'es-caping from Germany' — in other words, becoming human again, no longer being an outcast.

Now the word 'survive' had taken on a fresh and deadly serious connotation for us.

In the dining-room that evening Schilling called a general meet-ing for half an hour after supper. He wished to have a word with us about the changed situation. A murmur went round the tables. One *chaver* was heard to mutter, 'Wouldn't you know! Got to have his say.

* On the occasion of the boycott of 1 April 1933 the NSDAP gave instructions for placards — a 'yellow patch on a black background' — to be posted on the boycotted premises. Weltsch issued his celebrated watchword in the Zionist newspaper *Jüdische Rundschau* in April 1933.

You can't snuff it around here without Moritz holding forth.'

However, the meeting surprised us all. Schilling did indeed 'hold forth', but this time he struck exactly the right note. He told us that, for an indeterminate period, we were now prisoners; none of us knew what lay ahead. So now was the time to direct all our endeavours and focus all our plans on our future life in Palestine. How would it be, for example, if by our own efforts we got to the point, here in Germany, where we could speak fluent Hebrew?

Never had a suggestion from Schilling's lips met with greater approval. What a splendid idea, to set ourselves such a goal just when we needed one most!

The Hebrew language class enjoyed a dramatic revival. Since our working day left us with so little spare time and energy, we introduced new teaching methods. Labels were stuck on many of the objects in the dining-room and in the dormitories, giving the Hebrew word for each. As a result, we assimilated vocabulary without effort. Groups of volunteers formed who for certain periods of the day resolved to speak nothing but Hebrew. On Sundays, when some of the outside workers helped on the training farm, we allotted the jobs in such a way that those *chaverim* who were better at Hebrew could help the others.

The new drive to learn Hebrew was sustained for a long time. Even Schulze saw something of it. He happened to pop into our 'coffee hut' during a break one day when we were in the middle of reading a Hebrew novella. He took the book from my hand, looked at it in perplexity, held it sideways, turned it upside down, and finally said, 'You can *read* that? Makes my head spin.'

Only for a day or two did we appreciate the grisly significance of our yellow stars. Then we grew accustomed to walking around with them on our chests. We grew accustomed to the ban on emigration. We grew accustomed to living our difficult life day after day and to being appalled by each fresh curb on Jewish rights. Months went by. The yellow patches on our overalls got dirty and were duly laundered. Lethal was the last thing they looked.

Repatriations

In October 1941 three of our *chaverim* received a police order to pack their things and be ready to leave for Poland on a certain date. They were German born and bred, but they possessed Polish nationality. Altogether we had seven young people with Polish passports. The Neue Schleuse village policeman gave us to understand that the other four would be summoned shortly. It was a 'repatriation measure', he said.

Among those concerned was Lotte, Richard's fiancée. As they shook hands in parting, both were smiling. I shall never forget that farewell smile. In the evening I was overcome by a sudden attack of nausea. I went to bed immediately after supper and turned my face to the wall, wanting only to be alone.

Some time later a letter arrived for Richard from Warsaw. The other repatriates also sent word. Lotte wrote that she was in a labour camp, helping in the kitchen. In that and her ensuing letters, Lotte kept up her attempt to reassure Richard. She was having an easier time of it in Warsaw than she had had at the training farm, she wrote. How typical of Lotte! From letters smuggled out from other deportees, we learnt that Jews in Warsaw ate things we at Steckelsdorf threw in the dustbin.

Richard sent food parcels to Warsaw. Coming home from work in the evening, he might find a couple of slices of bread or a few potatoes on his bed, together with a note 'For Lotte'.

Towards the end of October two other *chaverim* received letters from their parents in Leipzig and Stuttgart respectively, telling them to pack their bags in a hurry and rejoin their parents, who had received notice of resettlement. In both cases the people concerned were of German — not Polish — nationality. The parents wanted their children with them for the move, lest the family be split up for an unforeseeable period.

Later we learnt that other Jewish parents had done the exact opposite: they had taken pains to find other people to look after their children in order that they, at least, might be spared the ordeal of deportation. There was a rumour that compulsory resettlement was directed mainly against older Jews and those who were unemployable. According to another rumour, Jews were being resettled by families whenever the family was living together. So complete was the general uncertainty regarding the actions of the authorities and the fate of the deportees that the most contradictory speculations flourished.

In the autumn of 1941 many a Jew learnt to say his prayers — after a lifetime of merely reeling off the prayer-book text.

A letter from father

In November 1941 I received an alarming letter from my father. It was not just the contents of the letter that I found disconcerting; my father's rashness worried me too. In the Third Reich, even children had learnt to express themselves in veiled terms when writing letters

141

or speaking over the telephone. My father's way of disguising what he said was hopelessly amateurish. Instead of putting dangerous information into some form of code, he simply sprinkled his German prose with Hebrew words and phrases. Anyone could have guessed that he was trying to hide something from the censor.

This time he did not even use Hebrew. No doubt it was his agitation that made him so incautious. I remember the letter well; it went more or less as follows:

Dear Ezra,
        I hope this finds you in good health. You would not believe what a delightful surprise your pound of peas gave us! With their help, Mama was able to cook a substantial lunch several days running. We had not eaten so well in a long time.

Mama's health is not quite up to the mark. The reason is Jakob's deportation, of course. I wrote to you about it. Now I am able to give you more details.

As you know, Jakob had to give up his job at the paint works after the introduction of forced labour for Jews. Since then he had been building roads. Five weeks ago, Jakob was suddenly sent home from work early. He was given only a short while in which to prepare for 'evacuation to a labour camp'. Mama packed him some provisions for the journey. He dressed in a great hurry. Then we had a fierce argument as we said goodbye. Jakob insisted on taking his violin with him. I advised strongly against it. Where's the sense in taking such a valuable instrument along to a labour camp? I wanted to keep it here until his return. But you know how obstinate Jakob is! He just wouldn't be told, and in the end he took the thing with him. Thank God, we had that sign of life from him from Posen,* as I mentioned. He has written twice since then. He is still in the same labour camp, and he urgently requests food parcels, although he knows full well how little we have to eat ourselves. That gives you some idea of the starvation rations they give them there. Naturally, we do what we can to help him. Compared to him, perhaps, we're still living well.

It is of the greatest importance for Mama's peace of mind that we manage to do more for Jakob. He's allowed post once a fortnight. For the whole two weeks all Mama thinks about is putting together Jakob's next food parcel. That's all she is concerned about. It is also her only consolation. Guess what! That kind shoemaker gave us a whole pound of sugar for the second parcel!

Leon is still working at the German Armaments and Munitions Factory, and Toni is still at the telephone works. Both firms are directly involved in the munitions industry, so we can be easy in our minds about those two. There is surely no risk of deportations for munitions workers.

I know how exhausted you must be after eleven hours' work. If it is

* Now Poznan, in Poland, some 150 miles east of Berlin.

hard for you to write long letters, then write short ones. Think of how much a couple of lines from you can do towards cheering up Mama.

May God bless and keep you.

With best wishes from us all,

Papa

PS. Make sure they let you come home on leave as soon as possible. There is an important matter I wish to discuss with you.

I should have given anything to be able to depart for Berlin immediately in order to discuss that 'important matter' with my father and at the same time warn him to be more careful. Unfortunately it was out of the question. With my yellow star I was not permitted to travel without police authorisation. Obtaining such authorisation involved a long-drawn-out official procedure. The village policeman in Neue Schleuse would not even accept my application until I could prove that my employer had granted me leave. And Schulze was certainly not going to give me time off just now. There was still too much to be done in the tree nursery before the frosts.

Once again we were planting saplings in the autumn drizzle. It made us oppressively aware of how much time we had already spent in that tree nursery. We had acquired additional experience, but it had cost us a precious — and arduous — year of our lives. And we were not one step nearer our goal: Palestine. Instead, in return for a starvation wage we had cultivated trees for the Third Reich. And now the whole performance looked like repeating itself all over again: pulling up dead trees, planting saplings, spreading dung, digging it in, repairing wire fences, grafting, hoeing, weeding, fighting greenfly, fiddling clandestine breaks in the latrine and tramping home to the training farm, hungry and exhausted, to be greeted at the gate with a 'Here, have you heard? They've brought out a new anti-Jewish law.'

And not a ray of hope in the whole depressing cycle. It was all becoming more and more dreary and harder and harder to bear. Schulze had gained a team of valuable assistants over the months. Our working hours had been extended. Even so, we were unable to cope with the harvest work and all the autumn jobs. As a result, Schulze finally decided to work us on Sundays as well, though with no corresponding reduction in our extended weekday hours, which stayed at the new level.

One comfort remained to us: the Sabbath. On the holy day we were free, the labour department having never got wind of our

143

private arrangements. Once a week we could still relax and murmur our prayers without having to keep one eye on the clock. The only difference was that our weary limbs no longer allowed us to celebrate Friday evening with senses fully alert. But we continued to spend Saturday in the old way. Our lives still revolved around a holy centre. Did we not have weekly proof of the fact that our community of ninety-five souls might feel safe in God's hands?

Chanukah 1941

As the evenings began to draw in, our working day became shorter again. In November evening classes were revived. We should even have had time to think about our situation but for our reluctance to spend our evenings worrying. Let the future bring what it would bring.

The Jewish festival of Chanukah was coming up (that year it fell in the third week of December).* We decided to make it as merry as possible. Preparations were put in hand four or five weeks in advance. Secret discussions were held behind closed doors. Sounds of hammering, the rattle of sewing machines and muffled giggles emerged from certain rooms. Anyone attempting to enter was vigorously repulsed.

In the wider world those weeks saw such events as gave civilised mankind cause to fear for its survival. The aggressive expansionism of the Axis powers — Germany, Italy, and Japan — reached around the globe. On 7 December 1941 Japan attacked the American fleet as it lay in Pearl Harbour, Hawaii. Four days later, Germany declared war on the United States.

Was it by divine favour or was it a divine punishment that we heard nothing of the slaughter of Jews going on in the East at the same time? In Riga, Vilnius and the Crimea, Hitler's troops perpetrated massacres in which more than 69,000 Jews perished in December 1941. During that same month a permanent gassing camp was built at Chelmno, near Poznan.†

Our principal — indeed, practically our sole — source of information about what was going on in the world was the newspaper. Consequently we had no idea of the mass murders being carried out by the German task forces. We did, however, read the official bulletins about the Japanese attack on Pearl Harbour, the American declaration of war on Japan and the German declaration of war on

---

* The festival of Chanukah commemorates the successful Jewish rebellion led by Judas Maccabeus against the Seleucid ruler, Antiochus Epiphanes, in 165 B.C.
† See Reitlinger.

the United States. The newspaper also explained why Hitler had appointed himself Supreme Commander of the Armed Forces:

What the German army is now fighting for in the East is not this or that strip of land; rather what is happening is that flexible tactics are preparing the way for the delivery of a crushing blow to the enemy in the New Year. In this fresh phase of the struggle, which has coincided with the extension of the war to the world front, the Leader [*der Führer*] has assumed supreme command of the armed forces. Decisions of enormous, even historical importance are required such as only the Leader himself can take.*

What consequences might all these things yet unleash? We did not even try to work it out. The world had become transformed into impenetrable chaos. There seemed no point in attempting to understand it.

Wrapped in our own immediate worries, we no longer thought about anything very much beyond Steckelsdorf and Rathenow. We went ahead with our preparations for the festival in spite of everything. How keenly we felt the need to shut out all major problems just for once! This was particularly clear from our cabaret, which made fun of a great many things, certainly, but what harmless fun it was! It never strayed beyond the circle of our own lives and our memories of the middle-class Jewish world of our past. Not a word, not a single gesture made the least allusion to the horrifying present.

The long-awaited evening of the feast arrived. We lit the Chanukah lights and said our evening prayers. Supper was a feast in itself: pea soup, boiled haddock and potatoes — a great deal more than we saw on our plates on most days. The kitchen even managed to conjure up a slice of apple tart for everyone.

No sooner was the meal disposed of than the tables were removed, curtains were draped across the verandah, and the benches were arranged in rows. In no time at all, the dining-room had become a theatre, filled with the excited chatter of an expectant audience.

At last there was silence. The curtain parted to reveal a small table at one side of the stage. On it stood a 'radio' made from a box and some gaily painted paper. At regular intervals the set emitted an interval signal that bore a strong resemblance to the traditional Chanukah melody.

'This is Radio Steckelsdorf,' came the announcer's voice. 'We now bring you the latest news from the farm. Minnie the cow calved last

* From *Das Reich* (the official government weekly, edited by Propaganda Minister Joseph Goebbels), Berlin, 4 January 1942.

night. The little bull calf and his mother are both doing well. A mouse has been found in the head gardener's cottage. It has not moved for three days and is assumed to have expired.

'That was the latest news bulletin. There now follows a ground-water report. The ground-water level in the greenhouse cellar currently stands at twelve and a half inches. The boiler is in imminent danger of drowning.

'There will now be a short break, after which I should like to introduce to you the celebrated marriage broker, Mr Havoc Wreaker.'

When the curtains parted again, the marriage broker was seated at his desk. He wore a crafty huckster's smile, had a pencil tucked behind his ear, and was studying a sheaf of letters, each with a photograph attached. He twirled his moustache and then rubbed his hands together.

'Gentlemen,' he announced, 'I am still in a position to assist a number of young men in their search for happiness. I am acquainted with three spinsters who are looking for husbands. They are no beauty queens, but' — he clicked his tongue before continuing with a gleam in his eyes — 'their dowries are not at all bad, and all three are well-educated, have hearts of gold, come from highly respectable families, and are blessed with sunny temperaments. In short, they possess most of the advantages that anybody can desire!'

The three spinsters came on, one by one. The first waddled like a duck. Her unsteady head was initially turned towards the broker, but then she swung round, showing the audience her great fat face. She gawked at us unashamedly through thick horn-rimmed spectacles.

The second spinster was carried in on a stretcher. 'May I present Miss Heady Fragrance?' the marriage broker said. 'She is obliged to take things very easy at the moment, having recently sustained a nasty road accident.' Miss Fragrance was encased in plaster up to her chin. The marriage broker asked her how she was progressing. Unable to move her lower jaw, she waggled the rest of her head up and down as she replied.

'Miss Fragrance, gentlemen, comes with a dowry of fifty marks and' — here he licked his lips — 'no fewer than forty years' experience in the kitchen, cooking *and* baking. She further enjoys universal esteem as a *femme du monde*. When she arrives, I am reliably assured, boredom takes flight!'

The third spinster then came tripping in, nothing but skin and bone from head to foot. A peculiar feature of her gait was that her knees bent backwards as she walked. On closer inspection, everything about her was back to front. A whisper went round the audience: 'It's Sabre!' The disguise was excellent, but there was no concealing that astonishing nose on the 'back' of the 'lady's' head!

The wireless broadcast the interval signal once again. Then the voice announced a general meeting. Six *chaverim* gathered round the table on the stage and one of them opened the meeting in a parody of Sholem Klein's manner.

The meeting over, a group of five men in tracksuits appeared and won applause for their acrobatic routine. They were followed by an Indian snake-charmer, and the snake-charmer by an astrologer, who read the horoscopes of many members of the audience, taking the opportunity to indulge in a great many personal remarks that provoked much laughter and not a few red faces.

Once they had played their parts the members of the cast came down and joined the audience, still in costume. Little by little the audience itself took on the appearance of a theatre troupe. Scattered among the marriageable spinsters, Bedouin tribesmen, acrobats, conjurors and tramps were one or two figures who had not appeared on stage at all. Berta Fröhlich occasioned general merriment in her nurse's uniform. Everybody knew that Berta's one ambition was to become a nurse.

It was nearly midnight but no one seemed in a hurry to go to bed. Faces radiated gaiety. Someone had the idea of moving all the benches out to make room for some *hora* dancing.

Those who wished to dance formed up in a large circle with arms folded. Together, they all began to move. Soon the room was shaking beneath the rhythmic stamping of their feet. They sang as they danced and danced as they sang — slowly at first, then louder and louder and wilder and wilder, literally until their lungs gave out. There followed a short pause, during which many of the dancers laid aside jackets and jumpers. Then, perspiring and happy, they quickly re-formed and began all over again.

It was agony getting up next morning and an irksome chore going back to work. But the memory of that Chanukah festival outshone all our gloom for the next few days.

Ice age

It was bitterly cold. Fields, meadows and tree nursery lay beneath a blanket of snow and ice. The biting wind froze the moisture in one's nose at every breath. Gathering and chopping the necessary wood for the kitchen and the laundry was becoming a struggle. The deportations had thinned our ranks considerably, leaving us short of labour. Only the office, the sickroom and the sewing-room were heated now.

147

The pumps froze up, no matter how thickly we lagged them with straw. The towels in the bedrooms froze to brittle boards.

The only warm place was bed, and the nightwatchmen had a terrible time of it, shaking the exhausted sleepers awake and coaxing them out of their cosy nests into the ice-cold dormitories.

Most of the *chaverim* were poorly equipped for such a winter. We all had to make do with the clothes and shoes we had brought with us from another life. None of us had expected to be in Germany still, two years into the war. Anyone without a warm hat wrapped a scarf or sweater round his ears. Grotesquely muffled up, our eyelashes white with frost, we would set out for work in the morning, staring at one another in astonishment at our disguises. I remember someone chaffing me, 'Take a look in the mirror, will you! You look like a caricature of yourself!'

Arriving back from work in the evening, most of us did not take off our coats and scarves at first. Walking had helped to keep us warm, but it was when we got inside that we really needed to protect ourselves from the cold. Our hands became chapped and sore, and wounds were slow to heal. Cases of purulent inflammation of the skin became more and more common. Lacking medicaments and dressings, there was little we could do about them.

Suffering is far easier to bear when you can see that all those around you are suffering just as badly. One relief was a reduction in our working hours. In winter we reverted to an eight-hour day, and most of our employers who worked the land were unable to offer enough work to fill eight hours. However, they made sure they did not lay off any help, fearing that the labour department would then grab us for factory work. They knew they would not get us back come the spring.

Schulze had us painting signs to be stuck in the earth in front of each row of trees, indicating the different sorts of fruit. Temporarily, the 'coffee hut' became a paint-shop.

Grateful to have a warm place to work in during that terrible winter, we sat ourselves down around the table and began to paint: Cox's Orange, Golden Reinette, James Grieve, Nancy Mirabelle, Reine Claude, White Pearl, Early Victoria, Morello and so on. The fruit trees had beautiful, noble-sounding names. The fire was crack-ling in the stove. Everything was fine — except that the work was proceeding rather too fast. What should we do once we had painted the 1942 supply of signs? Not only did the problem exercise us, who were loath to see the end of our warm indoor job; Schulze, too, was beginning to scratch his head uneasily.

So we set about painting the remaining signs in a different style. It was no longer enough that the letters should be clearly legible; they must now be masterpieces of calligraphic brushwork. Schulze looked on with raised eyebrows, an ironic twitch playing about the corners of his mouth. Yet he seemed happy enough that there was still work to keep us busy.

In this way the winter days brought a certain amount of relaxation after the strain of the autumn months. But we felt ashamed of the farce we were playing, and we were fed up with the waste of an irreplaceable slice of our lives. Schulze was ashamed, too, appearing only infrequently in the 'coffee shop' as if he had no wish to know too much about how we were passing the time.

'Have you heard?' someone called to us at the gate as we arrived back one evening after the usual long tramp through the snow. 'There's a new decree. Jews are required to surrender all woollen and fur clothing! They're allowed to keep one of each kind of woollen garment but no furs at all!'

We were used to a lot by this time. Jews might not own bicycles or use electrical appliances; Jews were no longer allowed to use public telephones. However, this one about woollen and fur clothing sounded so utterly mean and spiteful that we said we wanted to see it in black and white. Sure enough, there it was in the newspaper.

Everyone went to his or her cupboard and sorted through the woollen things, keeping what was in the best condition and putting the rest on one side to hand in. The things for handing in were placed on a pile in the sewing-room. Each person was given a further opportunity to take garments from the pile and exchange them for poorer ones.

The new enactment was no mere trifle. It obliged us to wear our best and only warm items of clothing even when doing the dirtiest jobs. But the most irritating thing about it was the way in which, at a time when our minds were preoccupied with far more serious matters, it forced us to debate the footling question of how exactly the order was to be interpreted. More and more relatives of our *chaverim* were being deported; who would be the next to be 'resettled' with his parents? Did rabbit-skin insoles count as items of fur clothing within the meaning of the decree? Was it true that deportees were no longer allowed to receive food parcels? What about woollen socks, was it *one* pair only of them too?

We returned from work two days after the woollen and fur garments had been surrendered to find the girls' rooms in chaos. Two Gestapo officers from Rathenow had suddenly arrived by car, ostensibly to verify whether we had surrendered our woollen and fur clothing in full compliance with the new regulations. They rummaged through all the cupboards and, without bothering too much about numbers and totals, took away another thirty girl's pullovers.

A case of evacuation

What was the difference, we wondered, between 'resettlement', 'repatriation' and 'deportation'? Or was there no difference? Were they perhaps just different words for one and the same thing? Etymologically speaking, 'repatriation' could apply only to Jews of foreign nationality. Did that mean there *were* differences? The officials of the Jewish congregation in Berlin used another word again: *Abwanderung*, 'migration'.

What did all these terms actually mean? No one would give us a straight answer, and little by little we grew tired of asking. But when there was a rush of reports of fresh deportations, and when people were taken from among us at Steckelsdorf and sent away, the issue once again became urgent, jerking us out of our leaden torpor.

For some time now an elderly Jewish country doctor from Neue Schleuse, of whose existence we had hitherto been in complete ignorance, had been living with us on the farm. As a Jew he had of course had to give up his practice long before. He was a man of about seventy years of age. The Gestapo had given him twenty-four hours to 'move in with the other Jews on the training farm'. We had vacated the nightwatchmen's room in the summer villa for him.

On our way to work we would occasionally be stopped by villagers asking after him and sending him their best wishes.

Dr Samuel must have found life in our community very different from what he had been used to. This was clear from the great attention he devoted to everything we said and did: the religious ceremonial, our Zionist German and the whole style of our collective existence. He began, out of politeness, to keep his own hat on during meals, and he even appeared in synagogue now and again.

A bond of diffident sympathy soon formed between the old man and ourselves. He bore with astonishing equanimity the fact that he must now reside in a single, tiny room not three miles from the house that he had had to himself for many years. He spent much time in the reading-room, and he frequently went on long walks around the farm with a remote, meditative expression on his face.

Towards the end of December Dr Samuel was ordered by the Gestapo to report to the village police station on such and such a date for 'evacuation'. What might this new term denote?

As it happened, I was on nightwatchman duty on the night before the appointed date. Making my rounds as usual, I pushed open the

150

door of Dr Samuel's room. My breath caught in my throat and cold sweat began to trickle down my spine. The good doctor, whom a couple of hours previously I had seen bent over his books in the reading-room, was now lying motionless on his bed. His ashen face was hideously swollen and distorted. His eyes were closed. Never having seen a dead man before, I was not sure at first. But all the signs were there: the way he looked, the lack of chest movement, the smell in the room.

He'll not suffer any longer, I thought. A shot of morphine has put him out of his misery. The Gestapo can do nothing to him now. He's ready for evacuation. Take him away.

If the worst comes to the worst

The uncertainty of the future was a crushing burden. It filled our thoughts from the moment the gong roused us in the morning; it tormented our minds until, exhausted after a seemingly endless day's toil, we fell into bed in the evening.

If we could only have known what the future held in store for us! The Gestapo had informed our manager that we should be summoned for resettlement in due course. Resettlement! What was one to understand by that?

As spring came, our working day climbed back up to eleven hours; later, a twelfth hour was added. Our kitchen staff, much reduced by deportations, could no longer cope. We decided at a general meeting that we should all remain seated at table after supper each evening to prepare the potatoes and turnips for the next day.

The mounting difficulties placed in our way kept us in our seats after the vegetables were all finished to discuss further emergency measures. Some *chaverim* wanted to shorten morning prayers. Others resisted the move. A girl from the sewing-room suggested we bind rags round our feet in place of socks.

Things eventually reached a point where we were all getting on one another's nerves. Harsh voices were sometimes raised at general meetings.

'Have you heard?' one heard over and over again. 'Jews aren't allowed to subscribe to newspapers any more! Only to the *Jewish News* [*Jüdisches Nachrichtenblatt*] — and that never has anything in it but announcements of anti-Jewish legislation.'

'Have you heard? Jews now have to stick a Star of David on their front doors!'

The endless succession of anti-Jewish enactments no longer

scared us. We saw them as portents of our approaching deliverance. When that deliverance would come, no one knew; but come it must!

On the way to the tree nursery in the mornings, we indulged in comforting fantasies about the future. They all began with the words 'When the war is over . . .'. What had to happen in order for the war to come to an end was something we did not even attempt to think about.

'When the war is over,' Richard would imagine for us, 'we'll stop doing this forced labour. We'll go to old Schulze and say, 'Goodbye, Mr Schulze! Find some other help now, if you don't mind. We're off to Palestine, where we shall be opening our own tree nursery. Many thanks for all you've taught us and for the relatively humane way in which you have treated us. But before we go would you mind paying us our wages for the work we've been doing for you for so long — in money that we can buy something with!'''

On another occasion we talked about what might lie ahead for us if the war were to last for a long time.

I spoke up: 'Here at Steckelsdorf, for all our wants, we still have a certain amount of freedom of movement. We wouldn't have that in Poland, and we'd starve even worse than we do here. They'll squeeze the last drop of strength out of us, and then. . . .'

Richard disagreed: 'I tend to think they'll dump us in some remote spot and leave us to our fate.'

I find it impossible to recall those conversations without a shudder. Why were we not moved by the courage of despair to try to do something about getting away? But, you see, we did not believe what we were saying ourselves; it was literally beyond our power to imagine.

By March 1942 we had already lost something like twenty members. Most of them had decided to accompany their deported parents. The dissolution of our community became a very real prospect. Schilling implored us to hold out at Steckelsdorf. 'We *must* stay together', he told us in forceful tones. 'Through thick and thin! In doing so, we shall prove to the world that *nothing* can deflect us from our goal of reaching Palestine and establishing our own country there!'

As Schilling was speaking, someone was heard to mutter, 'It's easy for him to preach loyalty to the community — he's got his whole family with him!' Several *chaverim* asked for the floor and spoke up in favour of obedience and loyalty to our parents. The choice between the two courses was the subject of fierce arguments for weeks afterwards.

Was there a third alternative? Richard had been to see his parents

152

in Berlin and had brought back some sensational news. There were Jews who were tearing the yellow stars from their clothes, destroying their identity cards and disappearing from their homes to 'go underground'. Some had managed to get through to Switzerland. Most of them, however, were presumably still in hiding somewhere in the capital.

In hiding! What about going into hiding? The idea soon became an obsession with us. We discussed it at great length over our hoeing and weeding.

What sort of a hiding-place would one need in order to be tolerably comfortable and if necessary even get by for a year or more? What gymnastic exercises would one have to perform daily if one was not to seize up completely? We quickly agreed that, from the point of view of obtaining food, it would be best to find a place with a farmer or landowner. Thinking of our employers, for example, which of them might be prepared to conceal one or two of us? Only Habermann, the proprietor of the wholesale market garden, was even a possibility. But he had masses of children and a very large staff. How would he manage to enjoin all of them to silence? So it came down to a hideout in the big city after all.

The conclusion we came to was this: anyone who did not have an 'Aryan' friend who was prepared to bring him food and to make enormous sacrifices for him should not even contemplate going underground.

On leave in the shadow of the star

Despite my warnings, father had continued to send incautious letters summoning me to Berlin to discuss that 'important matter'. In the end, my travel permit cost me a few white lies. Spring work in the tree nursery was in full swing, and Schulze was very reluctant to give anyone time off. The village policeman kept me waiting for weeks with his bureaucratic chicanery.

In April I set out, laden with sufficient documents for a world cruise. The railway journey — my first wearing the yellow star — went off without incident. One or two of my fellow-passengers glanced briefly at me, but I was not molested.

After the bombing, my parents had been given a new flat. It was in Agricolastrasse, near the NW 87 post office, about ten minutes' walk from the old one. With a beating heart I climbed the stairs to the first floor, stopped outside the door with the yellow Star of David on it and rang the bell.

I heard footsteps and became aware of someone examining me

153

through the spyhole. A bolt was drawn back, a chain released. The door opened a crack and father's face appeared. Keeping one hand on the handle, he beckoned me inside and hurriedly closed the door behind me.

'How are you, dad?' I was on the point of asking, but my father, with a wave of his hand, bid me wait a moment. He pushed my suitcase aside, took another look through the spyhole, double-locked and bolted the door, and replaced the chain — all this at around eleven o'clock in the morning! Only then did he turn to face me. 'Ah, here you are! At last!'

Mother wiped her fingers on her apron and shook my hand, smiling weakly. She seemed even more tight-lipped than usual, undoubtedly as a result of Jakob's deportation.

Father wanted to know all the news from Steckelsdorf at once. But when I began to talk about the training farm, he paced impatiently up and down the room, only half listening. At one point he even interrupted me with a sharp 'Psst!', crept to the front door and peered out through the slit of the letter box. When he came back into the room I did not even attempt to resume my account at first.

I had imagined the moment of reunion very differently, despite all our troubles. Who, after all, was better at greeting visitors than my father, with his welcoming 'Ah!' and his way of asking them how they were getting on, eager to hear all the details?

What had come over my father? Did he think it became the dignity of a rabbi to kneel down in front of a letter box and inspect the stairwell through the slit or put his ears to the walls and listen? He was behaving like a gangster in a house that the police have surrounded. I had seen something like it in a film once. What crime could my father have committed? I knew no more scrupulously law-abiding man.

Father was still officiating as rabbi in the synagogue in Münchenerstrasse. He started giving me news of his congregation.

'Do you know?' he said abruptly. 'One Sabbath recently, the Gestapo people took up positions outside the synagogue, and when people came out after prayers, they examined them all individually to see whether they were wearing their stars in exactly the pre-scribed place. Imagine, they even arrested one or two for having sewn their stars on a fraction of an inch too low down or too far over the left!' Father spoke more in naïve surprise than in anger.

'Dad, what was the important matter you wanted to discuss with me?' I asked, finally losing patience. It had to do with escape plans, my father replied. However, it emerged that he had no definite plans in mind as yet. He wanted to do everything in his power to try to get

Leon, Toni and myself to a neutral country — any neutral country. He was hoping that his many Jewish acquaintances would somehow enable him to contact the 'right people'.

None of this aroused any great expectations in me. My father had often come out with vague plans of one sort or another. The fact that he had gone so far as to summon me to Berlin for so nebulous a reason I put down to his desperation. He wanted at all costs to spare Leon, Toni and myself the fate that had overtaken Jakob.

Towards evening, Leon came home from work. 'But you're not wearing your star!' I said to him in amazement.

'What, me walk around with a yellow star on my chest? I'm not daft! I'm not going to sabotage all my options for the future!'

This struck me as extremely dubious. Granted, in terms of the general perception of such matters, no one in our family looked 'Jewish'. That fact might possibly be of vital importance at some time in the future. Might it even justify the risk of infringing police regulations?

'But what do you do about it at work?' I wanted to know.

Leon proceeded to demonstrate. The yellow star on his coat was sewn on only halfway round. The top half thus formed a flap, which with the aid of an arrangement of press studs could be fixed in either the up or down position. In the down position, the star was completely invisible.

'But, Leon, isn't that dangerous?'

'Nowhere near as dangerous as walking round with it showing the whole time!' he retorted.

Toni had adopted an even riskier stratagem: she used her handbag to cover up her yellow star.

Although I was in Berlin only for a short stay, I too began to worry about being recognised as a Jew. As a result, I went out only rarely and saw hardly anyone except the visitors who came to the flat. Apart from my parents' Jewish friends, I met a number of foreign workers there.

We had my brother Leon to thank for these unusual visitors. When we lived in Gross-Strehlitz, Leon had already taken a lively interest in foreign languages and seized every opportunity to enter into conversation with foreigners. He would have given anything to be able to spend the school holidays in France, Italy or the Balkan countries. But then he had been too young. Now the war had washed up all sorts of nationalities in Germany. The country was teeming with 'foreign workers', as they were called.

Obviously these foreign workers stood on very different rungs of the social ladder in the Third Reich. On the lowest rung were the Poles and *Ostarbeiter*, workers from eastern Europe. Voluntary workers from countries allied to Germany enjoyed the highest status. Somewhere in the middle were the workers from the occupied countries of western Europe.

Foreign workers were not always under particularly strict surveillance, a fact my brother took advantage of. He used to go walking in the Tiergarten on Sundays, trying to get into conversation with foreign workers in their mother tongue. As a result, he made friends with an Italian in the first year of the war and with two Frenchmen and a Bulgar subsequently. These friendships did not come to an end when we were required to stick a yellow star on our front door. Presumably our visitors were not aware of any danger to themselves.

Curiously enough, it did not occur to anyone in our family to think what a hazard such acquaintances might represent to us — not even to my father, who was otherwise so quick to scent danger everywhere. It did us good to associate with people who treated us as people.

On the fifth day of my leave, a letter arrived from my brother Jakob. Clearly he had managed to get it past the camp censor. The trouble was, he had not stopped to think that unveiled remarks might also endanger the people to whom they were addressed.

Jakob wrote to say that the last three food parcels had arrived empty. One of the camp officers was opening all food parcels and selling the contents on the black market.

So that was what father and mother were going hungry for! Father stamped his foot in rage and called down all manner of curses on the camp officer's head. Mother, her face rigid and expressionless, said nothing.

Jakob asked explicitly for no more food parcels to be sent. Mother wanted to go on sending them anyway, as long as there was still a shred of hope that some of them might reach him.

Not only were my parents leading a wretched existence materially, there was now appreciably more tension between them. Why were we at the mercy of an uncertain fate? Why had we not for years already been living a life fit for human beings in some safe haven abroad? In a barrage of nagging remarks, mother chided father for his lack of initiative. So bitter had she become that her reproaches were beginning to direct themselves against father's religious outlook on life.

My mother had grown up as the daughter of a family of pious Jewish craftsmen. It would never have entered her head to turn against the faith of her fathers because of the way in which Jews were being stripped of their rights. Yet her faith in my father's spiritual leadership was beginning to waver. She had decided that

1. Family group in Wurzburg, 1922. Left to right: Mother, Ruth, Toni, Jakob, Father with me on his knee, Leon.

2. Myself at eight years of age in Gross Strehlitz.

3. My sister Toni in the uniform of the German-Jewish Youth League, 1934.

4. Myself at the Steckelsdorf training farm, 1940.

5. A group of *chaverim* peeling potatoes at the Steckelsdorf training farm, 1940.

6. The Lewetzowstrasse synagogue, the collection point for Jews awaiting deportation, 1942–3. (In contrast to the Kaiser Wilhelm memorial church — which was rebuilt, this memorial to the deported Jews of Berlin was actually pulled down after the War.)

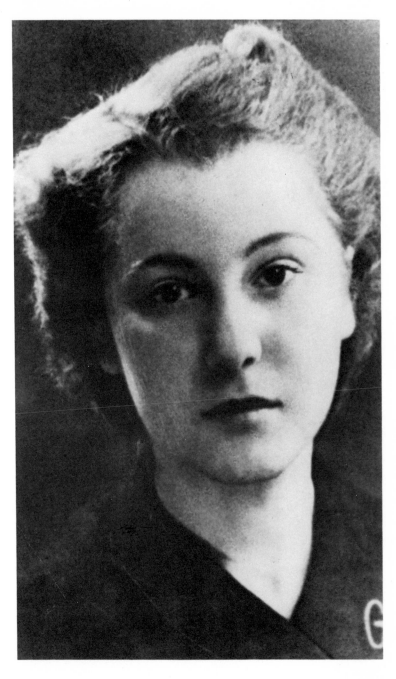

7. Lore, friend of my brother Leon, 1940.

8. My brother Leon in his 'uniform'.

9. The crocodile hall in the Berlin Aquarium.

10. Myself in 1944, after my flight from Germany.

there was something very wrong with my father's attitude. Was it not his job as a rabbi to give a lead to his family and his congregation? Was it not verging on the absurd to offer spiritual guidance when what the congregation needed was political guidance, to confine oneself to the cure of souls when it was a question of saving people's skins? Might one not expect of one's rabbi that he should meet the exceptional predicament of the present age with exceptional acts and decisions? The only decisions my father took consisted of certain concessions to sheer physical necessity. The food rations for Jews were very meagre. In order to make the most of them, he allowed all varieties of cheese to be eaten, there being no more kosher cheese. On every other matter his only advice was to invoke God's aid.

I once heard my mother cry out angrily, 'Call yourself a rabbi? Call yourself a man?'

Destination Istanbul

One day, when two friends from the Jewish congregation were with us, we had a visit from a Turkish Jew with whom my father had recently become acquainted. He immediately became the focus of our small gathering. We all listened to him with rapt attention, my parents and brother and sister, the two friends and myself.

His whole appearance bespoke the elegant, urbane man of the world. With his upright bearing, self-assured manner and virile features he looked like a diplomat of the old school, or possibly a general-staff officer. The situation of Berlin's Jewry caused him deep concern. However, he did not stop at expressing sympathy for his co-religionists' plight; he proceeded seriously and objectively to consider what, in this desperate situation, could still be done.

The next day he called again. This time the conversation revolved mainly around myself. He believed I was in greater danger than Leon and Toni because I was not employed in the munitions industry. It was high time I got away to a neutral country, he said, adding that it was his wish to help me do so. He intended to get hold of a Turkish passport for me and take me to Istanbul as 'his son'.

To Istanbul! At first we saw him as a well-meaning but impractical dreamer. However, the Turk very soberly laid out the details of his plan for our benefit. Eventually my parents urged him to come again on the following day to continue the discussion.

To my delight, I realised that my father was already won over to the idea. He saw the Turk as a guardian angel sent from above. Mother took a deep breath and said nothing for a while. The whole

157

business struck her as just too miraculous. Father's precipitate enthusiasm only made her more sceptical. She found it impossible to say 'yes' so quickly. If the adventure came off, we might never see one another again. And who knew what consequences might ensue if the enterprise were to fail? Nevertheless, it would be irresponsible not to take advantage of this unique escape opportunity. By the time the Turk returned next day, my parents had decided, after much soul-searching, to place me in his hands.

In order not to arouse anyone's suspicions, I was to return to Steckelsdorf for the time being. As soon as the Turk had my passport, father would send me a message in a prearranged code. I was then to make my way to Berlin, with or without a police permit.

Schulze was making preparations for grafting. None of us had grafted a tree for months. He reminded us how to do it and repeated his earlier advice: 'I'll let you have a bundle of shoots and you can practice your grafting under the pew in the Jewish church while the preacher's spouting. All you need is practice.'

My mind was full of images of Constantinople, as seen in various paintings. Serried ranks of sumptuous beak-prowed ships rocked at anchor in the Golden Horn. Snow-white mosques with golden spires and soaring minarets lay under a clear blue sky, reflected in the waters of the Bosphorus. And from there, two days in the train would bring me to Palestine!

The Turk had impressed upon me that I must speak to no one of our plan. It was more than I could do, though, to keep it from my closest friend. As soon as the two of us were alone, I burst out: 'Richard, I may soon be practising my grafting under the pew in a mosque!'

'What's that supposed to mean?'

When I told him the details, he grinned. He told me he had noticed that my thoughts had been far away ever since my return from Berlin. He was unreservedly glad for me, with just a touch of that harmless envy that is possible only between friends. One day, he said, we should see each other again in Palestine.

And if Hitler were to win, what then? We did not even contemplate it. Our condition had become so oppressively wretched that we blocked off all thoughts not in harmony with our hope of eventual deliverance. One day the war would be over and our difficulties at an end. Then our plan to live in Palestine would — nay, *must* — become reality.

More than three weeks had passed since my return from Berlin. Richard, tactful as ever, did not ask what had become of my plan.

Then I heard from father that the arrangement with the Turk had fallen through. It was not entirely clear from father's guarded intimations what had actually happened to the Turk, except that he had been arrested for being in possession of forged passports with which he intended to take a number of Jews to safety in Turkey.

So the Turk was in the hands of the police! For him, as a citizen of a neutral country, there was some hope. But what of the Jews he had been trying to rescue?

It was in the tree nursery that I came back down to earth. All around me stood the silent witnesses to our wretchedness: the tool-shed with the spades and hoes, the little latrine hut for stolen rest periods. From Schulze's house came the continuous drone of the radio: '. . . local offensives on the eastern front have led to advances all along the line . . . . In April, British and American supply convoys suffered losses totalling over 500,000 gross register tons . . . . A cultural agreement has been signed between the German Empire and Slovakia . . . .'

Creeping despair

When express letters or registered letters arrived at the training farm during these months, we almost took it for granted that they contained news of fresh deportations. Some parents asked their sons and daughters to return home immediately and go with them. Others wrote to bid their children farewell. But not one of those letters contained the least indication as to where those concerned were to be resettled.

What lay in store for us Jews? Must we all expect to be dragged off to Poland like Richard's fiancée and my brother Jakob, there to perform hard labour on starvation rations?

For some Jews the order to 'be ready on such and such a date' was a signal for suicide. We also heard of people who, having gone underground, had been discovered by 'Aryan' neighbours and been duly reported to the police. Others again had tried to find refuge in Switzerland but had either been caught by the German frontier police or been sent back by their Swiss counterparts.

And what did we do? We simply sat and waited for our own resettlement without lifting a finger. Did we completely fail to understand why Jews were going underground or attempting to flee across the Swiss border? Had we no suspicion as to what was prompting men and women to hoard sleeping pills and lay in a supply of rat poison?

The fault lay with our short-sighted instinct of self-preservation. It prevented us from thinking further. No one at Steckelsdorf would have been capable of rousing himself to commit any kind of desperate deed.

We just went on living. The sun tanned our faces and our busy arms. For thirteen hours a day we gave our all, tumbling exhausted into bed and rising exhausted next morning.

We went on living. Have you heard? They've enacted a new anti-Jewish law. General meeting after potato peeling! Sal Burg is sure to come up with some constructive ideas. He's a practical man; fought at the front in 1914–18; is calculated to have cut his finger-nails a total of 600 times in his life (he'll be an old man before he gets to Palestine!). And why was Moshe Heilborn still listening to such nonsensical discussions? He had spent years waiting for a certificate and yet more years waiting for a ship. And what had he got from it all? A yellow star on his chest and police permission to drive a horse-drawn vehicle to Rathenow twice a week!

We went on living. And Lea Wittner went on looking at herself in the mirror — a study in melancholy. She was not getting any lovelier, only thinner. Lea kept taking out the testimonial she had received on her dismissal from the Halberstadt furniture firm where she had worked. It spoke in glowing terms of her competence and abilities, but no one asked to see it now.

We went on living, we went on working, we went on starving. Yet food did not tempt us. We simply swallowed what appeared on our plates. We would as indifferently have spewed it up again. We sat at table in silence, not talking, not even looking at one another any more. Even Fred said nothing. He had run out of jokes.

Schulze clearly felt no hint of queasiness as he came striding along between the rows of trees, his pipe clamped in the corner of his mouth. 'Right, peaches next!' he announced.

Even the Polish and Ukrainian prisoners-of-war seemed cheerful compared to us. They spat in their hands and shovelled and hauled earth the same as ever in their tattered clothing with the 'P' or the 'Ost' (for the east Europeans) on the front. Our yellow star was worse. Did they realise that? Did we?

The summer villa, the farmhouse, the barn and the hothouse still stood where they had always stood. The training farm had not altered its appearance. Beyond the rye field the trains still clattered by — passenger trains, Red Cross trains, goods trains from all over the world laden with war machines, closed goods wagons and so on. We wondered what they contained.

The villages of Neue Schleuse and Steckelsdorf had not changed either. Apart from the stone-faced policeman, few showed us any malice. No cause for panic, then.

160

Ah, but it was not panic that paralysed us. It was that incomprehensible mixture of lassitude and nausea.

Deliverance

'We don't go to work tomorrow!' one of the *chaverim* called out to us from the gate of the farm. It was 21 May 1942 and we were just coming back from the tree nursery.

A letter had arrived from the Gestapo. We were to report for resettlement in three days' time. Only fifteen *chaverim* were to remain behind: the group that was working in the optical industry and the staff of the farm itself, including Herr Blumenfeld. These fifteen were to be resettled at a later date. (Sholem Klein, of course, was excepted from these resettlement arrangements, being a Hungarian and as such a citizen of a friendly power.) Nothing was known about our destination. The Gestapo had informed us only that it lay in a cold region. They were therefore letting us take two blankets per person. Otherwise we might take only what we stood up in, plus our washing things and food for three days.

Should we argue? Ask questions? What was the point? No one ever knows what lies ahead. All we knew was what lay behind us. Now, suddenly, all that was at an end. We did not have to go to work the next day! Was it possible? What had God chosen us for now?

Eighty sweaty, dusty young men and women ate supper in silence that night. There had never been such silence at table, not even before the holy Day of Atonement itself. Supper ended and we sat on in the gathering dusk. No one got up; no one drew the blackout curtains across the verandah doors and switched on the light. It was like the last hour of the Sabbath. The figures on the verandah side of the room stood out as silhouettes against the reddening sky. The outlines of the rest dissolved into darkness. Only the faces of one's immediate neighbours could still be seen, some staring into space, others, their eyes wide open, apparently gazing into some remote, indeterminate region that lay beyond the walls.

On the morning of 22 May the farm buzzed like a beehive when the bees are about to swarm. From the post office in Rathenow telegrams to parents sped off to the four corners of Germany. They closed with words of reassurance: 'NO UNDUE CAUSE FOR CONCERN'. 'DO NOT WORRY IF FURTHER NEWS NOT IMMEDIATELY FORTHCOMING'. 'TILL WE MEET AGAIN WITH GOD'S HELP'. I, too, sent a farewell telegram to my parents.

Soon the summer villa and the farmhouse resembled the packing

161

and dispatch department of a large store. Suits, dresses, caps, shoes, blankets and cooking utensils littered the tables and covered the floors. The clothes we must leave behind were piled up in the reading-room, where once again anyone with worn-out trousers might swap them for a better pair. Shoes were tried on, books exchanged. Those who wished to amass a great many possessions could do so now. Schilling recommended that we should not take suitcases but only a rucksack. 'We don't know, we may have to cover some distance on foot!'

We all had rucksacks, having bought them for the Danube steamer. We took Schilling's advice — except that most people filled a suitcase as well.

The kitchen staff set to work feverishly. They really did their utmost to make our last meals just that little bit more nourishing. The *chaverim* who were staying behind relinquished their bread ration for the next three days.

The sewing-room staff cut up sheets and sewed them into bags for soap, toothbrushes and other toiletries.

'Shame about those sheets,' someone said.

'Huh, what do we want sheets for now?'

Frau Schilling had brought her nine-year-old son along to the sewing-room and was letting down his coat.

In the upstairs corridor I bumped into Hans Untermann. He was beaming. 'Hans, you'll be glad we're all staying together, I dare say!' He nodded. Now he need no longer fear that his Gerda might leave him to let herself be deported from Leipzig with her parents.

I tried to find Richard. The only person in his room was Kurt Levin. With all his worldly goods disposed around him, Kurt was leaning over an open suitcase, whistling the shepherds' song from the last movement of Beethoven's *Pastoral Symphony*.

'Seen Richard?'

'He'll be back soon. He's just gone over to the farmhouse.'

'What are you so pleased about then, Kurt?'

'I just feel so *free*! Have done since yesterday evening. No more bloody Hörnke, devil take the fellow! He was here this morning, you know, at the crack of dawn, wanting to know what had happened to his minions. Well, now he can lug all his sacks round himself, the slave-driver!'

'What makes you so sure we won't fall into the hands of another Hörnke in Poland?'

'Nothing scares me now. Things couldn't be any worse! You've no idea what it's like to be at the mercy of a swine like that. Your tree nursery was a play-school in comparison!'

162

Suddenly, there at the door of the summer villa stood Schulze. I had never seen him on our farm before. He was the fourth employer to have turned up at Steckelsdorf in person that morning. He wanted more details about where we were going, and he seemed put out when we were not able to tell him anything and did not appear to pay much attention to him.

'I can't make head nor tail of it!'

'No more can we, Mr Schulze!'

He shoved his pipe into the corner of his mouth and scratched the back of his head. 'So you're off day after tomorrow? What about giving me a hand to finish the apples and peaches, at least?'

'Sorry, but we've other things to attend to before the day after tomorrow, as you can see for yourself!'

'Well, give me back my billhooks and pruning-knives, at any rate!'

He was right. The knives were still in the pockets of our work-clothes. Property is property! Schulze collected his, mounted his bike, and rode away, pale with shock.

The hours were flying by. I set about packing. It took a lot of working out, how to make the best use of the space in a rucksack. What was essential and what not, and of the essential things, which were most essential? Like the others, I optimistically packed a small suitcase as well. In the rucksack, apart from my toilet things, I put my thin-paper edition (published by Schocken) of the Torah with commentaries, a small-print Hebrew pocket Bible, a prayer-book, my phylacteries, Goethe's *Faust*, a selection of Goethe's poetry, some family photographs that I had removed from the album, my identity card, my birth certificate and a roll of sticking-plaster.

I did not want to give up the books and clothes that I was not taking with me. My family in Berlin would, I knew, be able to make good use of them in this time of need or alternatively swap them for food. So once my rucksack and suitcase were packed, I filled a number of strong cardboard boxes, tied them up with string, and addressed them to my parents. I gave the boxes to Sholem Klein with the request that he post them at the first available opportunity. Sholem and his wife worked tirelessly, pitching in wherever help was needed.

The final day before our resettlement arrived and still most *chaverim* were not ready for the road. They were still busy exchanging worn garments for better ones, making repairs and alterations in the sewing-room, and deciding what to take and what to leave behind. Meanwhile, a series of postmen called at the farm with express letters from mothers and fathers replying to their children's telegrams. As the day wore on, one person after another was summoned to the telephone in the farmhouse for a final conversation with his or her parents.

Jews were not, as private persons, allowed either to own a telephone or to use a public telephone booth. The Steckelsdorf training farm was exempt from the ban because it was a recognised public institution. But how did all those parents manage to ring us up? Did they all have good, non-Jewish neighbours from whose telephones they were able to make the calls?

At last I was more or less finished with my packing. I decided to have another look to see what Richard was doing. On the stairs I passed Rifka Berger, our youngest member.

'Shall I take my school reports?' she asked me.

'Yes, put them in anyway! They won't take up much room.'

Rifka had no one to whom she could have sent a telegram. She had lost both parents shortly before the war. Her only brother was in Dachau concentration camp, and she had not heard from him since his incarceration.

I found Richard in his room, surrounded by clothes, books and photographs. He was leaning on his elbows on top of a half-closed suitcase, staring into space.

'Richard! What's the matter? Don't tell me — your thoughts are in Warsaw, aren't they, with Lotte? But listen, you never know, we may be sent to Warsaw too! Then you'll be together again and needn't spend so much time waiting for each other's letters. Come on, old pal, snap out of it! What's the use? Time's getting short! We've got things to do!'

'Tell me, Ezra, did you never hear from your Turk again? You could do with him now!'

'That's all over, Richard. Nothing doing.'

'Then we'll be staying together!'

'Of course we'll be staying together. Look, which of your books are you taking with you? These ones here? I thought so. Listen Richard, would you like to have some of the books that I'm leaving behind?'

'Ah, I'd be glad if I could take a tenth of my own books with me.'

'You'll be taking your own poems, I expect. I just hope that secret code doesn't get you into trouble. They might think you're a spy.'

'Well, I can always clear myself if I have to. I only have to give them the key to my alphabet.'

'That's true. Hey, I've just thought of something else! You said yourself they might dump us in some God-forsaken spot in the wilds of Poland. I reckon we ought to take some potato and turnip seeds with us, just in case. We can hide them away in a waistcoat pocket, and they might come in very handy! You never know!'

'Trust you to think of something like that!'

'Yes, but we must go and collect the seeds immediately. There are plenty of plants in flower. Potato seeds are something we certainly won't be able to buy, and anyway we can't go into town any more! What's the matter? Aren't you coming?'

'Oh, do please shut up about your potato seeds! I really couldn't care less at this stage.'

I heard my name called from downstairs.

'Telephone? For me? Coming! Listen, Richard, you'll have time enough for brooding the day after tomorrow, when we're sitting in the train. We've got a day and a half left. There are still things we can do, and now's the time to do them!'

'Come *on*! You're wanted on the telephone from Berlin.'

'Berlin? Right, I'm coming! It's all this luggage lying around, I can hardly get through!'

I passed Herbert Frohwald outside the kitchen.

'You left your slippers in the reading-room,' he called out to me. 'May I have them?'

'Help yourself!' I shouted over my shoulder as I set off at a run along the path to the farmhouse.

'You took your time,' the manager told me. 'Your father's on the telephone.' And he disappeared into the next room, leaving me alone in the office.

Father's voice was jerky with emotion. 'Is that you?' he shouted. He always shouted on the telephone. Then, recognising my voice, he started speaking Hebrew. This threw me completely. Using Hebrew on the telephone was one of the hundreds of things expressly forbidden by the state police.

Undeterred, my father proceeded to bellow in Hebrew: 'Drop everything and come here to us immediately! I don't want you to go under any circumstances! I'll get you out of the country. Will you . . .'

To avoid attracting attention, I interrupted in German: 'Right! Rely on me. I'll do everything you say.'

Escape from deliverance

I rushed back to Richard.

'Richard, it seems to be working out with the Turk after all. That was my father on the telephone.'

'Is the Turk out of gaol, then?'

'Father didn't say. All he said was that he'll get me out of the country. Maybe he's discovered another escape route.'

'Look, just disappear, Ezra! Don't say a word to anyone. I have a feeling you're going to make it!'

And as if in confirmation of this belief, he went on to ask me to look up his brother in Palestine. I should probably find him at Kibbutz Sde Eliyahu, he said, although he might be serving in the army. At any rate, the people at Sde Eliyahu would point me in the right direction.

I did not know the times of the trains from Rathenow to Berlin. Since it was already late afternoon and I still had one or two things I wanted to do, I decided to make my getaway next morning, on the day before our scheduled departure.

The first thing I did was to unpack my belongings. The most essential things I now put in my little suitcase, stuffing my rucksack into another cardboard box and wrapping it up for the post. Then I went to Sholem Klein and once again asked him, in confidence, to make sure my parcels were dispatched to Berlin.

After that, I went on a tour of the farm. I wanted to take a last look at the *chaverim* to whom I could not say goodbye. I sought out the ones I was most fond of: Fred the joker, Franz Wertheim, the lad from Berlin, the young violinist Achim Gadiel, the lovely Henny and others. They were all busy packing and took no notice of me. I began to be assailed by doubts: ought I to obey my father's summons or stay with my *chaverim* — not because I wanted to 'show the world', in the sense of Schilling's challenge, but quite simply because I had become attached to these people?

When I awoke next morning I was surprised to find that I had slept deeply, despite my indecision. I made a second tour of the farm to see my friends once again. Then I returned to the villa. I found Richard alone in his room. We agreed that he should say goodbye to the other *chaverim* for me as soon as enough time had passed for no one to come looking for me. We shook hands over his open suitcase. He grinned: '*Shalom*! See you in Palestine!'

Carrying my suitcase, I walked through the wood and out of the gate. Everyone was too busy to notice me. On the path leading to Neue Schleuse I took out my scissors, cut off my yellow star and stuffed it into my pocket. Before I reached the road I met Moshe Heilborn coming in the other direction. He waved while he was still some distance away. I held the suitcase against my chest to hide the fact that my star was missing.

'Hello, Ezra! Where are you off to, then?'

'Just taking this case to the station. It's going to my parents in

Berlin.'

Farther on I ran into Hans Untermann. The same pantomime was repeated.

I kept a particularly sharp lookout as I passed through Neue Schleuse. The man I was most anxious to avoid was the village policeman. Fortunately I spotted him before he spotted me, and I managed to slip past unobserved.

At last I was in the train. The one and half hours' wait in the station restaurant had been an ordeal. The stupid waitress had insisted on cross-examining me. As far as I could recall I had said nothing careless in reply. At worst I might perhaps have watched her a little too closely. But what did any of that matter now? I was sitting in the train, and the train was rolling towards Berlin.

If they notice my disappearance, I reflected, they will have time to notify the station police in Berlin. And what do I do if there is an inspection on the train and everyone has to show his identity card?

That reminded me! Locking myself in the toilet, I pulled the yellow star from my pocket and took out my identity card with the 'J' on it. Using the scissors, I cut both into small pieces, dropped them down the lavatory, and flushed the bowl several times. Afterwards I returned to my seat in the compartment and sat looking out of the window.

My friends were still caught up in the turmoil of preparations for 'resettlement'. I had escaped that turmoil. The telegraph poles flashed past the window; the woods and fields slid by more slowly. Why me, especially? Why was it being given to me to get out of the country? When should I see Richard again?

I glanced at the clock. A third of the distance covered; another thirty miles and all would be decided. I should find myself either locked up in the police station or at liberty.

Find myself at liberty? Was I not already free?

CHAPTER 8

Underground in Berlin

Another friendly reception in the capital

What was going on in the world during those weeks that were of such crucial importance in my life? After the war, wishing to know in retrospect at least, I consulted the history books and combed archives and libraries for newspapers dating from the period. For the months of May and June 1942 I found, among others, the following news items:

— The German 'Africa Corps' advances on Tobruk.
— The German southern army group launches its summer offensive, aimed at the Don, Stalingrad and the oil-rich Caucasus.
— Japanese armed forces overrun Burma, attack Oceania and the Dutch East Indies and threaten Australia. The expansion of the Axis powers approaches its zenith.
— Czech patriots shoot Himmler's henchman Reinhard Heydrich. Germany exacts a terrible revenge, flattening the village of Lidice and killing all its inhabitants.
— The yellow star is introduced in France and Holland.
— The German gassing and shooting industry in Poland moves into top gear. The first 'selection' takes place in Auschwitz.
— Seyss-Inquart, the German governor of the Netherlands, organises hostage-shootings and deportations of Jews. The Vienna Philharmonic Orchestra pays homage to Seyss-Inquart as a patron of the arts.
— Molotov visits London. A twenty-year Soviet–British mutual-assistance pact is signed.
— Saukel, Hitler's Commissioner for Labour, forces millions of citizens of occupied countries to perform slave labour in Germany.
— The Vienna Burgtheater gives a performance in Amsterdam with

Goethe's *Torquato Tasso*.

Had I known more about these events at the time, had I witnessed for only five minutes the way in which prisoners in Auschwitz were forced to tear the gold-filled teeth from the mouths of the murder victims, would I still have made such efforts to save myself? It was not until long after the war that I began to ask myself that kind of question. At the time of my flight from Steckelsdorf, my ignorance shielded me from despair. In my naïve self-absorption my sole concerns were how to get out of Germany as quickly as possible and how to arrange my escape in such a way as to avoid placing my parents in jeopardy.

From the station I made my way through the familiar streets of the Hansa quarter. My goal was a particular house in Lessing-strasse. I had no idea whether Herr Schlesinger, the headmaster of the former Jewish *Gymnasium*, was still in Berlin. He might have been deported. Clutching my little suitcase, I slipped stealthily into the entrance hall of the building. I stood there listening for a moment, started to climb the stairs, stopped again to listen, then went on up. Eventually I arrived, rather out of breath, at the door of the Schlesingers' flat. The name-plate was still there, with the regula-tion yellow star affixed above it. The lock had not been sealed by the Gestapo. I knocked. Inside the flat, footsteps approached the door. An eye appeared at the spyhole. The door opened immediately and Herr Schlesinger himself let me in.

I briefly described my situation and asked his advice.

'You'll stay here for the present!' he said without the slightest hesitation, and he dispatched his twelve-year-old son to tell my father I had arrived.

I had been right to take the precaution of not going straight to my parents. Next morning two officials turned up at their flat. To his 'astonishment' and 'dismay', my father learnt that his youngest son had been missing since the previous day. He begged both officials to let him know as soon as his son was found. However did father contrive to play his part so convincingly? Lying was certainly not his strong point.

But what a merciful turn of fate that no one was blamed for my disappearance — neither my parents nor my *chaverim* back at Steckelsdorf!

I stayed with the Schlesingers and their large brood of children for forty-eight hours. Meanwhile my parents found another temporary refuge for me with an elderly widow, Frau Gold, a friend of my mother's who lived on her own. She rented a ground-floor flat in the rear part of a house in Lewetzowstrasse, only five minutes' walk from my parents' place.

Frau Gold put me up in a long, narrow room containing a sofa, a round table, two chairs and a bookcase. The first thing she did was to warn me to be very quiet: only a thin partition separated the room from the communal stairwell of the house. And I must never open the curtains: she would see to it that I had enough air.

The day I moved in, Frau Gold made several trips to my parents' flat to fetch bedding and other necessities. She also brought me food, some from my mother's kitchen and some from her own.

I did not see my parents until the next day, when they visited me in my hideout one at a time. I immediately asked father how things stood with the Turk and when I could expect to continue my flight. His answer came as a shock to me. It seemed I had misunderstood him over the telephone: there could be no question of my continuing my flight in the immediate future. The Turk was presumably still in prison, he said, if he had not already been expelled from the country. At any rate, he had not been in touch again. We could no longer count on him.

And that was it! My father had no alternative escape plans for me. It was the usual vague intention: he meant to 'pursue his inquiries' among his friends and acquaintances in an attempt to 'make fresh contacts'. And for that I had abandoned my *chaverim*!

'Don't look so glum!' father said. 'You're with us now. There's still a wealth of possibilities open to us.'

'And meanwhile I'm to remain here indefinitely, eating your starvation rations and putting your lives in danger — is that it?'

'But don't you understand? If you'd been deported with your friends, it would have been too much for Mama. She'd never have borne it! You've seen how disturbed she has been ever since Jakob's deportation.'

I had no means of knowing it at the time, but my father's telephone call to Steckelsdorf had laid the foundation stone for my eventual rescue.

I soon forgot my bitterness. Shortage of sleep, aggravated by the physical strain of the past months, hung heavy in my limbs. I collapsed on the sofa. In fact, I spent most of the next few weeks on that sofa, little realising how short a distance separated me from the desks and filing-cabinets of Heinrich Himmler's Reichssicherheits-hauptamt, the headquarters of all the police forces in the Third Reich. A stroll through the Tiergarten was all that lay between me and Department IV B 4, which directed the 'final solution of the Jewish question'.

I felt very cramped in my hideout. If I peered through the net curtains, blank walls and gable ends blocked my view. If I lay on the sofa, the old-fashioned brass chandelier filled my field of vision. To my left, the world lay hidden behind a papered wall; to my right, it was obscured by a curtain running the whole length of the room. I lifted the curtain once — to find I was living in only half a room. The other half was piled high with furniture.

Shielded and confined between walls and curtains, I buried myself in the books father had brought me. But every time I heard footsteps on the stairs outside, my ears pricked up. Who was it, and were they coming or going? Was it one of the 'Aryan' occupants or one of the Jews (Frau Gold had told me that almost as many Jews as 'Aryans' lived in the house)? Or did the footsteps belong to a stranger? The postman, perhaps? A Gestapo agent?

I made a great effort to be as quiet as possible all the time. Nevertheless, there were days when Frau Gold would warn me to be particularly silent for the next few hours. Such and such a Jewish family expected to be fetched for deportation that afternoon. The Gestapo might arrive at any moment. She would say all this in a whisper — though calmly enough — before scurrying back to her kitchen, leaving me alone. At such times I would lay aside my book and try to imagine what the future might hold for the Jewish tenants upstairs.

Frau Gold knew only that the Gestapo agents took Jews designated for deportation to the synagogue up the road. The Lewetzow-strasse synagogue, a huge building with a columned portico, was a smoke-blackened survivor of November 1938. Now, SS men stood guard between the columns. The Jews locked inside had to wait in the house of God until 1,000 of them were assembled and one of the special trains stood ready at the loading ramp. Sometimes they waited for two or three days. Then they were escorted to the station and 'loaded'.

But if — to use the official term — this 'evacuation' of Jews was in the interests of a better deployment of labour, why were old people, children, war cripples and the sick taken along too? And why did the authorities leave the officers of the Jewish congregation completely in the dark as to the train's destination?

The synagogue stood near a busy crossroads, right next to a large post office. However much of a hurry they were in, the people of Berlin who passed that way cannot have failed to notice the city's Jews, young and old, trudging into the house of God loaded with rucksacks and hand luggage. Later, when I began to venture out of my hiding-place, I saw with my own eyes that they noticed.

How were the *chaverim* from Steckelsdorf faring while I lay back on the sofa in my hideout, staring up at the brass chandelier? Frau Gold told me shortly after I moved in that two days before some fifty youngsters of both sexes wearing yellow stars had been marched into the Lewetzow synagogue. With their suntanned faces and coarse clothes, they looked 'very country', she said.

My *chaverim* — no doubt about it! The night after my flight I had slept only a few blocks from them! The difference had been that the doors of their billet were guarded by SS sentries. I never heard any more about what happened to them, not even after the war.

The German Reich inherits an estate

Weeks went by. It looked as though the Gestapo had stopped trying to trace me. My father and mother were not summoned for interrogation, and the house search they dreaded did not materialise.

I put it to my parents that I could now come to them, at least for lunch and supper, to spare them the laborious business of bringing me food. 'No, no — far too dangerous!' father objected. However, when he heard that in Frau Gold's house 'stewards' of the Jewish Council (of whom more later) and Gestapo men came and went, he agreed. Perhaps after all their flat was no less safe than my present hiding-place. I should pay a trial visit first, he said. But I must observe certain rules. These he impressed upon me with a wagging forefinger. 'Never use that noisy bell on the door of our flat but only our secret knock.' He demonstrated it for my benefit: knock, knock-knock, knock-knock. 'But you must never knock at the door when a stranger can see you on the stairs. When you're with us in the flat and friends come, you must hide in the next room — never mind whether they're Jews or "Aryans". I don't want anyone burdened with the secret unnecessarily.'

Three weeks after moving in with Frau Gold I ventured my first visit. We had agreed in advance the exact time I should arrive. First, like someone who has just spent several weeks in bed, I had to get used to traffic again. I had no difficulty in slipping into my parents' flat unobserved. It was not even necessary for me to use the secret knock. Father was already in position at the spyhole. The door opened as I came up the stairs, and it closed behind me without a sound.

Towards the end of the afternoon Leon and Toni came home from work. Leon had a front-door key; Toni gave the secret knock and was admitted.

For supper we each had two potatoes boiled in their skins, a slice of bread covered with a spread prepared from baker's yeast, and a cup of barley coffee sweetened with saccharine. What a miserable family meal that was! None of us said a word. We stared gloomily down at our plates, lifted our forks to our mouths and chewed mechanically, each far away in his or her own thoughts. I felt an almost irresistible urge to break the silence. But one look at mother's face was enough to drain me of all desire to talk. Her grief hung over the supper table like a nightmarish presence.

It was mother herself who finally spoke. There was one potato left in the bowl. Mother said she was full, and she pushed it towards Leon. 'I couldn't!' insisted Leon, pushing the bowl on to father. The potato went backwards and forwards across the table. In the end it was left in the bowl, untouched.

After supper there came another knock at the door. Leon quickly went out into the hall and looked through the spyhole. At a wave from him, I disappeared into the next room before he opened the door. Toni slipped into the room a moment later and said that Lore, Leon's girlfriend, had come. I knew Lore only from a photograph that Leon had once shown me. How I should have loved to meet her in person! Now, though, that was forbidden me. I could not even go to the lavatory until Lore had left the flat.

The return journey to Frau Gold's went off without a hitch. I took advantage of the blackout. In the days that followed I ventured further visits to my parents, staying with them from lunchtime until nightfall. There were no untoward incidents, and my parents and I quickly grew accustomed to my comings and goings. Only once did it happen that someone was climbing the stairs behind me. I passed my parents' door as if I had been heading for one of the upper floors. The man followed me all the way to the fourth-floor landing. There I pretended to have made a mistake and turned back down. The man disappeared into one of the top flats.

Living underground — that is to say, illegally — means being condemned to solitude. This became clearer to me with each day that passed. During my last leave in Berlin, I had experienced embarrassment at meeting other people wearing the yellow star: we suffered the same shame, yet there was so little we could do for one another. Now, walking round without a star, I found such encounters awkward for another reason. Whatever happened, any sign of recognition, let alone any exchange of remarks, must be avoided. The time I encountered Herr Schlesinger in Lewetzowstrasse I had to walk straight past with an air of utter indifference. He did the same.

But who would ever have thought that I should one day have to hide from the imbecile Guli? One afternoon when I was with my family we heard footsteps on the stairs. They were followed by Guli's personal call-sign: he let the flap of the letter-box shut four times. For security reasons we could not let him know our secret knock.

'That'll be Guli!' Leon hissed to me. 'Quick, into the other room! Hurry! If he sees you, he'll go blabbing to everyone.'

From the next room I heard Leon ask, 'Tell me, Guli, what do you think of the way the war is going?' I caught only the inevitable 'Well, for instance. . . '; the rest was inaudible.

Fifteen minutes later, it happened. Leon came into the room where I was hiding in order to fetch something — and Guli followed him.

'Hey, it's you!' he exclaimed, his voice cracking. Then he simply stared at me in speechless amazement until, seeing me smile, he recovered himself and burst out laughing.

It was too late for recriminations. Leon did his best to impress upon Guli that he must tell no one he had seen me. Guli gave his solemn promise. He even showed us, by pressing a forefinger to his lips, how silent he intended to be.

Four weeks after I had moved in, Frau Gold gently broke it to me that I would have to leave her flat that same day. My room, she told me, had previously been rented from her by someone called Feigenblatt. It was his furniture piled up behind the curtain. Summoned for deportation, he had taken poison. Now Frau Gold had received an official letter — she showed it to me — requiring her to be present in her flat on the afternoon of 23 September 'for the purpose of identifying the Feigenblatt furniture'. By way of explanation, the letter added that the state was authorised to impound the property of Jews in the event of death or deportation.

Frau Gold had discussed the matter with my parents, and between them they had decided that I should stay there until Feigenblatt's 'estate' had been removed. Carrying nothing but a briefcase, I went straight to my parents' flat. Frau Gold said she would bring the bedding round later.

Father was already waiting for me behind the door. He immediately began to instruct me in all the particulars of life in their flat.

'But I already know all that!' I protested. 'It's not as if this was my first visit!'

'No, no, you don't know it all!' father contradicted me impatiently. 'We still have to arrange how you . . .' He paused, holding up a hand to silence me. He listened for a moment. With a sign to me to stay put, he tiptoed out into the hall, bent his head to the spyhole in the front door and raised the little cover. Holding his breath, he peered out at the landing and the stairs. Then, having satisfied himself that there was no one there, he let the little cover fall back, checked that the door was properly locked, and returned to the room.

'Now, where were we?' father resumed. But already his gaze was wandering back towards the hall.

'Dad, there's not a lot of point in walking on tiptoe. The floor-boards creak so badly they can surely be heard outside. And why on earth do you . . . ?' But I did not bother to finish. It was clear from the glazed look in my father's eyes that he was not listening.

Mother came in. 'You can sleep on your old folding bed,' she said. 'And if anyone comes in the night. . . What are we going to do if someone comes in the night?'

'If that happens, I'll quickly toss the bedclothes over to Leon on the sofa, fold up the bed, and hide somewhere.'

'Yes, but where?'

'That's what we have to discuss,' said father. 'Perhaps he might . . . No, that wouldn't . . .'

'He could slip into the larder quickly,' mother offered.

'Sorry? In the larder, you said? Aha! That would be a good place. But no — people might . . .' Putting a hand up to adjust his skullcap, father turned back towards the hall.

As my parents continued the discussion. I was struck once again by how much weight they had both lost in the two months since my last official leave. Indeed, how could they not have done? They did not even eat the whole of the meagre personal ration allocated to Jews, always holding back at table for the benefit of Leon and Toni, who had to do factory work all day long. And every two weeks they sent a food parcel off to Posen. Now my arrival had added another mouth to feed without bringing an extra ration card.

Why had father's walk become so hesitant? And why did he leave so many of his sentences unfinished? It was as if he was thinking of something else the whole time, as if his mind was permanently elsewhere. Come to think of it, mother was no longer entirely herself either. Two months earlier, when the Turk had visited us, she had still been capable of listening with great attention. Well, no, actually she hadn't even then, I realised. But now I was shocked by the absent-minded air with which they discussed a matter that was clearly of crucial importance to them!

After a period of reflection, father said, 'I think the best hiding-place for you is the big oak wardrobe.'

'The one we used to play hide-and-seek in when we lived in Heilbronn? Oh, dad! Do you mean the big oak wardrobe we used to play in when we were kids?'

'Eh? Oh, yes, that's the one. If anyone comes, you can climb in there quickly and hide behind the clothes. Let's give it a try right away. Wait a second, though — I want to make sure there's no one on the stairs first.'

I climbed into the huge wardrobe and found it a far more practical hiding-place than the larder. To start with, it stood in the semi-darkness of the hall. I was still small enough to fit inside it. Even with both doors open, I could squeeze so far in that a casual glance revealed nothing but suits and coats.

'And what shall I do if an air-raid warning sounds?' I wanted to know.

'You'll do the same as us — stay up here.'

Within hours of the move I became aware that I had not brought peace to my parents' home.

It was getting on for five in the afternoon, the time when Leon and Toni were due home from their factories. Father's shoes creaked in an irregular rhythm as he paced up and down. The piano on one side of the room and the sideboard on the other forced him to turn in mid-stride. This clearly disturbed father's thoughts. He lifted the lid of his desk and began to search for something. His fingers drummed on the raised lid. Then he shut it again, went out into the hall, tried the front-door handle to check that the door was well and truly locked, lifted the cover of the spyhole, bent down to look out, walked back across the creaking floorboards to the living-room, resumed his pacing, stopped in front of the mirror, pulled his tie straight and went out into the hall again to see whether the afternoon post had come. Holding his lower lip between his teeth, father then came back into the room, cautiously approached the window and peered out through the net curtains: nothing out of the ordinary appeared to be happening in the street.

There! We could breathe again! That was unmistakably Leon's step on the stairs. We heard him insert his key in the lock and turn it. Leon came in, put down the leather briefcase he had made himself and always carried with him, and removed his coat. He sat down and crossed his legs.

'Can't you ever stand still, dad?' he said after a while, clearly irritated. 'Drives a chap crazy, your endless pacing up and down!'

'Go and lie down for a bit on the sofa in the other room,' father replied. 'You're tense and overwrought.'

After a moment father paused again in his pacing: 'Listen, there she is at last!' he cried with a sigh of relief. Sure enough, a few seconds later we heard our secret knock at the front door. It was hurriedly repeated. Leon dashed to the door and let Toni in.

She sat down, breathing heavily. She was also grinning like a child who has just pulled off a really terrific stunt. She had had a reason for being in such a hurry to be admitted: the caretaker had been trudging up the stairs behind her.

Proudly, Toni unpacked her handbag to reveal the priceless treasures she had brought home with her: four tomatoes, a fish and two packets of imitation powdered egg! Things that according to the law of the land Jews were not allowed to possess! Thank God she had not been stopped in the street carrying that lot!

'The fish comes from the fishmonger by Bellevue Station,' Toni whispered, 'and the egg is from the shoemaker!'

'From the shoemaker!' asked father. 'Ah, where should we be without the shoemaker!'

I had already noticed during my April leave the extraordinary importance that the front door of the flat had now acquired. It served as both bastion and drawbridge, while the spyhole was our watchtower against the persecutors, both uniformed and plain-clothes, with whom Germany teemed. The door, which was double-leaved, consisted of some fifty square feet of timber; it was fitted with an iron lock and a patent cylinder lock. The two leaves could be fastened together with a heavy iron bolt about two feet long as well as with a guard chain.

Beyond this wooden bulwark lay the hostile outside world. It extended right up to the coat of white paint covering our front door. A stranger who rang the bell might stand there for a long time, contemplating his distorted reflection in the glossy surface. The flat would remain as quiet as the grave; no one would open to him.

Only members of the family and friends who knew our secret knock found their way into the fortress. The Star of David posted outside showed visitors that the enclave behind the door did not belong to the hostile world. Once admitted, with the door safely shut behind them, they could speak freely, albeit only in an undertone. Yet that same Star of David also showed how insecure the fortress was, for all its locks and bolts.

My parents' most dangerous guest

The sudden need for me to flee from Frau Gold's flat pointed up the impossibility of my situation. After supper I discussed the matter with my parents in the kitchen.

Mother suggested that they should start by trying to find me lodgings with some obliging Christians. Once installed with them, I could make plans to escape to Switzerland, or possibly Sweden, more calmly and collectedly.

Father countered by saying he would rather look for an escape route out of the country immediately. Then I would not need a hiding-place.

I had heard this before. Father had often spoken in similar terms since my arrival in Berlin. I knew nothing would come of it.

I was about to ask mother whom she meant by her 'obliging Christians' when suddenly the doorbell rang. Leon, who had been about to step in the hall, froze and stood rooted to the spot. The tap was turned off in an instant. We exchanged questioning looks. Father moved to flick off the hall light, but Leon waved a hand to stop him. My emergency hiding-place in the big oak wardrobe turned out to be useless; I dared not cross the creaky floorboards to reach it and open the equally creaky door. We all stood stock-still, as if an evil wizard had cast a spell on us. A second ring tore through the silence. Father, panicking, started towards the hall and could be restrained only with difficulty. Mother was shaking all over. Toni's teeth chattered audibly, and Leon angrily signalled to her to clamp her jaws together. My heart was beating violently and seemed to be accelerating all the time. And the awful thing was, all this was solely on my account! Shhh — keep quiet! If only whoever was out there would go to the devil! Even then we knew we must remain silent for a while longer. Realising that Jews always pretended to be out, they had adopted the ruse of noisily descending the stairs as if they had grown tired of waiting, then tiptoeing back up to listen at the door. Now, though, we could no longer hear anything outside. Had they really given up and gone away? No, listen — wasn't that a floorboard on the landing that just creaked?

The letter flap was raised. A voice called my father's name, then asked, 'Why are you keeping me waiting all this time?'

Father ran to open the door. 'Frau Gold! It's you! Come in, come in! You can't imagine what a fright you've just given us all! Whyever didn't you use our secret knock?'

'Oh, I'm terribly sorry! I did knock, but you can't have heard me. Then some people started coming up the stairs, and I didn't want them to catch me with all this bedding.'

When we had all calmed down again, father returned to the subject of possible escape routes for me. He drew Frau Gold into the conversation. She knew of one Jew who had contrived to get himself smuggled onto a troop train bound for Norway and had leapt to freedom on the way through Sweden. Others were said to have reached Switzerland in coal trains. They had been nailed up in crates and the crates placed in trucks and buried beneath a load of coal. She believed the trip cost 10,000 marks.

It was pointed out to her that, even supposing there was any substance to these rumours, one still had to contact the right people. One could not just go up to any old train driver or shunter, ask if one might have a word in private, and then spill the whole plan. Frau Gold shrugged and gave a resigned smile.

About a week after I had moved to my parents' flat Frau Gold called to tell us that the Gestapo had now identified Feigenblatt's furniture and taken it away. I was welcome to return to her flat. So I went back to my old hiding-place and to my habit of spending only a few hours with my parents during the day.

In July, two months after my arrival in Berlin, I was still at Frau Gold's. All attempts to get in touch, through her, with former Jewish school-mates for the purposes of seeking their advice had ended in failure. Other attempts to find avenues of escape had met with no more success.

My parents decided at this point that it would be a good thing to introduce me to the shoemaker of whom I had heard them speak so highly.

A rendezvous was arranged, and I turned up at his shop one day at the same time as Toni. I had my first glimpse of him through the shop window. He was sitting by himself on a stool behind the counter. As we entered, he interrupted his hammering to hold a broad, manly hand out towards me.

'Toni has told me so much about you,' he said with a smile. 'You've been working in a tree nursery, I believe?'

According to my parents, the shoemaker was around seventy years old. He looked no more than fifty-five. It was not until he stood up that I discovered what a giant he was. Yet his face was not that of a giant. There was shrewdness in it, together with a hint of boyish mischief. His eyes were narrow and slightly foxy. Were they always like that, I wondered, or only when he smiled? The smile, which was one of pure friendliness, never left his face the whole time I was with him. After all I had heard about him, I saw predominantly good qualities in his face.

Two days later I heard from my parents that the shoemaker had gained a favourable impression of me. It was not out of the question that he might do something towards my rescue.

The 'lists'

During the summer of 1942 the tide of Jewish deportations continued to rise. Those of us who were not at that time swept away by

179

it knew only what happened up until the moment when the deportees were taken to the loading ramp and put into goods trains. That much, however, we knew in great detail.

A person designated for 'resettlement' first received a fat envelope containing a great many questionnaires, all of which he had to fill in. We called them the 'lists'. On these forms he was required to enter all his possessions, movable and immovable.

Anyone who had the 'lists' delivered to his home must reckon to be fetched a fortnight thence. When the Gestapo officials arrived, he had to hand them all his keys together with the completed 'lists'. The officials would then seal his front door and escort the 'resettler' to the nearest collecting-point. The Lewetzowstrasse synagogue was one such collecting-point; other synagogues served the same purpose. There the Jews were held in custody until between 300 and 1,000 were assembled, depending on the size of the transport available.

Everything that Jews owned — goods and chattels, bank accounts, real estate — had long since been designated the inalienable property of the state. The purpose of the 'lists' was to help the relevant authorities to sort those possessions and assign them to 'appropriate utilisation'.

On orders from the Gestapo a 'Jewish Council' had been set up, ostensibly to look after the interests of the Jewish population and to represent them *vis-à-vis* the Gestapo. The offices of the Jewish Council were in the annex of the huge synagogue in Oranienburgerstrasse in the city centre. From there Jewish 'stewards' were dispatched to every corner of Berlin to lend assistance in connection with 'resettlements' and furniture removals.

The members of the Jewish Council were themselves required to select the candidates for the individual 'resettlement operations'. They did so in the evident belief that by carrying out the Gestapo's orders they could prevent something worse from happening.

My parents, too, like many other people, were convinced that the Jewish Council helped wherever it could. Certain individuals who had already received their 'lists' tried, with the aid of the Jewish Council, to evade deportation. Anyone who could prove that his or her job was vital to the war effort had a chance of being allowed to remain in Berlin.

In July 1942 I gained at first hand a fleeting impression of what went on inside the Oranienburgerstrasse synagogue annex. I forget why, as a Jew not wearing a yellow star, I ventured into a place where I risked being recognised by Jewish acquaintances and where Gestapo informers almost certainly lurked.

180

The longer I had been living underground, the more my initial caution had given way to a feeling of confidence. So far nothing untoward had happened to me. No one had quizzed Frau Gold as to who was living in her flat. No Gestapo men or Jewish Council stewards had come ringing at my parents' door. All this had made me bolder. As I entered the building that day, I used my briefcase to cover up the place on my chest where the yellow star should have been.

The magnificent synagogue with its gilded dome was as silent as the tomb. It presented a stark contrast to the administration building next door, where an apparently endless queue of people thronged the vestibule. What, I wondered, had brought all those yellow-starred supplicants there? Were they all trying to prove that their jobs were vital to the war effort? I preferred not to ask. Their faces showed that they had come to plead — and that they awaited the verdict in fear and trembling. Each person had had a queue number thrust into his hand at the door. From the length of the queue it was obvious that the petitioners would have a long wait before being heard. But then they were used, were they not, to standing in line for hour after endless hour, a damp, sweaty scrap of paper with a number on it clutched in one hand, in the other the handbag containing the identity card, ready to be presented as required?

A postman — an 'Aryan' — began to push his way through the throng. People drew back as though before some high-ranking dignitary. Crestfallen faces and forlorn glances took in his uniform, his cap, the Nazi national emblem. Eyes searched his features as if in an attempt to detect some trace of human sympathy. Coldly, looking straight through their wretchedness, the postman went on his way.

Women wearing old-fashioned flowery hats pressed their handbags to their bosoms and waited and waited. How worthy and well-behaved they all looked! Respect for German laws, uniforms and rubber stamps had been instilled in them since girlhood.

In the corner was the office, the holy of holies that none approached without a quickening heart-beat. A Jewish steward stood at the door, checking numbers. The door opened and an elderly woman emerged. She held a handkerchief to her eyes and was sobbing.

'Next, please!' the steward called. 'Number 83!'

I never did get to the bottom of what those poor, tormented souls were after. Feelings of suffocation and mounting nausea soon had me elbowing my way towards the exit. Still clutching my briefcase tightly to my chest, I stumbled out into the street. My head was throbbing, the pulse at my temples racing.

How cut off we were from the world! We were almost wholly dependent upon news and rumour of the sort that went from mouth to mouth.* The raw material for this was provided by the few 'Aryans' who were still prepared to speak in confidence to their Jewish friends. It took some courage to do so, for 'Aryans' who received Jews in their homes or visited a 'Jewish domicile' had to be constantly on their guard against informers. As for stopping in the street to talk to a person wearing a yellow star, that was a liberty no 'Aryan' dared take.

The few scraps of news that reached my parents' flat came together from three sources. The occasional report from the front as well as fragments of other official bulletins reached us across the courtyard whenever a neighbour had his radio turned up too loud. Leon used to bring us information gleaned from his French, Italian and Bulgarian friends. And the rest we learnt from the Jewish oral news chain.

With regard to the most burning question of all — 'What lies ahead for us Jews?' — we remained totally in the dark. The men from the Jewish Council with whom my father had some dealings answered his questions with a helpless shrug. Soldiers on leave from the eastern front might have been able to tell us more, but which of us was likely to come into contact with them?

One thing was certain: Berlin's Jewry was in the process of rapid dissolution. Every day brought news of fresh deportations. The Jewish friends who visited my parents during July 1942 spoke of little else.

I remember one such conversation. Frau Gold and another woman called Seligsohn, an elderly member of the Adass-Isroël congregation, had popped in for a chat. In addition to my parents, Guli was present. The two women, still clutching their shopping bags, chattered away across the table. Guli listened open-mouthed.

'Have you heard?' Frau Gold said. 'The Gartenfelds were fetched yesterday. So was Königsohn, with his eight children. And Gold-berg's packing his bags — his lists arrived first thing this morning.'

'If only we knew when it will be our own turn!' Frau Seligsohn sighed. 'There appears to be no system at all in the deportations. Last Monday they took only old people. Then Friday they took a consignment of 300 children, from infants to fifteen-year-olds. Just

* We even had a saying about it: 'Vom Mund['mouth']funk haben wir mehr als vom Rundfunk', 'We learn more from . . . than from the radio'.

took them away from their parents. Said they were sending them to a children's home in Poland. And at this moment there are 1,000 people locked up in the synagogue, waiting for their transport — old and young, single folk and whole families, all thrown in together!'

Somebody's friend had heard that Berlin was to be 'Jew-free' by the end of 1942. The Gestapo chief from Vienna had been summoned especially to see to it. He was an expert, apparently, at 'purging' cities of their Jews. In the congregation building in Grosse Hamburgerstrasse, Jews who had been fetched from their homes were packed into the cellar — men, women and children. A maniac had torn into them with a dog-whip. Recently a consignment of Jews had been found to be several persons short. The Gestapo had promptly arrested the same number from the staff of the local congregation. Nothing had been heard of them since.

Guli felt compelled to react in some way to these appalling disclosures. 'Well, for instance,' he drawled out of his lopsided mouth, 'the Nazis don't like Jews with hooked noses!'

'Don't like them!' Frau Gold echoed with a pitying glance at Guli. 'Do you know what Königsohn said before he was taken away? "There are times when one feels like despairing of everything!" And him a shining example of a God-fearing man! I'd never have thought to see such a one lose hope.'

My mother did not usually contribute much to these conversations. This time, however, she could not contain her anguish. 'How can God allow it all to happen?' she cried, turning angrily on my father. 'Isn't he supposed to be just? Is this what he has chosen us for? The "Chosen People"! The damned, more like it! It's right what the street-urchins shout: "Damned Jews!" What have Königsohn's little kids done to deserve this? Tell me that! What was the point in them even being born? This dog's life we lead is not worth lifting a finger for!'

'You shouldn't blaspheme,' was father's shocked response as he sought to pacify mother with his gentle tone. 'God gives us many heavy burdens to bear, but he will never forsake us!'

'Regrettably the subsequent whereabouts of the above-named person(s) cannot be ascertained'

The date was 12 August 1942. Mother forced herself, as she did every morning, to make the effort of tidying up and cooking. Father sat down to work at his desk in the living-room, though he kept getting up to check whether the front door was properly locked and peer through the spyhole. I was reading.

From the courtyard came the tinkle of a piano, the blare of a radio and intermittently the chatter of two pneumatic drills demolishing a bomb-damaged house nearby.

From one of his repeated trips out to the hall father returned with a bulky envelope in his hand. He seemed to be in two minds about opening it, as if the day had been the Sabbath. Then he took his paperknife, slit the envelope and drew out the contents. The colour drained from his cheeks as he read. Resting his head in his hands, he stared at the papers spread out before him.

'What's that letter?' mother asked anxiously.

After a momentary hesitation, father said quietly, 'It's the lists.'

'The lists?' Mother and I ran to him.

'Yes. But look,' he added for mother's benefit, 'there's no need to alarm yourself. We've got two weeks. We'll sort this thing out by then — you'll see. The Jewish Council is bound to do something for me. Haven't I got my congregation to look after?'

Mother said nothing. She looked at father; she looked at me.

'Tomorrow I'll have a word with the people I know on the Jewish Council,' father went on quickly. 'First thing in the morning! No, I'll do something about it now!'

The Jewish Council was miles away across town, and Jews were not allowed to use transport of any kind. Father took his hat and coat and went out to seek advice from friends who lived nearby in the Hansa quarter. He was still out when Leon and Toni returned from work.

Less than an hour later we heard father running up the stairs. He came in white-faced. 'Would you believe it?' he gasped. 'They're not waiting fourteen days any more! I've just seen Dr Adler. He had the lists this morning too, and he's packing as fast as he can. He told me he knows for a fact that they'll be coming to fetch us today!'

I shall never forget what followed as long as I live. I can see it all, in every detail. And yet I am unable to put those last few hours with my parents into words.

The sounds of the tinkling piano, the blaring radio and the two pneumatic drills still reached us from the courtyard. Eventually mother brought herself to say to me: 'Quick, be off with you!' She pulled me out into the hall. 'That would be all we need, if the Gestapo were to catch you here! You make sure you get through to Switzerland, and if that doesn't work, you've always got the shoe-maker to fall back on. I told you, didn't I? He gave me his solemn promise not to leave you in the lurch as long as the war lasts. Leon and Toni have their munitions jobs. That way, at least you three will survive this war!'

And without a kiss or even a handshake she thrust me out of the front door.

Back in my hiding-place at Frau Gold's, I threw myself on the sofa in the gathering dusk and stared up at the old-fashioned brass chandelier.

When I returned to the flat next day, Leon told me what had happened.

Half an hour after I had left, as father and mother were hurriedly preparing to run away and look for somewhere to hide, the doorbell rang. Everybody froze. Father, however, too flustered to be capable of remaining motionless, stole across the creaking floorboards to the front door, lifted the cover from the spyhole, and looked out.

A voice from the landing called, 'Come on, open up! I know you're in there!'

Father opened the door.

The young man in civilian dress was not impolite. He even allowed father and mother time to finish packing their things.

As father went out of the door, he paused for a moment to make Leon and Toni promise to keep the flat on until the end of the war, come what might. Then my parents accompanied the young man down the stairs.

I can picture the scene as if I had been there myself. And I can just imagine what my father must have felt: here was a young man with whom one could communicate in a civilised fashion, so probably the rest of it would be all right too, or at any rate not as bad as he had feared.

Everything in the living-room was as it had been the day before — the slender grandfather clock, the desk with all its drawers pulled out where father had searched for things in a mad rush. The tinkle of a piano and the drone of a radio still came from the courtyard. The two pneumatic drills fired occasional bursts of shrill chatter, now singly, now in tandem.

Toni, tidying up the clothes that had been left lying around, discovered that mother had forgotten her little sponge-bag and had inadvertently taken the key of the flat with her. She wanted to go round to the synagogue there and then. Leon and I both urgently advised against it. It was true that, were she to be arrested, she could show that she was a munitions worker. However, the synagogue no longer formed part of the predictable, human, trustworthy world.

Toni would not be dissuaded. 'Mother must have her sponge-bag,' she reasoned, 'and from our point of view the key is irreplaceable. We'll never be able to get another.'

Leon and I spent an anxious half-hour before Toni returned. Her plan had succeeded. At her request, someone had gone to find mother. She had appeared at the door of the synagogue, escorted by an SS man, and had stared at Toni in glassy-eyed confusion. Looking as though she was only half-awake, she had handed Toni the key and taken her sponge-bag. Silently she had followed the SS man back inside the synagogue as Toni descended the steps to the street.

Four weeks later, having given prior notice of his intention, an official called on Leon and Toni. Clutching a sheaf of papers, he explained politely that it was his job to take possession of the effects our parents had left behind. I ventured out of hiding to steal a glance at the man. I remember thinking that he looked more like a commercial traveller than a Nazi official.

'Is the flat now in your name?' he asked Leon, and when Leon said yes he smiled and made a dismissive gesture. In that case, he said, he would take with him only those items of my parents' clothing for which Leon and Toni had no use. With a broad wink he gave them to understand that he was content to fulfil the letter of his instructions only.

Toni went to the big oak wardrobe, selected a small number of worn-out garments, stuffed them into an old pillowcase and gave them to the official to take away.

In December 1958, after years of fruitless attempts to discover more about what had happened to my parents, I received an official communication from Berlin. The sender was *Der Haupttreuhänder für Rückerstattungsvermögen, OFP Aktenverwahrstelle, Berlin* (The Chief Trustee for Refundable Assets, [Office of the] First Financial President, Records Office, Berlin).

To my disgust, the communication consisted of an official printed form with only my parents' personal details typed in and the inapplicable bits duly deleted. The form certified that my parents ' . . . *was/were deported to* Riga *on the* 18th East *transport on* 15.8.1942. *Regrettably the subsequent whereabouts of the above-named person(s) cannot be ascertained.*'

Living on tiptoe

I moved in with Leon and Toni and lived with them on what they were able to buy with their two 'J'-stamped ration cards. This would have been scarcely tolerable without the help and support of good friends, chief among them the fishmonger and the shoemaker.

About a fortnight later my brother Jakob wrote from Posen to say how hungry he always was but that there was no point in our sending food parcels; they benefited only the camp officers. It was his last letter.

I spent the next few months virtually under twenty-four-hour house arrest. Only very occasionally did I slip out into the street. During the day, when Toni and Leon were out at work, I had to maintain complete silence.

How little experience I had in the art of keeping my existence a secret from the world! It was sounds coming through the ceiling from the flat above — a chairleg grating, the hum of a vacuum-cleaner — that first made me aware of how easily one can give away one's presence. I promptly took off my squeaky leather shoes and stole about the flat on bare or stockinged feet. But that was not the end of it. A door not properly closed snapped shut by itself. The tap in the kitchen emitted a high-pitched whine. Saucepans and particularly saucepan-lids slipped from my grasp. And the struggle I had with those groaning hinges! The kitchen door could be closed only by grasping the handle firmly and pivoting the leaf very, very gently. Lubricating oil was no longer available in the shops, so I asked Toni to bring some castor oil from the chemist. I spent the next two hours oiling every hinge in the flat.

After a few days I found I could live more or less without making a sound. I had learnt to stack china plates silently, to fill the bathtub without splashing, to open and close windows while remaining well out of sight behind the net curtains, to avoid the areas of the hall floor that creaked the most noisily, to suppress coughs and sneezes — and, when they would not be suppressed, very quickly to bury my head under a cushion — and to tidy up, sweep up and wash up as carefully and quietly as if the furniture and the dishes had been made of wafer-thin glass.

I became familiar with a great many sounds from the outside world. The hysterical nagging of a neighbour and the beer-sodden mumble of an old man came from the same gound-floor window across the courtyard, just to the left of the carpet-beating rail. Every day at half past twelve the sentimental tones of an accordion struck up in the courtyard of the house next door. The tinkling piano opposite was an old acquaintance. I recognised the postman's footsteps when he was still half a flight below our landing. I could tell exactly when the young woman in the flat above us went out and whether the old people she left at home were in the room above our kitchen, above our living-room or above our hall; I could also hear when they were listening to the radio, when they made telephone calls and even when they used the lavatory. It was vital, whenever they emptied their bath or flushed their lavatory, to seize the opportunity to do likewise.

I was so quiet the whole time that it was scarcely necessary for me to freeze instantly whenever the doorbell rang. Nevertheless, I did — with a start — each and every time. And I remained in a state of chronic nervous tension until I heard the stranger redescend the stairs.

I got into the habit of making frequent use of the spyhole. Like a caged animal, I would pace back and forth between the kitchen and the front door, or between the front door and the bedroom, or across the living-room from the piano to the sideboard and back. When Leon and Toni were due home from work my 'spying' became particularly restless.

Our flat also had a window overlooking the street. Through the net curtain it was possible to see part of the facade of the house opposite. To see the entrance of our own house it would have been necessary to open the window and lean dangerously far out. For a long time Leon and I toyed with the idea of mounting a pair of mirrors outside the window. We never did it, though. None of the houses in the Hansa quarter had such mirrors, and we knew we must avoid drawing attention to ourselves in any way.

Once my brother and sister were home, life assumed a semblance of normality for the space of a few hours. The moment when they left me alone again early next morning marked the beginning of another anxious day of tiptoeing about in a phantom world filled with trivial, everyday sounds.

A glance through the net curtain into the courtyard; upstairs neighbours in, downstairs neighbours in; a creaking floorboard, a groaning cupboard door, a singing water tap; footsteps on the stairs, footsteps overhead, the grating sound of the radio from the court-yard; a quick look through the spyhole .... Ah, the caretaker coming up the stairs! Too late to creep away from the front door. Slide the cover slowly over the spyhole and wait! Good, he's gone! Go and lie down for a while. Do some reading. But check that the front door is locked properly first. Is the night bolt in the correct position for Leon and Toni to be able to open the door from outside? What's that droning noise? A mosquito? Quick, kill it with a tea towel! Quietly, though! What's the matter with that lavatory cistern? Will the damned thing never stop hissing? I know, I was going to lie down. I'll read by the light of the bedside lamp. No, that shows through the curtain. Let down the blackout blinds! That's no good either: blackout blinds down in the middle of the day might attract attention. That old man upstairs spends all day pacing back and forth too. Is he another Jew in hiding?

The longer my house arrest lasted, the more strongly I felt the need to arrange my day according to a set programme.

Part of that daily programme took care of itself. I saw to it that my brother and sister came home to find the flat tidy and the table laid. Preparing the few boiled potatoes and the other unchanging items of our diet called for no great culinary skills.

I also conducted experiments to determine the practical nutritional value of caraway seed and aniseed. These were among the very few edible items that could be bought without ration cards. We chewed the things literally *ad nauseam*. I tried — not without some success — to get rid of the strong taste by heating the seeds to a high temperature, the idea being to turn them into a calorie-rich foodstuff.

Any time that was left to me after the housework I spent reading.

Books

I had plenty of time for reading. It was no longer a question of having to lock myself in the latrine with a paperback. I now had limitless hours at my disposal. My father's library comprised some 3,000 volumes, and I had quite a collection myself. The time seemed ripe for me — now twenty years old — to pursue my education by my own efforts.

I resolved to set aside a regular portion of each day for the study of Jewish religious literature and another portion for general subjects. In addition to history and literature, I wanted my old predilection for physics, chemistry and medicine to come into its own once again, though of course the practical side was out of the question.

How naïve my plan was. It was based on the educational ideal I had inherited from my father and from the Adass-Isroël school: the combination of German humanistic culture with a late rabbinical bourgeois world-view. I gave no thought to what education is really about or to how it needs to be attuned to its context. Thinking such questions through properly would in any case have been well beyond my powers.

The first scientific book I started to read was entitled *Recent Findings in the Field of Organic Chemistry*. It was soon back on the shelf. I did not even take down the remaining books in the natural sciences section but merely stared in repugnance at the spines: 'Gattermann, *Practice of Organic Chemistry*', 'Hertwig, *Evolution of Man and the Vertebrates*'.

I went on to look at various works of *belles lettres*, sampling a

189

passage here and there before closing the book and trying another one. Schiller's poems were too erudite for me, too heavily laden with emotion; Heine's satire and elaborate wit were more than I could stomach. Nietzsche's brilliant prose no longer worked its magic, and even Goethe had nothing to say to me any more. Were the books dumb, or was I deaf? Had I become a numbskull, or had fear and hardship warped my outlook?

It was only in retrospect that I understood why books had suddenly come to seem so dull and insipid. What I yearned for unconsciously at that time were standards by which I might have assessed and accounted for the appalling present, words that might have made it easier for me to deal with the world of 1942. The German classics were of no use to me in my mute helplessness.

I found myself reaching for the Greek tragedians. Shakespeare's history plays also held my attention. When, after the war, I saw a copy of Thomas Mann's radio broadcasts to the German people, I saw more clearly what had been lacking in my life at that time: a voice that called a spade a spade.*

The search for reading matter suitable for a person in my position led me to a renewed preoccupation with Holy Scripture. For the third time in my life I began systematically to read through all twenty-four books of the Bible in the original Hebrew. My father's library offered me a large selection of dictionaries and commentaries to help with the more difficult texts. Many chapters needed to be worked through laboriously; nevertheless, I reached a point where I was hearing the speeches of the prophets with the same sort of immediacy as if I had been standing in the crowd in Jerusalem two and a half millennia before.

On one occasion, when some stranger rang the doorbell of the flat, I started and involuntarily slammed the Bible shut for fear the powerful voice of the prophet Amos should give me away. And I had been reading to myself!

Sheer spiritual hunger drove many Jews and Christians to study the Bible at that time. While one sought comfort and hope in its visions of the Last Days, another clung in a spirit of magical superstition to the redeeming power of Holy Writ. A third learnt from the Psalms how the people of Jewish antiquity were able to

* In the autumn of 1940 the BBC invited the self-exiled Thomas Mann to talk to his fellow countrymen on the air. He did so in fifty-five addresses delivered between October 1940 and 10 May 1945 (three days after the German surrender). Published after the war as *Deutsche Hörer* (German Listeners), they are collected in Volume 13 of Thomas Mann's *Gesammelte Werke*, Frankfurt am Main, S. Fischer Verlag, 1960–74.

speak to God in their need. The fulminations of the prophets against all forms of idolatry and their wrath at the inversion of good and evil proved effective defences against the insidious power of Nazi propaganda. None of that requires justification. The problems arise when I try to explain why my Bible studies gave me strength despite the fact that I also read the sections that, judged by the moral criteria that we have extracted from other parts in the Bible, appear immoral.

I never got to the bottom of such questions. But nor did they undermine my faith. The sense of outrage that the biblical figures themselves felt at God's amorality, their doubts as to whether there was not something radically wrong with the world, engendered a deep moral earnestness and a dissatisfaction with the godless life. That in itself had sufficed to keep them going.

My reading was badly disturbed by noisy radios. It was not possible to tell how many loudspeakers were going in the courtyard at any one time, for usually they all blared in unison, pouring out the same unremitting sequence of reports from the front, light music, news, Nazi battle songs and plays. I should have worn earplugs had my ears not needed to be on permanent guard duty.

My daily Bible study brought home to me once again not only the beautiful speech melody but also the conciseness of the Hebrew language. Anyone who is obliged to read the Bible in translation can have only the dimmest perception of the mighty eloquence of the prophets and psalmists.

Jewish tradition refers to Hebrew as the Holy Language because, with the exception of a few Aramaic sections, it is the language of the Bible. For me there was a further sense in which it partook of the nature of the holy: it had never been so deeply profaned as my German mother tongue. Hebrew words had suffered a certain amount of devaluation in the course of time. But no Nazis were in a position to commandeer Hebrew and misuse it for propaganda purposes and for the perversion of every concept.*

What a fearful pass things have come to when one can no longer trust one's mother tongue, the language one loves, but must turn

* The author cites the following (essentially untranslatable) examples of Nazi usage:
—'Der Reichsmarschall überzeugt sich von der Einsatzbereitschaft seiner Mannen.'
— 'Der Fraueneinsatz bei Luftangriffen erfolgt im Einvernehmen mit den Ortsfrauenschaftsleiterinnen.'
— 'Zur Freizeitgestaltung gelangen überall Rundfunkgeräte zum Einsatz.'
— 'Der vom Reichspropagandaminister einberufene europäische Schriftstellerkongress hat unter Beweis gestellt, dass die weltanschauliche Ausrichtung aller Kulturschaffenden bereits weitgehend zur Durchführung gelangt ist.' [Tr.]

191

every word over to examine whether it has not been drained of all meaning or acquired some new and ominous connotation! Despite the loathing I felt for Nazi jargon, I occasionally caught myself using some of its expressions. Even today I have to guard against doing so.

The fact that I was able to escape from the corrupting influence of all the loudspeaker-German and immerse myself in the unspoiled purity of Hebrew — as in a cleansing bath — certainly helped preserve my self-respect at that time.

Behind the tightly drawn curtains of my 'prison' I resolved to learn to speak fluent Hebrew. Between that resolution and its execution, not a day passed unused. I had brought an excellent manual of colloquial Hebrew with me from Steckelsdorf. It was written in a lively tone with no trace of academic heaviness or boring pedantry. Reading it, one could with very little imagination picture oneself in some Jewish settlement in Palestine. I helped with the orange-picking near Petach Tikvah. At Haifa railway station I inquired when the next train left for Jerusalem and spent the time waiting for it in the station restaurant. And all the people I had dealings with, whether on the orange plantation or at the station, whether grown-ups or children, spoke Hebrew without stumbling over a single problem of grammar. Thrusting my way through the crowded streets of Tel Aviv, I looked up from the book and peered out through the net curtain into the courtyard. Another propaganda broadcast had just finished. The neighbour's radio now offered the joyful voices of a large choir: 'For we're off,' they sang, 'for we're off, for we're off to fight the Eng-er-lish!' From the window just to the left of the carpet-beating rail came a burst of hysterical nagging and bass mumbling from the quarrelsome couple. Then everything went quiet; all I could hear was the restless pacing in the flat upstairs. Someone flushed the lavatory up there. I hurried to flush our own under cover of the noise, then stole back to the living-room on stockinged feet and sat down again to my Hebrew book.

Sometimes stange doubts would assail me. Was I perhaps the only person still bothering with Hebrew? I noticed that the textbook had been printed in Vienna in 1937 — the year before the Nazi takeover there. It will take miracles, I told myself, for such a book ever to be printed in Vienna again. And who will be learning Hebrew in Berlin now, in the summer of 1942? No one! You are the last person still doing it. Maybe you're the last in the whole world. Maybe everything you ever heard about Palestine is pure fantasy. Rattled, I would pace back and forth for a while between the table and the bookshelf and between the bookshelf and the curtained window before sitting down at the table again to continue studying.

Soon the little exercise pieces in the book were no longer enough for me; I wanted literature. I hunted through my father's library and my own collection and pulled out everything I could find by modern Hebrew authors.

For anyone who has got to know Hebrew through the Bible and the rabbinical writings, the language acquires a dignity far in excess of what might be accounted for by its beauty alone. There is beauty in all human languages. Speaking Hebrew, however, means continually evoking the Bible. Had it not been so, could Hebrew ever have been awakened to new life?

I have to admit that the writers of modern Hebrew literature rather disappointed me. At the focus of their work stood the secular Zionist ideal. In the context of the apocalyptic events of the Hitler war, they had little to say to me beyond 'If you had only been a bit smarter and emigrated to Palestine in time!'

When my brother Leon found me yet again buried in Hebrew books, he shook his head: 'Listen, are you completely off your rocker? Now you're mugging up Hebrew. Shouldn't you be making sure you get out of here alive first?'

He was right, of course. But how in the world was I ever going to find a way of escape?

Some months later, when Leon no longer had his job in the munitions factory and was as much an outlaw as I was, he took down my old textbook and began to study Hebrew himself.

Autumn 1942

My life of secrecy and confinement continued. Only rarely was the monotony of my existence broken by external events and personal encounters. Let me mention one or two of these that occured during this period.

Four months had passed since my flight from Steckelsdorf, one since my parents' deportation. Worrying about what had happened to my parents and to my Steckelsdorf *chaverim* was a constant preoccupation. It left me no peace. Leon and Toni tried in vain to extract some information from the offices of various Jewish institutions.

It dawned on me that the Hungarian youth leader Sholem Klein might still be at the training farm. I persuaded Toni to try writing him a letter, inviting him to visit her and Leon.

Sholem did indeed come. And he beamed with joy when he found me at the flat as well. He told us he had thought there must be something behind the invitation.

Sholem told me what had happened at the training farm after my flight. When my absence was brought to the attention of the manager (fortunately not until the evening, by which time I was safely in Berlin), he felt that he had no choice, given his duty to protect the interests of the Steckelsdorf community, but to inform the village policeman in Neue Schleuse and the Gestapo in Rathenow immediately. (That explained why two officials had called at my parents' flat the day after my flight.) Blumenfeld's action had the desired effect: the police made neither him nor the *chaverim* pay for my disappearance.

Sholem went on to describe the day that had followed my flight, the day of the 'resettlement'.

The village policeman and a number of Gestapo officers arrived at the farm. The fifty were made to form up in ranks and marched to Rathenow station. The suitcases had to be left behind; the *chaverim* were allowed to take only their rucksacks and haversacks.

After they had gone, the abandoned suitcases, swinging cupboard doors and other signs of frantic and partly futile preparations gave the farm a forlorn appearance. The next day the village policeman and two Gestapo men came back — this time, as Sholem put it, to 'divide up the loot'. The sight of them rummaging through the deportees' cupboards and cases in search of the choicest items had so disgusted him, he said, that he had actually vomited.

In August the whole ghastly business of deportation had been repeated at Steckelsdorf with the fifteen *chaverim* left behind the first time — repeated in every detail from the farewell telegrams and feverish travel preparations to the sharing out of the spoils. Since then the only people living on the training farm, apart from the Hungarian nationals, had been the head gardener, Rotschild, and his 'Aryan' wife. The *chaverim* had never been heard from again.

Sholem told us that they were expecting the farm, which was the property of the Reichsvereinigung, to be confiscated by the authorities within the foreseeable future. He and his wife had not yet decided what to do with themselves. They were not keen on the idea of returning to Hungary.

After Sholem's visit, the hostile outside world seemed to tighten its already effective stranglehold around our flat. I never set eyes on any but a handful of people: Frau Gold, a French civilian worker friend of Leon's, and Lore, Leon's girlfriend.

My illegal existence having become a permanent state of affairs we had decided to take Lore into our confidence, and I got to see her for the first time. God, she was lovely! I silently congratulated Leon

194

on having won the love of so beautiful a girl.

Lore belonged to a family that had become completely estranged from the Jewish tradition. She had been unaware of her Jewishness until the Race Laws were introduced. There was something touching in the way she asked about details of our religious customs and tried to understand the links between the Jewish faith and the persecutions, ancient and modern, suffered by Jewry.

Lore was a half-orphan. In the autumn of 1942 she frequently came round from her mother's flat to ours, where she found as much security as a boyfriend living behind a door with a yellow star on it could offer her.

Frau Gold, mother's friend, was the only person who had access to our flat while Leon and Toni were out at work. She mothered me to some extent, and in her matter-of-fact voice she told me the latest news — most of it bad.

One day she had a story about a girl who had leapt from a fourth-floor window into the street when the Gestapo came. Another time she told me about a 15-year-old boy who was to have been taken from his parents. The boy promptly took to his heels, dashed down the stairs, and disappeared round the corner of the street, with the Gestapo man shouting 'Stop that boy!' from the balcony as if after an escaped criminal.

According to Frau Gold's information, the Gestapo had changed their tactics. Since more and more Jews were going into hiding the Gestapo had stopped sending out 'lists' and had taken to driving through the streets of Berlin in an enormous pantechnicon — like a dog-catcher's van — loading up people with yellow stars whenever they could lay hands on them. Jews now had to keep abreast of where the van was currently stationed in order to avoid running straight into the hangman's noose, as it were. Frau Gold urged me to be extremely careful: even without my yellow star, I might easily get caught in one of these round-ups.

Jews in hiding were apparently discovered more often by neighbours than by police patrols. Consequently I was more frightened on the stairs than I was in the street. If a trip to the shops was unavoidable, some quick-change artistry was called for. Nothing about my outward appearance must betray the fact that I was a starving outlaw who spent the day creeping around on stockinged feet behind heavily curtained windows. I donned my leather boots, examined myself critically in the mirror, took a look through the spyhole, and listened carefully for whether there was anyone on the stairs. When the coast was clear I cautiously opened the door and as cautiously closed it behind me, letting the patent lock spring back as quietly as I could. Then it was a matter of walking down the stairs with a normal-sounding step and at a natural, unhurried pace.

I wondered, though, how my neighbours would account for the fact that, after a period of complete silence, steps were suddenly heard descending from the first floor, and that on my return the sound of ascending footsteps was so abruptly followed by, again, complete silence. In the street I endeavoured to present the appearance of a senior schoolboy who has not a care in the world. I did not look my twenty years.

Waiting at the hairdresser's was always an ordeal. Even while I was being attended to I could feel curious eyes on my back. I found myself exchanging glances in the mirror with suspicious-looking customers in civilian dress. Were they waiting for a haircut or were they waiting for me? Why were they looking at me like that? Was there something odd about my appearance?

The hairdresser, a man in his early fifties, once inquired between snips of his scissors as to my military status. I mumbled something about belonging to an anti-aircraft gun crew and attempted to steer the conversation back to hairdressing. However, the man was determined to talk about subjects of global importance. Quite unsolicited, he offered me his view of the future: 'Oh, yes, they'll make it up to us after the war. The British and Americans and Russians are going to have to rebuild everything their bombs have destroyed. They'll supply the materials *and* do the work, while we keep an eye on them. We shan't be able to do the work ourselves — we'll need all our people to occupy their countries.'

I responded to these remarks by looking as pleased as I could. My haircut was now finished. 'Heil Hitler!' I said as I went out of the door. It was the first time the words had passed my lips. I was surprised and appalled by the naturalness with which they did so.

I remember walking past a bombed house one day. Some workmen were busy removing the debris. I would have taken no further notice of them had I not spotted a policeman with them. 'Why do you not have an identity card?' I heard the policeman bark at one of the men. 'A German always carries an official identity card, complete with photograph, about his person!'

I missed the answer: the workman spoke much too quietly. But I saw the look of desperate entreaty that accompanied his protestations to the uniformed figure standing in front of him. If anyone were to stop me, I realised, I had no proof of identity to present either. The challenge 'Your ID card, please!' would mean curtains for me.

The air-raids increased in frequency. When bombs were falling and the sky was torn by anti-aircraft and machine-gun fire, Jews could relax a little. No one would be coming up the stairs to fetch them just then. All the sounds in the stairwell were made by the 'Aryan' occupants of the house hurrying down to the cellar.

Of all the air-raids on Berlin in the autumn of 1942, one sticks in my mind with particular vividness. We had remained in the flat, as always. There were some heavy strikes not far from the house. As soon as the all-clear sounded, we dashed outside.

The sky glowed red and smoky with the reflected light of burning houses. A block of flats on the corner of Altonaerstrasse and the Schleswig Embankment was burning fiercely. That was very close to the shoemaker's place! Quick, we must go to him! Hansa Bridge was jammed with fire-engines and ambulances. A large crowd was following the grim spectacle with horrified fascination. We attempted to work our way through the crush. It was hopeless. A human chain of air-raid wardens, policemen and stewards had sealed off the entrance to the Schleswig Embankment against the excited crowd. Someone shouted that he had lost his home and everything he possessed. Someone else raised his voice in protest at the obstruction. Was the crowd about to start demonstrating?

The air-raid wardens were letting no one through. One of them addressed the crowd in calming tones. His face shone redly in the light of the flames. I was standing only a few feet from him, and I heard him say, 'Now then, don't get excited! It's all been taken care of. There are Jewish flats waiting for you all, fully furnished. And if there aren't enough, we'll soon empty a few more!'

The words hit me with a physical impact. I heard no applause from the crowd, but no more complaining either.

CHAPTER 9

The Shoemaker

'Come on in and make yourselves at home!'

As 1942 gave way to 1943, the Second World War entered a crucial new phase. The German Sixth Army was cut off around Stalingrad. Montgomery drove Rommel and his Africa Corps out of Cyrenaica and Tripolitania. Landings of American and British troops led to the formation of a second front in North Africa. Douglas MacArthur began to inflict heavy defeats on the Japanese in the Pacific.

It was the evening of New Year's Eve 1942. The sirens were silent; the Gestapo, accordingly, were all the busier.

Toni was doing the washing-up; Leon was lying on the sofa; I was reading. Suddenly we heard pounding footsteps: someone was coming up the stairs in a great hurry. Next moment there was a hurried knock at the door: knock knock-knock knock-knock. Leon leapt up and opened the door. The person who came bursting in was Lore — but Lore as we had never seen her before: white-faced, trembling, perspiring, gasping for breath. She blurted out, 'They came! They wanted to take us away — mummy and me — for deportation! I just ran — out from under their noses! They started to chase me. . . .'

Lore had been talking for no more than a few moments when the doorbell rang. It was them! One of us flicked off the light. We all froze where we stood. The bell rang and rang. 'Open up!' came a shout from the landing. They yelled, they banged on the door, they rattled the handle, they kicked the panels. We remained glued to the spot; the devil himself would not have shifted us. Abruptly, silence fell outside, though we could still hear breathing. They listened, held a whispered consultation. Then they took a run and hurled themselves at the door with all their might. How the timbers creaked and groaned! Don't let it give way! I prayed — for God's sake, don't let it give way!

198

'Open up there!'

Leon started to tiptoe towards the door. I guessed what it was he wanted to do under cover of the din they were making outside. Don't try it! I silently implored. They'll hear! You'll get us all into such trouble! But I could see he was determined to make the attempt. God, what a racket they were making on the landing. My heart came into my throat as. . . . He's done it! I rejoiced inwardly, as the heavy iron bolt slid into place. Good old Leon! Now let them ram it with their heads if they want to!

They descended the stairs. We listened with bated breath as the footsteps receded. Don't let them fetch a locksmith or a builder! Don't let them come back with saws and crow-bars!

We held a council of war. We could no longer stay in the flat, that much was clear. We must drop everything and leave immediately. But where in the world were we to go, so late in the evening? Toni believed she could persuade the shoemaker to offer her shelter, and possibly me too, but not all four of us.

We knew immediately what Toni was thinking. It would be unwise to expect the old man to hide the four of us. To Toni and myself he had made promises, and that was already a great deal; his three boys were under fire on the eastern front, and he was prepared to offer us two shelter and protection in their rooms — where every stick of furniture must inevitably remind him of his absent sons. We ought not to risk forfeiting his goodwill by asking too much of him.

That was where we began. We wound up our deliberations just before midnight with the apparently weird decision that, while accepting that we must abandon our parents' flat with all speed, we would spend one last night in it and make our getaway just before dawn. Toni and I would move to the shoemaker's first thing in the morning. Leon and Lore must find their own hiding-place elsewhere during the course of the day. We resolved to say nothing to the shoemaker about their predicament.

Where we found the courage to lie down and go to sleep in a flat that was effectively under siege, I no longer know. Possibly it was not courage at all so much as utter helplessness. I suspect Toni went round to the shoemaker's place and he made an urgent request that we should not come until the morning. But here my memory lets me down.

In the grey first light of New Year's Day, we set out. We could not have asked for better weather conditions: a heavy snow flurry. The few pedestrians who were on the streets were all battling, head down, through the swirling flakes. None of them paid any attention to the four figures who, laden with bulging quilt-covers, crossed the

Spree over Hansa Bridge at fifty-yard intervals.

It was about ten minutes' walk to Cuxhavenerstrasse. The shoe-maker was waiting for us at the door of his shop, which also gave access to his ground-floor flat. He greeted us with a friendly nod. 'Come on in,' he said, 'and make yourselves at home!'

The shoemaker had given my mother a solemn promise that he would never leave me in the lurch. He was now keeping that promise. Even so, when he received us so warmly and we felt the firm ground of his flat beneath our feet, we could scarcely believe our good fortune.

Accommodating Toni and myself was no great problem. Toni took over the housekeeping, thus fulfilling one of the old widower's fondest desires. She 'made herself at home' amid the old-fashioned furnishings of the flat's 'Berlin room', a spacious connecting room with a window looking onto the courtyard that was a feature of the nineteenth-century apartment buildings of Berlin. The shoemaker gave me the use of a small room with a window overlooking the courtyard.

And Leon and Lore? We gave the shoemaker to understand that they had found accommodation elsewhere. They followed us into the flat as if they had simply been helping us transport our belongings. Actually they were bringing their own things in too in order to be able to pursue their search unencumbered.

How they were to find a hiding-place within the space of twelve hours, I simply could not imagine. And yet they *had* to — at any cost! A night with nowhere to stay would have meant the end for them. Before Leon and Lore went on their way, we held another council of war in the room the shoemaker had assigned to me. For Toni and myself it was intolerable to think that Leon and Lore faced a yawning void when we had found safety. We felt we could not simply let them go.

'Look, if you don't find anything at all,' Toni told them, 'you come back here and sleep in Ezra's room without the shoemaker knowing.'

'All right.' Leon concurred. 'In a real emergency. But it probably won't be necessary. I have a very definite address in mind.'

When the evening was already far advanced and Leon and Lore had not returned, I began to feel easier in my mind: presumably they had found somewhere. To be on the safe side I decided to stay awake until midnight. The shoemaker had retired to bed a long time before.

Suddenly I heard tapping on the windowpane. Our secret knock! Quick — light out, blackout blind up, window open; in over the sill from the darkness of the courtyard into the darkness of the room; window shut, blackout blind down again, light on. Luckily there was a folding camp bed in my room. Preparations for the night were quickly made. Lore slept on the couch. Leon stretched out across a couple of chairs. I took the camp bed. Leon and Lore did not undress; in fact, they even kept their coats on. Early in the morning, before the shoemaker was up, they left the flat by the back door.

The overnight stay — doubly illegal — had gone off without a hitch. Leon and Lore had been saved for another day, and the shoemaker had been spared a conflict of conscience that he might have found too much for him. Now Leon and Lore had a whole new day in which to find somewhere to stay.

What would we do, we wondered, if they were still unsuccessful? Should we take the shoemaker into our confidence, thus gambling with all our fates when it might only be a question of one or two nights more? Which was more considerate towards the old man as well as towards ourselves: to own up or to risk one, perhaps two more doubly illegal overnight stays? We decided that the right course was to spare both the old man and ourselves any extra trouble.

As a result, these overnight stays were repeated on the following days, for Leon and Lore had still not found other quarters. They did not even have anywhere to spend the evenings, so that they sometimes smuggled themselves into the shoemaker's flat by the back door in the early evening. They would sit down in my room without removing their coats. When the shoemaker came into the room, they had 'just dropped in for a visit'. The unsuspecting old man would even greet them cordially.

The shoemaker would not have been more severely punished if four people had been found living illegally in his flat rather than two. The fact was, we considered the danger to which we were exposing him trivial in comparison with that which hung over our own heads. A seventy-year-old widower with three sons at the front would be treated with indulgence even by the Nazi authorities, we thought.

It did, however, weigh heavily on our consciences that we had to deploy such odious wiles against a man to whom we owed so much. How degrading it all was! Yet we could think of no better course. We had to resign ourselves to this solution, distasteful though we found it. It was a question of saving four people's lives.

Leon still did not dare to go underground completely. He continued to report each morning to the German Armaments and Munitions Works. When he left the factory at the end of the afternoon he fastened down his 'two-way' yellow star and began the illegal part of his day. I nearly said that he came home as an outlaw; but he had nowhere he could call home. For the first two weeks of January 1943, Leon and Lore had no other base than the shoemaker's flat.

I pointed out to Leon how illogical he was being: did he think he was halving the risk by going underground for only half the day? Of course he would rather stay away from work, he retorted. The trouble was, he did not know where else he could spend the day in that cold weather; the factory was still the safest and warmest place. Added to which, if he did not go to work he would not receive his food allowances. It was bad enough that Toni, Lore and I were already wholly dependent on the shoemaker's kitchen.

What Lore did during the first half of that January I cannot recall with any degree of certainty. Having fled from the Gestapo on New Year's Eve, she presumably had to stay away from her place of work as well. It was not easy for a girl to find somewhere to spend the daylight hours, though it was easier than for a man of call-up age. Lore had the additional advantage that her whole appearance — particularly her blond hair — was more 'Aryan' than Jewish. She no longer wore her yellow star, of course.

Leon and Lore had to get by in this makeshift fashion for quite some time, with Leon asking around among his Jewish friends and among the foreign civilian detainees he met at work. After much agonisingly fruitless searching, Leon and Lore billeted themselves in an abandoned flat that had belonged to some friends of ours: Guli and his parents! As far as Leon could discover, they had been deported in December. Leon still had the key Guli had once given him.

Guli deported? So the methodical German civil service had not even overlooked a poor imbecile!

'But, Leon, there'll still be a yellow star on the door of the flat!' I exclaimed in dismay.

'Of course there is. But you needn't worry. The flat has been sealed, you see. I simply remove the Gestapo seal and reattach it. There's no safer place for two illegal Jews to hide than behind a door sealed by the Gestapo! They can really sleep soundly: no one's going to come looking for them there.'

Some time later, Leon and Lore moved into rather less comfortable but considerably less risky lodgings. Lore had managed to find an old lady living on her own who badly needed some help with the housework. The lumber-room she offered Lore was just large enough to sleep two.

I never learnt where that lumber-room was, nor what it looked like. Nor did I discover anything about the other hiding-places they used over the following months. I saw Leon and Lore only at our permanent rendezvous: the shoemaker's flat in Cuxhavenerstrasse.

The shoemaker's flat

The art of living one's life while keeping it a secret from the world takes some learning. I had had seven months' experience to draw on. So I was appalled at the speed and confidence with which Toni took the step into outlawry.

After our flight from our parents' flat she did not return to her job at the telephone works, wanting to devote all her energies to looking after the shoemaker and ourselves. She took up her new duties as soon as she was installed in the shoemaker's flat. She dusted everywhere, pushed the vacuum-cleaner round the flat and lit the wood-burning stove. She dropped her identity card and her yellow star into the flames, put a couple of saucepans on top, and proceeded to cook the lunch, warbling a song the while.

She said she had nothing to lose but her ration cards stamped with their 'J', and that loss was nothing in comparison with the freedom she had regained. Indeed, so far as getting hold of food was concerned, we were extraordinarily lucky. The shoemaker was able to provide for us without any difficulty. His customers brought him little gifts of sugar, potatoes, jam and other foodstuffs in order not to have to wait weeks for their shoes. Particularly important were his relations with the Hansaplatz baker and the Lessingstrasse green-grocer. As a rule Toni was able to bring me enough to eat in my room, and often she managed to put something by for Leon and Lore as well.

But living outside the law involved other worries than getting enough to eat.

'You simply must start taking more care!' I remonstrated with Toni one day. 'Don't you realise the danger we're living in?'

'How can I take more care? I go out as little as possible as it is, but I have to do the shopping!'

'I don't mean just that — here in the flat as well! What are the customers going to think when they hear footsteps and doors banging the whole time? They know the shoemaker lives on his own. And *must* you sing so loudly in the kitchen?'

'Oh, you worry too much! The shoemaker has already introduced me to several people as his niece. I can't start being all secretive now, otherwise they'd really be suspicious. Besides, don't you think it would make the shoemaker himself pretty nervous if we tiptoed around the place all day?'

The shoemaker's flat might have been designed to accommodate people on the run. It had two entrances (and exits!): through the shop, and via the stairwell. Moreover, there was no need to pass any doors with spyholes through which inquisitive neighbours might have spied on us.

The shop itself was spacious. It contained a grinding and polishing bench and a great many shelves for shoes. There was a permanent smell of leather and glue as well as of freshly sawn pine, because the front part of the shop, including the large window, had been twice renewed following bomb damage. Seen from the street, the window offered a display of gleaming new men's and ladies' shoes. Half-hidden behind an advertising board that stood at a slight angle, was a small butter tub. The customers ensured that this was kept well topped up.

On the hotplate against the back wall a kettle stood permanently on the boil. Its singing, however, was audible only when the so-called *Volksempfänger*, the 'people's receiver' on the little table beside it, was silent.* That was not often. The shoemaker liked to have the radio keep him company; he could not stand what he always referred to as a 'deathly hush'. Only when, say, a frail old lady came into the shop and the shoemaker, try as he might, simply could not understand her feeble piping, would he condescend to reach for the knob and turn the volume down. Everyone else had to bawl his or her lungs out. The seventy-year-old shoemaker was hard of hearing. He liked people to speak up.

Behind the counter, out of the customers' sight, was a trapdoor leading to the cellar.

The shoemaker proudly gave me a guided tour of his domain. The 'Berlin room' behind the shop led into the shoemaker's own bedroom off to one side and into the passage straight on. This was much encumbered by wardrobes and chests. In the only free part a pair of antlers hung on the wall above crossed swords, some ancient pistols and a group of pictures. When I asked the shoemaker whether he had used the weapons himself, he pointed to a large framed photograph of a Mecklenburg uhlan of the 1890s.

'There you are,' he said. 'That's me serving the emperor, and now my own sons are at the front.'

'That's you?' I asked in astonishment. 'That dashing young soldier? Why, the uniform suits you to a T.'

---

* The *Volksempfänger* radio set was sold at a special low price to encourage the populace to listen to the government's propaganda broadcasts.

The build and the ramrod bearing were the same. I also recognised the chubby cheeks, now reddened with cold. But the young uhlan had yet to acquire the foxy look of the old man.

'Was your father in the army too?' I asked.

'He certainly was. Fought the battle of Sedan in 1870,' the shoemaker announced with pride.

The passage led to my little room, the lavatory and the kitchen.

The windows of the bedrooms and the kitchen overlooked the courtyard. All except the kitchen window were fitted with net curtains. One of the first things Toni did was to make net curtains for the kitchen window as well.

A door leading straight from the kitchen into the stairwell of the house provided the flat with the second exit that was later to be of such importance to us.

Toni and I entered and left the flat by the shop, as if we had been customers. If we returned from whatever errand we had been on to find real customers waiting, we would wait beside them in front of the counter until they left the shop.

At such times I overheard many conversations. The talk turned mostly on the shortage of good butt leather, the burden of work currently being shouldered by the older generation of craftsmen, the much missed sons away at the front and the terrors of the air-raids. Politics was never discussed. The shoemaker had a habit of reinforcing his remarks with an emphatic 'And that's a fact!' He might observe, for instance, 'The folk in the air-raid shelter ought not to chatter so much. Then at least between the bombs dropping we'd have a bit of peace, and that's a fact! They make more noise down there than the guns!' With each 'And that's a fact!' his face would take on an aggrieved expression quite out of keeping with his gigantic stature.

Waiting in front of the counter could become a nuisance when fresh customers kept coming in. Then we would leave the shop as if we had been in a great hurry and use the kitchen entrance. As a rule, though, we preferred to use the shop in order to keep to a minimum the number of occasions when the caretaker and the neighbours might catch sight of us in the courtyard.

The small side-room where the shoemaker installed me belonged to Fritz, his youngest son. I found it well furnished and cheerfully appointed. It felt as though the son had only just left, whereas in fact he had been away since the beginning of the war. Two photographs of him stood on a small writing-table. In one he wore the uniform of a sergeant in the German army; the other showed him in civilian dress, accompanied by his girlfriend. His uniform fitted his sturdy body well. He was clean shaven and well groomed, and he looked out at the world with an air of self-assurance. I could see no great likeness to his father. The conventional photographs gave away little of his character. I tried to form a clearer idea of him from the way in which he had arranged his room.

But neither was there anything very personal about the room. Nothing in it gave any indication of his profession, for example (he was a hairdresser). Apart from the writing-table, the furniture consisted of several chairs, a sofa, a wardrobe and a bookcase. The wardrobe contained two Sunday suits, an incomplete Hitler Youth uniform and a raincoat.

Of the books in the bookcase I recall the following: *Fridericus Rex*, the patriotic poem by Willibald Alexis, a book entitled *With the Migrant Birds to Africa*, the Bible in Martin Luther's translation, Hitler's *Mein Kampf*, an obscene publication disguised as something called *Faust and Gretchen: An Interlude Based on Goethe*, a Karl May novel (*Unter Geiern*) and the memoirs of Otto von Bismarck.

Naturally I made as few changes to the room as possible. Even after Leon and Lore had found a place of their own, I continued to sleep on the uncomfortable camp bed in order to preserve the sofa. The books I had brought with me I hid behind Fritz's books.

From what my mother had told me of her pact with the shoemaker, I had hoped he would teach me his trade and have me working for him in the cellar. I never stopped to think what his customers would have made of all the underground hammering! I could have worked for him in the kitchen, of course, or in my bedroom. But I never managed to persuade the shoemaker to let me. It would have made things far too complicated for him, in any case, having to commute between his workshop and my room all the time.

So I sought to make myself useful to him in other ways. I welcomed every opportunity: greasing a leaky gas-tap in the kitchen, replacing a broken broomstick, locating a short circuit, mending an iron, chopping firewood in the cellar in the evenings.

However, such trivial chores were a poor substitute for what I might have done for him in the workshop, and I found it depressing to meet the shoemaker during his working hours when my own hands were idle. I preferred to remain silent and still in my room, burying myself in my books. I also read Sergeant Fritz's books. Every now and then I would make a discreet sortie to see if there was anything else I could do to help.

A typical day went something like this. I used to get up around half past six and go to the lavatory before the shoemaker rose.

Around half past eight, provided there were no customers in the shop, I would pop my head round the door to say hello to the shoemaker and spend a few moments chatting with him. Then it was back to my room, where Toni brought me something to eat. There followed a period of Bible and Talmud study and Hebrew translation exercises. As I read and wrote I was aware of Toni passing to and fro between the kitchen and the workshop. Through the pane of obscured glass in the door of my room, I occasionally glimpsed the giant figure of the shoemaker gliding past.

'Toni!' he might shout in the direction of the kitchen. 'I'm just off to the barber's. If any customers come, tell them I'll be back in half an hour.' Or, 'Toni! That Ukrainian who works for the baker was here again. He had this half-made tart up his jumper. It's still piping hot. He almost scorched his tummy, poor devil! See if you can finish it for our supper. He was stammering something in Ukrainian and kept pointing at his feet. I really must do something about those shoes of his some time. We might need the fellow again, and that's a fact!'

Around eleven I popped into the workshop again for a couple of minutes. The shoemaker was hammering at a shoe while the 'people's receiver' disgorged an unbroken stream of words and music. Another bulletin from the front had just finished.

It suddenly struck me how strange the radio had come to seem. We Jews had not been allowed to own one for the past two years. We had heard only scraps of indistinct loudspeaker noise from a distance. Now at last I had an opportunity to study in greater detail the kinds of programme currently being broadcast, for the shoemaker had his 'people's receiver' on virtually all the time. The announcer's voice sounded much more human from close to than it had when it came bawling at us from the neighbour's window opposite. More human, more personal — and so much more suggestive! Had the shoemaker no fear that the steady trickle of Goebbels's propaganda might undermine his judgement and poison his soul? Did he feel that his critical faculties were still intact? He probably never even thought about it.

As a source of information, the radio did not have much to offer us. One learnt little more from the newspapers on sale at every street corner. It would have been different had the shoemaker tuned in to a foreign station occasionally, but the idea never occurred to him. Nor did I ever try to put him up to so perilous a venture. (It was illegal, and the penalty could be death.)

The bulletin from the front was followed by highlights from the last act of *Carmen*. The shoemaker hammered busily as he listened.

'This is where he stabs her!' he shouted to me, wrenching a bent nail from the sole of the shoe.

'You seem to know the story well.'

'Oh, I used to go to the opera a lot in my young days. I've still got the opera guidebook from that time. Always used to read the plot before I went. Otherwise you don't get a lot out of it, and that's a fact!'

A stranger approached the door of the shop. I disappeared and returned to my books: Graetz, *History of the Jews*. 'Chief heresy hunter Hoogstraten backs a permanent court of inquisition against the Jews. . . . Misuse of the Dominicans against the advice of Reuchlin. . . .'

Around half past twelve I heard a sudden burst of radio noise in the passage, followed by the shoemaker's heavy tread. 'Toni! I'm going round to the baker's. Where's the bailiff's bag?'

The shoemaker was on intimate terms with the baker in nearby Hansaplatz. He was therefore permitted to use the back door of the bakery. There were times when he had to wait unattended for several minutes before he was noticed and served. But waiting between shelves laden with fresh bread and pastries was a very different matter from queuing in the shop behind a long line of housewives while the baker fussed over bread coupons and totted up columns of figures. This did not prevent the shoemaker from repeatedly giving vent to his irritation with the baker. 'The fellow's always stuffing himself,' he would snort, 'while he lets his customers half starve! And that's a fact!'

The shoemaker saw it as no more than trimming the scales of justice to 'seize' the occasional item from the inordinately mountainous heaps of loaves and rolls. There was no need for him to stick it up his jumper, like the poor Ukrainian. He had a special bag for the purpose, a briefcase with gleaming buckles such as might fittingly be carried by an officer of the court.

'Toni!' I used to hear the shoemaker shout whenever, around lunchtime, he slipped into his coat and reached for his hat. 'Where's the bailiff's bag?' And off he would go to the baker's as customer, old friend, forager and law-enforcement officer rolled into one. The old man took an evident pleasure in combining so many roles. He usually returned from Hansaplatz wearing a satisfied smile.

Around one o'clock the shoemaker and Toni sat down to lunch in the kitchen. Toni brought me lunch in my room. I had suggested this arrangement to the shoemaker myself, lest the neighbours hear too many voices coming from the kitchen. After lunch I went back into the workshop for a few minutes.

'Tschibel,' the shoemaker said to me, 'could you put a bit of wood on the fire, do you think?'

'Tschibel' (pronounced 'Cheeble') had been my pet name as a child. It was a name more usually applied to a young rooster, and I had come to dislike it heartily. However, it was what Toni still called me, and now the shoemaker had adopted the wretched name! Still, I was pleased that the old man had also adopted the familiar form of address and warmly called me *du*.

I stoked the fire. Meanwhile, the sound of the radio filled the shop as usual. A reporter from the propaganda corps was describing a tank battle in the south section of the eastern front. Each Russian tank, he said, was a complete fortress in itself. Our soldiers, combating these steel monsters in the bitter cold, were performing superhuman feats.

'Tschibel,' the shoemaker called above the noise, 'could you fix this plug for me? It sparks every time I start the motor.'

The voice on the radio had reached the end of its report. There followed a many-voiced rendition of 'We're Off to Fight the Eng-er-lish'. The loudspeaker kept up a never-ending sequence of music and speech, speech and music. The shoemaker had donned an apron and was back on his stool. Spotting a customer as he approached the door, I dropped everything and disappeared. Five minutes later the shoemaker came knocking at my door: 'Tschibel! He's gone! You can come out now!'

The plug mended, I went back to reading in my room. A poem by the Hebrew poet Tschernichowsky (written — in Hebrew — in Swinemünde* in 1925!). Bismarck's *Thoughts and Reminiscences*. My Hebrew translation exercise: a paragraph from *With the Migrant Birds to Africa*. Try as I might, there were two words for which I simply could not find a translation. If I survive this war, I thought, I'll ask someone in Palestine.

Tired of sitting and writing, I stood up to stretch my limbs. There was not much room for pacing to and fro; I kept bumping into things. I heard footsteps in the courtyard and peered through the curtains. The caretaker was rummaging in the dustbins.

The door of my room opened. It was Toni, bringing me a cup of black 'coffee' (it even had sugar in it). I pulled down the blackout blind and switched on the light. Toni hurried away, saying she still had a lot to do before supper. I continued my studies with a piece from the Mishnah: instructions as to how a Jew should behave towards idolaters. I followed this with two chapters from Thomas

* Now Swinoujscie in Poland.

Mann's novel *Buddenbrooks*, including the scene where the men tuck into a feast. The scene is so vividly described that one can actually smell the roast meat and wine. I broke off as the third course was about to be served and skipped to where the meal was over.

At half past six the door opened and in came Toni with my supper. The first course was a bowl of soup made from dried vegetables. It was accompanied by a slice of bread — doubtless from the 'bailiff's bag'. The main course consisted of a synthetic product known as 'Migetti' (ersatz noodles), together with a herring. At seven, when the shop had long been closed to customers, I opened the trapdoor behind the counter and climbed down into the cellar to chop firewood.

I remember expressing surprise, the first time the shoemaker showed me the cellar, at the quantities of discarded furniture and smashed window-frames it contained. I was even more surprised to find, lying beside them, a pile of windows in excellent repair. In the building in which the shoemaker lived, nearly all the windows — on all five floors — were still intact.

'Am I to chop everything up for firewood?' I asked. 'Isn't that rather a shame? Those windows could easily be used in a house.'

The shoemaker disagreed. 'Come off it! They won't be building any more houses till the war's over. By then these will all be rotten, and that's a fact!'

'And the chairs and wardrobes, are you going to burn those too?'

'Why, certainly, Tschibel! Don't you worry, I've got new ones to replace them. Firewood is worth far more to us now. We'll never get through the winter on that bit of coal they allow us, and that's a fact!'

Now I understood what Toni had meant by the shoemaker having a lot to thank the air-raids for: new, modern wardrobes and chairs instead of the old junk, a gleaming new gramophone in place of the rusty old screech-box. The shoemaker was lucky, though, that he had been bombed in January 1941. At that time the policy had been to make good all damage immediately. Now people received tokens — to be cashed in 'after the ultimate victory'.

So I set to with saw and axe. But what was this I saw — an undamaged oak chest of drawers and two leather-covered chairs with only three legs apiece? How was the inspector from the bomb-damage department to know whether the chairs had not already been lame before the raid — or whether the *coup de grâce* had not been administered with a hammer afterwards? It was no concern of mine; my job was to strip off the leather and rip out the steel springs and bronze fittings with a pair of pliers to prevent the stove from

210

becoming clogged with scrap metal.

I heard footsteps upstairs. Friend or foe?

'Come on up, Tschibel!' the old man called down through the hatch. 'You've chopped enough wood for today, and that's a fact!'

Later that evening I was sitting in my room reading by the light of the desk lamp. I looked up to find Leon and Lore standing beside me. 'Tonight and tomorrow night we can't sleep at Lore's place,' Leon said. 'Her landlady's got a visitor.'

'Then you'll sleep here.'

'Is that all right? Really?'

Eventually they sat down, still with their coats on, and allowed Toni to persuade them to eat something. We were just thinking about preparing the beds when the door opened.

'Ah, Leon and Lore are paying us another visit!' the shoemaker exclaimed cordially. 'How are you both?'

And he sat down with us and struck up a conversation.

A quarter of an hour later Leon got to his feet: 'Well, I think we ought to be going,' he said. 'Good night, all! See you again soon!'

The shoemaker showed them out of the back door.

At half past ten I heard tapping at the window: knock knock-knock knock-knock. Quick, light out; blackout blind up; window open!

'Has the shoemaker gone to bed?' Leon whispered.

'Yes, Come on in, I've got your beds ready.'

At a quarter to twelve the sirens began to howl an air-raid warning.

'That's it!' Leon cried. 'I knew there was a reason why I felt I wanted to go to bed in my coat! Look, we'll run to the public shelter in Altonaer Street. After the "all clear" we'll wait for a quarter of an hour and then come back here.'

The shoemaker had taken to staying in the flat during air-raids to keep Toni company, for she never went to the cellar. Against all the dictates of common sense, he would sit himself down in an easy chair in the shop — as if his plate-glass window afforded the surest protection against shells and shrapnel. Also — God knows why — he used to roll up the blackout blind, so that the reflections of the tracer bullets from the anti-aircraft guns and of the beams of the probing searchlights danced all over the workshop walls. 'Oh dear, oh dear!' he groaned at each fresh explosion. But all our remonstrations failed to persuade him to retreat farther into the flat.

That night I sat with him. Neither of us spoke as we endured the terrifying hail of bombs. As things were beginning to calm down a little outside, I noticed that the shoemaker's already narrowed eyes had disappeared completely beneath their drooping lids. He had fallen asleep in his easy chair.

On Saturdays Toni did no shopping, and she restricted her housework to the most urgent tasks. Even so, she found herself compelled to do things on the Sabbath that she would never have done under normal circumstances. Where should we have been, after all, had she not made herself useful to the shoemaker seven days a week? My help was very much less important to the old man. I could therefore allow myself to refrain from nearly all prohibited activities. Sometimes I went for a walk along the river; otherwise I spent practically the whole day in my room, saying my prayers or reading. I preferred not to show myself in the workshop.

So closely did I adhere to traditional Sabbath observance that I did not even switch the electric light on and off. My desk-top lamp and my electric fire came on and went off automatically at set times. It never occurred to me that anyone could keep the Sabbath without clockwork time switches — as of course Jews had been doing for three thousand years. Fleeing from our parents' flat, I had decided without a moment's hesitation that the two time switches must form part of our emergency luggage.

There was no holy day in the shoemaker's life. For him, Sunday was a public holiday, pure and simple, and he was not going to sit in the workshop while the rest of Berlin went out. Even the foreign workers might stroll through the streets at their ease. On Sundays, too, we 'illegals' felt in less danger on the streets than on weekdays.

On every Sunday in January 1943 there was a mild frost. The sun tempted many people out of doors. For one thing, they wanted to view the latest ruins.

Our shoemaker used to like to go out with Toni and mingle with the crowds. Sometimes he would take her to a café or they would go to see a film.

On one occasion I joined them. I remember approaching Tiergarten Station and seeing a throng of Berliners and foreign workers, soldiers and civilians pour in motley confusion across the pavement and the roadway to reach the Charlottenburger Chaussee. We allowed the stream of people to carry us along, following the line of the railway through the park. Suddenly there loomed up out of the trees the gigantic green-painted concrete tower of the 'Zoo Bunker' with its battery of anti-aircraft guns, whose thunder we had to put up with almost nightly. It was said to have walls twenty feet thick and to be capable of accommodating vast numbers of people and huge stores of munitions. Ever-increasing numbers of strollers passed us in both directions, pausing to look at the bunker in an attempt to gauge its size. Many of them were speaking Italian, Hungarian and other foreign languages. Most of them — Germans as well as foreigners — gave the impression of having few cares in the world.

We did not meet a single person wearing a yellow star. Had the authorities achieved their goal of making Berlin 'Jew-free' by the end of 1942? It almost looked as if they had. I knew from Leon, however, that there were still many star wearers working in the munitions industry. What had happened to Frau Gold, I wondered, or to my old headmaster, Dr Schlesinger, and all his brood? Had they been deported, or had they gone underground like us? God alone knew what had become of them! Since fleeing to the shoemaker's we had had very little contact with our Jewish friends.

We came to the planetarium and the entrance to the zoo. The shoemaker wanted to go into the station restaurant. I tried to put him off the idea: 'It's always so crowded in there. You have to stand around for hours, waiting for a table, and then it's ages before you're served!' Actually it was something else that was worrying me: stations were magnets for police patrols and Gestapo informers.

My ploy was successful. The shoemaker drifted back into the dense crowd slowly circling the Emperor William Memorial Church.*

How that crowd bristled with uniforms! It was as if half the German armed forces were on leave. And they said the south section of the eastern front was having trouble holding out against the Red Army! Officers, each with an elegantly dolled-up girl on one arm (the other hand toyed with a dress dagger), armoured infantrymen, mountain infantrymen, machine gunners, Hitler Youth members from the air-defence corps, naval officers, ratings — they were all there. SS officers and military police swaggered past looking almost serene. Military attachés from allied and neutral countries strutted among them. Civilian males counted for nothing in that glittering array of daggers and cockades. Civilian females were another matter, provided they were young and pretty. Members of the League of German Girls and female staff assistants showed a preference for air-force and army officers. The splendidly braided foreign officers

---

* The Kaiser Wilhelm Gedächtniskirche was built in the 1890s in memory of Wilhelm I, King of Prussia, who had become emperor of a united Germany in 1871. It suffered severe bomb damage during the Second World War. When it was rebuilt in 1959–61, the ruined nineteenth-century tower was incorporated in the new structure and the whole building was rededicated as a war memorial. By contrast, the synagogue in Lewetzowstrasse, which had served as a collection-point for thousands of Jews before their deportation to the death camps, was demolished and cleared away after 1954 and replaced by an inconspicuous memorial tablet.

from neutral countries appeared to be less in demand.

I wondered what had drawn the shoemaker to that place. The Memorial Church? The magnificent streets that radiated out from it? Or had he simply drifted along with the crowd? He circled the Memorial Church twice before deciding to patronise a café in Joachimsthalerstrasse.

The café, too, bristled with uniforms. With some difficulty we found a vacant table. The shoemaker took out his ration card and ordered tea and cakes. The tiny cakes smelled of artificial sweetener, the tea like an extract of marsh marigold and dandelion. We peered through the shroud of tobacco smoke and the reek of beer at the teeming confusion around us. We ate up the remaining cakes and pushed our way back out into the fresh air.

Good morning — good night

In the last week of January I noticed a change in our shoemaker. The narrowed eyes in his wrinkled schoolboy's face grew even narrower. He gave mumbled answers to my questions and kept muttering to himself unintelligibly.

I wondered what had put him in such a bad mood. Was he worried about his sons at the front? The shoemaker usually had Toni read their letters to him. According to the letters, all the sons were fine. None of them belonged to the Sixth Army, the one the Russians had encircled near Stalingrad. Nor had any of them been wounded.

I began to feel uneasy. The shoemaker was far friendlier towards Toni than he was towards me, and when Leon and Lore visited us he positively radiated joviality.

Since it appeared to be something about my presence that upset him, I took to avoiding the workshop when there was not actually a job for me to do there. I placed myself under virtual room arrest. Before stepping into the passage, I checked whether the shoemaker was in his shop. I went out only after dark, when I could use the back door.

I managed, in fact, to make myself pretty scarce as far as the shoemaker was concerned. On some days he saw no more of me than was absolutely necessary for a 'good morning' and a 'good night'.

But was that really all we had left to say to each other — 'good morning' and 'good night'? Did the man who had always been so friendly and helpful now bear some grudge against me?

Sitting in my room one morning, I heard the shoemaker step into the passage and shout in the direction of the kitchen: 'Toni! Where's

Tschibel? What does that boy do with himself all day, then?' Alarmed, I closed my books, thanking my lucky stars that it so rarely occurred to the shoemaker to open the door to my little room.

So that was it! I was of no use to him any longer. The window-frames and furniture in the cellar were all sawn and chopped up, ready for the stove. What had needed repairing in the house was repaired. Now I was an idle waster who selfishly allowed others to do all the work.

I reflected that when, six months previously, the shoemaker had told my mother that he was prepared to shelter me for the duration of the war, he had almost surely been prompted by a generous impulse: he had not looked for any advantage for himself. Now he had begun to see things in a different light. His three sons were still fighting at the eastern front. He himself was still doing a full day's work in his old age. Toni gave him indispensable help with the housework. But Tschibel? What did he get out of Tschibel? Tschibel only got in his way and crowed 'Good morning' or 'Good night! And that was a fact! A strapping young fellow — and what did he do with himself all day? Sat in his room and frittered away his time with books!

That must be roughly what he was thinking when he turned grumpy, I concluded. He was incapable of understanding our situation. What did he know about the identity checks that made every step we took in the street a risky enterprise? The barrack yard and the parade ground had set the bounds of his experience: the police state was beyond his comprehension. This was made crystal clear by something that happened one day when Toni was out with him. The shoemaker was stopped in the street and asked for his identity card. His answer was an impatient 'I don't need an identity card! Everyone round here knows me!' The patrolmen, totally disarmed by such naïvety, exchanged dismissive gestures and let him go. The shoemaker proceeded on his way, looking most aggrieved and mumbling his 'And that's a fact!' In his eyes, the identity check had been a bit of pompous showing-off on the part of the two policemen.

I further reflected that it was this naïvety of the shoemaker's that we had to thank for our shelter and our survival. Yet that same naïvety might also be our undoing. Relations must not be allowed to deteriorate further! The shoemaker must be kept sweet at any price, otherwise four people might lose the very foundation of their existence!

Or was I making a mountain out of a molehill? Must you immediately fear the worst, I asked myself, just because the old man happens to look a little sour one day? The best of friends have their misunderstandings.

I tried to reassure myself, but I was unable to dismiss my forebodings entirely. We had moved in with the shoemaker in a mood of effusive gratitude. Barely three weeks had passed since then, and already there was this perceptible tension between us. What might happen over the next few weeks and months?

The picture I had formed of the shoemaker began to cloud. He was showing a new side of himself. He was starting to think of his own advantage. What was he getting out of me in return? Normally I should have seen this as the pardonable weakness of an old man. In our particular circumstances, however, it struck me as a blemish, a betrayal of his essential good nature.

How could he think only of material advantage when people like us faced deportation, detention behind barbed wire, forced labour, unimaginable distress, perhaps even death? It did not occur to me that he had little conception of these dangers. We had deliberately avoided alarming him with all that we knew or suspected.

Had I thought the whole thing through, had I tried to put myself in his position, had I entered into his state of mind with a little more understanding, I should doubtless have judged his behaviour less harshly. But I was incapable of that kind of objectivity. I was too obsessed with the question: will he go on helping us or not?

I did not forget that without the shoemaker we should have had neither shelter nor food and might well have fallen into the hands of the Gestapo long since. I did not forget that at all. But I expected more of him. I expected him to make up for all the wrong being done by all the other Germans — those who carried out Hitler's orders with a sadistic pleasure, those who did so with a bad conscience and those who turned a blind eye to what was going on. I expected him not only to help us but to do so out of pure kindness. Having indeed shown our parents and ourselves nothing but kindness for so long, he had become an ideal figure in my eyes. I was deeply disappointed in him.

Passing time

The shoemaker looked a lot happier, I noticed, since he had been seeing me leave the flat around half past eight every morning. Did he imagine I was going to work? He did not inquire, appearing to be satisfied with the impression that my life had somehow or other acquired the respectable rhythm of a day's labour followed by an evening's leisure.

216

As for me, striding through the shop at 8:30 a.m. with a ringing 'Good morning!' and pulling open the street door with a confident gesture, I had only the vaguest idea of how I was going to spend the day. Something would come to me once I was outside, walking down the street. Berlin was a big place, and ultimately it mattered less where I went than that I should keep going. The last thing I must do was look idle.

So I walked myself warm, trying to decide which direction to take and meanwhile maintaining an air of determined purposefulness. An icy wind blew off the river. Two or three gulls were patrolling the stretch of water between the Hansa and Schleswig embankments in a melancholy fashion.

The piercing cold and the biting wind gave me the idea of taking a ride on the *S-Bahn*, the surface rail network that serves the city and suburbs of Berlin. I bought a ticket at Tiergarten Station and elbowed my way onto the first train that came along. I found myself wedged between a wheezing fat man in horn-rimmed spectacles, a sister from the National Socialist People's Welfare, and a young fellow in the uniform of the Waffen-SS, the 'fourth arm' of the German army. The carriage was crammed full of policemen, school-children, foreign workers from the Balkan countries, Japanese students, housewives with bags of shopping, military police, several grey, unclassifiable civilians with briefcases under their arms and one 'non-Aryan' outlaw — all of us breathing the same foul air. However faint one felt in the crush, it was impossible to fall over. The loathsome warmth of bodies in Nazi uniforms pressing against me eased the stiffness from my frozen limbs.

'Beware! The enemy is listening!' warned innumerable little placards. Not that a spy would have found much worth listening to there. The Berliners stared stolidly straight in front of them. Only at stations did anxious voices pipe up from the middle of the carriage: 'Where are we?' 'Is this Halensee already?' 'Are we at Westkreuz?' 'Let me through, please!' 'Excuse me! Excuse me!' 'The polite man is always the better man,' Goebbels preached to the — by this time — rather surly Berliners, along with 'Save money now [it was compulsory] and spend it after the war.'

Later in the morning the trains were slightly less crowded. I managed to find a seat. It was unlikely that police patrols would try to push their way through the crush, but for safety's sake I changed carriages several times and kept getting out at random and taking the next train in the opposite direction.

If only the day were over already and I could slip back to the shoemaker's! Toni would be sure to have saved some food for me.

217

But it was only half past eleven. I got out at the Zoo and made my way towards the giant Kaufhaus des Westens, the Department Store of the West. The air in the shop would be less stale than in the train, I reasoned, and I should be able to wander round unnoticed amid the hordes of customers and sales assistants.

But there were no hordes! The marbled halls of that palace of luxury were almost deserted. The lifts were not working, though fortunately the central heating was. A few women stood in front of counters here and there, looking gloomily around for someone to serve them. I climbed the stairs to the record department, had myself shown into a booth, and listened to Beethoven's *Prometheus Overture* followed by his *Fifth Symphony*. During the final bars of the last movement I was already preparing my excuse: I would inquire the price, and when the girl told me that I must surrender old records in part-exchange I would feign surprise and say I would go home and fetch some. I pushed open the door of the booth to find that I need not lie. What luck! The girl was nowhere to be seen. Quick: into another department! What an awful thing to do, though; she was so friendly! Still, out of here fast! It was a quarter to two. Beethoven's stirring music had brought the end of the war an hour closer. How should I spend the afternoon? Go to the cinema and see one of the films passed by the official censor? Better not. Cinemas were said to be the scene of frequent identity checks.

I went back to the *S-Bahn*, took a train to Lehrter Station, and from there walked to the Natural History Museum. This was a place I had often visited in the years before the war. Ah, the blessed silence that filled its galleries! Wandering through the museum's many departments, I came across only two other visitors. A moustached attendant who walked with the aid of a crutch — probably a 1914–18 war invalid — limped over to me and asked what I was looking for. I'm looking for a sofa, I felt like telling him, where I can lie down and spend the rest of the afternoon reading. This endless walking about on an empty stomach is making me weak and confused. Don't you understand? I can't show myself back at the shoemaker's until half past five!

'I'm sorry,' I told him. 'Could you please direct me to Tropical Amphibians?'

Expeditions with a sledge

One day it suddenly occurred to the shoemaker to ask Toni what household effects we had left behind in our parents' flat.

'And you're just going to let the thieves have it all?' he exclaimed.

'That would be an awful pity! You ought to go round there some time, you know, see if you can't salvage some of it, and that's a fact!'

What was this, a bad joke? Was the old man serious? Talk about a hare-brained idea! We could only hope he would soon forget it. But he didn't; he kept harping on the subject. What on earth were we to do?

We held a council of war in my room. It lasted the whole evening — and the whole of the next evening, too. Leon and Lore, keeping their coats on as always, sat on the sofa. Toni and I pulled our chairs close to them to enable us to keep our voices down. Whenever the shoemaker used the passage, we froze in silence until he had gone again.

Lore thought frankness was the only way. Toni must make it clear to the shoemaker that such a reconnaissance trip would be utter folly. Toni and I had reservations: the old man must not hear too much talk of danger.

The first evening, Leon sat fairly quiet, sunk in thought. By the second evening his mind was made up. We must risk it, he said. It was important for us, too, that we should salvage some of our possessions. The few garments we had would soon be worn out, and we should have nothing to replace them. We also needed valuables, not just to keep the shoemaker happy but also to use for barter. And some of them we must turn into cash. 'We need money, too. I'm the only one earning at the moment!'

'But the flat is sure to have been requisitioned long ago!' I put in.

'Is the house still standing, even?' Lore wondered. 'Maybe it's been bombed.'

Leon smiled. 'No, it hasn't. I've been to look. There's no seal on the door of the flat yet, and there's no one inside.'

'You've been snooping around there?' Toni cried in dismay. 'But the Gestapo may well have the place under — '

'Now listen to me!' Leon interrupted. 'And above all keep your voices down or the shoemaker will hear us! We've got to think this through calmly. Things can't go on the way they are with the shoemaker. We have to take the risk. If necessary, we'll even bring away furniture.'

After a brief pause for thought I said, 'Right, I agree. But how do you see it working out in practice?'

Leon rose to his feet, paced the available area of carpet for a moment, then stood looking down at us.

'There's only one way: we must do it quite openly. Then the neighbours will assume we're from a removal firm or agents of the welfare department. No one will dream that Jews living in hiding are calmly taking furniture from the very flat the Gestapo have down as their last known address!'

The shoemaker was full of enthusiasm. In fact, he could hardly wait. He was even keen to come with us: he could still hump furniture, he said.

We set out on a pitch-dark night. Bluish pools of light in the snow-covered street reflected the obscured headlamps of the occasional passing car. Leon and Lore led the way. I followed, pulling the shoemaker's sledge, and the shoemaker and Toni brought up the rear.

When we reached Agricolastrasse, Leon went ahead to reconnoitre. At a wave from him, we entered the building and climbed the stairs to the first floor, taking care not to make too much noise — but not to make too little either. Only the shoemaker went clumping up the stairs quite unconcerned. With our hearts in our mouths we inserted the key in the lock and turned it. The door opened.

It was soon closed again behind the shoemaker and Toni. Black-out blinds still down — good. Light on. It was true: the flat looked as though nothing had been touched since our hasty departure several weeks previously. The water was still on, and the central heating was still working. No one had broken in, and there was no one lying in wait for us under the sofa or behind the larder door.

Right: the thing to do was to choose wisely and decide quickly what we were going to take. We began throwing clothes into a suitcase. Meanwhile the shoemaker prowled around, examining everything. He pointed to the carpet in the hall, the wall-clock in the living-room . . . And we, of course, had to act accordingly.

We rolled up our sleeves and opened the front door as wide as it would go. Each of us shouldered a burden and carried it downstairs. Lore stayed with the sledge while the rest of us went up for a second load. We were all amazed to find how much we could get on one sledge, as long as it was well stacked and properly tied up.

'That'll do now, though!' Lore warned. 'Otherwise the sledge will tip over!'

'Don't you worry, young Lore!' the shoemaker reassured her. 'That won't tip over! Anyway, there are plenty of us to steady it, and that's a fact! We can easily go up and get another lot.'

But we managed to dissuade him. The procession set off into the winter night, with one person pulling and four pushing.

Later, we celebrated our success in the shoemaker's workshop over a cup of barley coffee and a pastry from the 'bailiff's bag'.

The shoemaker had quite recovered the friendly manner of the first days of January. Even the doubters among us were convinced that the expedition had been worth the risk.

Imagine our dismay, though, when a week later the shoemaker suggested a second visit to the wretched flat! The man was becoming a menace. Our guardian angel, my father had called him — sent to shield us against hunger and possibly worse. And so it had indeed turned out. But now, having once set eyes on the flat, our guardian angel refused to leave us in peace.

Deeply uneasy, we agreed. All right, once more. Just one last time. But we were unable to suppress a nagging fear that after that 'last time' he would want a very last time and then a very, very last time.

Which is exactly what happened. Every second or third evening we would set out on the ten-minute journey to Agricolastrasse, and each time we would come back pulling and pushing an overloaded sledge. When not prevented by air-raid warnings, we even went out on consecutive evenings.

We were extraordinarily lucky. No one ever challenged us. Fortunately we had always, even in our parents' time, made ourselves as unobtrusive as possible. None of the other occupants of the house seemed to recognise us. One was even so good as to hold the street door open for me as I came marching down the stairs, toting a full-length mirror.

Our expeditions went off so smoothly that we began to play the 'removal men' with fewer and fewer inhibitions. Indeed, so industriously did we bustle up and down those stairs that we forgot all the appalling things that were happening in the world. We even forgot our own problems for a while.

Of the easily removable household effects, we found we had recovered the most valuable. Our guardian angel then decided he wanted to salvage the major items of furniture as well. The sideboard and the bookcases could be dismantled, he pointed out. And if we were taking the bookcases, why not also take the books? 'Shame to leave them behind. Be a shame to leave the cooking pots and the china, too, and that's a fact! And it would be a crying shame not to take those lovely washing troughs and zinc tubs. You can't buy those anywhere now!' the shoemaker said.

A kind of comradeship-in-arms grew up between the shoemaker and ourselves. Each fresh expedition reinforced it. I lost my feeling of awkwardness about showing myself in the workshop during working hours. The shoemaker was in a constant state of delighted anticipation, for we had not yet removed half of what the flat contained.

The shoemaker's workshop was beginning to take on a rather

221

curious appearance. Between the shelves of shoes there now stood several fine pieces of antique furniture, while Titian's *Girl with a Fruit Dish* and the *Returning Reapers* hung on the back wall. We worried about what the customers would think. On the sideboard between the counter and the shoe-stand the shoemaker had set up the silver Sabbath lights. Between them, the eight-branched *Chanukah* candlestick of gleaming brass had been given a place of honour. Now he decided to hang up a large brass dish engraved with Hebrew script as a wall decoration.

We could have told him that it was what we called a *Seder* dish and that it was used during the celebrations for the Passover festival. The inscription was a verse from the Bible: 'Seven days you shall eat *mazzoth* [unleavened bread].' But the shoemaker did not ask.

My parents owned a second, even more magnificent *Seder* dish. It was not so easy to find a suitable place for this. As an interim solution the shoemaker put it in the shop window.

He was busy in the workshop until late, swinging his shoemaker's hammer to bang hooks and nails into the wall, hanging things up, then stepping back a few paces and cocking his head on one side to make sure they were straight.

A sudden, irresistible urge to burst out laughing drove me from the shop. In my room I found Leon, Toni and Lore already in stitches.

'What is it?' I spluttered. 'Are you laughing about the *Seder* dish in the shop window?'

They nodded wordlessly, wiping tears from their eyes.

'The old man's out of his mind!' Toni exclaimed. 'He has no idea what he's doing!'

'Lucky the blackout blind's down!'

'Yes, well, that luck won't hold beyond daybreak,' Lore said soberly. 'You've simply got to speak frankly to the shoemaker. You've got to explain.'

'Toni can do that best. He thinks more of her.'

'Explain?' Leon broke in. 'Have you seen what he's done with father's Talmud books? He's put them on show in the bookcase where everyone coming into the shop will spot them immediately! No, explaining won't do any good — not with the shoemaker. We'll have to go about this differently.'

I returned to the workshop. Sure enough, there they were: three fat volumes of the Babylonian Talmud and two of Maimonides's Code. What did the old man think he was doing? It can hardly have escaped his attention that the spines carried gilded inscriptions in Hebrew lettering!

222

As I wished the shoemaker good night, he gave me a broad wink. 'Good night, Tschibel! Got another good load in today, didn't we? And that's a fact!'

When the shoemaker had been asleep for about an hour, Toni and I took a torch and crept back into the workshop. Working as quietly as we could, we opened the trapdoor, carried the two *Seder* dishes, the *Chanukah* candlestick, and the Hebrew tomes down to the cellar, and stowed them away in a large chest. Fortunately the shoemaker never thought to ask what had become of them.

CHAPTER 10

Refuge among the Reptiles

The defeat at Stalingrad was announced in the press and on the radio, though not so much from any love of truth as in order to capitalise on it for propaganda purposes. I was in no position to assess the historical importance of the event. It may be that I was involuntarily influenced by the official version. In any case, I was far too wrapped up in my own predicament to have been able to spare much thought for what was going on in the world.

It was not until after the war, when historical studies became available and a great many memoirs were published, that I was able to form a picture of the international situation in the first two months of 1943. I became aware then that 'Stalingrad' had not only been a crucial event militarily, representing an appalling blood sacrifice on the part of the Russian and German peoples;* it had also been a defeat for the regime that invented the practice of human extermination on an industrial scale.

Indeed, it was only in retrospect, in the light of our knowledge of the German extermination camps, that all the events of the Second World War took on their true significance: the victories and defeats of the Axis powers, the victories and defeats of the Allies, the enslavement of the prisoners-of-war, the establishment of the ghettos, the deportations and even our humble fate in the home of the shoemaker. During the war we knew nothing of the extermination camps. That meant we lacked the principal yardstick for assessing

---

* In November 1942 six months of rapid German advance towards the Caucasian oilfields ended when the German Sixth Army was cut off near Stalingrad (now renamed Volgograd) by a Russian counter-offensive. Ordered by Hitler to stay put, General Paulus offered futile resistance, losing 300,000 men in the process, until he was forced to surrender at the end of January 1943. Russian losses were similarly horrendous in a battle that, together with Montgomery's victory over Rommel at El Alamein in Egypt in October 1942, constituted the turning-point of the Second World War.

our own situation.

How narrow was our field of vision! I realise just how narrow when I compare my reminiscences of that period with those of other people.

Bernard Goldstein, a Polish Jew and a leading figure in the resistance movement, told us in his memoirs about the penultimate phase in the saga of the Warsaw ghetto. On 18 January 1943 the Germans were taken by surprise by the first armed resistance on the part of the Jews. After killing several thousand people, the Germans called off their attack and withdrew from the ghetto.*

Anne Frank's diary entry for 13 January 1943 refers to things 'going better for the Allies' but speaks of Amsterdam's Jews still being 'dragged off with nothing but a rucksack and a little money . . . . Families are torn apart, the men, women and children all being separated. Children coming home from school find that their parents have disappeared. Women return from shopping to find their homes shut up and their families gone.'†

From the same period we have the 'autobiographical notes' of Rudolf Höss, then commandant of Auschwitz concentration camp:

> The two large crematoria I and II had underground undressing rooms and gassing chambers capable of being ventilated and evacuated. A lift brought the bodies up to the ovens, which were above ground. The gassing chambers were capable of accommodating 3,000 persons each. These figures were never achieved, however, because the individual transports were never so large. The two smaller crematoria III and IV were said by the builders — Topf of Erfurt — to be capable of cremating 1,500 each in a 24-hour period.‡

The three statements, uttered from such different viewpoints, do not contradict one another. Indeed, they complement one another. As personal testimonies they all supply vivid details to help build up an overall picture of Europe at that time.

What personal testimony have I to contribute? We humped furniture to keep the shoemaker happy and to boost our own reserves of clothing, barter material and ready cash. We had no opportunity of hearing the news as broadcast by the BBC. We knew less about the world situation than the fourteen-year-old Anne

---

* Bernard Goldstein, *The Stars Bear Witness*, New York, 1949.
† *The Diary of Anne Frank*, tr. B.M. Mooyaart-Doubleday, London, Vallentine Mitchell, 1953.
‡ *Kommandant in Auschwitz, autobiographische Aufzeichnungen von Rudolf Höss*, Stuttgart, 1958.

Frank. Yet my recollections also fit into the overall picture of that period.

The expeditions to my parents' flat and the refurbishment of the shoemaker's workshop kept us so busy that we did not even pay much attention to the 'withdrawal movements' and 'front corrections' being carried out by Hitler's armies. Let me just mention, as they come to me, one or two minor — and major — incidents that occurred in my limited world during those weeks.

The shoemaker received a letter from the front. It was from his son Fritz, in whose room I was living. Following his usual practice, the old man got Toni to read the letter aloud to him. Fritz wrote that he hoped to be granted a fortnight's leave quite soon.

We discussed the matter in our 'council of war'. Since we did not know Fritz's attitude towards the persecution of the Jews, Toni urged me to make sure that he found no trace of my occupancy of his room. The best course would be for me to stay away from the shoemaker's flat altogether. She alone should remain there, she thought. Where I should sleep during Fritz's leave was something we were going to have to work out later. Fritz himself did not seem to know when his leave would come up, and in any case the eastern front was a long way from Berlin. In fact, it was nearly half-way to the north-west frontier of China!

The tenth anniversary of Hitler's appointment as chancellor was celebrated on the radio with a series of major speeches. 'Where should we be now without our Leader?' was the recurring theme. In the evening we spent two air-raids sitting in the workshop. 'Oh dear, oh dear!' the shoemaker groaned repeatedly. Was it only the bombs and the thunder of the anti-aircraft guns that he was thinking of, I wondered, or was it also his Führer?

The four days of national mourning ordered by Goebbels to commemorate the defeat at Stalingrad did not affect the shoemaker's workshop. The old man, unabashed, continued to trade as usual.

The weather was bitterly cold. I paced the streets of the Hansa quarter, hands thrust deep into my overcoat pockets, wondering yet again how I was going to pass the time until evening. Our former good relations with the shoemaker were now entirely restored. Nevertheless, I was keen to maintain the fiction that I had a job somewhere during the day.

The walls and the street-corner advertising pillars featured a bright new poster. (However did they manage to stick posters in that weather? How did they keep the glue from freezing?)

I took a closer look at it. A young giant, his face contorted with rage and his jaws tightly clenched, led a symbolic representation of the German nation: farmers carrying scythes over their shoulders, blacksmiths, artists, scientists, engineers — all the 'labourers of brow and fist', in that outlandish Nazi phrase — were quitting their workplaces to repulse the dangers threatening the Third Reich. 'TOTAL WAR!' the poster screamed. 'National comrades', Goebbels had asked in the 'Palace of Sport', 'do you want total war?' 'Yes!' the crowd had roared. 'Yes!' echoed a million loudspeakers throughout the length and breadth of Germany.

Total war! What did the term mean? What did it imply for us? Many shops and small businesses were said to have closed down in order to enable their proprietors to devote wealth and health, not to say life itself, to prolonging the Nazi regime. Compulsory 'labour service' had been introduced for women and girls. Soon the whole of Germany would be one vast forced-labour camp, with only children, old men and invalids exempt.

What about us, who had gone underground? We too would be exempt. The rabid giant would not draw us in his wake. The writ of the labour department did not run amongst us 'illegals'. As the drama of world history unfolded, we were safely off-stage, behind the scenes.

We soon found out that we were wrong. The drastic changes affecting civilian life made it far harder for us to remain safely 'behind the scenes'. With the switch to total war the Nazi state reached its highest pitch of perfection. Everything that happened in town or country became subject to control. Now that women and girls were also ordered to work Toni and Lore could no longer show themselves in the street as freely as before. Forged papers had become almost as vital for them as for Leon and myself. Yet none of us possessed such papers, nor did we know where we could get hold of them.

How many Jews were still living in Berlin when total war was proclaimed? It was a rare occurrence to meet someone wearing a yellow star in the street. Only in Berlin's munitions industry were many thousands of Jews still doing 'labour service'. Then there were the Jews living underground. How numerous they were, we did not know; nobody knew. We had virtually no contact with our Jewish friends and acquaintances nowadays; only Leon occasionally encountered Jewish workers at his factory.

One day he dropped in after work with some startling news. He had been reluctant to believe his eyes at first, he said. Among the wretched figures who worked in his machine room he had suddenly recognised Dr Seligmann, our dentist from Gross-Strehlitz.* The

* See Chapter 3, pp. 33–4.

227

poor man had aged appallingly and lost a lot of weight.

So the arch-Zionist, whom we had long believed safely in Palestine, was himself now a slave of the German munitions industry! Toni thought we should invite him round.

Leon would have none of it. 'Where to?' he wanted to know. 'Here in the shoemaker's flat — is that what you had in mind?'

Leon described in scathing tones how abjectly Seligmann complied with all the National Socialist decrees. He would never dare go about without his yellow star. Jews were forbidden to use any form of transport, so Seligmann walked for miles across Berlin to and from the factory. Leon said he could never arrange to meet such a rabbit in the street; in fact, he must avoid getting too involved with him altogether. He could not even do the disappearing trick with his patent yellow star in Seligmann's presence.

It was easy for Leon to talk. Seligmann could never have taken the liberties that Leon took. He would have been recognised as a Jew immediately.

An evening in the first half of February 1943. The time: half past ten. We had brought yet another load from the old flat and found a place for everything. The shoemaker had gone to bed. The flat was silent. Weary after all the removal work, I meant to go to bed myself shortly. I decided to do a little Hebrew translation, just a paragraph from *With the Migrant Birds to Africa*. Fortunately, on one recent expedition I had brought away father's big scientific dictionaries. Now, how did Hebrew distinguish between 'drive' and 'instinct'?

There was a knock at the door. Oh well, the shoemaker was safely asleep by now. I looked up. 'Come in.'

The door opened — and on the threshold stood a young Wehrmacht sergeant in cap and greatcoat. We faced each other. I said nothing. He said nothing but simply stood there, staring at me — coolly, steadily, in utter astonishment. It was impossible to believe that he had just arrived from the front: he looked so neat and well-groomed. His smooth face was unmarked by strain or hardship. I remember thinking that it bore little resemblance to the shoemaker's. He was hardly taller than I. For a second he looked me full in the face; then he let his glance slip past me into the room, taking in the desk with the reading-lamp, the portable stove by the window, the two time switches (what did he make of those? I wondered), the camp bed with my pyjamas lying on it, the Hebrew dictionaries (would he recognise the script as Hebrew?). And again, still saying nothing, he looked straight into my eyes.

'Good evening!' I blurted out, and before I could restrain it my

228

right hand, by way of explanation, had executed a sweeping gesture in the direction of the camp bed and the pyjamas. Searching his face for some sign of a smile at my performance, I caught myself mumbling empty, meaningless words. Still he said nothing. Then, outraged, he swung on his heel and strode smartly away down the passage.

Better get out of here immediately, I thought. No, that might be quite the wrong course. His father will explain everything to him and with any luck calm him down.

I closed the door, turned the light out and crawled into bed. A few minutes later Toni slipped into the room and whispered, 'We must disappear first thing in the morning!'

At the crack of dawn, carrying two bulging briefcases, I left my hiding-place by the back door and made my way to the only refuge available to us: our parents' old flat.

Once there, the first thing I did was to take my boots off. In stockinged feet I began to pad around, just as I had two months earlier, between kitchen, living-room and bathroom. I stood stock-still and listened, peered through the spyhole at the landing and the stairs, crept over to the window and looked out through the curtains. Outside, nothing seemed to have changed. From the courtyard came the all-too-familiar blare of radios. I could hear footsteps. They belonged to the occupant of the flat upstairs — a man too old for military service, labour service or any other kind of 'service'. I heard him hobble from his kitchen down the passage to his lavatory. I took the opportunity to visit the lavatory myself, waiting to pull the plug until he pulled his. After that I unpacked the two briefcases and began settling in.

Two hours later I heard our secret knock. I hurried to the front door and admitted Toni. She had brought a full shopping-bag, which she also began to unpack.

As she did so, she heaped reproaches on me: 'It's all your fault this has happened! Didn't I tell you only yesterday to go to bed and not always work so late? If Fritz hadn't seen the light shining through your door, he might never have gone in there!'

'How does the situation look now?' I asked in order to divert Toni from her pointless chiding. 'Has he explained things to his son? Do you know how long Fritz is staying?'

'We'll have to hold out here for two weeks at least, but I'm not at all sure we'll be able to move back to the shoemaker's immediately. There was a dreadful scene at breakfast this morning. I couldn't very well stay in the room, of course. But I'd dearly love to know what the two of them said to each other!'

'Do you think Fritz is capable of giving us away?'

'I don't think so, because he'd be giving his own father away too if he did. But what worries me most is how upset the old man was after the row with his son. He was in a terrible state. God knows what will happen now. I may be able to tell you more this evening.'

'What, you mean you're going back?'

'Of course I am! What do you think? We don't want the old man getting it into his head that he can do without me. Otherwise we shan't stand a chance with him. I'll try to keep running his household during the daytime at least.'

'You really have got guts.'

When Toni returned in the evening, she brought Leon and Lore with her. She had intercepted them just in time at the back door of the shoemaker's flat.

In the days that followed we waited anxiously for every scrap of news that Toni brought in the evening. The situation at the shoemaker's remained unresolved. She had overheard only snippets of the arguments between father and son.

The shoemaker had insisted on Toni's continuing to keep house for him. My name had not been mentioned. The sergeant knew that we were Jews, of that there could be no doubt. He also knew that in the occupied areas of eastern Europe Jews were interned in ghettos or vast 'labour camps'. There was talk of 'sinister goings-on' in such places. Yet he showed no sympathy with our having gone into hiding. He once told Toni in so many words, 'One shouldn't attempt to evade one's destiny!'

Arguments between father and son recurred throughout the latter's leave. Even their farewell clearly failed to bring about a reconciliation, for the shoemaker was left deeply upset.

Toni moved back in with him immediately. After three days she persuaded him to let me return too. But things were no longer the same. We racked our brains day and night for ways of restoring our former understanding with the old man. This time the suggestion that we resume the expeditions with the sledge came not from him but from us.

27 February 1943

I had known Herr Max Löwenzahn in the years before the war as a member of the Adass-Isroël congregation. My school-mates told me he had once held a high-ranking position in one of the Bavarian ministries. Desperately casting around for fresh sources of help and advice after Fritz's visit, I thought of Löwenzahn.

I knocked at the yellow-starred door of his flat in a house in nearby Siegmundshof. And there he was. It was almost as if his home stood under extraterritorial protection. In his elegant study there was nothing, apart from the blackout blind, to remind one of the war and of the peculiar situation of the Jews. Pacing the carpet with measured tread, Löwenzahn listened carefully to what I had to say.

If he had known how to find a good hiding-place, he told me, or how to get across the Swiss frontier, he would no longer be there himself, living in that luxurious mousetrap. He went on to talk about the military situation in general. It was from him that I first heard of Rommel's retreat and the conference of the Allies in Casablanca. How did he come to be so well informed? Did he listen to so-called enemy broadcasts?

Although Herr Löwenzahn was unable to give me any practical advice, I drew encouragement from his words and above all from his astonishing composure. I asked if I might visit him often.

'But of course!' he said. 'Come whenever you like!'

I had occasion to be grateful for his being so well informed shortly afterwards. One of the chief things he had done was to warn me about the coming 27 February. On that day, he told me, all 15,000 Jewish munitions workers in Berlin were to be taken from their workplaces and deported. For weeks and months there had been a hard-fought tussle in progress between representatives of the munitions industry and the Gestapo, with the representatives of the industry maintaining that their Jewish workers were indispensable: they spoke German and they were more intelligent than most foreign workers. However, the Gestapo had now decided that all Jews without exception were to be deported. Löwenzahn urged me repeatedly, 'Warn your brother and all your other Jewish friends about that day!'

That fateful day was now drawing near. I was back with the shoemaker. Leon, finding himself once more without a billet, had moved into our parents' old flat with Lore. I told him Herr Löwenzahn's alarming news. He simply shrugged in disbelief.

On the morning of 27 February Leon was actually standing on the platform of Tiergarten Station, waiting for the train to take him to work, when his French friend Raymond came running up and begged him on no account to go to the factory. Raymond had also got wind of an imminent 'operation' against the Jews.

That moment marked the beginning of a new chapter in Leon's life. He went straight back to our parents' flat and burnt his identity card and his patent two-way yellow star. In doing so, he took the final step into illegality.

That same day we heard evidence of how frighteningly well-founded the warnings had been. It was not only from factories that Jewish workers were dragged from whatever they were doing and driven away in lorries; the operation extended to homes displaying the yellow star. Never before had Jews been so openly rounded up and removed. Toni told us how she had seen SS men going from house to house, shouting, 'Are there still Jews living here?' Any Jews they found were driven into the street with rifle-butts and bayonets and loaded into waiting SS vehicles.

On 28 February, the day after the round-up, there was a ring at the front door of the flat in Agricolastrasse. Leon, alone in the flat at the time, kept as quiet as a mouse until he heard footsteps redescend the stairs. Then he ran to the window. He was just in time to see his friend Raymond disappear round the corner of the street. He rushed out after him and caught him up.

'Raymond! I didn't realise it was you at the door. I thought it was someone from the Gestapo. That's why I was keeping so quiet in the flat. Tell me, what happened at work?'

'You had luck, my friend. All the Jews were arrested at nine o'clock Saturday morning. The SS came with lorries — about fifty of them — and simply grabbed all the Jews, men and women, where they stood or sat at their benches or their machines. You are the only one who escaped. It's what I came round to tell you. But do not stay in your flat. They may come for you at any moment.'

Toni and I no longer remained in the shoemaker's workshop during air-raids. The shoemaker, possibly influenced by something Fritz had told him, had expressed misgivings: maybe the cellar would afford better protection against shrapnel, he suggested. We must also face up to the worst that might happen. For example, if 'Tschibel', as he still insisted on calling me, were to be found dead in his workshop, the discovery would place him in an extremely awkward situation.

He was right: even as a corpse I could be a danger to him.

The air-raid that Berlin suffered on the night of 2/3 March 1943 was worse than any previous attack. The nearest public shelter still in use was in Flensburgerstrasse, some 500 yards from the shoe-maker's flat. We ran as fast as we could. Yet even before we reached Hansaplatz the hellish thunder and lightning had started up all around us behind the momentarily and eerily illuminated silhouettes of the surrounding buildings. At last we arrived at the shelter and ran breathlessly down the stairs.

The room set aside for the protection of the public during air-raids had once been the coal-cellar of an apartment building. We arrived to find it already half full of people. Huddled in their overcoats, they sat in attitudes of grim anxiety on the garden chairs and benches arranged around the white-washed walls. When the anti-aircraft guns were silent for a moment, the diffused hum of hundreds of aero-engines became audible. Explosions — each one sounding closer — made the floor quake underfoot. Hunched forward, the people sat and waited. The bombers must be right overhead now. There — that terrifying howl! In seconds it was upon us. Involuntarily, every torso bent even farther forward. A single thought ruled every mind. From somewhere outside, a muffled detonation broke the tension.

After two seemingly endless hours the sirens sounded the 'all clear'. The surrounding streets were bathed in a ghastly red light. Fire engines dashed in all directions, hooting and shrilling. Ambulances, emergency services, crowds, traffic jams, police, blazing roofs, whole houses in ruins.

A bucket chain was being formed. Part of the crowd began hurriedly to disperse. An air-raid warden shouted after them: 'No shirking, you folk! Come over here and lend a hand! There'll be a bonus tomorrow — half a pound of rice!'

We ran back to the shoemaker's through streets littered with broken glass. Thank God! Cuxhavenerstrasse had not been hit.

Next day the people of Berlin could be heard muttering to one another behind their hands, 'That was retribution for the mass deportation of Jews on 27 February.'

At a personal level, too, the air-raid of 2/3 March affected me deeply. Three days after that dreadful night, I once again set out to visit Herr Löwenzahn. I turned the corner into Siegmundshof with a sense of grim foreboding. Only one wall of the house still stood. A bizarre skeleton of beams and fragments of masonry showed where floors and rooms had once been. Above bleak heaps of rubble, the door of Herr Löwenzahn's study swung idly in mid-air. Walking past, I heard someone say that not all the bodies had yet been recovered.

Warm baths for free

We were torn, the whole time, between paralysing grief and our determination to survive. We oscillated violently between dull despair and wide-awake terror, between hope and revulsion, bitterness and frivolity. We faced inconceivable horrors every day of our lives — but we were healthy young people, and we were still capable of laughing. In the midst of all the perils, there were some irresistibly comic moments.

The old comradeship between the shoemaker and ourselves was now restored. Our furniture removing was already so far advanced that we decided to go on and clear the place. The only item that, with the best will in the world, we simply could not transport on the sledge was the piano — much to the old man's chagrin.

On one occasion we found the shoemaker gazing pensively at the bathtub. 'Pity we can't take that with us', he said. 'Does the thing still work, in fact?' He indicated the gas water heater. 'I'd love to wash my hands!'

Toni lit the pilot light and showed him how to operate the appliance. 'Hey, this is marvellous, children!' he crowed happily. 'Next time we'll have a bath! All the hot water you want at absolutely no cost, and that's a fact!'

We exchanged rapid glances behind his back. There was no doubt about it: the old man was serious. The devil himself must have whispered this notion in his ear!

And how did he propose to get away — how would any of us get away — when he was sitting in the bath and suddenly the Gestapo knocked on the door? That was a question neither devil nor angel appeared to have whispered to him. However, since the object of the exercise was to keep the shoemaker happy, we too held our tongues and went along with the idea. Let him have his bath, for God's sake!

When the expedition set out the next evening, we took with us soap and five hand-towels — because by now it went without saying that we must all bathe in turn.

If the shoemaker had only gone about things a little more circumspectly! But he slammed every door he went through, and while his bath was running he conversed with us in those empty, echoing rooms as if we had all been hard of hearing. As soon as we could hear him splashing, puffing and snorting away behind the bathroom door, we held a council of war. Lore again favoured speaking frankly to the old man.

Toni objected strongly: 'No, never! We don't want any more talk of danger. I'm only pleased that he's beginning to forget Fritz's warnings.'

'Perhaps it would be best if we were all to talk quietly', was Lore's next suggestion. 'Then he'll automatically start talking quietly too.'

At this point the bathroom door opened and the shoemaker called from the hall: 'Toni, are we going to leave the wet towels here or take them home?'

Toni replied in a whisper, 'I'll see to the towels.'

'What?' he asked, shouting even louder. 'I can't hear you. Shall

234

we leave the towels here on the central heating?'

'Yes, all right, let's leave them here,' Toni said quietly.

'But aren't we going to take the curtains down first?' he bellowed.

Toni threw him a despairing, imploring look and pressed a forefinger to her lips in an attempt to bring him back to reason. He still did not understand.

We were unable to contain ourselves any longer. Gesturing towards the floor and ceiling in a pantomime of admonition, we told the shoemaker in no uncertain terms that he simply must start thinking of the neighbours. Otherwise. . . .

At the words 'police' and 'Gestapo', he caught his breath in alarm. 'Police?' he croaked, adding with a shake in his voice: 'Sh-shall we be off, then?'

It was the moment, of course, for a word of reassurance, but the sight of that huge bear of a fellow, that grizzled giant, suddenly transformed into a shivering overgrown baby was just too much for us. The poor man! His question went unanswered as, one by one, we averted our faces and stole from the room.

In the kitchen the four of us gave ourselves up to helpless laughter until our breath was coming in gasps.

'We mustn't — leave him alone — otherwise — he'll think we've cleared off,' Leon urged me. 'You — go back to him — at least!'

'You go back to him! I can't!'

'Whatever will he think? You go to him, Lore!'

Suddenly Toni cried, 'Stop laughing, all of you! He's coming!'

But this served only to set us off again. We quickly closed the kitchen door and leaned our combined weight against it, still laughing uncontrollably.

The shoemaker tapped at the door. He tapped again. We realised, then, that there was no putting the moment off any longer: we had to open up.

'What's going on?' he asked in some irritation.

'Nothing,' Toni replied. 'Nothing. It was just a joke.'

'All that was just a joke?'

'Yes, of course it was! Oh, except for the bit about the police!' And once again Toni went off into peals of laughter.

Later, unloading the furniture and arranging it in the workshop, we were careful to avoid the shoemaker's bewildered but deeply suspicious eye.

Many thanks? Is that all?

By the beginning of March 1943 the Agricolastrasse flat was empty.

The highpoint of our enterprise had been the removal of the huge oak wardrobe in which we children had once played hide-and-seek. The expeditions had had the desired effect. There was no longer any need for us to feel that we were impoverished refugees who had no means of thanking our benefactor beyond helping a bit with the housework and uttering the occasional 'May God reward you!' The old man was now very much friendlier.

The overcrowded workshop looked more like an antique shop. But the wardrobes, chairs and pictures had brought with them something of the atmosphere of our old home, and it did us good to see that the shoemaker was now living in our domestic context, so to speak, rather than simply we in his.

He ought not to have worn father's velvet smoking jacket, though. In fact, it was wrong of Toni to give it to him. But what did Toni *not* do, after Fritz's departure, to restore the old man to a more pleasant mood!

Before a fortnight was up, however, we knew for certain that the shoemaker was a changed man. His peevish moods returned. There were days when I kept out of his way completely lest I irritate him even further. I used to leave the flat by the back door early in the morning, despite the fact that in doing so I exposed myself to the prying eyes of the caretaker and the other occupants of the house. Toni lacked this escape. She had to stay with the shoemaker all the time and simply put up with his tantrums.

Clearly he had forgotten his protestations of friendship towards our parents, together with the 'sacred promise' he had made them. Our warnings to him after his bath that day, when we had mentioned the police and the Gestapo, must have made him think. He really had started taking more precautions at first. But before long the new secretiveness had begun to get on his nerves. He wanted to throw his windows and doors wide open again, not sit behind drawn curtains and be forever on his guard against strangers.

The shoemaker certainly enjoyed the many fine pieces of furniture, the bright lamps and knick-knacks, the cutlery, clothes and linen that we had brought into the place. But as the days went by and the beautiful things always looked the same and were no longer being added to, he seemed to stop seeing them. Did it ever occur to him to wonder whose property they now were? Not a word on the subject ever passed between the shoemaker and ourselves. The worrying thing was that the question now occurred to *us*. How sad it all was! We actually began to calculate — repulsive, indeed impossible though the exercise was — how the life-saving assistance provided by our fickle benefactor measured up to the material

236

considerations he had received in return.

The question of the ownership of the salvaged furniture and household effects remained unsettled. We thought the best course was to keep the old man on tenterhooks. There was no knowing how long our present indigence would last. And if we survived the war, we did not wish to be left entirely without possessions — not least because we wanted to be in a position, when it was all over, to give the shoemaker some tangible expression of our gratitude.

Meanwhile, he would occasionally be presented with a small gift from among my parents' possessions: a woollen scarf, a crystal vase, something like that. Initially the shoemaker used to thank us very warmly each time. Later he would receive our presents with no more than a conventional 'Thank you very much!' And finally he was simply taking them with a muttered 'Right! Many thanks!' This had the effect of arousing our suspicions. Did he look upon our parents' property as his eventual reward? Having now stockpiled all our worldly wealth in the shoemaker's flat, had we played our last card, as it were?

I wondered whether the shoemaker perhaps resented my eating his food. I had indeed been sharing his provisions for some time, but I had done so in the knowledge that he had more than enough for himself. Did he really think he was going short on my account?

From then on I endeavoured to eat as little as possible of what the shoemaker provided. And what Toni was able to put aside for Leon and me she gave us as unobtrusively as possible. When we managed to get hold of some food ourselves, we even gave some of it to the shoemaker, pretending that we had plenty.

Occasionally it was possible, through barter, to offer him some rare delicacy. Then Toni would say: 'Tschibel brought that back today!' or 'Look what Leon has produced!'

One day the department store in Leipzigerstrasse that old Berliners still referred to as 'Wertheim's' was selling little packets of fruit paste unrationed. We took our places in the queue — Lore, Leon and myself. The queue was so long that we were able, once served, to join the end of it again without anyone noticing. A lady standing in front of me turned round after a while and asked me under her breath, 'What are they selling here, in fact?'

That evening, disregarding our rumbling stomachs, we gave two of the packets to the shoemaker. The sacrifice was worthwhile: the old man beamed at us. And Toni made it up to us later with liberal helpings of other things. But it was not every day that we were able to share some of our 'surplus' with the shoemaker.

One evening Lore produced a whole loaf of bread from her

237

handbag. 'I found it in a telephone kiosk!' she said, delighted with her luck. 'Let's hope it didn't belong to someone in hiding like us!'

A place of our own

By March 1943 there was already extensive bomb damage in certain parts of Berlin. Almost miraculously, it seemed, the *S-Bahn* was hardly touched. When the train traversed a district that had been destroyed, the passengers would crowd to the window to gaze at the deserted streets and endless rows of hollow-eyed façades. I too would push my way towards the window with my ears pricked up. Yet I never heard a single word of outrage or dismay. The passengers did not even exchange glances. They simply stared out of the window in silence. It was an eerie silence, charged with fear and bitterness. But bitterness against whom? Against the British bomber pilots who visited Berlin almost nightly? Against the ravagers of Rotterdam and Coventry? Against the Gestapo agents who might be standing amongst them, also looking out of the window? I should have loved to know what my fellow-passengers were thinking. But their lips remained sealed as they gazed fixedly at that picture of desolation. Where only a short while before the sun had shone on the roofs of dwellings teeming with life, now it reached right down into the cellars and threw the shadows of bizarre, ruined shapes on the piles of rubble that lay all around. Nothing moved. Only occasionally a gust of wind, whipping across the scene, would lick at inexhaustible reserves of powdered mortar, shattered brick and bare earth to send a fresh cloud of dust whirling into the surrounding streets.

Berlin grew smaller with each night that the bombers came; more and more houses disappeared, more and more people were made homeless, and we, who legally did not exist, kept up a constant search for new quarters and if possible new sources of food. Since the shoemaker's most recent angry outbursts, we had ceased to cherish false hopes in that direction. If we were to hold out until the end of the war, we had to find fresh hiding-places. Not just for Toni and myself; Leon and Lore also needed somewhere more secure. There was also the fact that their present place was not always available. They still needed to spend many evenings and nights in my room. And without the leftovers that Toni put on one side for them, they would have gone very hungry.

Leon was tireless in his efforts to end our dependence on the shoemaker. My father had once owned a house in Wedding, the part of the city that lies to the north of the Hansa quarter. We calculated that Ruhnke, the man father had put in to manage the property, must now be eighty — if he was still alive. How we hoped and prayed that he was! Surely he would not leave us in the lurch! The old Prussian was not only a reliable property manager; he called himself a 'friend and admirer' of my father and remained devoted to him even after Hitler came to power and the house fell into 'Aryan' hands as a result of a compulsory purchase order. Why had we not thought of Ruhnke long before? Ah, God grant that he was still in the land of the living!

He was. Opening the door in person, he gave Leon a cordial reception. He was still hale and hearty — a giant of a man, and ramrod-straight like one of the *Langen Kerls*, the famous 'Tall Guards' of Friedrich Wilhelm I of Prussia. Ruhnke had been widowed some years before. Since then he had been living all alone in his four-roomed flat. Leon's hopes rose: the old man might even be glad to have a few youngsters around to keep house for him.

My brother put his case with care. Ruhnke was shattered when Leon told him what had happened to our parents. He continued to listen attentively and compassionately until, on hearing that we were 'in hiding' and 'not registered with the police', he began to twiddle his Kaiser Wilhelm moustache nervously. Thereafter the conversation came to a swift end.

'I can't understand an old dodderer like that clinging so tight to his little bit of peace!' Leon exclaimed bitterly on his return. 'He just gave a sympathetic shrug and showed me to the door.'

Berlin was getting smaller, but it was still inconceivably vast. There must be a hiding-place somewhere in that sea of houses, we thought. Somewhere among those millions of people there were surely some who would dare to help four Jews in hiding? But how were we to find those valiant Berliners, and how were we to gain their confidence? After all, they would have to hide their goodness behind a mask of inhuman zeal for the law, and we should have to pretend to be loyal servants of the ruling powers of the Reich.

After the disappointment with old Ruhnke, Leon turned his attention away from looking for plucky protectors. He saw more future in our seeking out hiding-places where we could stay without the knowledge and assistance of courageous 'Aryans'. There must surely be such places in a huge city like Berlin? My brother spent day after day roaming the streets and open spaces of the capital.

One Sunday he asked me to come with him to help him look. He also wanted to show me one or two places that he had already identified as possible hideouts or at least bases.

We joined the stream of pedestrians pouring along the pavement beside the Charlottenburger Chaussee in the direction of the city centre. It was good to mingle with so many people strolling simultaneously through the Tiergarten. The more people there were around us, the safer we felt, though we were still careful to keep our distance and to speak in low voices for fear of being overheard. The sun, shining warmly through the great camouflage net that covered the avenue along its entire length and breadth, cast a grid of shadow onto the asphalt. The fresh breeze blowing from the depths of the park bore a hint of spring.

I had often taken that same walk with Leon — through the Tiergarten and on up the avenue called Unter den Linden to the old Royal Palace — in the years before the war. How different Berlin looked now! And how differently we looked at Berlin now! Our eyes examined everything in terms of its potential as a hiding-place. We cursed the Prussian love of order that neglected no path and left no litter-bin unchecked. We envied the birds their nests. Later, when we came across a number of trees that had been damaged in the air-raids, we felt sorry for the birds because they were so helplessly exposed to bombs and shrapnel. We wondered whether the many strollers ahead of, behind and to right and left of us were also preoccupied exclusively by accommodation problems.

Leon told me what he had found so far. In the vicinity of the Reichstag building he had noticed a long-disused construction crane. He wanted to convert the cab of the crane into living-quarters. And in the south-west corner of the Tiergarten he had seen an empty furniture van that also appeared to have been abandoned. There was a third possibility, he said, that he wanted to take me to now. Leading me away from the road, he showed me a wooden hut near the rose garden. In the winter the hut was used for storing deck chairs. Throughout the summer, Leon assured me, it stood empty. But rather than wait for the summer he wanted to check as soon as possible whether there might not be room for us somewhere in among the stacks of chairs. It was simply a question of getting hold of a skeleton key with which to pick the lock. The only disadvantage was that during air-raids we should be in just as much danger as the birds. We should have to dig ourselves a secret shelter somewhere in the bushes.

All Leon's plans were equally desperate. He had only to put them into words to appreciate how impractical they were. He would then begin to pour ridicule on them himself. But he remained insistent. We must continue to comb the residential areas and parks of Berlin until we found something. We must spare no pains in our attempt to make ourselves independent of the shoemaker.

We returned to the main avenue and rejoined the stream of pedestrians. The Brandenburg Gate loomed ever clearer out of the misty distance. Its columns looked as if they were actually supporting the camouflage net. Not until we reached the end of the net did the crowning figure of Attica driving her quadriga come into view. The sky brightened and the grid of shadow disappeared from beneath our feet.

Unter den Linden stretched before us, bathed in sunlight and strewn with the mortar and brickdust of bombed-out houses. This crunched beneath the soles of our shoes at every step. We had never seen Berlin's most splendid avenue in such a state. And what an extraordinary sound! The babble and chatter that filled the air was made up of twenty different tongues. Foreign workers with dark hair growing down over the collars of their proletarian Sunday suits swarmed over the whole width of the street, calling to one another and gesticulating noisily. At crossings they gathered in a knot before bursting across the carriageway in waves, completely ignoring the traffic signals. They did not look at all discontented with their lot, even though within the German sphere of influence it was very much that of second-class citizens. Polish prisoners and *Ostarbeiter* (workers from occupied eastern Europe) were not in evidence. The scene was dominated by people from the Mediterranean and Balkan lands. Only very occasionally did we hear a German voice, and on turning to look we could be virtually certain of seeing a uniform.

Leon joked that we had better stop speaking German if we did not wish to make ourselves conspicuous. Soon, however, what had begun as a joke was causing us serious concern. The people around us were, in effect, all identified either by their appearance or by their language. Where did we fit in? What role should we be playing?

We hurried on in the direction of the Arsenal, where a recently captured Russian armoured car was said to be on display. As we went, Leon tested me on how well I remembered what Unter den Linden had looked like before the war, asking whether I knew which monument lay hidden beneath this or that heap of sandbags.

The Russian armoured car was the size of a railway truck. We calculated that it was built to take a crew of twelve. There was not much left of its internal fittings or of its armament, but the empty, burned-out steel shell alone struck fear in the heart. Leon examined the monster enthusiastically. 'There would be a hideout for us!' he said with a sigh of regret. 'No need to be afraid of shrapnel inside that. Pity they had to stick it next to the Arsenal, of all places.'

Leon's tireless researches were not wholly unsuccessful. He did discover a tiny hideout — not in the Tiergarten, not in a bombed-out building somewhere in Berlin, but where we had least expected to find one.

Sneaking into the shoemaker's flat by the back door one day, he spotted another door in the stairwell that none of us had ever noticed before. It was right next to the door of the shoemaker's kitchen. Where did it lead? Down into the cellar? Into the next-door flat? Unable to contain his curiosity, Leon knocked on it. No answer. He pushed down the handle, entered — and found himself in a lavatory.

On one side a thin partition separated it from the shoemaker's kitchen; on the other, a window overlooked the courtyard; and to all appearances it was no longer in use. Leon reckoned we could not have wished for a more ideal emergency hideout. If we needed to leave the shoemaker's flat while there were people in the courtyard, we could wait in the lavatory until the coast was clear. Coming in from the street, we could hear in the lavatory if the shoemaker happened to be in the kitchen. And we could perfectly well wait there for hours on end, because after all it was a lavatory. In an emergency, someone could even spend the night in there.

We inspected the tiny room. The seat looked rather like that of a simple farmhouse privy. However, the lid lifted to reveal not a cesspit but an enamelled bowl. There was even a cistern to flush it.

What was the lavatory doing there? Years ago, presumably, it had been for the use of all the occupants of the building. Now that every flat had its own plumbing, it was redundant. That would also account for the absence of the customary smell.

Redundant! We positively leapt to the conclusion that no one ever used the lavatory any more.

The place had only two drawbacks. No one could sit there for any length of time; the seat was too uncomfortable. And people could see in from the courtyard. Leon, however, had a solution to both. He found a wide plank to place over the seat and he got Toni to make a net curtain for the window.

Our new base was quickly fitted out. Leon even wedged a small wooden box high up beside the cistern to hide books in. For safety's sake he did not remove the round lavatory seat but simply stood the plank against the wall in readiness.

By the time we gathered in my room on the following Sunday afternoon, we had already used our new base several times. The operation had gone very smoothly. '*Please* let nobody notice anything!' Leon implored aloud. 'It's just what we've always dreamed of: a hundred cubic feet of space where we shall be left in peace, where we can go and not have to keep out of the shoemaker's or anyone else's way!'

242

Hearing footsteps outside in the courtyard, we sprang up and peered through the curtains. It was the caretaker. He plodded past and disappeared into the entrance leading to the shoemaker's back door.

A few minutes later we saw the caretaker go plodding back across the courtyard. This time he had a length of plank tucked under his left arm and a wooden box under his right. Smiling grimly, we watched him carry them both away.

'Let's hope he recovers from his surprise without feeling driven to investigate too closely!' Lore remarked.

Leon was gnashing his teeth: 'Damn the man! Damn all caretakers and porters and spying doormen!'

Despite this disappointment we still got plenty of use out of Leon's discovery. We continued to refer to it as our 'secret privy', even though it was no longer entirely secret.

Mimicry

In March 1943 the inhabitants of Berlin were ordered to clear out their attics by a certain date. The idea was to provide the incendiary bombs with as little fuel as possible, thus making the work of the fire brigades easier.

Inspired by the attic-clearance order, Leon promptly formed a plan. The people of Berlin were all suffering from overwork and chronic shortage of sleep, he reasoned. They would gladly give us a bite to eat in return for some help. And we were experienced furniture removers, were we not?

He lost no time in putting the plan into effect. His foreign-worker friends gave him the addresses of some people who were interested. Possibly as a result of their mediation many of the people for whom we cleared attics and humped coal took us, too, for foreign workers. Once we were aware of this, we spoke as little as possible and did everything to maintain and even reinforce the illusion. Fortunately, people did not inquire too deeply. Delighted to have found helping hands, they used to reward us with dishes of steaming potatoes.

Only once did we find ourselves in a tricky situation. Leon had been given another address for an attic clearance: a girls' boarding school in Lützowstrasse, over on the south side of the Tiergarten. The Spanish headmistress, despite the fact that she had been living in Germany for many years, still spoke German with an accent and seemed not to have a particularly sharp ear for the accents of others. Speaking broken German, we introduced ourselves to her as Bulgarians.

243

Speaking one's own mother tongue in a convincingly broken fashion is not an easy thing to do. For all our inventiveness, we should have made a poor job of it had we not ourselves spent so much time listening to foreign workers. But speaking broken German was only part of it. The Spanish woman was entitled to expect her two Bulgarians to converse together in their own tongue.

We gave her a foreign language, all right. During the lunch break she invited us into the kitchen, and as she served us a hot meal, Leon and I chatted away in Hebrew. Actually, most of the chatting came from me, while Leon did most of the listening (I was rather ahead of him in Hebrew). The lady of the house listened in amusement.

Between the soup and the potato dish, she began, in her well-meaning innocence, to ask us some extremely awkward questions. She wanted to know how we liked Germany, whether we did not feel homesick for Bulgaria, whereabouts in Berlin we lived, and so on.

To give us more time to think, Leon hit upon the idea of repeating the Spanish woman's questions in execrable German. The conversation went something like this:

The Spanish woman: 'Tell me, do all the men in Bulgaria have to go to the front, too?'

I gave her a bewildered, helpless smile.

The Spanish woman (turning up the volume): 'IN BULGARIA, ALL MEN GO TO THE FRONT?'

Still smiling, I looked inquiringly at Leon.

Leon: 'Lady ask, eez in Bulgaria vor? Oll men in Bulgaria shoot bang bang?'

The last touch brought me dangerously close to hysteria. It cost me a tremendous effort to stifle the laughter welling up behind the bland mask of my smile.

I nodded earnestly to the Spanish woman: 'Yurss. Vor no good. Eez vurking much, itting no much.'

Despite our laboriously feigned misunderstandings, the Spanish woman persisted with her questioning. Not until the third day did she look like giving up. 'I know!' she said then, after a moment's thought. 'I have a cousin who knows Russian. Russian is supposed to be very like Bulgarian, isn't it? I'll ask her round tomorrow. Then we can have a proper chat.'

But the two 'Bulgarians' were never seen again.

We had been lucky: the woman's suspicions had not been aroused. Still, the episode made us think. Not everyone in Berlin was as naïve as our Spanish headmistress. We must consider how we intended to present ourselves in future. And we must have an identity card. Any old scrap of paper would do, provided it had a stamp on it!

Once again it was Leon's friendly relations with his foreign acquaintances that came to our rescue. An Italian mate of his had started taking Leon to the 'Fascio', the League of Italian Fascists in Berlin. The building was also frequented by Germans attending Italian evening classes.

One evening Leon came home and pulled an official-looking card from his pocket. Not much larger than a folded postcard, it bore a genuine passport photograph of Leon with the 'Fascio' stamp across one corner. The Fascist national symbol, the bundle of *fasces* or rods with a projecting axe-head that had been carried before high magistrates in ancient Rome, was prominently displayed on the front.

For our benefit, Leon translated what it said on the card. As I recall, it went something like this: 'This is to certify that the holder of this membership card is enrolled in the language course of the Fascio Organisation in Berlin. For each month of the course the appropriate receipt stamp is to be affixed to the card.' Leon's card had a single stamp on it, for March 1943.

We shook our heads. Apart from the holder's name, the card gave no personal details. It was simply a piece of printed paper with a receipt stamp stuck in it. Were the police likely to fall for that?

Leon had his own view: 'It's not ideal. No intelligent policeman is ever going to accept it as an identity card. But most of them are duffers anyway. When they see the indecipherable text, together with the national emblem and that huge rubber stamp, they'll all bow down and worship! In any case, when they're checking a whole lot of people they don't have time to examine every card in detail.'

Toni, Lore and I remained sceptical. However, when Leon promised to get cards like it for us, we ran round to the photographer's the very next morning and had passport pictures taken.

In the interests of caution, Leon took us along one at a time, on three separate evenings. I went first, then Lore and finally Toni.

The villa that housed the 'Fascio' was decked out with Italian emblems. Leon took me straight to the cash desk to enrol. The girl behind the counter issued me with the coveted card immediately. All she asked was my name. Before I could open my mouth, Leon answered for me: 'Wilhelm Schneider.' Afterwards Leon took me into a deserted corner of the splendid entrance hall and whispered, 'From now on your name is Wilhelm Schneider — got that? Never use any other name!'

We surrendered our coats and followed the stream of people up the marble staircase. The classroom was adorned with swastika and fasces flags. Many of the benches were already occupied by our fellow students. And what fellow students! I found myself sitting amid a motley crew of policemen, army officers and SS men — with just a few civilians thrown in!

We had certainly got ourselves into fine company here! I threw Leon a doubtful look. But then it dawned on me what he had meant by hinting earlier that in this building we should be safe from identity checks. Who, indeed, among the policemen and SS officers taking up so much room on those benches, would ever have dreamt that two Jews living in hiding from the law would one day march in and sit down beside them?

How harmless, how positively genial they all looked! They had removed their caps and placed them on the desks in front of them, and it was as if in doing so they had laid aside all their quality of inhuman officialdom.

Suddenly the comfortable chatter was stilled. An attractive signorina had appeared on the podium in front of the blackboard. Speaking the most delightfully accented German, she introduced herself as our teacher and went straight into the lesson. From the classes I attended over the next fortnight, I have retained perhaps two rules regarding Italian pronunciation. I also learnt to leave the room with an 'Arrivederci!' My goal as a language student had been achieved before the first lesson began.

Soon Lore and Toni also had their 'Fascio' cards and could manage a handful of Italian expressions. Only Leon spoke Italian properly. He had been studying the language as a hobby for years. Consequently he was the only one of us capable, when it came to it, of acting the part of an Italian.

In fact, Leon was so resourceful that he manufactured a second identity card for himself. He still had his pass from the 'German Munitions and Armaments Works'. He scraped the 'J' off it with a knife, and over the scraped area he neatly glued the firm's symbol, 'DMW' (Deutsche Munitions- und Waffenfabriken), which he had cut from an old pay-packet. Proudly, he showed me his new 'document'. Now in an emergency he could claim to be a German munitions worker.

The new card really did look most convincing, as long as it was not removed from its celluloid sheath. But how did Leon intend to masquerade as a German munitions worker without being able to prove simultaneously that he was exempt from military service? What worried me even more was the fact that he kept changing the part he was playing. He now had two identity cards. Moreover, in his curious outfit he felt he could get away with even more roles. He had taken to going about in his homemade black 'uniform' again, the one that was reminiscent of both the SS uniform and the Italian Blackshirt get-up. However, since he had neither cap nor badges, Leon believed he could also pass as a civilian.

But was there not a danger that so ambiguous a disguise might actually attract the attention of police patrols? In a time of total war, even men in genuine, regulation uniforms had to reckon with identity checks at any and every moment. Surely, I thought, the best way to present oneself confidently and convincingly was to decide on a particular role and stick to it? Yet when I attempted to do so, like Leon I ended up with a rather dubious compromise.

I was now twenty-one. According to all my friends, though, I could easily pass for sixteen or seventeen. The most suitable disguise for me would therefore seem to be that of a member of the Hitler Youth. It struck me as unlikely that a lad in Hitler Youth uniform would be asked to show his identity card. A civilian of military age was at far greater risk.

In the war years the Hitler Youth no longer wore the brown outfit of 1933 but a uniform not unlike a ski suit. That made it easier for me, because I owned a ski suit. All I lacked were the Hitler Youth badges. However, I hesitated to deck myself out in swastikas. What would the shoemaker say, for one thing, if he saw me thus attired? For another, I shrank from wearing the emblems of the Third Reich.

Leon found the incompleteness of my disguise far more alarming than that of his own. 'How is your uniform supposed to tally with your "Fascio" card?' he asked me. 'And if someone stops you and asks which Hitler Youth unit you belong to, what are you going to tell them? Just you mind you don't bump into any genuine Hitler Youth members!'

There is a knack to studying the faces of passers-by without appearing to look at them. I practised it the first time I ventured onto the street in my 'uniform'. The rehearsal went off successfully. It was clear to me that no one was paying me any particular attention, and slowly but surely I grew accustomed to the strange, strange role I was playing.

Leon's experience was no doubt similar. In order not to erode each other's self-confidence, we stopped criticising the incompleteness of our respective disguises. We both knew that a self-assured exterior mattered just as much as our 'Aryan' faces, our phoney identity cards and our protective camouflage.

Lore and Toni did not need to wear any disguise. However, the fact that they had no other proof of identity to show than their 'Fascio' membership cards worried them too. Since they could not in fact speak Italian, they had had the cards made out in German-sounding cover-names. How were they going to explain to the police why German girls were carrying Italian papers?

Despite our misgivings, we were all four of us glad to have at least something to show if required. But we were in no hurry to try out the effectiveness of our 'identity cards'. If we saw something down the street ahead of us that looked like a police checkpoint, we would execute a swift about-turn. We even went out of our way to avoid the Wehrmacht patrols that seemed to be everywhere in Berlin. We did not know that they were only allowed to stop members of the armed forces.

Refuge among the reptiles

I have spoken in some detail of what happened to me in March 1943, but I have not yet told the whole story. A great many momentous events occurred during that time within the narrow circle of our lives. Increasingly we felt that we were losing our footing in the world. My own situation in particular became critical. In only one respect had the pressure on us eased: no longer did we receive visits from Jewish friends who frightened us with bad news. We heard no further talk of 'lists', 'collections' and 'deportations'. We were like fossil Jews who had somehow survived into Berlin's new post-Jewish age. There were times when it seemed to us that in all the world there were only four examples of the Jewish species left: Leon, Lore, Toni and myself.

I have since read, in history books dealing with the Second World War, of what was happening in the world at that time, and I hold it up against my own recollections:

March 1943: Under massive coercion from Germany, the government of Bulgaria co-operated in deporting Greek and Yugoslav Jews from Bulgarian-occupied areas. However, it drew the line at deporting Bulgarian Jews. Hitler's planned genocide foundered in Bulgaria on the rock of hostile public opinion.

Himmler and Ribbentrop meanwhile set the wheels in motion to deport the Jews from the Italian-occupied part of France. Their plans foundered on the humane behaviour of French officials and Italian soldiers.

Neutral Sweden offered protection to Norway's Jews by granting them Swedish nationality — much to the annoyance of *Reichskommissar* Terboven, the German ruler of occupied Norway.

March 1943: Liquidation of the Kraków ghetto. Most of Kraków's Jews were interned in a labour camp, though many had already been murdered in the ghetto. A transport left for Auschwitz and arrived just in time for the opening of the first new gas chamber. A Jewish detail was ordered to sort out the spoils in the ghetto.

March 1943: German troops, fighting with the courage of lions, retook Khar'kov.

March 1943: The shoemaker was subject to increasingly frequent bouts of rage. Everything got on his nerves — the everlasting secrecy on account of his protégés, the air-raid warnings, lack of sleep, letters from his sons at the front.

After one heavy night attack on Berlin he read in the paper that people affected by the air-raids were entitled to receive free medical treatment; all they had to do was to report to their nearest Red Cross post.

'Just what I need!' the shoemaker said as he pulled on his coat. No bombs had actually fallen anywhere near us during the previous night, but he had a distinct feeling that something was not quite right with his innards, no doubt as a result of all the excitement.

But what rotten luck! At the Red Cross post they gave him a slimy white liquid to swallow and X-rayed his stomach and intestines. The shoemaker insisted that the white liquid had now made him really ill. He felt awful, he said.

After that I kept out of his way as much as possible. The sight of his permanently scowling face with its shrewd, foxy eyes had begun to make me feel ill. And we owed the wretched man our lives! He still constituted our mainstay in the Nazi Reich!

Once again I started doing the rounds of the museums and galleries of Berlin. The art museums had packed their treasures away in the cellars, but the Natural History Museum, a short *S-Bahn* ride away in Invalidenstrasse, was still open to the public. I had already been through it several times. Perhaps, though, I had not explored it thoroughly enough. Perhaps there was, after all, a remote corner somewhere in the building, a cupboard or a disused stock-room, where I might spend the night undetected?

My explorations did not take me long. The rooms were either full of glass cases or they contained impossibly exposed displays of skeletons or stuffed animals. It would have been difficult to hide behind any of the stuffed animals; behind the skeletons, of course, it was out of the question. And everywhere — among the dinosaurs, behind the anatomical specimens in jars of alcohol, even in the museum's splendidly hygienic lavatories — there were attendants in peaked caps that were stretched as tight as drums.

Disappointed, I left that haunt of dead animals and took a train to the zoo. It was not by chance that I sought refuge particularly in the Natural History Museum and in the zoo. Both places were familiar to me. My interest in animals had often drawn me to them in the years before the war, and I had acquired a far more thorough knowledge of zoology than is expected of the average zoo visitor. Now that persecution of the Jews had assumed such inhuman forms, I felt even more strongly attracted to the innocence of the animal world. I also considered it unlikely that many other people living in hiding would show themselves in so public a place — and equally unlikely, therefore, that the Gestapo would come looking for them there.

The green expanses of the zoo lay bleak and abandoned-looking. I could see no police patrols. I took the risk of resting for a while on one of the benches, but the cold soon moved me on.

To get warm I ducked into the tropical houses, visiting in turn the lions and tigers, the parrots and the monkeys. I found I could not stand the noise and stench of the animals for very long. Possibly in time of 'total war' they were ventilating less in order to save fuel. It then occurred to me to look in the aquarium building for a place where I might stay for a while.

The aquarium, too, I knew well from my pre-war visits. The lower floors accommodated, in gleaming chests of crystal, an overwhelming abundance of the creatures with which God filled the seas and rivers on the fifth day of Creation. The upper floor held a large terrarium. Primitive insects, millepedes, dragonflies and butterflies spun, wriggled and pupated in the everlasting tropical summer of the heated insectariums.

I walked unhurriedly through the darkened rooms and passageways, eyeing the bright, colourful aquariums but also studying the other visitors. There were not many of them. 'Total war' left Berliners little time for contemplating the wonders of Creation. But neither did I encounter a single person in uniform, which made the silence I found amid all that teeming wildlife doubly delightful. The building was pleasantly warm from the basement to the very top floor. There were benches everywhere, and if I sat down I caught only the dim reflection of the lighted aquariums. I could rest there for half an hour without making myself conspicuous. I could even eat a sandwich. And the building was well equipped with lavatories and wash-basins.

I hurried back to the ticket office. 'Can one also buy monthly — no, yearly season tickets for the aquarium?'

'You certainly can,' the ticket clerk said. 'Costs ten marks. You'll need to bring a passport photo, though.'

Next day I had in my breast pocket a yearly season ticket to the aquarium, complete with my photograph, the stamp of the zoo administration, and the signature of Wilhelm Schneider.

The aquarium provided me with a precious base in a thoroughly insecure existence. My daily round began to assume a rather more tolerable form. I still left the shoemaker's flat at half past eight every morning, but now it was with a definite goal in mind. And what an excellent effect it had on the nerves, studying salamanders and watching turtles glide silently through the water, wreathed in air bubbles and surrounded by the darting shapes of fluorescent fish! Even the predatory billfish and the monstrous hammerhead sharks looked peaceful in comparison with warring, war-mongering Germany!

In what enviable luxury were the crocodiles billeted! They had a whole house to themselves, with a built-in tropical river landscape and every imaginable crocodile comfort — all to make the creatures feel at home in Berlin. They could have a bath whenever they wanted. And while an icy wind howled outside, they were able to lounge on the beach or crawl about beneath palm trees and exotic climbing plants. If the fancy took them, they could open their jaws and hold them open for as long as they felt like doing so. The only thing they possibly did not enjoy was being stared at and occasionally interfered with by the zoo visitors crossing the bamboo bridge above them. But no one was after them constantly — no shoemaker and no police. And when visiting hours came to an end, they did not have to leave the aquarium and ride round in circles on the *S-Bahn*.

Tired of walking, I sank down on one of the benches in the twilight of the viewing-rooms. My stomach was rumbling. Where on earth did the zoo management find the food to keep all those swimming, slithering, crawling creatures alive? Taking out the slice of bread that Toni had given me as I left the flat, I ate my lunch in the company of 3-metre-long Komodo dragons, fearsome-looking frilled lizards, and the three-eyed tuatara, which looks as if it is wearing a permanent smile. They really are still with us, the antediluvian reptiles, still flicking out their tongues at the speed of lightning, just as they did in the Jurassic and Cretaceous periods.

In our council of war I spoke enthusiastically of my new refuge and urged Leon to join me there each day. He simply laughed at me: 'I expect the fishes and snakes know you pretty well by now. Let's hope your face doesn't become too familiar to the attendants!'

CHAPTER 11

Festival of Freedom

An underground munitions worker

The shoemaker now made no secret of the fact that he wished to be rid of me. He hurled insults at me that under normal circumstances I should certainly not have let him get away with. Mindful of everything I owed him and of my present dependence upon him, I stood there and made no reply. I cannot even say whether the shoemaker blushed at some of the things he said. A shamefaced reluctance to witness his shame — and even more to witness his lack of it — kept my eyes on the floor. The old man interpreted my embarrassed silence as an admission of guilt, which only made him more sure of himself.

'What?' he would ask me reproachfully, ' — the rest are all fighting at the front or working hard on the home front, and you just want to wait around here till the war's over?'

Seeing him and being seen by him became so intolerable to me that in order to avoid an encounter I would even hide from him in his own flat. I recall one particularly painful scene. The caretaker was sweeping the courtyard. I was standing in the kitchen with my coat on, waiting for him to finish and leave the coast clear for me to go out. Suddenly I heard the shoemaker coming along the passage. There was no time to slip out of the back door and into our 'secret privy'. In any case, the caretaker was working in that direction and was by now quite close to the stairwell door. I darted into the larder and pulled the door to after me. The shoemaker entered the kitchen. I kept as quiet as a mouse. Holding my breath, aware of all my pulses racing, I listened as the shoemaker made a great clatter with cups and plates only a few feet away from me. Suddenly the larder door was pulled open.

'Hello, what are you doing in there?' the shoemaker demanded.

Blushing furiously, I stammered a few meaningless words and

forced myself to smile in an attempt to make a joke of the whole thing.

Ugh, how that smile disgusted me! How it must have disgusted him! How nauseating I suddenly found the whole world, how odious the whole business of living! No, that was not right: the fault lay not with life but with me! No one on earth stood as much in my way as I did myself! Humanity had decreed that I should not live. So why was I still hanging around in a world in which there was no place for me? Why was I not a tiny ant, capable of crawling into a safe hole somewhere? Why did my tiresome body everlastingly demand light, air, food, sleep? Would it not be marvellous to be rid of such a burden?

The classified advertisements sections of the newspapers always contained plenty of job opportunities. After carefully combing through them, I took down the address of an electrical and precision engineer who was looking for a part-time assistant. Meeting such a man might open up fresh possibilities, I thought. Perhaps I would be able to sleep at his works without anyone knowing or spend the night there as a volunteer nightwatchman. If on the other hand the engineer was a conscientious Nazi working hand in glove with the Gestapo, that would put an end to me and my problems.

The factory was situated in a quiet side street in nearby Charlottenburg. From outside it looked no different from the other residential houses in the street. Only the brass plate — 'Helmut Sell, D. Eng., Electrical Engineer' — marked it out.

There did not appear to be many applicants for the post. I was promptly admitted and taken before a gentleman in his middle years. Dr Sell, clearly delighted that someone had answered his advertisement, shook me by the hand and indicated the seat across the desk from him. I sat down.

Everyone is familiar with the kind of polite chit-chat that goes on in such circumstances. Its purpose is to put a human face on the painfully self-evident question, 'Can I use you?' However, at that particular moment I very much hoped that my questioner would confine his interest to my skills and abilities and leave personal matters out of it. I wondered what I might expect from 'Helmut Sell, D. Eng., Electrical Engineer'. His gaze told me little; in fact, his steel-blue eyes looked in slightly different directions.

I told him I was a student at the 'Italian High School', saying that I wished to earn a little pocket money in my free time and that I was very interested in engineering.

'Well, I'm blowed!' said Sell, genuinely astonished. 'I knew there was a French high school — I didn't realise there was also an Italian high school in Berlin.'

His astonishment was entirely justified. The 'Italian High School' was an invention of my own. It was the best lie I could think of to enable me to explain, if I had to, why a schoolboy wearing the uniform of the Hitler Youth should produce an Italian identity card.

However, the engineer did not pursue the matter, nor did he ask to see my papers. He showed me round the machine rooms and workshops. Afterwards he remarked: 'Total mobilisation has meant that most small businesses have had to consent to being absorbed by the giants. I managed to get permission to go on running my little works myself because I supply specialised precision instruments for the munitions industry. It's a distinct advantage to be able to remain at least partially one's own master. I think you'll like it here. You seem to know something about engineering. In fact, it's my belief, Mr Schneider, that if you come and work for me you will stand a very good chance of making a career in the field.'

The 'Mr Schneider' gave me a bit of a jolt. It was the first time anybody had called me that in good faith.

We were soon on the point of agreeing terms. The only snag was that Dr Sell could not understand my reluctance to register with the labour department.

'The thing is, sir, I should like if possible to stay on a trainee basis,' I said rather hesitantly.

'Ah, I see!' he replied. 'You mean: otherwise the labour department might order you around and make you go where *they* wanted?'

This comparatively daring remark made me sit up. I was encouraged to respond with a certain frankness of my own. 'That's right,' I agreed. 'I should like to remain my own master for as long as I can.'

'I understand. But in that case I'm afraid I shan't be able to take you on. The law lays down heavy penalties for anyone employing people without an official work book.' His eyes wandered upwards and focused pensively on one of the blackout blinds. 'Wait a minute, though — let me check the regulations!'

A little while later Sell looked up from his books and files. 'Yes, I'm afraid it's just as I said. The new regulations leave us virtually no leeway. You may not work more than eleven hours a week without registering with the labour department,' he explained resignedly.

Disappointed, I looked down at the papers spread on his desk. Then, after a suitable 'pause for thought', I brought out what had long been on the tip of my tongue: 'Please sir, if you're interested, I'm quite prepared to work for you for eleven hours. I can find myself another eleven-hour job somewhere else. I haven't got more than twenty-two hours' free time anyway.'

Sell's gaze wandered back to the blackout blind. 'All right, Mr Schneider,' he said at last. Let's give it a try. Perhaps you'll feel differently about registering when you've worked here for a bit.'

I had not been in his employ for more than a few days when the engineer stopped looking at his watch altogether. He did not even appear to notice that I was neglecting my studies at the 'Italian High School' and for three days in the week placing myself at his disposal not only in the afternoons but in the mornings as well. Did my uniform not occasionally make him stop and think? As a member of the Hitler Youth I ought to have been involved in anti-aircraft defence or other home-front duties. Sell never embarrassed me with awkward questions.

Sometimes he had me working at a vice in the workshop; sometimes he sent me out on errands. My new job brought me precious rewards, and I do not mean only the few marks that the engineer paid me in accordance with the official scale laid down for errand-boys. As I hurried busily to and fro between Sell's works and various factories and stores in Berlin, I carried in my rucksack and my briefcase instruments and appliances for the air force and the navy. If a policeman were to ask me for my papers, I could show him an order form or an invoice marked 'Urgent! First priority! Materials vital to the war effort!' Possibly I exaggerated the power of those bits of paper. But they certainly made me feel a lot safer.

My new job made a big difference to my life. I still spent the day riding round Berlin on the *S-Bahn* and the Underground, but now it was no longer in order to alight after ten or a dozen stations and take a train in the opposite direction; it was because I actually wished to reach a particular destination.

Sell's invoices and order forms opened doors to me that were marked 'Unauthorised persons not admitted' and 'Beware of spies!' The doors revealed machine rooms that were a jumble of thundering transmission drives and slapping belts. In one room 100 women sat winding electrical coils. Hitler's picture occupied a prominent position on one wall, surrounded by inspiring slogans: 'Forward to ultimate victory!' and 'Leader, command us — we shall obey!'* On another occasion I left a factory rather more swiftly than I had entered it because the police were in there, arresting two workers.

My encounters with storemen who handed me parts across counters or through hatches or took delivery of items from my bags sometimes led to conversations. My semi-uniform never prompted

* 'Vorwärts zum Endsieg!' and 'Führer befiehl — wir folgen!'

anyone to ask me embarrassing questions. Only on one occasion did anyone take an interest in me personally. A departmental manager to whom I had to deliver some orders sized me up with a big smile on his face and said: 'You're not a Berliner, are you? I'd say you came from Stuttgart — am I right?'

'Almost,' I replied. 'I'm from Heilbronn.'

'There you are! I could tell by your accent. It doesn't take me long to know who I'm dealing with', he added, winking sagely.

The longer I worked for Sell, the more cruelly my conscience tormented me. Now I too was actually helping to arm the Nazi war machine! The measuring instruments that I carried from factory to factory would serve, I knew, to build more submarines and aircraft for Hitler's armed forces. I decided that somehow or other I must offset my share of responsibility.

Deciding was as far as I got, of course. My visits to the various munitions works were too brief to have afforded any worthwhile opportunities for sabotage. And anyway, I was never on my own in any of the larger concerns.

My best chance of committing some act of sabotage would have lain in the engineer's own small factory. I was already fairly familiar with the workshops and with the various employees' jobs and working methods. I might also, when entrusted with precision instruments for delivery to other factories, have smashed them on the way. One simple consideration held me back: the culprit would have been obvious immediately.

But that was not all that prevented me. In Sell's factory I never once heard or witnessed the Hitler salute. No pictures of the Führer hung in the workshops. Moreover, Sell himself occasionally made remarks that may have meant nothing in themselves but that made me prick up my ears.

One morning we were busy fitting new windows in the workshops following an air raid. I was up the ladder; Sell was holding it down below.

'You have a pretty strong grip, I believe, Mr Schneider,' he said. 'Would you mind tightening that screw in the top left-hand corner?'

I could not manage it. Sell waved a hand: 'Don't worry, Mr Schneider. Leave it if it's too difficult. It's hardly worth it, if you ask me. How long will it last, I wonder? The fellows will be back tonight or tomorrow night, and then we shall be lucky if we only lose the windows!'

That was no Hitler supporter speaking! I was reminded of my first interview with Sell, when I applied for the job. The way he had spoken then about total mobilisation suggested, rather, that he was a secret anti-Nazi. Possibly that was indeed what he was. In which case I must certainly not damage his works: I should only be delivering him into the hands of the Gestapo.

So there were several reasons why I refrained from committing an act of sabotage. There was in fact one more: I very much doubted whether I should be able to withstand interrogation under torture without giving away my secrets. If I was caught, it would be almost bound to mean hideous consequences for Leon, Toni, Lore and the shoemaker.

Today I have no illusions on this score. Anyone who merely desires to be a resistance fighter without being firmly determined to carry it through will easily, just as I did then, find a whole string of perfectly respectable excuses. I doubt whether I had it in me to be a hero. The atmosphere in which I had been living for years was not congenial to the spirit of rebellion. It was the will to survive that governed our lives.

Consequently, I too went on doing my bit for German armament — just like the countless host of prisoners of war and foreign workers who were assigned to the munitions factories.

A helping hand from Budapest

I had made no progress in my search for new lodgings. Sell's little factory comprised three workshops and two storerooms. One of the storerooms was almost empty. There would certainly have been room for me to sleep in there. The trouble was, I could find no excuse for remaining in the factory after work finished for the day.

For the engineer's benefit I maintained the fiction that my lessons at the 'Italian High School' took up three full days a week. I used those days in attempts to tap fresh sources of help.

My attempts were not wholly unsuccessful. Towards the end of March I made the acquaintance of one Jenö Farkas, a Hungarian Jew in his mid-thirties. Farkas, who was from Budapest, lived alone in an elegant flat in Lützowstrasse, on the south side of the park. I had heard he was looking for a cleaner.

After I had introduced myself and dropped a few cautious hints to the effect that I was living underground, he questioned me until he knew as much about me as he thought it desirable to know. All this took fewer than five minutes.

It looked as if he had entertained guests the previous evening. The signs were everywhere: half-empty tea glasses, overflowing ashtrays, sticky liqueur glasses. A plate of leftover sandwiches stood on a low table. The carpet was littered with cigar ash and breadcrumbs.

It took me only a few days to realise that this opulent mess might well have been created without the assistance of guests. Farkas was a bachelor. The total mobilisation of labour meant that he was unable to employ a maid.

He was delighted that I had offered my services. I was to come three times a week to sweep the flat out, push the vacuum-cleaner round, wash up and so on. In my breaks I was allowed to fortify myself with sandwiches and tea, a permanent supply of which stood on the low table.

'Don't be afraid to help yourself!' he said by way of encouragement. 'Please, tuck in! There's no shortage here. On top of my ration cards I receive regular food parcels from Hungary.'

Pretending that sandwiches represented the summit of my ambition, I set to with vacuum-cleaner and cleaning-rags in a bid to give the Hungarian maximum satisfaction. Wealthy folk living in comfortable circumstances ought not to be confronted too brusquely with other people's poverty, nor should one immediately bombard them with requests, for fear of souring their self-sacrificial mood.

However, the Hungarian puzzled me more and more. From what Sholem Klein had told me of the legal status of Hungarian Jews in Germany, I could appreciate why Farkas chose to remain in Nazi Germany rather than return to his own country. But why did he always have so much to do? The way he spoke and the way his flat was furnished suggested a man of education. Farkas owned an extensive collection of gramophone records of classical music and a library in which German titles outnumbered Hungarian. Yet there was nothing to indicate an academic profession or even a particular specialist training.

His conversations with me were invariably brief and to the point. He told me almost nothing about himself. I never saw him smile. Often I would find him pacing up and down the room with eyebrows raised and forehead knotted in a frown as if he faced some crucially important decision. From him I learnt details of the military situation such as I had previously heard only from Löwenzahn. He clearly had excellent sources of information and a good political brain. I felt naïve in comparison, for all my not inconsiderable personal experience. But how did the man's evident seriousness of purpose chime with his luxurious life-style?

As I went about my tasks I overheard many of his telephone conversations, which were conducted almost exclusively in German. He appeared to associate with a great many 'Aryans', both German and foreign. Clearly he occupied a position of some privilege. For years now we German Jews had been confined within invisible ghetto walls. There were times when I suspected that all his feverish activity simply represented an escape from taking a sympathetic interest in the fate of his German co-religionists. That was until I learnt that Farkas had family connections with German Jews. He had a female cousin in Berlin who was living underground. Later he also mentioned a nephew in Birkenau concentration camp. The names Auschwitz and Birkenau meant little to me at the time. However, I had a feeling that the deep disquiet in Farkas's manner had other causes than mere business worries.

In the days that followed we came slightly closer. As soon as Farkas heard about Leon, Lore and Toni and the circumstances in which they were living, I no longer needed to put my request into words. He knew without my saying anything that I should prefer to receive my wages in food than in money.

Toni's eyes used to widen when I returned in the evening and unpacked my briefcase. One day there might be a packet of sugar or flour, another day rice or even such delicacies as tins of goose fat or meat. Naturally I did not neglect to show the shoemaker that once again I had something to offer. Laden like Santa Claus, I felt I could probably return to my old custom of entering the flat by way of the workshop. The shoemaker had recovered his former friendliness towards his 'Tschibel'.

Now that I was working three days a week for the engineer and three days for the Hungarian, I was rarely stuck for a place in which to spend the daylight hours. My most difficult day was still the Sabbath, with no work. I generally spent it with the crocodiles and turtles.

Farkas honoured the religious tradition of the Sabbath himself. Wondering why he would not let me spend it with him, I immediately suspected that the reason was the caretaker, who was constantly in and out of his flat. The caretaker knew I came to tidy up three times a week. He sometimes exchanged a few words with me. What would he have said, though, if he had seen the Hitler Youth regularly spending Saturday sitting around in Farkas's flat?

I was right: that was what Farkas was afraid of. He once told me that, although Hungary was regarded as an ally, Hungarian nationals in Germany were kept under surveillance and were constantly at risk from informers. If he were to be caught aiding and abetting Jews who were living underground, that would have been the end of his protected position as a foreigner.

One day I found four men of Farkas's age gathered at his flat, together with an extremely beautiful young woman. He told me they were friends of his, also Hungarian Jews living in Berlin. I might speak as frankly with them as I did with him. He introduced me to them there and then, using the cover-name 'Herbert'.

Suddenly I was filled with fresh hope. Taking the bull by the horns, as it were, I explained my situation to the group of strangers sitting comfortably around the low table in Farkas's living-room. I asked their advice. Immediately they launched into a vigorous discussion in their own strange-sounding language. Two words kept recurring, always with the stress on the wrong syllable: *Ber*lin and *Ges*tapo. They were the only ones I understood. Finally they turned to me and addressed me in German.

What their advice boiled down to was that it would not be a good idea to seek refuge with people who were themselves, as aliens, under the eye of the police. I should be glad that I already had accommodation with an 'Aryan' shoemaker. That was the best that anyone in my situation could hope for.

I had achieved a great deal through Farkas, I reflected. Just not my main objective.

Where to now?

One evening in April I returned from Farkas's flat and unpacked my wages: a tin of liver pâté and a pound of flour. Toni accepted the tin and the bag with no great show of delight over these valuable additions to our larder.

'What's wrong, Toni? Did the shoemaker throw another tantrum today?'

'Not today, no — not at all,' she replied. 'He's not said an unfriendly word.' Yet her face wore a troubled look.

'There's something the matter, though. Aren't you going to tell me?'

Toni sighed deeply but said nothing.

'If you keep it to yourself, I'll *really* worry.'

'Oh well, you'll find out soon enough anyway. Another letter has come — from the front.'

'Fritz again?'

'No, the second son, Klaus.'

'He's coming home on leave?'

Toni nodded.

'Oh, God! Oh, God! When's he coming? Will we not know for sure again?'

'Middle of April. No, it's definite this time. Look, you must eat something first. We can talk about it later.'

'Will he be staying a fortnight too?'

Again Toni nodded.

'What does the shoemaker say?'

'He said: "As long as Klaus is here, Tschibel is not to set foot in the flat!"'

'I wouldn't have done anyway. But him saying so. Not set foot in the flat — just like that! And where shall you sleep?'

'He says I can stay here. I'll be all right. Listen — maybe you could sleep at the Hungarian's? Tell him it will only be for a couple of weeks!'

'It's not even worth asking him. It would be hopeless. I'm under no illusions there. And when the two weeks are up, the shoemaker will never have me back.'

'Try it — have a word with your Hungarian! The worst he can do is say no.'

Next morning I went to the telephone kiosk in Hansaplatz and rang the engineer: 'Dr Sell? Wilhelm Schneider here. If it's all right with you, I'd like to have today off and come in to work tomorrow instead. I have an urgent matter to attend to.'

'Fine, Mr Schneider — that will be quite all right.'

I then telephoned the Hungarian: 'Mr Farkas, it's Herbert speaking. Could I come round and see you for a couple of minutes? There's an urgent matter I'd like to discuss with you.'

'Yes, but come quickly! I'm going out in half an hour!'

As I left the telephone kiosk, I noticed a civilian standing outside. Had he perhaps overheard me making two consecutive telephone calls as 'Wilhelm' and 'Herbert'? I did not wait around to find out.

I had to leave the Hungarian without having been able to broach the subject. The caretaker was with him and would not stop talking. Farkas paced nervously from one corner of the room to the other, powerless to get rid of the man — who smelt strongly of alcohol — before it was time for him to go out himself.

In despair I caught another bus going back towards Hansaplatz, though I had no particular destination in mind. Everything started to get on my nerves: the stolid faces of the matrons with their bulging shopping-bags, the broad shoulders of the SS man blocking my view, the centrifugal forces generated whenever the bus went round a corner, pressing everything against the side of the vehicle willy-nilly: the women's bulging shopping-bags, the SS man and me.

I alighted after several stops and walked east along Tiergartenstrasse, past the villas that housed the embassies of neutral countries. I intended to walk into one of them and ask for asylum. The policemen marching up and down on sentry duty changed my mind for me.

I turned back and headed for the zoo. Perhaps there was still just a chance that in the dimly lit viewing-rooms of the aquarium I might find a hiding-place where I could spend fourteen nights? As the building came into view, my hopes faded. By the time I reached the entrance they were gone. Nevertheless, I stubbornly insisted on completing my tour of the building. Eventually, muttering a bitter 'I knew there'd be nowhere!' I left the luxury animal hotel.

Once again I found myself drifting through the shopping streets around the Emperor William Memorial Church. I ambled past cafés and restaurants, pursued by the relentless loudspeaker music: 'It'll all be over some time, it'll all be past and gone. . . .'* They were the words of a sentimental song that had recently become popular, no doubt at the instigation of the propaganda department, as 'ultimate victory' receded into the distance. Several passers-by were whistling the tune.

Arriving back at the shoemaker's flat after a day of fruitless efforts, I paused for a moment in our 'secret privy'. The same song was coming from the kitchen. Clearly not even Toni was aware of its Nazi lineage.

Because of my arrangement with the engineer I had to let two days go by without doing anything about emergency accommodation. On the third day I saw Farkas again. He could not attend to me immediately because his Hungarian friends were with him. They were sitting around the low table, discussing something in Hungarian. This time the only words I could pick out of the bubbling stream of talk were two place-names: Berlin and Budapest. I noticed the men were leafing through timetables and making notes.

At last they went. Alone with Farkas, I decided to come straight out with my request. Farkas, however, was in an even greater hurry to tell me something himself. 'Listen,' he said, 'there's a new decree: foreign Jews must shortly leave German soil. I have to pack today. In fact, I'm very glad you've come — you can help me! I'll pay you well.'

Pay me well! Was the whole world conspiring against me? I was seized with a savage envy of those Hungarians, who appeared to have no more serious worries than train connections and hotel rooms.

'Listen Mr Farkas, couldn't you take me with you? In a wardrobe trunk, maybe? Or as freight?'

'Certainly! Just hop in this case!'

'No, I'm serious! I'll gladly put up with anything — hunger,

* 'Es geht alles vorüber, es geht alles vorbei. . . .'

262

thirst . . . I don't care if I arrive covered in bumps and bruises, so long as I arrive!'

'But you're talking like a child, Herbert! If it were as simple as that, hundreds of people would have had themselves nailed up in packing-cases before now!'

'And if I somehow smuggled myself through? Don't you think I'd have a chance of surviving the war in Hungary?'

This question set Farkas thinking. Once I was on Hungarian soil, he said with conviction, I should be safe. Life would not be easy for me there either. But I would not have to starve, and I need not fear deportation. Nor would I have to sleep in the street. The worst thing that could happen to me would be if the Hungarian police caught me. In that event I should be interned. Internment in Hungary, however, was a very different matter from internment in Germany. There it did not begin to carry the threat of death. And I would certainly not be extradited to Germany.

I asked Farkas whether he could help me get hold of Hungarian papers — or any other papers, for that matter, with which I might attempt to make my way across the border.

He made a rueful gesture. He would love to help me, he said, but with the best will in the world there was nothing he could do. There was nothing he could do for his own cousin and his two Austrian friends, either. They were all three living underground, and he had already explored every possibility of getting them safely out of Germany.

He plunged his head in his hands and began to think. If I could manage to reach Vienna, he said, I should be over the biggest hurdle. In Vienna it was easy to find smugglers who would take you across the border for a few hundred marks. Yes, if I could just manage to reach Vienna! But Farkas raised an admonitory finger: I should not imagine that the train journey to Vienna was a simple matter. Passengers were subject to rigorous checks. A number of refugees had already been caught on that stretch. And then, of course, it was a question of getting in touch with the right people in Vienna. Perhaps it would be best if I consulted his friend Wolfsohn about that. Wolfsohn was a native of the city and still had contacts there.

I nodded enthusiastically.

Right, then, he would let me have his address. But I must not write it down; I must memorise it.

Farkas did indeed pay me very generously for helping him pack. He also gave me several gramophone records from his collection. Five days later, he and his Hungarian-Jewish friends left Berlin.

Wolfsohn, a former officer in the 'Imperial and Royal' (Kaiserliche und königliche) Austro-Hungarian army* who had fought in the 1914–18 war, was living illegally in a hideout in the centre of Berlin. I first met him towards the middle of April. Farkas had already told him the details of my plan.

'Well, aren't you a fine sight in your uniform!' he said by way of a greeting. 'I very nearly slammed the door in your face! And you're 21? Incredible! That's your trump card, that is.'

Wolfsohn urged me to attempt the escape to Hungary. Farkas was already in Budapest; I stood a good chance of meeting up with him again in the near future. He gave me two addresses in Vienna there and then: that of a family of Swiss Christians, and that of an elderly academic by the name of Herzberg. Dr Herzberg, he said, was one of the few Jews still allowed to remain in Vienna for the time being. He was involved in the administration of the Jewish congregation. I should contact these two immediately on my arrival.

If I made the journey to Vienna successfully, Wolfsohn went on, it could even be that other Jews living underground would follow me. My function would be that of a reconnaissance patrol. In fact, he said, he would have followed me himself if he had only been younger and looked as 'Aryan' as I did.

As soon as I arrived in Vienna, I was to send a telegram to his 'Aryan' friend in Berlin. We agreed the wording of the telegram there and then. HAVE FOUND WRISTWATCH would mean: I was not asked for my papers; the journey went off without a hitch. CAN TAKE AT MOST ONE CHILD (TWO CHILDREN, etc.) FOR HOLIDAYS would mean: my papers were checked once (twice, etc.) on the train.

Leaving Wolfsohn's hideout, I went straight to the nearest travel agency and bought a ticket to Vienna, valid for two months. I then returned to my room in the shoemaker's flat and began to pack my belongings in secret.

Toni and Leon found me bent over an open suitcase. They smiled at my 'boy-scout notions'.

'He'll get over it,' Leon jeered. 'We all have our weak moments.'

Only when I showed him my train ticket did he take my plan seriously. He reacted with alarm.

'But that's pointless!' he remonstrated with me. 'The Nazis are in Hungary too. You want to risk your neck to live as illegally there as

---

* From 1867 to 1918 the emperor (*Kaiser*) of Austria was also king (*König*) of Hungary, so that all his institutions were prefaced by the adjectives 'Kaiserliche und königliche' (written 'k. u. k.' for short).

you do here? Besides, you don't speak a word of Hungarian. You needn't give up hope just because the shoemaker's son is coming home on leave. We'll find somewhere for you to stay. You can always come and sleep at my place. Listen, think it over once again before you do anything stupid!'

But I was deaf to reasoning. Envy of Farkas and his friends proved more powerful than Leon's thoroughly justified warnings. And I was too much in love with my daring escape plan to drop it now.

Afterwards — and incidentally — rational considerations occurred to me in support of my decision. Hundreds of homes were being destroyed in Berlin night after night. I did not believe that we 'illegals' would be able to survive the war if we remained in the city. Moreover, I wanted to stop being a burden to my brother and sister and to the 'Aryans' assisting me.

The unquestioning, utterly natural way in which Wolfsohn helped me to plan my journey strengthened my resolve. It is possible, even so, that I would have come to my senses and thought twice about undertaking the trip. However, events moved too fast for that.

The calendar tells me that the first day of the Jewish Passover festival fell on 20 April 1943. Easter was on 25 April. This enables me to attach approximate dates to my experiences at that time.

It must have been on 7 April that the second letter from Klaus arrived, announcing his arrival for 19 or 20 April.

What should I do? Leave for Vienna immediately? Was there any alternative? At a pinch, I thought, I could ask the engineer to help me. I had wanted to study Sell's reactions for a little longer before saying anything. But now everything was pressing me to make an immediate decision. I must risk it. I had known the man for several weeks by this time, and in the Third Reich one developed a sixth sense about people. I did not know whether he would help me, but I was confident that he would not give me away. The worst he might do would be to shrug regretfully and escort me off the premises.

I went to see Wolfsohn to ask his advice. He listened to what I had to say, paced the room a couple of times from corner to corner, then stood for a moment in thought.

'No,' he said. 'I would advise against both courses. Don't rush into anything! Your journey to Vienna must be meticulously prepared. Around this time, coming up to Easter, they check the trains very strictly. I get to hear things. Over the last fortnight, apparently, several refugees have been caught on that stretch. We'd do better to wait for a while — just until the situation calms down a bit. As for talking to your engineer, are you out of your mind? There's one rule

265

you must adhere to: for as long as you're living underground, admit to anything rather than to being a Jew!'

'Where am I to sleep, then, until I leave for Vienna?'

'Tell me, is the Passover festival important to you?'

'It certainly is! Very important indeed. My family has always honoured the Jewish tradition. Just now, though, I'm more concerned about where I'm going to sleep!'

'Well, I may be able to help you. I'll give you an address where you can join in the *Seder* tomorrow evening. They may also find you a corner where you can bed down for the night. But you must take some food with you! The other guests will all be illegals too.'

I called on the Friedmann family, with whom I was to celebrate the Passover, that same afternoon. Their hideout was not far from Alexanderplatz. How did they manage to live in hiding in their own flat, without 'Aryan' cover, right at the heart of Berlin? In the circumstances, I could hardly ask them.

I entered to find Frau Friedmann and another woman baking *mazzoth* — loaves of unleavened bread for the festival. My contribution of a pound of flour was gratefully received and put to immediate use. Herr Friedmann invited me to the *Seder*, the Passover meal and did indeed promise me accommodation for three nights.

Three nights without worrying about where I was going to sleep! I returned to the shoemaker's flat much relieved.

Very early the next morning there was a ring at the door. The shoemaker opened up the shop, and in came the son home on leave from the front. Still only half dressed, I hurriedly packed my pyjamas, toothbrush, and other essentials in two briefcases and disappeared out of the back door. After completing my morning toilet in the 'secret privy', I took to my heels.

It was too early to go to the engineer's, so I spent an hour and a half riding round on the *S-Bahn*. The first thing I did on arrival at the factory was to stow my two briefcases in a corner of the workshop.

The fitters were not in yet. Sell was the only person there. My head was in a whirl: should I say something, or should I keep quiet? Before I could make up my mind, the telephone rang, and by the time Sell had finished on the telephone the staff were at their machines. I spent the day working at a vice and running errands. There was no other opportunity to speak to the engineer alone.

Festival of freedom

After work I made my way to Alexanderplatz, clutching my two

266

briefcases. I gave the prearranged knock. As he let me in, Herr Friedmann asked me neither to introduce myself to the other guests nor to inquire the name of anyone present. Before I had my coat off there was another knock at the door. Friedmann gave the newcomer the same instructions as he had given me.

Some ten men as well as several women and girls were already gathered in the living-room. We greeted one another with nods and smiles of tacit complicity. I was surprised to see a face I knew: a youth leader I had once met on a Zionist course in the first year of the war. He also recognised me.

'What, you still here?' he whispered to me. 'In hiding too?'

At last we were all assembled. We took our seats around the frugal festive board. The *Kiddush* — the blessing to inaugurate the festival — is traditionally pronounced over a cup of wine. We had no wine, so we made do with lemon extract. At this point the head of the household — in our case the tenant of the illegal flat — is required to read aloud from the Haggadah. This is a collection of stories, legends, homilies and prayers for the occasion of the Passover festival.* Friedmann confined himself to reciting the printed text without, as is usually done, glossing it with contemporary observations. The assembled company struck up — but in a whisper, of course — the traditional hymns of thanksgiving. None of us referred by so much as one word to our present desperate plight. No one asked why God, having once released the Jews from slavery, now allowed them to be borne away in cattle trucks, or why the wheels of those trucks did not fall off, or why the officials of the state railway company did not refuse to carry out their criminal orders.

Can anyone present on that occasion have helped being reminded of the Marranos, the Spanish Jews who had been forced to accept baptism and who continued to celebrate the Passover in secret underground chambers, spied on by the informers of the Catholic Inquisition? The similarity between our Passover and theirs was too striking to require spelling out. But we left our thoughts unspoken, giving ourselves up to the gaiety that arises when a festive mood is wrested from a condition of mortal fear, the kind of gaiety that can be experienced only by people who are aware of God's protective nearness, people who can look back over 4,000 ineradicable years of history and who, in this instance, knew little of what was happening

---

* Begun in antiquity but completed only in medieval times, the Haggadah contains the narrative of the exodus from Egypt together with reminiscences of the suppression of the Jews by Babylonians, Syrians, Romans, and Christians, the whole accompanied by prayers of thanksgiving for the Jews' repeated deliverances by the hand of God.

in history's present hour.

We raised our glasses of lemon extract and gave thanks for Israel's deliverance and for the breath of freedom that had been granted to us in the midst of danger. We had no idea that the events of that day were to fling down a bitter challenge to the prayers of all God-fearing people.

Consulting the calendar of events of the Second World War I see that on 19 April 1943 tanks commanded by Major-General Jürgen Stroop of the German police rolled into the Warsaw ghetto to crush the desperate revolt of the remaining Jews there. His 2,100 soldiers included SS cavalry, armoured infantrymen, sappers and security police. He also had some Polish police and a number of Lithuanian militiamen. The German tanks, heavy artillery and incendiary and fragmentation bombs proved too much for the wretchedly armed and totally isolated Jewish task forces. Stroop's leather-bound photograph album survived the war to provide the prosecutors of the Nuremberg War Crimes Tribunal with a detailed record of exactly how his forces set about those 50,000 starving, exhausted ghetto dwellers, how in the flickering light of whole streets of burning houses they dragged men, women and children from the sewers where they had sought refuge and carted them off to their deaths.

And we, in Alexanderplatz, Berlin, were giving thanks to God. At the end of the meal a number of those present, who lived in the neighbourhood, went 'home'. Most of us stayed, though, and soon the Friedmanns' flat resembled an improvised refugee camp, with mattresses and blankets spread all over the floor.

We came together again for morning prayers, greeting one another like old friends, despite the secrecy in which each of us remained wrapped. I spent the whole of that day at the Friedmanns'. In the evening I saw the others again at the second *Seder*. This proceeded very much like the first except that, just after the thanksgiving psalms, the sirens began to howl. We leapt up from the table and scattered, Friedmann telling us how to reach the nearest public air-raid shelters. After the 'all clear' we reassembled, and the meal continued.

Another night went by. The astonishing composure and cheerfulness of the others had a calming effect on me. But as the next day wore on and morning gave way to afternoon, I found myself glancing repeatedly at my watch and counting the hours. Just one more night, I said to myself; you have a promise of shelter for one more night, and then where will you go?

Friedmann listened sympathetically but could neither give me an address nor offer me any advice. Later I got into conversation with the former youth leader. I told him of my plan to flee to Hungary and of how I meant to take the engineer into my confidence.

'You're crazy!' he exploded. 'You and your blind, childlike trust! You must never, never tell anyone that you are a Jew. Do you hear? Not anyone! As long as you remain in this fiendish Nazi empire, that fact must remain a secret.'

Next morning, with a silent handshake, I took my leave of the Friedmanns.

A private matter

Citing some pretext or other, I had asked the engineer whether I might come to work at eleven o'clock on this particular morning. He had agreed readily and made a note in his diary. I had been so confident that I would need the morning hours to move straight from the Friedmanns' flat into new quarters. Now, with nothing to do in the free time, I decided to turn up at the factory around nine after all. In the train I changed my mind again, preferring to stick to the arrangement I had made with Sell. But that meant I had to while away the hours until eleven.

From Zoo Station I made my way to the aquarium. Checking that my two briefcases were firmly closed (they contained my toothbrush and pyjamas, among other things), I handed them in at the cloakroom. I wanted to go over everything in my mind once more in the peace and quiet of the viewing-rooms.

I stared for ages at a pair of Japanese giant salamanders, incapable of rousing myself to take an interest in the creatures. Nor did I succeed in even collecting my thoughts, let alone in bringing them into any sort of order. In the end I turned up at the factory around ten o'clock. The engineer was in the middle of a discussion with one of his mechanics. Dumping my briefcases in a corner, I waited until he was alone at his desk.

'Dr Sell,' I asked, speaking in an undertone, 'might I have a word with you about a private matter?'

'Of course, Mr Schneider! Come this way.'

He led me back through the workshops to a storeroom that was currently out of use. Apart from an empty shelf unit covering one wall, it contained only a table, some chairs and two or three abandoned packing-cases.

I came straight to the point. 'I wish to tell you something in confidence,' I said quietly (though my voice seemed to echo in the bare room). 'I am a Jew. Since the day that I was to have been deported I have been living in Berlin illegally.' And I gave him a brief description of my situation.

The engineer had a habit, when spoken to, of fixing his gaze on some object in the room. This time, however, as I blurted out what I had to say, our eyes met for the space of a second. He rose from his seat, paced up and down the room, then came to a halt.

'Well, this is quite a revelation you've just sprung on me! I've thought for some time that there was something a bit fishy about Wilhelm Schneider of the Hitler Youth. But this! Heavens above, man — how do you get away with it?'

He resumed his pacing, sunk in thought. 'You realise, don't you, that you're like an unexploded shell in my house, now that you've let me into your secret — a bomb that may go off at any moment?'

I looked at him in consternation.

'Oh, you don't have to worry about me,' he added quickly. 'I'm an old Social Democrat. But what the hell are we going to do? Clearly I can't leave you in the lurch now. It's my duty as a human being to help you.'

What he said next received no more than half my attention. I was too full of what he had just told me. 'An old Social Democrat. . . . My duty as a human being to help you. . . .' The utter straightforwardness with which he had spoken the words!

Sell was now pacing the storeroom in earnest, talking with the garrulity of a man who has had to keep silence for too long. In swift succession he covered the military situation, the increasing atrophy of education and training, the plunder of the nation's economic reserves and the godless Nazi cult with its corrupting effect on the young. He appeared not merely to have forgotten my admission; he appeared to have forgotten my presence altogether.

He threw all caution to the winds. His voice, which had begun in an undertone, rose in a rapid crescendo of anger.

'I'm forced to let my son and daughter join the Hitler Youth, and then I have to be constantly on my guard against my own children! Day and night that fiendish propaganda hammers away at one's eardrums. I'd like to smash every wireless set and loudspeaker into little pieces. Soon we shan't be able to tell right from wrong any more. They stand everything on its head with their lying and their ranting. . . .'

I was growing uneasy. A fine 'private matter' this had turned out to be! The engineer was shouting as if he had been addressing a hall full of people. He was quite unaware of my agitation and of my anxious glances at windows and doors whenever he bellowed such phrases as 'Nazi riffraff!'

'Oh yes, the enthusiasm's falling off now. Suddenly we're getting pangs of conscience — ever since what happened at Stalingrad! Many people now admit — in the privacy of their own homes — that there's something not altogether healthy about this Third Reich. Now, with things starting to go wrong, we're seeing signs of remorse. When France was overrun, how the rabble adulated Hitler! But now we're hearing people's excuses, the reasons why they voted for him. He wasn't as bad as his speeches, they thought. To begin with he seemed quite moderate. He just had a bee in his bonnet about the Jews; otherwise he was quite a decent fellow. How could the fools think such a thing possible? An anti-Semite who was otherwise "quite a decent fellow"! The most depraved hoodlum in the land — and they elected him head of state! In error, they now claim. To stop something worse happening! They swore allegiance to a criminal fanatic! By mistake!'

'Dr Sell!' I broke in imploringly. 'Dr Sell! We can be heard! Do please keep your voice down! We'll have the police here!'

But my warnings went unheeded. Pounding the table with his fist, Sell thundered on: 'They've kept one of their promises all right, the Nazi scum! They've made history — ineradicable history! They'll never be forgotten! Not for all eternity! One tries to picture the future, and one is seized with horror. . . .'

For my part, I was seized with fear and happiness in roughly equal proportions. So there were still men in Germany! There was still some feeling for human dignity and justice! I gritted my teeth to hold back the tears.

Suddenly the engineer appeared to recall my presence. He reached for his briefcase, which was lying on the table.

'You're hungry, I dare say. My wife packed me a couple of sandwiches. Here, help yourself! No, I mean it. I get plenty to eat. And you've nowhere to sleep, you say? Well, you'll sleep at my house for the time being. Wait here a moment, I'll go and telephone my wife now.'

He left me and ran through to his office. In three minutes he was back in the storeroom. 'Right, that's all arranged. We'll expect you for supper at seven this evening, and afterwards you'll stay with us.'

'Wh . . . What can I do for you, Dr Sell?' I stammered.

'Do for me? How do you mean?'

'I mean for the firm. What is my job for today?'

'Ah, yes. . . .'

He began to pace the room again. After some reflection he told me he thought it inadvisable that I should continue to work at the factory. What was I to do instead? Well, that was something we could discuss in detail at his home in the evening.

As we were about to leave the storeroom, he stopped me. I would also be meeting his son and daughter that evening, he said. He had already mentioned to them that I had some experience in the cultivation of fruit trees. It would be a good idea if I confined any conversation with his children strictly to the subject of arboriculture. That would help to keep the atmosphere relaxed. He would rather not burden his children with the secret, though he would of course be taking his wife into his confidence.

Before leaving the workshops I carefully studied the faces of the fitters and mechanics. Had they been eavesdropping? Had the engineer's shouting reached their ears? They appeared to take no notice of me.

Out in the street, I ran and ran. No space seemed vast enough for me to grasp what had occurred. I looked at my watch. Sell expected me at his house in six and a half hours. I had time to mull over that hour in the storeroom.

My legs carried me on and on. The passers-by slipped behind me like shadows. The huge bulk of the Technical University loomed up — and gave way to the terraces of Hardenbergstrasse. Rising above the street noise, the engineer's voice still rang in my ears. Oh, the power of the truth when it is uttered at the risk of the speaker's life!

I felt cleansed, liberated, fearless — as if no man could harm me now.

A second visit to a chemical works

'May I introduce Mr Wilhelm Schneider?' The engineer and his wife greeted me with cordial handshakes, and we sat down to supper immediately. The son and daughter would not be home till later, they said; there was no point in waiting for them. I propped my two briefcases against the coatstand in the hall, pulled my collar straight in the mirror and did my best to slip into the role of house guest in which I had so unexpectedly been cast.

But what a clumsy oaf I felt, seated at that elegant, stylishly laid table! I had quite forgotten how to behave in society. Surreptitiously I studied how the engineer held his knife and fork.

After supper we lounged in comfortable armchairs in the smoking-room. I had to tell Dr Sell and his wife the story of my life. They asked me what my real name was. (They did not notice how I flinched.) They wanted to know everything: 'Have you heard from your parents? Have you heard lately from your brother in Posen? Have you ever heard from your training-farm friends?'

But we did not spend the whole time talking of these terrible things. The engineer also told me something about his life. Before the war he had had many contacts with British firms and had paid many visits to that country. He knew stories of refugees who in the early days of the war had reached England from Germany in small boats, defying both the coastguards and the North Sea storms.

I told him of my plan to flee to Hungary. Sell became thoughtful for a moment. Then he said that he personally knew little about the opportunities that would be open to me there and the risks that such an undertaking might involve. However, his friend Stressmann, another old Social Democrat, was a top manager in a major chemical works and had a great many valuable contacts as a result. Stressmann would certainly be able to advise me.

The engineer went out into the hall to telephone to his friend immediately.

'Right, that's all arranged,' he said as he returned to the room. 'Stressmann will expect you at eleven o'clock tomorrow morning. You can of course be as frank with him as you are with me.'

Waking next morning after a deep and dreamless sleep, I rubbed my eyes to find myself in a real bed with clean pillowcases and snow-white sheets. The towel on the chair beside my bed smelled freshly washed.

I heard a knock. 'You get up just whenever you like!' Frau Sell called through the closed door. 'I dare say you need the sleep! There's no hurry — breakfast will be ready when you are.'

The name 'Wilhelm Schneider' had suddenly become a magic password. The doorman had only to hear the name and the great gate of Riedel & de Haen's Chemical Works in Tempelhof was thrown open to me. At every window, checkpoint and information counter the spell proved effective in securing young Mr Schneider the most courteous treatment until he was shown into the office of the works manager himself.

Stressmann, a man in middle age, shook me warmly by the hand. He radiated the self-assurance of someone who is accustomed to giving orders and seeing them obeyed.

'Mr Schneider!' he boomed. 'Take a seat and tell me what's on your mind!' He appeared not to notice my anxious sideways glances towards the window and the door.

With lips pressed together in a firm line, he listened to what I had to say. When I had finished, he gave a single nod. 'Your plan to flee to Hungary seems to me a very sensible one. Let me think for a moment. . . . Yes, I would advise you to leave tomorrow. On Easter Saturday the trains are sure to be overcrowded. Then you probably won't face so many identity checks. Wait just a moment — would you mind?'

He reached for the telephone: 'Fritz? Georg here. You've just come back from Vienna; tell me, were there many checks on the train?'

Again I turned towards the door, quaking with fear. The man clearly took no precautions whatever. Holding the receiver to his ear, Stressmann was making a note.

He hung up. 'Right. You have to be able to prove that your journey is vital to the war effort. Just a second, please!'

He reached for the telephone again, spoke to someone, replaced the receiver, rose to his feet, and handed me a sheet of paper.

'There you are! Go straight from here to Alt-Moabit. I've written down the full address for you. There you will be given a letter confirming that you are travelling to Vienna on behalf of the firm of Hagenhorst & Co. The document will also state that the purpose of your trip is "to transact business vital to the war effort". It will be waiting for you when you reach Alt-Moabit — I shall arrange that by telephone. And if you should need me again, I am at your service. May I wish you a pleasant journey and the very best of luck?'

To my surprise, the address in Alt-Moabit belonged not to a munitions factory but to a private flat on the third floor of an apartment building. The lady who handed me the letter — which was indeed waiting for me — said she well remembered the days when the firm of Hagenhorst & Co. had still existed. Ah, but those had been good times! Then, after the dissolution of the firm, there had been all this headed notepaper left. 'And as you see,' she said with a smile, 'it still comes in useful at times!'

I had to promise her that I would destroy the letter as soon as I reached Vienna.

See you in Budapest!

Later I too had to shake my head in amazement over the amount of luggage I took with me when I fled from Berlin. The two large suitcases, already carefully packed, contained shirts, underclothes, a suit, towels, a pair of shoes, a Hebrew Bible, a German–Hebrew dictionary, those two classics by the German psychologist Eduard Spranger, *Psychology of Youth* and *Life Forms*, Thomas Mann's *The Magic Mountain*, three Hungarian books (a language textbook, a miniature dictionary, and a phrasebook), a map of Vienna, photographs of my parents, my brothers and sister and some of the Steckelsdorf *chaverim*, and finally a 'teach yourself Arabic' manual.

This had been a last-minute purchase, made hurriedly in the

middle of preparations for my journey. I thought it unlikely that I should find any German-language Arabic textbooks in Budapest. That I must learn Arabic was something I had decided long before this. How could one contemplate living in Palestine without being able to communicate with all the inhabitants of the country in their own language?

The weight of the suitcases was considerably increased by the gramophone records that Mr. Farkas had given me. These included Beethoven's *Kreutzer* and *Spring* sonatas. Such treasures might never come my way again, I thought, carefully slipping the precious books and records between layers of clothing. And of course the two clockwork time switches had to go in too; I could not possibly leave them behind. A small silver goblet that had stood on my father's table completed my equipment.

I had only hours left in which to make my final preparations. My first call was at the shoemaker's flat.

We had told the shoemaker nothing of my plan as long as everything was still uncertain. Only when my journey was an immediate prospect had Toni said to him: 'Tschibel is doing a flit to Vienna. He says *please* could you resole his shoes?'

The shoemaker had reacted with amusement. 'Well, well — so Tschibel's doing a flit to Vienna? In that case we must stick him on some new rubber soles. Then he'll be able to flit even better!'

Sure enough, my shoes were ready.

I had called at a good time. The son home on leave happened to be out, and the shoemaker was in one of his more benign moods. But my delight at the fact that at least for our farewell he should be showing his better side once again was soured at the last moment. As I carried the two tightly packed and bound suitcases out of the door of his shop, the old man could not resist remarking from his seat behind the counter, 'What's all that you've got with you, then? Just so long as you haven't taken too much from here!'

Puffing and sweating, I dragged the two cases to Zoo Station and dispatched them as freight to Farkas's Swiss friend in Vienna, whose address Wolfsohn had given me. Under 'sender' I wrote on the labels 'Jenö Farkas'.

The clerk behind the luggage counter took my two suitcases and placed them on the scales. As he was weighing them and filling in the forms, I became aware of a ticking noise. It sounded as if the clerk had an alarm clock in his trouser pocket. Only on my way back through the Tiergarten did it dawn on me: that was no alarm clock in the man's trouser pocket; that was one of my time switches, ticking away inside the suitcase! God almighty, they're bound to open the case to see if there's a bomb hidden in it! How stupid of me! I should have stuffed some paper into the clockwork mechanism. Quick, back to the station! I stopped, turned round, ran a few steps, then turned again, deciding against trying to do anything about it after all. With any luck the general noise level in the station would be high enough to drown the ticking.

I spent my last night in Berlin in the hospitable comfort of Dr Sell's house. Again I was fortunate in missing the son and daughter. The engineer and his wife supplied me with food for the journey and bread coupons. They wanted to know if there was more they could do for me.

In the morning, as we shook hands in farewell, Sell said, 'You will write, won't you, when you arrive safely? A postcard will do — just send greetings. In fact, make sure it is only a postcard! That'll be safest.'

By arrangement, an hour before the train was due to leave I met Toni, Leon and Lore in the Tiergarten. They were already waiting on the bench. As I approached, I saw them looking my uniform up and down. My ski cap came in for particularly minute inspection.

Leon said, 'Well, you've certainly got yourself up this time! Don't you think that's going a bit far—pinning a swastika on as well? You're taking a big risk there!'

'On the contrary,' I replied. 'I'm trying to reduce the risk. Now I have to play my part up to the hilt. Half measures would be far more dangerous.'

I had asked for the Hitler Youth badge in a uniform shop and been sold one with no questions asked. A fat man wearing SA uniform had served me.

I gave Leon Dr Sell's address. Toni had brought me some sandwiches and a couple of bread coupons. She also slipped a golden tooth crown into my purse, not wanting me to arrive in Hungary without any valuables at all. After we had agreed a number of code words for correspondence purposes and discussed everything else that had any bearing on my enterprise, we still had forty minutes to kill.

We asked Toni how things were with the second son home on leave. Much better than with Fritz, she told us. This time she was not aware of any tension. The shoemaker was also in a relatively good mood these days. It had made a big difference, of course, that Klaus had not actually set eyes on me. But he also gave the impression of being very much less of a fanatical Nazi than his brother. He had once explained — in Toni's presence—why he saw it as his duty to go on fighting the Russians: 'If the house is on fire,

276

you have to put the fire out, never mind who lit it.'

There were still twenty-eight minutes before my train was due to depart. Conversation had ground to a halt. None of us could think of anything to say. Concern about the outcome of my adventure weighed heavily on all our minds.

To cheer us up, I said, 'If I reach Budapest safely and find life is better there than here, you must all come too!'

Leon, Toni and Lore smiled as if I had just cracked a joke.

'Shall we bring the shoemaker?' Leon teased.

'Yes, the old man ought to see Budapest some time,' said Lore. 'And that's a fact!'

'How are you going to earn your living in Budapest?' Toni wanted to know. 'Shall you be Farkas's skivvy again?'

All three of them thus managed to laugh with me one more time. But the pallor did not leave their faces. Leon in particular looked as if he was heaping silent reproaches on himself for having failed to persuade his kid brother to drop the whole foolhardy plan.

Yet was there any alternative? Our last talk took place not between the safety of four walls but—flouting all the rules of caution—on a park bench. That was the kind of situation we were in.

There could be no question of their coming with me to the station. We sat on in silence for a while, the four of us on that bench in the park, glancing every few seconds at the advancing hands of the clock. Then we tore ourselves apart.

'See you in Budapest!'

They nodded resignedly, smiling.

Epilogue

The train bore me away from the capital of Hitler's Germany towards saving frontiers. I recall my successful escape — yet I do so without joy. A glance at the map shows that the first half of my journey coincided with the route from Berlin to Auschwitz. On the very rails that bore me to safety, unnumbered thousands were freighted punctually to their deaths. The self-same permanent-way inspectors and crossing keepers did duty for both sorts of traffic as far as that point in Upper Silesia — no doubt indicated in some timetable — where the line branched off to the biggest of the German death camps. Where was the parting of the ways, in Oppeln or in Ratibor?* The managers of the state railway company knew. Hitler could count on them. And who could doubt the utter reliability of the lesser officials of the *Reichsbahn* — the stationmasters, the drivers, the pointsmen? I have not heard of a single instance of a train bound for Auschwitz being accidentally switched to Vienna. My train turned south. The smoke clouds of the crematoria were well out of visual range. In any case, I had long since been rocked to sleep by the rumble of the wheels.

Auschwitz — I had yet to hear the name.

That was the beginning of my journey to the Holy Land. Eighteen months were to pass before I reached my goal. They were not a time of idle waiting.

What did I do in Vienna on Easter Monday 1943, for example? I began by turning my back on the splendid edifices of the former *Kaiserstadt*, residence of the Emperor of Austria and King of Hungary. St Stephen's Cathedral merely served me as a landmark in my

* Now Opole and Racibórz in Poland.

search for the insalubrious alleys where Jews still lived, marked out by their yellow stars. There was only a handful of them left. The Gestapo had granted them a stay of execution to minister to the dying remnants of the third largest Jewish community in Europe.

I was clearly on the right track: above a doorway I spotted a Hebrew inscription. It was a verse from a psalm: '. . . . enter his courts with praise!' I caught a whiff of the pestilential stench of SS that hung about the hall of the Jewish congregation.

I was referred to a Herr Färber. He was said to be the most experienced adviser for 'U-boats', as Jews living underground were called. Färber received me in his yellow-starred flat with an air of hopelessness. 'Most of the U-boats that have tried to get away to Hungary so far this year have been picked up,' he said. 'And how do you propose to find a Hungarian smuggler? Maybe through one of the Gestapo agents who go around Vienna wearing yellow stars and offering to put people in touch with smugglers? No, Vienna's no place for you. With your northern accent, wherever you go you're going to stand out like a sore thumb. Actually it must have been easier for you to disappear back home in Berlin, what with the air raids causing such chaos. If I were you I'd go straight back to Berlin!'

His greeting set the tone for the two harrowing and extremely hazardous months that I was to spend in Vienna.

Herr Färber had not been exaggerating. Stalingrad had put paid to Austria's enthusiasm for the Führer and his 'Greater German Empire'. Vienna, safe from air raids, had become one vast field hospital. You came across whole groups of crippled servicemen in the streets. A new symbol adorned the walls of public lavatories: the swastika shown hanging from a gallows. A growing feeling of bitterness against the Nazis combined with the Austrians' traditional contempt for *Piefkes* (their word for arrogant Prussians)—as if Hitler and many of his vilest henchmen had hailed from Prussia and were not Austrian at all. Nor was it long before I got a taste of this ill will towards *Piefkes* myself — reassuringly in one sense, but also greatly to my disadvantage. In spite of my Swabian burr I was in fact taken for a Prussian member of the Hitler Youth. The good people of Vienna cordially pointed me in the wrong direction, ignored my presence in shops and prevented me from boarding the tram.

I spent day after day hurrying and being harried from pillar to post through that once great city, now so sadly diminished and provincialised. I got to know many of its tight-packed streets of antiquated houses, seedy-looking carriage entrances and airless back courts where janitors hovered in dark doorways, following

279

every stranger with their gimlet eyes (they doubled as informers). At ten I had a rendezvous outside the Urania Observatory; at twelve-thirty, in response to a vague hope, I was waiting in front of the Opera House; at a quarter to three I kept an appointment with a man who was said to know someone whose aunt had apparently heard about this smuggler. . . .

But how superbly the invisible network of the 'U-boat' helpers operated! Rarely did I have to risk being seen twice by the same janitor through spending two nights under the same roof. Each helper told me where to find the next, and they all took in gladly the refugee who placed their lives in jeopardy, be he or she a Jew, a half-Jew (or the husband or wife of a Jew), a Catholic or a Communist.

Actually Färber himself found me a Hungarian inside ten days. This was Janos, who had no desire to fight for 'Greater Hungary' but was happier living as a foreign worker in Vienna — and happier still when he could earn his living through contraband. The train taking us on the short journey to Hungary was thoroughly checked by an SS officer, and to my dismay Janos was arrested on suspicion of smuggling meat. From a village that lay practically on the Hungarian border, I caught the next train returning to Vienna. All the way back I practised saying, 'I'm so sorry, dear Viennese helpers — but here I am again!'

The nerve-racking quest for another smuggler, coupled with my daily changes of accommodation, drove me back onto the streets of Vienna. There I sometimes found myself almost rubbing shoulders with the black-uniformed Austrians who, under orders from Adolf Eichmann, were dragging Vienna's last few Jews from their homes. After a further six weeks in Vienna, weeks packed with escapades but made heavy by tragedy, I made contact with a second smuggler, Imre. With him I made good my escape across the rural frontier and arrived in Budapest. Towards the end of June 1943 I once again set eyes, for the first time since the outbreak of the war, on a big city that was still teeming with life.

The president of the Zionist Organisation in Budapest received me with evident misgivings. He appointed a committee of three young men to investigate this self-styled 'Jewish refugee from Berlin'. 'Your Hebrew isn't bad, but you can cut the German accent with a knife!' one of them told me with a smile. It was some weeks before their mistrust began to dissipate. But in the meantime they helped me out with money and meals. Not with accommodation, though: my three examiners were themselves refugees from Slovakia and had nowhere they could call their own. Imre helped me find my first billet — with a shoemaker (yes, another shoemaker!) in Buda, the part of the city that lies on the west bank of the Danube. The shoemaker was unable to interrogate me closely since he spoke only Hungarian.

The committee's mistrust vanished completely when first my brother Leon and subsequently Lore and Toni turned up in Budapest with Imre. The bases and contacts back in Vienna had by now evolved into a small organisation. Imre smuggled nearly twenty refugees across the border, most of them Viennese but including a few from Upper Silesia who had somehow contrived to reach Vienna.

I got in touch with Jenö Farkas again — my old employer in Berlin — and made the acquaintance of some of the leading members of the Jewish congregation in Budapest. Among these was Fülöp Freudiger, who a year later became one of the first victims of Eichmann's dupery. These solidly middle-class representatives of Hungarian Jewry simply could not understand the 'sheer obstinacy' of the 800 or so Jewish refugees from Poland and Slovakia and the few of us from Berlin who were living in Budapest at that time. 'If you will only register with the police,' they urged us, 'your staying here will be legal and we shall not be threatened with internment if we help you!' But registering with the police was something we had a deep-seated aversion to doing. We preferred to take our chances as vagrants. Life in Hungary struck us as relatively tolerable and involving so little risk that we determined — we Zionist refugees—to continue our journey to the Holy Land only when the war was over.

So for the time being we scraped along with some illegal financial assistance and a variety of casual jobs. And in the evenings, behind closed doors and drawn curtains, we listened with beating hearts to the BBC's reports from the front.

For a time I worked for a Jewish locksmith and gave German lessons in private houses. Leon, Lore and Toni also managed to get by with casual jobs. Towards the end of 1943 I was asked to teach a group of ten- to fourteen-year-old Jewish orphans who had been rescued from their native Poland, where they had lost everything, and brought to Hungary. They were living in two basement rooms of a Jewish old people's home. One of the things I did with them was to take them for walks in the woods around Buda. And what do you think my young charges played? Why, variants on the 'cops and robbers' theme that they called 'Jews and Police' or 'Jews and SS'! Who do you suppose possessed more maturity and knowledge of the world —those children or the management of the old people's home who had taken them under their wing?

All of this came to an abrupt end when on 19 March 1944 the German tanks overran war-weary Hungary. Without delay the hyenas and vultures of the Gestapo and the SS set about their work of murder and pillage. The matron of the old people's home could not understand why I and the orphans flatly refused to comply with the new law requiring us to wear the yellow star. 'A quarter of a million Jews — one in four of the population of Budapest — wear the yellow star!' she shouted, beside herself. 'And you want to be different! Well, in that case I can no longer have you and the children here!'

'We said this would happen,' clamoured the weeping orphans, '— that the Germans would follow us here and murder all the Jews!'

The catastrophe that actually befell the 900,000 Jews still living in what was called 'Greater Hungary' was something we had not imagined in our wildest nightmares. At the time, one thing was clear: 'Every man for himself!' was the wisest counsel. The bodies most capable of acting quickly and organising escape routes for groups and individuals were the Zionist associations and in particular the Polish and Slovak Jews who had already fled from the Germans once. We refugees saw our most pressing duty as being to warn the many Jews who as Hungarian citizens allowed themselves to be lulled into a false sense of security: 'Drop everything! Fly to Tito! Escape to Rumania! Any of you with Christian friends, go underground immediately!' It is terrible to have to be a prophet of misfortune. It is worse to meet only with disbelief.

Misfortune was an understatement for what the Hungarian *házfelügyelö* (a special breed of janitor/informer) brought upon the persecuted Jews of Budapest. Desperately I searched for a house without a *házfelügyelö*. Should I be alive today, I wonder, if the flower-grower opposite the municipal park had not happened to be looking for a lad? I said I should be happy to work for him if I could sleep in the greenhouse.

Heilbronn Swabian is perceptibly different from the dialect still spoken by those Swabians whose ancestors migrated to Hungary more than two centuries ago. Nevertheless, the fact that Budapest had a Hungarian–Swabian Hitler Youth unit enabled me to play my part convincingly. But although I was now my own *házfelügyelö*, I did not think I should be able to hold out in a greenhouse until the Allies arrived to liberate Hungary. At the beginning of June I and a group of young Zionists took the train to Szeged, a town near Hungary's south-eastern border. The smugglers were waiting for us in the frontier village. After wading for what seemed like hours through total darkness, accompanied by a chorus of croaking frogs, we at last reached Rumanian soil. A railway worker had been bribed to hide us in a goods waggon belonging to the Rumanian Post Office. However, we were discovered en route and taken by the police to an internment camp near Târgu Jiu. For the first and only time I forfeited my hard-earned freedom. But compared to the German concentration camps the place was a sanatorium.

Two months later the Rumanian king announced that Rumania was now fighting on the side of the Allies against his former ally, Hitler. We were released and allowed to proceed to Bucharest, which by that time had been severely damaged as a result of a revenge raid by the German Luftwaffe. Bucharest was swarming with soldiers belonging to the Red Army. At synagogue on the Jewish New Year's Day I bumped into a grey-haired officer from a sapper unit of the Soviet army. He understood Hebrew and spoke a very antiquated form of the language. I told him my story but obviously failed to convince him, for he reacted with monosyllabic mistrust.

Three months after that, I and about 500 young refugees from Poland and the Balkan countries found ourselves aboard a Turkish ship bound for Palestine. Towards the end of 1944, filled with a deep, deep joy, I set foot in the Holy Land. I was aware that I had escaped a catastrophe but only vaguely aware of its extent.

We were taken to a reception camp hear Haifa that was surrounded by barbed wire. There we were kept under guard. It took about a fortnight for the new arrivals to be questioned and examined by British Intelligence and released from the camp one by one. Unlike the others, I was interrogated not once but eight times — and everything was written down. Friends had advised me to simplify my story somewhat in order to make it more credible. But I had had enough: I wanted a chance, at long last, to tell the plain unvarnished truth.

Not until 1946 was I able to contact Budapest again. My sister Toni, posing as an 'ethnic German' domestic help, had lived through the German occupation to the bitter end — only to experience the horrors of the Russian conquest. Toni survived the war. Leon and Lore, I learned, had fallen into the hands of the Hungarian police in July 1944. Soon afterwards they found themselves in a goods waggon, bound for Auschwitz.

283

Chronology of Events

In compiling this table I consulted the following works: Walther Hofer (ed.), *Der Nationalsozialismus. Dokumente 1933–1945*, Frankfurt am Main (Fischer Taschenbuch 6084), 1968; William L. Langer (ed.), *An Encyclopedia of World History*, London, 1947; Golo Mann (ed.), *Propyläen Weltgeschichte*, Vol. 9, Frankfurt am Main, 1960; Gerald Reitlinger, *The Final Solution*, 2nd edn., London, 1968; Gerhard Schoenberner, *Der gelbe Stern*, Hamburg, 1960.

Contemporary Events	*Chapters of this Book*
1922–29	
Murder of Walther Rathenau (24 June 1922)	1. Boyhood in Heilbronn
French and Belgian troops occupy the Ruhr (11 January 1923)	
Hitler's 'beerhall putsch' in Munich defeated (8–11 November 1923)	
New York bank crash triggers world economic crisis (October 1929)	
1930–32	
Brüning governs with the aid of President Hindenburg's emergency powers	2. The Brown-uniformed World
German–Austrian customs union founders on French resistance (March 1931)	
Hitler receives 13.3 million votes (13 March 1932)	
Chancellorships of Franz von Papen and Kurt von Schleicher	
Six million unemployed in Germany	

1933

Hitler invited to form a government (30 January)

The Reichstag fire (27 February)

Hitler's Enabling Bill receives a majority in the Reichstag (23 March)

Constitutional rights abolished

Construction of the first concentration camps

The first anti-Jewish measures introduced

Founding of the Gestapo (26 April)

Public book-burnings in the Reich (10 May)

Concordat between Pope Pius XI and Hitler (20 July)

3. 'Dad, Everyone's Emigrating!'

1934

Hitler murders his rivals for power: Röhm and many others (30 June)

Hitler assumes the powers of the deceased president (19 August)

1935

Compulsory military service introduced in Germany (16 March)

Anglo-German naval convention (18 June)

The Nuremberg Laws remove Jews' civil rights (15 September)

1936

Germany and Italy assist General Franco in the Spanish Civil War

Olympic Games open in Berlin. Nazi Germany plays host to the world (1 August)

1937

Mussolini visits Germany (25–28 September)

4. Exciting Berlin

Hitler decides to launch a war of conquest
shortly

Britain recognises Italian possession of
Abyssinia (16 November)

<hr>

1938

<hr>

Hitler assumes command of the Wehrmacht
(4 February)

Austria annexed (the *Anschluss*) (13 March)

The Munich Conference: Britain and
France leave Czechoslovakia in the lurch
(29 September)

Jews' passports stamped with a 'J' (5 October)

Synagogues set on fire throughout Germany: the November pogrom (9 November)

Residential restrictions for Jews introduced
(28 November)

Britain and France sign non-aggression
pacts with Hitler (6 December)

<hr>

1939

<hr>

Protection abolished for Jewish tenants
(17 January)

Hitler prophesies 'the destruction of the
Jewish race in Europe' in the event of war
(30 January)

Anglo-French guarantees for eastern and
southern European states (March–
April)

German troops invade the rump of Czechoslovakia. Hungary and Poland also grab
bits of the booty (15 March)

Germany's Jews are placed under the
Reichsvereinigung der Juden in Deutschland (4 July)

Stalin and Hitler sign a non-aggression pact
(23 August)

Anti-Jewish laws enacted in Hungary

Hitler starts the Second World War (1 September)

286

SS and Wehrmacht organise numerous po-
groms in Poland (1–21 September)
The yellow star is introduced in the
German-occupied part of Poland (23
November)

5. Preparing for Palestine

1940

First deportation of Jews from Stettin (12
February)
German troops overrun Denmark and Nor-
way (9 April)
First ghetto under guard in Lodz (30 April)
German troops overrun Holland, Belgium
and Luxemburg. Germany invades
France (10 May)
Armistice in France (21 May)
The German Foreign Office and Adolf Eich-
mann put forward the 'Madagascar Plan'
— to settle 4 million Jews in Madagascar!
(15 August)
Second Vienna arbitration by the Axis pow-
ers: Rumania loses territory to Hungary
and Bulgaria (August)
The pro-Hitler Jon Antonescu becomes
Rumanian head of state (4 September)
German troops in Rumania (7 October)
Establishment of the Warsaw ghetto or-
dered (16 October)
Deportations from Baden, the Palatinate
and Saarland to southern France (22 Oc-
tober)
Italy attacks Greece (28 October)
Mentally ill persons murdered in Germany

6. Schulze's Tree Nursery

1941

Rumania enters the war (17 February)
Bulgaria enters the war (1 March)
Forced labour introduced for German Jews
(7 March)
Germany invades Yugoslavia and Greece
with the support of Hungarian, Italian
and Bulgarian troops (6 April)

Britain puts down a pro-Hitler rebellion in
  Iraq
Special squads formed in Saxony to exter-
  minate the Jews in the occupied eastern
  territories (late May)
Germany attacks the Soviet Union (22
  June)
German-inspired pogrom in Kaunas (28
  June)
Göring places Heydrich in charge of the
  'deportation' of Europe's Jews (31 July)
Test gassings at Auschwitz (23 September)
Massacre of 34,000 Jews in Kiev (28–29
  September)
Official decree: property of deported Jews to
  be confiscated! (25 November)
The first Jews from the Reich arrive in Riga,
  Minsk and Kaunas (November)
The Japanese attack Pearl Harbour (7 De-
  cember)
Massacre in Riga and Vilnius ends
Permanent gassing camp set up at
  Chelmno, near Poznan
Germany declares war on the United States
  (11 December)

7. Creeping Despair

1942

The Wannsee Conference: Heydrich an-
  nounces to representatives of various min-
  istries, the SS and the police guidelines
  for the 'final solution of the Jewish ques-
  tion' (20 January)
The Belzec death-camp is set up (16
  March)
The massacres of the 'Reinhard Mission'
  begin
The first Paris–Auschwitz train (28 March)
Jews from 'Greater Germany' are deported
  to Polish death-camps (April–June)
The yellow star is introduced in France and
  Belgium (1 June)
First selection in Auschwitz (23 June)
Hitler repeats his public prediction regard-
  ing the destruction of Jewry (30 Septem-
  ber)

8. Underground in Berlin

288

'Resettlement' in Warsaw ended (3 October)

The Minister of Justice transfers responsibility for Jews and people from the eastern territories in the Reich to the Gestapo (18 October)

The Allied landing in North Africa (7 November)

1943

The first resistance to deportations in the Warsaw ghetto (18 January)

Transports from Holland go to Sobibor death camp and from Vienna, Luxembourg, Prague and Macedonia to Treblinka death-camp (March)

The first new crematorium is opened at Auschwitz (13 March)

The Warsaw ghetto uprising (19 April to 16 May)

German surrender in Tunis (9 May)

Himmler orders the liquidation of all ghettos (11 June)

9. The Shoemaker

10. Refuge among the Reptiles

11. Festival of Freedom

Postscript to the English Edition

I see no reason to alter anything in this account of my early life in Germany, written some thirty years ago. But I should like to add certain things that have been much on my mind ever since.

Among the letters that I received from readers I was particularly moved by those from young Germans. While feeling — quite justifiably — that no blame attached to themselves, they saw it as their moral duty to demand an explanation of their parents' and grandparents' conduct. Some of them even came to see me and voiced their indignation at the fact that Nazi lawyers and criminal members of the medical profession had gone unpunished after 1945 and continued to enjoy high-ranking positions and public respect. The honesty and sincerity of those young people made a deep impression on me.

Readers of the Arabic edition have also told me of their emotion in letters and in personal encounters. Unlike the other foreign-language editions, however, most of the Arabic edition is still stacked in the warehouse. My friends Mahmud Abassi and Mu'ayyad Ibrahim had anxiously predicted such an outcome even before publication. As they bitterly remarked, the *Protocols of the Wise Men of Zion* (an anti-Semitic fabrication first published in Russia in 1905 and conclusively exposed as a forgery in 1921 by the London *Times*) still enjoyed wide circulation in every Arab country. Yet the reluctance of most Arabs to be brought face to face with the unexampled tragedy of the Jewish people was so deep-rooted that they were not even prepared to skim through such wholly non-political, untendentious books as those of Anne Frank and myself to see what they contained. I regret that every bit as much as Mahmud Abassi and Mu'ayyad Ibrahim, for it is our belief that peace between Jews and Arabs can never come about until both sides begin, *entirely without political calculation*, to take a humane interest in the special quality of

290

the other's affliction.

A similar unwillingness to listen to the testimony of survivors may be found in the West. A reproach commonly levelled at those who have written memoirs is that they have only accusations to make — as if there was nothing left in the world that was not defiled. To my mind, most of the writings of survivors actually prove the contrary, for they are addressed to readers who are still human and prepared to listen. Many an exhausted concentration-camp detainee would have succumbed at an early stage had the sacred duty to bear witness not filled him or her with the will to survive. Acutely aware of being cut off from the world of civilised humanity by those black-uniformed Germans manning the watchtowers, the prisoners also felt that the world was cut off from them. Once rescued and set free, they need only bear witness. Mankind would hear and act.

Today we know that they had too high an opinion of the 'outside world'. Roosevelt, Churchill, Stalin, Pope Pius XII — indeed, every government in Europe knew by December 1942 at the latest where the goods trains that traversed the European continent day in and day out were taking their human freight. They were the four most powerful and influential men of their day — and what did they say, what did they do to counter the greatest crime in history?

Four decades have passed since then. What task still remains for us survivors — grey-haired now and gradually dying out? To bear witness before mankind? There still seems to be a need for it. In fact, there seems to be a fresh need. In post-war Europe hundreds of thousands of young people have been able to grow up without acquiring any real knowledge of what happened to the Jews in the Third Reich or learning how the drive to hunt the Jews succeeded because virtually every country in the world had closed its borders to Jewish refugees.

When the film *David*, based on this book, was being made in Berlin, I fell into conversation with the friendly young policeman who provided a protective escort for the film crew. He asked me in some surprise why I did not wish to come back and live in Germany. This was while a heart-rending deportation scene at Bellevue Station was being filmed before his very eyes and while various walls and houses in Berlin carried venomous slogans against Israel, daubed in huge letters.

During the press conference after the film's première one young German journalist objected to the fact that the lad 'David' (as the person portraying me was called in the film), after successfully reaching the coast of Palestine, had been received and welcomed by Zionist settlers *without Arab acquiescence*. Whatever can that rabidly anti-Israeli journalist have learnt at school? Presumably the Jewish settlers and the young refugee ought first to have asked permission of that friend of Adolf Eichmann's and forerunner of the PLO, Grand Mufti Muhammad Amin Al Husaini!

Are we perhaps engaged in a vain struggle, we survivors with our shameful testimony, faced with the world's reluctance to hear us? I confess I have often been assailed by such doubts. But thanks to my readers and my interlocutors I have not given up trying. I cannot forget the young people from all over the world, but especially from Germany, whom I have met through writing this book, with whom I have talked, and on whose grave and seemly faces I have looked.

EZRA BENGERSHÔM
1988